FINDING BEAUTY IN THE OTHER

FINDING BEAUTY IN THE OTHER

THEOLOGICAL REFLECTIONS ACROSS RELIGIOUS TRADITIONS

EDITED BY

PETER CASARELLA

AND

MUN'IM SIRRY

A Herder & Herder Book
The Crossroad Publishing Company
New York

A Herder & Herder Book
The Crossroad Publishing Company
www.crossroadpublishing.com

© 2019 by Peter Casarella and Mun'im Sirry.

The text of this book is set in 12/15 Adobe Garamond Pro.

Composition by Rachel Reiss
Cover design by Sophie Appel based upon a poster done by Chantelle Snyder

Library of Congress Cataloging-in-Publication Data
available upon request from the Library of Congress.

ISBN 978-0-8245-2336-7 paperback
ISBN 978-0-8245-2335-0 cloth
ISBN 978-0-8245-2337-4 ePub
ISBN 978-0-8245-2357-2 mobi

Books published by The Crossroad Publishing Company may be purchased at special quantity discount rates for classes and institutional use. For information, please e-mail sales@crossroadpublishing.com.

CONTENTS

ACKNOWLEDGMENTS

The present volume is the fruit of the World Religions and World Church (WRWC) Inaugural Conference held at the University of Notre Dame in South Bend, Indiana (September 10–12, 2015). Without generous support from the University of Notre Dame, the conference and the publication of this book would not have been possible. A debt of gratitude is owed to Fr. John I. Jenkins, who generously opened the conference. Matthew Ashley, chair of the Department of Theology at the time, was very supportive of the idea of hosting the conference.

We would also like to thank the Office of the Vice President for Research, the Kroc Institute for International Peace Studies, and the Institute for Studies in the Liberal Arts at Notre Dame (and its remarkable staff, most notably Thomas V. Merluzzi, Alison Rice, and Elizabeth Kuhn) for their support. Three graduate students played a pivotal role in the preparation of this volume. Mourad Takawi was instrumental in maintaining contact with the speakers in preparation for the conference. Andrew O'Connor made the first pass at copyediting the entire manuscript in order to convert it from formless chaos into a readable text. In the final stages, Christopher Rios lent a sure hand as well. The editors are extremely grateful for these unsung labors. Finally, we thank Gwendolin Herder and Chris Myers of Crossroad for their remarkable support, encouragement, and help.

A NOTE ON TRANSLITERATION
AND TRANSLATION

Transliterations of Arabic follow the system utilized by the *International Journal of Middle East Studies* (IJMES) <https://ijmes.chass.ncsu.edu/docs/TransChart.pdf>. Various English Qur'ān translations have been used in this volume, depending on each contributor's preference. Some contributors may have used their own translation or a particular Qur'ān translation with some modifications.

The International Alphabet of Sanskrit Transliteration (IAST) system is used for Sanskrit/Devanagari; the "Hanuy Pinyin" system for Chinese; the "Revised Romanization" system for Korean; and the "Hepburn" system for Japanese.

INTRODUCTION

Peter Casarella and Mun'im Sirry

Finding—A Non-Dualist Process of Discovery

This volume treats the search for the beauty of the Other in an interreligious and intercultural framework. Having said that, there is nothing self-evident about the beauty of the Other. Even if one presumed that beauty is more internal and moral than external and cosmetic, the task of pinpointing the attractiveness of another's otherness is no small challenge. What keeps us from just looking for copies of ourselves? Can we really understand what is truly other, much less look for its genuine beauty?

The first set of questions that arises in thinking about the theme that undergirds this volume is, therefore, to explain the meaning of "finding." Across the religions of the world, the concepts of beauty, the idea of transcendence, and the goal of learning from traditions other than one's own differ sharply. Our goal in putting together this volume was to respect and explore these differences, not to discover exact replicas of what we already hold to be true. The academic area that we represent includes principally Christianity, Islam, Hinduism, and Buddhism, but the modes of diversity represented in the essays that follow go beyond differences in creeds or beliefs. In these essays, we encounter multiple types of difference: (1) the diversity of religious traditions, (2) the wisdom of Catholicism's global South (Africa, Asia, and Latin America), and (3) the internal diversity of each religious tradition and each continental reality.

In addition to highlighting diversity in the selection of contributors, we also learned about the process of discovering the beauty of the Other. One panel was arranged continentally, and others were set up to explore differences within the religious traditions on the question of beauty. We learned about the exchange of viewpoints and also about the to and fro of dialogue. In the final analysis, however, one participant boldly observed a salient point: there was no Jewish interlocutor in our discussions. This insight underscored the open-endedness of the process of discovery. We came upon a Pandora's box and were delighted to discover new things upon opening it.[1] So the first principle in finding the beauty of the Other is an openness to discovering something new about oneself and also about one's academic program.

The poet said that beauty and truth are one.[2] In this sense, the search for the beauty of the Other is without any doubt a search for truth. Western thinkers, influenced by the injunction of the Delphic oracle ("Know thyself!"), as well as its classic reformulation by the Platonic Socrates, have often embraced the learning that comes from unknowing. In a real sense, this tradition of recognizing the limits of one's knowing also guides the approach to beauty taken by the authors of this volume. In bumping up against the limits of one's knowledge of the truth, you also find that your grasp of beauty is equally, if not more, limited. Beauty is both familiar and attractive as well as foreign and novel. Otherness in this sense is built into the experience of beauty. In the Abrahamic religions, viz., traditions that foreground divine revelation (albeit in divergent ways), this openness to the unknown can be the beginning of what the divine Other beckons and enjoins.[3] In other traditions, the shimmering and evasive nature of beauty's call opens the eyes of the beholder in a different way to truth, or at least to a path that may yield it. Beauty may create its own path of discovery, one that resists being put under a microscope to the same degree that it rejects the relativistic principle that places it beyond the grasp of reason.

The German Enlightenment thinker Alexander Baumgarten (1714–1762) was the first to carve out a separate domain within philosophy for beauty. Even without agreeing with him altogether, in a certain sense we are still heirs to his own innovative idea that the new science of aesthetics operates as an "analogue" to reason.[4] More recently, the Harvard literary critic Elaine Scarry has claimed that beauty beckons us so strenuously precisely because it shows for us in a key quite different from cold logic why we are so often wrong about our perception of reality.[5] For both Baumgarten and Scarry (as for Plato long before them), beauty is not just irrational or contra-rational. Rather, beauty conjures up in the mode of a midwife a process or even a path that can lead to truth. Like the work of a midwife, all is not pretty or without effort in undergoing this process. Beauty can even wound the observer in the course of making manifest a new view of reality.[6]

To think about beauty in these terms is admittedly still very Western. The reflections in this volume on the oft-cited Sanskrit term *advaita* (non-duality) are thus worth recalling briefly. Non-duality can be a goad to engaging in dialogue, but much hinges on whether one develops an illusionistic or realist doctrine of non-duality.[7] The recognition of the immanence of a Brahman in the "you" of the Other could just be a shimmering image of the true Brahman that lies behind the appearance of another. A Judeo-Christian thinker could also take issue with the difference between a creationist reading of non-otherness (such as in certain psalms that treat God's wisdom in the created order) and the advaitic emphasis on the world as pure illusion. On the other hand, the Christian doctrine of Trinitarian unity in difference might also suggest a non-duality (and a distinctiveness) far deeper than the *advaita* doctrine.[8] In general, however, the doctrine of non-duality as it has been inherited from the Upanishads can still encourage finding beauty in the Other. The wonder and astonishment at the epiphany of the ultimate reality *in* our interlocutor signifies a newly discovered openness to reality. Bradley Malkovsky states the following in his essay in this volume about the modern interpreter of the Upanishads, Ramana Maharshi:

Notice the beauty, serenity, kindness, even holiness of
his face. His face shows us that non-duality is more than
a mere idea or theological notion. It is because of that
face that the words of Maharshi are so credible to so
many people of so many religions or of no religion at all.
Though his teachings are so challenging to our everyday ideas about ourselves and God, his face continues
to invite us to probe deeper into our self-awareness and
discover what is truly lasting and real about ourselves.[9]

That a Catholic theologian can praise a modern master of Hindu
non-duality in sincere and vibrant terms is a fitting testimony to
the relevance today of the challenging task of finding beauty in
the Other. Rather than a hide-and-seek theology of finding beauty
in the Other, the advaitic doctrine of non-duality helps us to recognize the fundamental mystery of the Other, a recognition that
requires a continual process of reorientation of the self and re-
discovery of what is real.

Beauty—Not Just in the Eye of the Beholder

The beautiful is infinite, and, as a result, there is no single instance of
beauty's self-manifestation that all will recognize as beautiful. Any
portal into the myriad forms of beauty will remain just that, a point
of entry into a mystery that eludes positive identification. Transcendent beauty is never just univocally beautiful, for the doctrine of
univocity claims that that which transcends our understanding and
that which stands before us as its surrogate are necessarily of the
same genre. In fact, to the degree that something is like the beautiful itself, the beautiful is also unlike that same thing. This process of
unity in diversity sets up a semiotic play of sameness and difference
that adds significantly to the earnest game of beauty.

A fitting window onto the dynamics of transcendent beauty
is the *kābôd* of YHWH ("the glory of the Lord"). The term has

many usages in the Hebrew Bible. For example, it is often used to signify the presence of God in the tabernacle. When the Israelites were constructing the tabernacle, we learn: "I will meet with the Israelites there, and it shall be sanctified by my glory."[10] After the tabernacle was finished, God brought his promise to fulfillment: "Then the cloud covered the tent of meeting, and the glory of the LORD filled the tabernacle"[11] (Exodus 40:34). Awe-inspiring and eminently worthy of respect and honor, the Israelites see the glory of God in their daily lives.

This "condescension" of the glory of God was itself the result of a transformation that took place in the history of Israel as the physical presence of the Ark of the Covenant became less important:

> With the disappearance of the Ark into the darkened sanctum of the Temple on Zion the ideas which it represented were transferred to the sacred site, which thus became the citadel of the imageless Yahweh-worship. These now underwent a strong process of sublimation. On the one hand they were associated with the prophetic conception of the universal God; on the other, through the priestly theological concepts of the *sem* and the *kabod*, the Name and the Glory of Yahweh, and through their identification with the tradition of the sacred Tent, they acquired a new significance. In time the earthly object to which these ideas were attached, the Ark itself, lost its importance, and its final disappearance, like that of the sacred Tent, occasioned no great distress. The fundamental principle, however, of which these two shrines were the focus, the concept of the distant God who yet condescends to be really present in the midst of his people and enables them to participate in the divine life, lives on in the symbolic language of the New Testament, which uses the image of the "tabernacling" to tell of the dwelling of the eternal God among men.[12]

The glory of the Lord (together with the name of God) thus remains fully transcendent but still radiant in the course of everyday life. This feature of being both "in" and "beyond" the ordinary is one of the key traits of beauty that we wish to underscore as we introduce the multiform approaches present in this volume.

Hans Urs von Balthasar was deeply influenced by the Hebrew notion of the glory of the Lord and gave it the kind of Christological meaning that we find, for example, in 2 Corinthians 4:4 or Colossians 1:15, which speak of an *eikón*, an "image" of an invisible God in Christ.[13] For Balthasar the glory of the Lord is not a generic reality. It is a unity more original than that of our finest artistries that is brought together by God into the midst of our lives. What von Balthasar calls *Gestalt*, or the form of the glory of the Lord, is one of several wholes that are greater than their individual parts in the world's religions.[14]

Jean-Luc Marion highlights the process of visibilizing the beautiful with even greater precision when he distinguishes between "*l'invisible*" and "*l'invisable*."[15] The former is that which is not seen, and the latter is that which cannot even be brought into view. In the latter case, we encounter a view of the radiance of beauty that is not even a view. It is the outer edge of making something viewable to the eye. The admiration of beauty thus transcends the science of empirical perception and enters into a realm of the impossible. The Hebrew Bible had already touched upon this extreme negativity in the encounter with the glory of the Lord: "But you cannot see my face, for no one can see me and live."[16] This suggests that in certain encounters with absolute radiance, *not* looking at transcendent beauty is the only proper response for the devout. With this insight, we come to the borders of iconoclasm, the religious insight whereby divine beauty can never be depicted in a representational form without profaning the divinity. If we stop our reflections here, then iconoclasm can quickly sink into becoming a blunt weapon for destroying beauty's myriad and subtle radiations into being.[17] Beauty is therefore a fragile reality, always on the brink of collapsing into nothingness. This weakness in beauty's form of perception actually adds force to the conviction that beauty really matters. Like life itself, beauty hangs on the edge of existence. Rather than preening with the self-satisfied smugness of a wealthy art collector, the true lover of beauty is aware of the tragic dimension of existence and beauty's unique ability, operating precisely out of its inherent poverty, to poeticize the *chiaroscuro* of life.

As the book of Exodus reminds us in equating the vision of beauty and mortality, beauty invokes a presence that is simultaneously an absence. We are commanded to withdraw from gazing upon the presence of the divine beauty precisely because beauty saturates and transfigures the everydayness of life with a presence that overwhelms our understanding of the finite. For this reason, we can say that transcendent beauty does not enter the stage of being as just another item on the ontological shelf. Transcendent beauty irrupts into the scenery of finite objects, blinding us with its radiance. Transcendent beauty questions many preconceptions that we hold about the divide between subjects and objects inasmuch as it questions both the arrogance of scientific rationalism ("beauty counts for nothing") and the shortsightedness of mere aestheticism ("beauty evokes a merely subjective feeling"). Transcendent beauty has the power to re-orient us and make us search for a new frame for understanding Being, beings, and the ontological difference between Being and beings. Dionysius the Areopagite introduced a play on words (*to kalon* ["the beautiful"], *kalleo* ["to call forth"]) that elucidates the beckoning quality of beauty. Beauty calls to us from beyond the world in which we normally are situated to a new frame of reference. There is no mystical flight into the unknown here. On the contrary, the wound of beauty calls the viewer to examine her or his own vulnerability even as the mystery of the call uproots the viewer away from the narrowness of the complacent gaze. In choosing the theme "Finding the Beauty of the Other," we opened ourselves to this vulnerability and sought contributors and interlocutors who would do the same.

Otherness—Recognizing Difference and the Difference that It Makes

In practical terms, we are all other to one another. No collective ever fully erases individuality, at least not without inflicting horrifying violence. In Spanish, the word *nosotros* ("we") combines the Latin root for "us" with "those who are other than ourselves."[18] Every time that the "we" is defined as the community that banishes the foreigner, we also exclude alterity. In making the world into a network of private clubs, we lose sight of something essential in the human constitution of we-ness as relation. In the spirit of WRWC, we desired to see this volume celebrate not only the otherness of religious diversity but also the wisdom of Catholicism's global south—namely, Africa, Asia, and Latin America. In Asia, for example, Christianity is always a minority presence. In Africa, sites that were once centers of genocide and tribal warfare are now viewed as historical wounds that need to be acknowledged and healed in order to create bonds of social reconciliation.[19] Even in Latin America today, Catholicism is feeling growing pains and dealing with questions of religious pluralism in ways that were practically unthinkable fifty years ago.[20] So the question of how to approach the Others of the Christian West is going to look different if we shift the point of view from the North to the South. Far too many of the present studies of world religions assume that the main dialogue partners are Euroamericans on the one side and the others of the West on the other side. This dialogue privileges Euroamerican discourses of pluralism without even acknowledging its limitations. Little attention has been paid to the new waves of thought and practice regarding pluralism that are emanating from the global South. In these cases, the South is not a mere "object" of scientific investigation that in its passivity confirms the value of the Western methods. The South, on the contrary, generates a new ethics of responsibility. This volume represents at least the possibility of beginning to think about the relationship between global religion and the North-South dialogue. From this point of view, the polarization between fundamentalism and secularism is no longer the main axis around which thought turns. Instead the questions of poverty and the legacy of colonialism need to be addressed.

The Lithuanian Jew Emmanuel Levinas is not treated directly in any of the essays that follow, but his brief (albeit cryptic) remarks about the glory of the Infinite in his book *Otherwise than Being* are still a good starting point for orienting our approach to the otherness of the Other.[21] These remarks sketch out what it might mean to glimpse a trace of God's beauty in the Other *as* Other. Levinas is the thinker of otherness *par excellence*, mainly because he strove so valiantly to question the foundations of what both the classical (metaphysical) and the modern (Hegelian dialectical) tradition had said about the notion. Levinas joins Talmudic glosses with profound insights into the shortcomings of Western metaphysics. In disavowing the language of being, Levinas turns the representation of beauty once again into a philosophical problem. If beauty can be represented as a reality that has a beginning and end in time, then its alterity is questionable. Truly transcendent beauty, the glory of the Infinite, comes and goes otherwise than as an essence. An artist's rendering of a field of flowers is not trying to evoke the essence of the scene, as if the infinite variety of perspectives on this one field could all be brought into a mode of seeing and knowing that pivoted around just one point of reference or style.

The Levinasian glory of the infinite passes into our lives as a trace of the Other. Respecting its otherness, Levinas would say that we glean its passing through the face of a stranger. If I, as a Western Christian or Indonesian Muslim, see a trace of the glory of the Infinite in the visage of a foreigner whom I have never met, then several claims about the beauty of the Other are being invoked. First, the face of the Other is not my own concept of God or the beautiful. Levinas would say (and here his anti-metaphysical stance might betray its own weakness) that one is grasped by a sincere act of responsibility for the Other as other before one grasps that the glory of the infinite exists as infinite glory. The purely passive recognition of one's own responsibility to the Other might, as Paul Ricoeur has argued, underestimate the resources within a properly dialectical notion of selfhood for recognizing alterity.[22] On the other hand, Levinas's breakthrough to ethics as a first philosophy leads to a profound new take on dialogue. Levinasian dialogue is thus not an exchange of niceties or an opportunity for academic progress or scientific advancement. Dialogue is inspired in the first instance by the requirement that comes from beyond being and remains otherwise than being ready to shelter, clothe, and feed the Other. The modern Western notion of tolerance, Levinas would argue, never took seriously enough the Biblical commandment: "Thou shalt not kill!"

The Levinasian injunction that we dialogue for the sake of offering hospitality (and not vice versa) helps to sharpen the meaning of "finding beauty in the Other." In sum, in the encounter with the Other we are searching for a beauty that will ground a new ethics of hospitality. We did exchange information in our meeting at Notre Dame, and feelings of tolerance and goodwill abounded. There is nothing wrong with this. But our goal in publishing these papers extends beyond providing a record of new data and newly gained mutual respect. The ethical mandate *to find beauty* and the ethical mandate *in finding beauty* were evident in our discussions and need to be reflected upon more as we move forward. The beauty of the Other can never be taken for granted.

Levinas also alerts us to "the amphiboly of the said."[23] In general, an amphiboly is a grammatical misstep that leads to serious ambiguity. If you write a sentence with an amphiboly, what appears at first glance as intelligible can actually have two opposed but grammatically correct meanings. But since Kant's *Critique of Pure Reason* and its Amphiboly of Concepts of Reflection (in which Kant decried Locke's sensualism and Leibniz's idealism as both amphibolies, but for different reasons), the term has gained a wider philosophical meaning. It thus signifies in Levinas not just a problem with one's grammar but the loss of meaning that results from a structural flaw in one's attempt to translate reality into philosophical concepts that privilege being as a first philosophy over the post-metaphysical call to ethical responsibility. Levinas claims that any attempt to congeal "saying" (*le dire*) into a system of signs that inhere into an expression that seeks to copy the structure of being (*le dit*) will result in the loss of meaning. All linguistic systems bear this inherent weakness, and the fallible act of translation is but the Achilles heel that betrays it. Every translation is a betrayal, so goes the saying, and the translation of the act of speaking beauty into a concrete form is likewise a departure from the original, pre-ontological epiphany of the showing. In this critique of both structuralism and metaphysics, Levinas is a loyal follower of Jacques Derrida, who had made a similar critique of Claude Lévi-Strauss and structuralist linguistics.

Levinas's claim for a rupture between the saying and the said has consequences for our understanding of the beauty of the Other if we want to take seriously the challenge of addressing the novelty of the Other—that is, of not colonizing and absorbing the Other into our own scheme of reality. In his groundbreaking book *Languages of Unsaying*, Michael Sells helps us to think with Levinas about the role of certain mystics in thematizing the difference between the saying and the said.[24] He connects the mystical posture of apophasis with the ethical notion of unsayability, a position that Levinas himself disavows. Sells's exploration of the hunt for unsayable wisdom is rich and exciting and takes him through a variety of texts, some well-known and others that were suppressed.

We will concentrate on his apophatic reading of Ibn 'Arabi as well as his retrieval of the Sufi notion of bewilderment (*hayra*). Ibn 'Arabi lived between 1165 and 1240 in Andalusia and, though not well known, is still acknowledged to be a grand master of the tradition of Islamic mysticism. While still an adolescent Ibn Rushd (Averroes) asked for a meeting with him. There is a hierarchy in Sufi mysticism based upon the notion of station (*maqam*), a testimony to his fame as a Sufi sage. The most sophisticated of Sufi mystics in the Middle Ages had developed a moral psychology with distinct levels of wisdom along the path of Sufism. In the Sufi interpretation of the figure of Noah in the Qur'ān, a certain station has been reached because Noah represents the triumph of the follower of Muhammad over the polytheists who perish in the flood. Ibn ʿArabi, with his strong language of the breath of the compassionate and the heart of the mystic being wide open to God, introduces a twist into this familiar reading.

Whereas the traditional reading attributes deception solely to the polytheists, Ibn ʿArabi says that both the polytheists and Noah are guilty of deception: "Noah had accused the polytheists of *makr* (deception, guise), but according to Ibn ʿArabi, both Noah and his rival party practiced deception, hiding the true apophatic dialectic behind the polemic between monotheism and polytheism."[25] Instead of positing a difference between Noah and those who perished as a difference between good and evil, the mystic turns the perishing of the polytheists into a moment in the dialectical interplay between transcendence and immanence. Rather than showing the higher station of Noah that undergirds the great hierarchy of being, the story of the flood represents "the station of no station." The bewilderment that the reader of the story of Noah faces in observing the perishing in the flood suddenly becomes a state of mystical contemplation: "Bewilderment is caused by an abandonment of the linear, dualistic logic represented by Noah's calling his people 'to' Allah."[26] The mystical "Muhammadian" thus begs for more bewilderment so that the mystic is carried further into a circular path that can never be abandoned. In a sense, Sells focuses on the said rather than the saying, for he is interested in highlighting the many wordplays that are inscribed into the mystics' poetry.

In the process, however, the text of the mystic deconstructs itself. Its beauty lies in its capacity to undercut the notion that the experience of God can be placed among one group of believers as opposed to another. All religions are *not* one, according to Sells:

> No attempt has been made to show a common religious experience, or a common mystical experience. The goal of this study has been an understanding of a similarly structured semantic event that takes place within various versions of the apophatic mode of discourse.[27]

The deft reading that Sells accomplishes by using the Sufi mystic as his point of departure allows for an understanding of difference that is truly difference. Difference makes a difference because he heeds the semantic differences within the mystical text and brings them to the fore. This is genuine alterity, and in the hands of a mystic being read by a Master, the beauty of difference is realized through and beyond the text. The languages of unsaying are therefore a powerful tool for questioning social hierarchies that find their way into religious discourse. Without the confrontation with the radicality of the mystic, readers of religious texts are likely to become prone to homogenizations of traditions and of differences between traditions that result from not attending to the full dimensions of the semantic event in the text.

How do we discover the beauty of the Other? We are left with two modes of discovering the beauty of the Other: the analogy of the said and the apophatic figuring of the unsayable. The former prioritizes the efficacy of language to communicate otherness and the value of representing that which is truly unrepresentable. The latter questions all attempts to place the Other into a system of thought that is generated by the subjective self. The former undergirds the project of von Balthasar and his predecessors. Sells shows how a mystical language of unsaying is central to Neoplatonic Christianity, apophatic mysticism, and Sufi love poetry. To assimilate this tradition into the tradition of the analogy of the Word might lead to a domestication of its wildness. At the same time the tradition of analogy, as Erich Przywara tirelessly demonstrated, always included a moment of dialectic whereby the "ever more" of unlikeness between Creator and creature is the very condition for the possibility of searching for likenesses.[28]

Beauty and Holiness

Levinas and Sells both take an an-archic approach to the beauty of the Other. This simply means that the revelation of beauty in difference takes away rather than posits the first principle or *arche*. Such discourse destabilizes the very notion of dialogue and can lead to a kind of preferential option for the otherness of the Other. That provocation represents a distinct gain in the discourse about dialogue. There is, however, a less radical but equally profound path to finding the beauty of the Other that contributes in equal measure to this volume. This is the path of holiness or sanctity. In this view, the command to heed beauty comes from above and is issued in prayer.

Here the otherness of the beautiful is just as radical, but the path to beauty is more directly connected to daily life. In speaking about the beauty of holiness, we are therefore not trying to put iconic religious figures on pedestals, as an elite core of devotees that the masses can then blindly follow. While holiness is not necessarily a universal desire of humanity, the idea of holiness as a way of beauty opens up a surprisingly broad notion of belief and interchange.[29] The beauty of the living witness of saints, especially saints who come from among the poor or from marginal groups in society, can subvert ingrained cultural traditions about exemplary behavior.[30] Often overlooked is the degree to which the cult of saintly figures is related to this desire to open up the way of holiness to a broader spectrum of followers. The cross-fertilization of models of holiness across religious traditions is another example of this phenomenon. For example, the religious influence of Gandhi on the doctrine of non-violence espoused by Dr. Martin Luther King is well documented but still has not received adequate attention.[31]

Reading and learning from the Torah bridges the gap between God and humanity, and this bridge makes the beauty of the Absolute a palpable reality in the daily lives of observant Jews.[32] In a manner somewhat akin to the Christian understanding of the real presence in the Eucharist (but at the same time without a recognition of its central premise), this view of Torah learning is the doctrine of communion of the observant Jew. Rejecting the doctrine of the incarnation, a Jewish lover of the wisdom of the Torah nonetheless sees God's embodiment in the people who read and heed the infinite mind of God found in the text. This aesthetic reflects a uniquely Jewish understanding of how the higher longs for and pines for the lower: "As the ancient sages stated, God himself studies Torah in the age to come, concerning himself with minutiae of human life brought under the sanctifying purposes of his commandments."[33] There is a new awareness of the meaning of the holiness of practical activities of religious followers that opens up a new view of the future:

> God gave the Torah to his people, planting eternal life among us. The desert is made into an Eden as Jews return to the Torah, making it present in action and study. Israel communes with God's infinite mind and lives in his eternity.[34]

To the non-believer, this may seem like an overly elevated way to describe the importance of mundane activities like reading a book, using the proper pots and pans in the kitchen, attending to the use of candles and wine at the Sabbath table, and the circumcising of a newborn male child.

These mundane activities nonetheless permeate and circumscribe the meaning of life. To see a shard of eternity in the midst of the everyday is a religious insight that cannot be lost if we earnestly seek to find the beauty of the Other. Serious problems occur when we relegate the beauty of such seemingly minute holiness to a domain outside the realm of reason and dialogue. Placing the beauty of the everyday at the center of a respectful and mutually enriching dialogue has great utility in many aspects of contemporary life. Greater understanding of the beauty of everyday holiness across religious traditions can break down the barriers that lead to intolerance and even violence.

It is beyond the scope of this introduction to develop a theory of how the beautiful and the holy relate to one another. But a brief comment on their distinction and relation is still warranted. Since the path of beauty cannot be fully disassociated from the search for pleasure, believers have been typically skeptical about the degree to which the path of beauty and the path of holiness could be equated with one another. Many great philosophers, not the least of whom is the enigmatic Søren Kierkegaard, have sharply distinguished between mere aestheticism, which continually rotates the insatiable search for a quenching of desire for constant novelty and transient material beauty with no higher end in mind, with true devotion to God.[35] One need not adhere to strict iconoclasm to see that there is a problem with identifying holiness too closely with beauty.

Can aesthetics be redeemed, or must it be relegated to the way of sensualism and sin? Rabbi Joseph B. Soloveitchik defends the aesthetics of prayer and, in the process, offers a modern notion of the redemption of beauty by religious belief.[36] Soloveitchik starts with a notion of prayer that recognizes the paradox inherent in looking at prayer as both anthropocentric and theurgic. His breakthrough lies in seeing that prayer as dialogue is an end in itself rather than a means to change or affect the Divine: "The basic function of prayer is not its practical consequences but the metaphysical formation of a fellowship consisting of God and man [*sic*]."[37] Prayer is not undertaken just to satisfy a human need. It arises out of a desire to serve God with one's entire heart. Prayer is a form of direct contact with the Creator.[38]

Building upon Kantian categories, Soloveitchik identifies four modes of relating to the divine: (1) intellectual, (2) emotional, (3) volitional, and (4) dialogical. All of these modes come into play when he speaks about the beauty of God. Particularly interesting is the way in which he explains the dialogical mode as an actual interplay between prophecy and prayer: "In prophecy God is the speaker and the prophet is the listener. In prayer, the roles are reversed and the person standing in prayer becomes the speaker."[39]

Soloveitchik is very careful to show that prayer grows out of an existential need basic to the human condition as such. He thus considers mystical interpretations of prayer as verging on elitism. He is particularly trenchant in noting that prayer is not an activity reserved for leisure time. Prayer is a call to God "out of the depths."

He also recognizes how in a scientific age the person who answers the call to prayer has the experience of God as *numen absens* ("a power that is absent").[40] Like Mother Teresa of Calcutta, the Rabbi knows that the feeling of "a grisly emptiness and chilling cruelty pervading the uncharted lanes of the universe" is no excuse for abandoning prayer.[41] On the contrary, persisting in prayer in the midst of the experience of boredom or divine absence is a basic element in the religious experience of the modern believer.

Where does aesthetics fit in? Like many post-Kantian religious thinkers before him, Soloveitchik observes that prayers of thanksgiving (as opposed to petitionary prayers) converge in a certain way with the aesthetic impulse to revel in the grandeur of God in creation. Petitionary prayers are equally necessary, but they arise as a response to the experience of God's absence. Prayers or hymns of thanksgiving, by contrast, are a response to having had direct contact with God.

> The beauty of God is experienced as holiness, as the *mysterium magnum*, the ineffable and unattainable, awesome and holy (*nora ve-kadosh*), as something that transcends everything comprehensible and speakable, which makes one tremble and experience bliss. Beauty and paradox merge—He is both remote and so near; awesome and lovely, fascinating and daunting, majestic and tender, comforting and frightening, familiar and alien, the beyond of creation and its very essence....[42]

The genius and also the limitation of the Rabbi's insights into the aesthetic consciousness come to the fore here. He assumes, as Kant does in his *Critique of Judgment*, that the differentiating point between the aesthetic and ethical consciousness is the issue of nonpurposiveness.[43] The aesthetic consciousness is oriented to the flux of reality as experienced through sensory perception. Whereas ethical reflection on good and evil is by its very nature linked to a final end, the aesthetic consciousness by itself cannot bring teleology

into view. The aesthete must therefore be redeemed by the purposiveness of ethical consciousness and the critical discernment that
is not only allowed but encouraged by the religious use of pure
reason. This dynamic interaction between a surge in the heart of
a prayer of thanksgiving, ethical normativity, and a healthy dose
of skepticism is what happens in genuine religion. "The experience
of beauty is redeemed by turning it into a religious experience."[44]

Soloveitchik thus outlines a theory of finding beauty in the Other
based upon the intrinsic connection between beauty and prayer.
One need not be an Orthodox Jew to recognize this path to beauty.
He underscores the communion that bridges the gap between the
finite and the infinite without ignoring the dialectical difference
between God's initiative to reach out to humanity and the human
need to give thanks to God. He also allows for a theory of divine af-
fectivity. Part of the beauty of holiness is the recognition that God is
affected by the prayers of the faithful. Soloveitchik does not ignore
the anthropocentrism of this claim but goes through and beyond
both anthropocentrism and theocentrism in developing his idea that
the beauty of the Absolute is best affirmed for the modern believer
by the religious transformation of humanity's sensory gaze at the
evanescent beauty of the world. This is no *deus ex machina* but a
dialectical movement that brings God and humanity into a communion that includes—in fact necessitates—radical difference.

Soloveitchik speaks for Jewish monotheism and provides a
model for thinking about beauty and holiness for all religions that
maintain that there is something beautiful and holy in the cleaving
of the human heart to one God. What about non-monotheistic
faiths or systems of belief that fail to acknowledge the deeply per-
sonalist dialogue with God that the Rabbi highlights? Even in the
cases where belief in the divinity does not involve an all-powerful
divine "You," Soloveitchik's path to holiness contains exemplary
reflections. In particular, he struggled with the problem of belief
in the modern era. He did not ignore the modern Western condition of alienation and certainly did not ignore the Kantian turn to
the subject or the post-Kantian account of religious experience as

founded upon a divorce between ethical teleology and sensualist non-teleology. Above all, he answered these formidable challenges from within the contours of his own system and practice of belief. Jewish prayers received a modern form of validity and normativity even as their content remained firmly within the Orthodox way of life and belief. In this sense, walking with Rabbi Soloveitchik on his path to faith in the contemporary era can teach people of multiple faiths what it means to find beauty in the Other.

Does the recognition of the beauty of holiness abandon the anarchic view delineated above? Perhaps. But the two questions are also quite separable. One can be an an-archic defender of *nomos*, the virtue of following the law as espoused in religious texts. The reader of the Torah becomes immersed in the wisdom of God's presence in a quasi-mystical manner. Levinas was no mystic, but he was quite insistent that the sincerity necessary for being responsible to the Other also involves a profound sense of obligation:

> Election traverses the concept of the ego to summon me as me through the inordinateness of the Other. It extracts me from the concept in which I continually take refuge, for I find in it the measure of an obligation which is not defined in the election. Obligation calls for a unique response not inscribed in universal thought, the unforeseeable response of the chosen one.[45]

For Levinas, obligation to another has a force that comes from beyond. It is not all based upon social utility. The anarchic sense of obligation to another may be unique to the worldview of the postmodern Talmudist, Emmanuel Levinas. On the other hand, it shows that surprising convergences can arise between the religious experience of *avodat Hashem* ("service of God") and the religious experience of metaphysical anarchism. In the essays that follow, one can encounter traces of both hypernomianism and antinomianism. This paradox is actually welcome, for it is undoubtedly part and parcel of the adventure that we have undertaken in convening this conference.

Significance of This Volume

In addition to exploring in this volume the different ways in which we can talk about and find beauty, broadly construed, in other religious traditions and cultures, we intended to foster interreligious conversations by way of addressing the very inner aspect of humanity. This is in line with Pope Francis's apostolic exhortation *Evangelii Gaudium*, in which he encourages Christians to foster "a renewed esteem for beauty as a means of touching the human heart." Convinced that beauty is indeed a means for touching the human heart, and recognizing the rich role of beauty in the history of Christian theological thought, this volume is an attempt to offer an alternative approach to looking at beauty as a framework for relating to one another, as well as a guiding principle for social interactions.

In times when misunderstanding, suspicion, prejudice, and violence are more commonplace than ever, openness to beauty can be seen as the way to escape narrowness and bigotry on the one hand, and, on the other, to embrace the Other and develop a theology of community. As such, the everlasting beauty of God will have a profound impact on the everyday lives of peoples of diverse backgrounds. In the Christian tradition, "the beauty of God has been shown to us in a supreme way in Jesus Christ, the 'epiphany of God's loving kindness' (Titus 3:4)."[46] As God created human beings in his own image (Genesis 1:27), a theology of beauty can open up to ecumenical dialogue among all mankind. In Islam, it is said in the Qur'ān that "to God belong the most beautiful names" (Q 59:24). The beauty of God's face, the Qur'ān asserts, will forever remain (Q 55:27). The Muslim prophet, Muhammad, is reported to have said, "God is beautiful and he loves beauty." The saving of souls through beauty is also a major theme in the Buddhist tradition.

Despite its importance in our religious traditions, beauty has not been at the center of contemporary theologizing. As Edward Farley puts it, "throughout the period of the modern, beauty rapidly disappeared as an important motif in itself and as a way in which Western peoples experience and interpret the world."[47] Farley traces this marginalization of beauty to "the postmodern turn [which] brought with it new forms of cultural alienation from beauty," which is typical of industrialized societies with their new economics, politics, modes of warfare, population growth, and urban cultures that show a low sensibility to beauty. We may disagree with Farley's characterization of postmodern societies' approach to beauty, yet we cannot overlook the need to bring beauty back to the center stage of any attempts to "humanize" our postmodern societies. How can beauty be a strategy for humanizing society? To borrow from David Bentley Hart: "How can one plausibly argue that 'beauty' does not serve the very strategy of power to which it supposedly constitutes an alternative?"[48]

There is no question that beauty thus has a profound impact on human life. "The more human beings fall captive to beauty," Hearne argues, "the more they are falling into the hands of God, and the more they become agents of liberation and protest."[49] It is hardly surprising that much of liberation theology takes the form of poetry and art. As the bearer of liberation, beauty becomes a new way of expressing the truth of and great ecumenical guide and inspiration for human relationships, friendship, and love. This volume takes a step further by critically examining the deep, even though not always obvious, contributions of the Catholic theology of beauty, as well as reflecting on the idea of beauty in other religious traditions. The latter involves Christian theological reflections on finding beauty in non-Christian religions and cultures with responses from scholars from those religions/cultures.

Growing out of a conference that took place at the University of Notre Dame over the period September 10–12, 2015, this volume is not only intended to address how beauty can be found in religions and cultures, but also how the beauty of the self and the Other have been and are still communicated in different religious and cultural settings. The conference itself was unique because it inaugurated Notre Dame's World Religions and World Church (WRWC) doctoral concentration. The WRWC area of study at the Department of Theology aims to explore new ways of thinking theologically about the study of world religions, cultural diversity in the Church, and the history of interactions between the Church and the religions of the world. As the place where the Catholic theological tradition and rigorous academic study of the religions and cultures of the world meet, WRWC is exceptionally important to the department and the university. In his opening remarks to the conference, in which he drew upon the inter-religious thought of St. Thomas Aquinas, Notre Dame's president, Fr. John Jenkins, CSC, underscored that WRWC is vital to the university. It is also important to the academy generally, as the way in which the study of religions and culture are put in conversation with the discipline of Christian theology, an approach that distinguishes WRWC from those at many peer universities. The inaugural WRWC conference reflects the kind of theological engagements that are scholarly and address broader audiences. The conference was truly collaborative in that scholars of different perspectives and backgrounds were in conversation with one another, and various approaches to beauty were critically discussed.

The chapters in this volume are grouped into five parts. The first deals with the question of beauty within the framework of Catholic theology of religions. Catherine Cornille begins her discussion by reminding us how little attention has been paid to the search for beauty in the Other among Catholic theologians, despite their awareness of its centrality in the realm of interreligious relations. Professor Cornille offers an analysis of recent developments that reflect a greater attention to the presence of truth and beauty in other religions as a result of a deeper understanding of those religions. Maria Clara Bingemer discusses an example of Christian-Muslim encounters in which beauty has been found and contemplated by embracing the otherness of Others. This part also includes important contributions by two Notre Dame professors: Peter Casarella and Lawrence E. Sullivan. The former addresses crucial questions of inter- and cross-cultural aspects of finding beauty in the Other by examining what he calls "tragic beauty" in the context of Latino/a theology. Casarella's critical engagements with Latino/a theological aesthetics can certainly be put in conversation with other modes of theological aesthetics in different settings. The latter, on the other hand, examines different ways through which the beauty of the Other can be discovered, including a process of eliminating the repulsive aspect from the beauty, perceiving the otherness as a form of beauty, and transmuting the ugly into beauty. Such transformation can and should be made possible by way of love and forgiveness.

In the second part, the authors focus on Islam and beauty. Gabriel Said Reynolds addresses beautiful names of God, especially those that reflect His mercy. After carefully examining those passages in the Qur'ān that deal with the nature of God's mercy and Muslim debates on this issue, he concludes that God's compassion and mercy are offered only to those who follow the right path. As for unbelievers and those who go astray, "the God of the Qur'ān is wrathful, even vengeful." Nayla Tabbara reflects on the phrase from Vatican II's *Nostra Aetate*, "The Catholic Church rejects nothing that is *true and holy* in these religions," and asks if such recognition of the divine in the Other can be justified from an Islamic perspective. She explores several passages of the Qur'ān that can be understood as scriptural resources for the Islamic recognition of what is *true and holy* in other religious traditions. How have those positive assessments of the Other in the Qur'ān been understood by Muslims through the centuries? Mun'im Sirry discusses this question by examining Muslim commentaries on Q 2:62, which is repeated almost verbatim in Q 5:69. This verse has often been interpreted as a Qur'ānic manifesto of religious pluralism and tolerance, yet most Qur'ān commentators have understood it to mean the opposite. For Sirry, "the lack of seeing the beauty in the other has led some Muslim scholars to obscure the peaceful message of the Qur'ān to such an extent that they strive to find ways to understand the inclusivist passages differently."

The third part, on beauty and Hinduism, includes contributions by Francis X. Clooney, Bradley Malkovsky, and Anant Rambachan. Professor Clooney elucidates in detail what he calls "travel the way of beauty" and offers possibilities of not only the search for beauty in the other, but also two-way traffic as how the beauty of other religions may find its way into our own religious experiences. For his part, Professor Malkovsky begins his paper with the most complex and, for outsiders, confusing notion of monotheism and polytheism in the Hindu faith, and he focuses his analysis on the Hindu teaching of non-duality (Advaita Vedanta). Despite subtle differences between the Hindu non-dualistic teaching and Christian doctrine and spirituality, Malkovsky contends that deeper reflection on this non-duality may enrich Christian theology and spirituality. This suggestion for possible theological conversations between Hinduism and Christianity is welcomed by Professor Rambachan, who further explores the different ways in which the non-duality teaching can be understood.

In the fourth part, which focuses on beauty and Buddhism, Donald Mitchell closely examines the use of the term "beauty" in the early Buddhist text (*Nikāyas*), where it has both negative and positive meanings, and explains the negative moral effects of the perception of beauty (*subha*) and ugliness and how Buddha lived beyond this duality. According to Mitchell, the positive reference to the "beautiful" (*subha*) can be understood as indicating (1) a subtle experience of beauty through mediation on a *kasina* that is the third of the eight forms of liberation, (2) the beauty of virtues lived through thought, word, and deed, and (3) the subtle beauty (*sugato*) of the Buddha's body, speech, and action expressing his attainment of Nirvāna. After explaining the notion of *Tathāgata-garbha* (womb/embryo of the Buddha), which is the source and reality of the subtle beauty of Buddhahood with oneself and the other, Professor Mitchell discusses the beauty of Buddha-nature as found in the teachings of Keiji Nishitani, the famous Buddhist philosopher and leader of the Kyoto School, and Shin'ichi Hisamatsu, the great Zen Master of the early Kyoto School. The second contribution in this part is written by Gene Reeves, the only practicing Buddhist to attend the conference. Reflecting upon Mitchell's contribution as well as a second paper by a scholar of Buddhism that could not be included in this volume, Reeves highlights the universalist dimensions of the *Lotus Sutra* tradition of Buddhism. He finds beauty not in a true self separated from the rest of reality but in the ordinary manifestation of reality, like the flowering of a whole plant, including its muddy roots.

The last part of this volume treats beauty in the African context. Teresia Hinga explores the diversity of African culture and the ways in which this reality of palpable difference(s) has been dealt with. She offers several examples to show that embracing the beauty and dignity of the Other is a moral imperative for a continent seeking a livable future. Conversely, Professor Hinga argues, the failure to adequately see, engage, and even embrace the beauty and dignity of the racially, ethnically, and religiously "Other" has too often led to (violent) conflicts that have radically compromised human and other forms of flourishing in Africa. The last—but certainly not least—contribution is presented by Paulinus Ikechukwu Odozor, C.S.Sp, and focuses on virtues and beauty in the Igbo community of Nigeria. Christianity constitutes the religion of the vast majority of the Igbo community, yet the nature of inculturation between Christianity and African Traditional Religion (ATR) is ongoing. It is oftentimes mutually enriching. Drawing from Thomas Aquinas's insights into beauty, Professor Odozor contends that "Traditional Igbo religion and Christianity share an important insight, namely, that it is all grace. Beauty in all or any of its forms, moral or physical, is grace."

Given the variety of issues and approaches herein discussed, the present volume is a unique contribution to the theological aesthetics across the different religious traditions and cultures. Looking at beauty as a point of departure, this book joins together questions concerned with Christian theology and cultural diversity with questions of Christian theology and religious diversity. At the heart of the mission of the World Religions and World Church (WRWC) initiative at the Notre Dame Theology Department is a conviction that these two areas of theological reflection are best studied together. The WRWC inaugural conference on "Finding Beauty in the Other," as reflected in this volume, has shown that the university's commitment to Catholic theology is in harmony with an interest in engaging in other religions. This interreligious engagement is possible because of Notre Dame's Catholic identity, and not despite that identity. This volume has embodied that commitment to foster academic reflection on religious diversity among Christians and non-Christians. Our authors have engaged and learned from one another to illuminate the possibility of finding beauty in the self and the other. Not only is the present volume designed to integrate the Catholic theological tradition and rigorous academic study of the religions and cultures of the world; it also provides a framework for discernment in rigorous engagement and dialogue among people of various backgrounds and disciplines.

Notes

1. As a result, this introduction highlights the insights of Jewish authors. In our area, Judaism is by no means excluded from discussion. But the two doctoral areas, World Religions and World Church (WRWC) and Christianity and Judaism in Antiquity (CJA), were conceived separately. As a result, it is up to the members of the two areas to seek to leap over these bureaucratic hurdles. This introduction represents one such leap.

2. "Ode on a Grecian Urn": "Beauty is truth, truth beauty,—that is all Ye know on earth, and all ye need to know." John Keats, *Endymion, and Other Poems* (New York: The Cassell Publishing Company, 1887), 184.

3. On this latter point, we consider the beauty of holiness below.

4. Cf. Paul Guyer, "18th Century German Aesthetics," *The Stanford Encyclopedia of Philosophy* (Winter 2016 edition), Edward N. Zalta (ed.) <https://plato.stanford.edu/archives/win2016/entries/aesthetics-18th-german/>.

5. Elaine Scarry, *On Beauty and Being Just* (Princeton, NJ: Princeton University Press, 1999), 1–53.

6. Cf. Peter Casarella, "'A Healthy Shock': Tradition and the Epiphany of Beauty," in *Tradition as the Future of Innovation*, ed. Elisa Grimi (Cambridge, England: Cambridge Scholars Press, 2015), 220–41.

7. What follows was aided greatly by the reflections of Bradley Malkovsky in his comprehensive essay herein, but the authors nonetheless take full responsibility for any distortions of advaitic doctrine that they have introduced in this section.

8. This approach is taken up by the late Stratford Caldecott in a rather apologetic fashion in his essay "'Face to Face': The Difference between Hindu and Christian Non-Dualism," *Communio: International Catholic Review* 34 (Winter 2007): 616–39. In the present volume we do not address the relationship between apologetics and dialogue. Needless to say, a defense of one's faith need not imply intolerance of the Other. This challenge of multiple theological discourses still needs to be addressed in future volumes.

9. See Bradley Malkovsky's essay below.

10. Exodus 29:43.

11. Exodus 40:34.

12. Walter Eichrodt, *Old Testament Theology* (Philadelphia, PA: Westminster, 1967), I:112.

13. Cf. Hans Urs von Balthasar, *The Glory of the Lord*, I (San Francisco, CA: Ignatius Press, 1982).

14. Von Balthasar himself never realized the potential of his own thought for pursuing the study of the world religions. For this criticism, see Louis Dupré, "Hans Urs von Balthasar's Theology of Aesthetic Form," *Theological Studies* 49 (1988): 299–318.

15. Jean-Luc Marion, *The Idol and Distance: Five Studies* (New York: Fordham University Press, 2001).

16. Exodus 33:20.

17. Immanuel Kant was no iconoclast, but in his *Critique of Judgment* he developed the idea of a beauty that always exists at the edge of natural understanding. This inherently disproportionate and unstable beauty Kant called "the sublime." For a trenchant evaluation of the unrepresentable "veil" of the Kantian sublime as a dominant *topos* of postmodernism, see David Bentley Hart, *The Beauty of the Infinite: The Aesthetics of Christian Truth* (Grand Rapids, MI: Eerdmans, 2003), 43–93.

18. Cf. Roberto S. Goizueta, *Caminemos con Jesús: Toward a Hispanic/ Latino Theology of Accompaniment* (Maryknoll, NY: Orbis, 1995), 76.

19. Emmanuel M. Katongole and Jonathan Wilson-Hartgrove, *Mirror to the Church: Resurrecting Faith after the Genocide in Rwanda* (Grand Rapids, MI: Zondervan, 2009).

20. See, for example, Patricio Merino Beas, *Teología latinoamericana y pluralismo religioso* (Salamanca: Publicaciones Universidad Pontificia, 2012).

21. Emmanuel Levinas, *Otherwise than Being or Beyond Essence* (Pittsburgh, PA: Duquesne University Press, 1998), 140–52.

22. On this point, a very instructive reflection can be found in M. Jamie Ferreira, "Total Altruism in Levinas's Ethics of the Welcome," *Journal of Religious Ethics* 29:3 (2001): 443–70.

23. *Otherwise than Being*, 6.

24. Michael A. Sells, *Mystical Languages of Unsaying* (Chicago: University of Chicago Press, 1994).

25. Michael Sells, *Languages of Unsaying*, 100.

26. Michael Sells, *Languages of Unsaying*, 101.

27. Michael Sells, *Languages of Unsaying*, 216.

28. Erich Przywara, *The Analogy of Being* (Grand Rapids, MI: Eerdmans, 2010).

29. The essay by Francis Clooney in this volume discusses the "way of beauty" at greater length.

30. Cf. Alejandro García-Rivera, *St. Martin de Porres: Little Stories and the Semiotics of Culture* (Maryknoll, NY: Orbis, 1995).

31. Cf. James Deotis Roberts, *Bonhoeffer and King: Speaking Truth to Power* (Louisville, KY: Westminster John Knox, 2005).

32. Rabbi Meir Y. Soloveichik, "Torah and Incarnation: Torah Learning Bridges the Gap between Man and God," *First Things* (October 2010): 44–49 <https://www.firstthings.com/article/2010/10/torah-and-incarnation>.

33. Meir Y. Soloveichik, "Torah and Incarnation: Torah Learning Bridges the Gap between Man and God," *First Things* (October 2010) <https://www.firstthings.com/article/2010/10/torah-and-incarnation>.

34. Meir Y. Soloveichik, "Torah and Incarnation: Torah Learning Bridges the Gap between Man and God," *First Things* (October 2010) <https://www.firstthings.com/article/2010/10/torah-and-incarnation>.

35. On "the method of rotation," see Søren Kierkegaard, *Either/Or* (Princeton, NJ: Princeton University Press, 1959), I: 279–96. Kierkegaard

writes (not without irony): "You enjoy something entirely accidental; you consider the whole of existence from this standpoint; let its reality be stranded thereon" (295).

36. Joshua Amaru, "Prayer and the Beauty of God: Rav Soloveitchik on Prayer and Aesthetics," *The Torah u-Madda Journal* 13 (2005): 148–76. This article is essentially a book review that covers the philosophy of religion contained in the posthumously published Rabbi Joseph B. Soloveitchik, *Worship of the Heart: Essays on Jewish Prayer* (New York: Ktav Publishing, 2003). This publication is based upon lectures delivered in the late 1950s.

37. Joseph B. Soloveitchik, *Worship of the Heart*, 35.

38. Joshua Amaru, "Prayer and the Beauty of God," 155.

39. Joshua Amaru, "Prayer and the Beauty of God," 153.

40. Joseph B. Soloveitchik, *Worship of the Heart*, 77.

41. Joseph B. Soloveitchik, *Worship of the Heart*, 75. For Mother Teresa's account of emptiness, see Mother Teresa, *Come Be My Light: The Private Writings of the "Saint of Calcutta"* (New York: Doubleday, 2007), 208–34.

42. Joseph B. Soloveitchik, *Worship of the Heart*, 66.

43. This connection is not surprising. Soloveitchik wrote his doctoral dissertation on the Jewish neo-Kantian Hermann Cohen. On the affinities and differences between *Worship of the Heart* and Kantian thought, see Joshua Amaru, "Prayer and the Beauty of God," 175, n. 21 and 22.

44. Joshua Amaru, "Prayer and the Beauty of God," 168.

45. Emmanuel Levinas, *Otherwise than Being*, 145.

46. Brian Hearne, "Beauty Is Truth, Truth Beauty," *Furrow* 41/1 (1990): 11.

47. Edward Farley, *Faith and Beauty: A Theological Aesthetic* (Burlington, VT: Ashgate, 2001), 2.

48. David Bentley Hart, *The Beauty of the Infinite*, 4.

49. Hearne, "Beauty Is Truth, Truth Beauty," 12.

Part I

BEAUTY AND THE CATHOLIC THEOLOGY OF RELIGIONS

Chapter One

BEAUTY AND TRUTH IN THE CHRISTIAN THEOLOGY OF RELIGIONS

Catherine Cornille, Boston College

In everything which gives us the pure authentic feeling of
beauty there really is the presence of God.
— SIMONE WEIL, *Gravity and Grace*, p. 137

An unobtrusive work of art can epitomize much patient
negotiation.
— HENRI DE LUBAC, *Catholicism*, p. 154

Of the traditional transcendentals, the category of "beauty" has
played a minimal role in Christian theology of religions. Official
Vatican documents have focused on what is "true and holy" (*Nostra
Aetate*) or on the presence of "goodness and grace" (*Dominus Iesus*
8) in other religions. And theologians themselves have been mainly
preoccupied with the salvific status of non-Christians and the presence of salvific truth in other religions and in relation to the truth
claims of Christianity. Reflections on the process of discernment of
truth in other religions have also centered predominantly on ethical virtues and the presence of analogous or homologous teachings
in other religions. *Nostra Aetate* speaks in positive terms of "ways
of conduct and life," of "precepts and teachings" of "good things,
spiritual and moral," and of "socio-cultural values," which are to be

33

respected and affirmed and which reflect a ray of truth. Throughout history, the process of inculturation has involved engagement of aesthetic elements of other religions: architecture, symbols, robes, dance, and so forth. But there has been little or no explicit discussion of the experience of beauty as a sign or expression of the presence of God's grace in other religions.

On the one hand, this neglect of the category of beauty is not surprising. The category of beauty has not been very central to theological reflection as a whole. While recognized as an expression of and a pathway to God, natural and artistic beauty has also been viewed with some suspicion because of its elusive and subjective nature, its elitism, its association with pleasure and desire, and because of the fact that it may also come to serve as a substitute for the divine. In addition to this, beauty is also often culturally and religiously particular or relative, and what is considered beautiful according to the aesthetic sensibilities of one culture may be considered ugly or tacky within another cultural and religious context. Moreover, questions of the discernment and valuation of beauty in other religions loom even larger in inter-religious than in intra-religious reflection. Finally, classical notions of beauty do not encompass the ways in which God may be revealed in other religions, where symbols of terror, ugliness, and disorder may also be of revelatory value.

On the other hand, Christian theology of religions has come to focus primarily on the Spirit as the means through which God may become manifest in other religions, and beauty is often associated with the Holy Spirit. Beauty may also be regarded as one of the most universal and unmediated expressions of the divine, as such providing a ready entry into or access to other religions. But it may play a more ambivalent role in Christian theology of religions. While sensitizing the tradition to the possible presence of truth in the other religion, it may also come to be defined in such narrow terms as to exclude the recognition of any traces of it in other religions.

Theology of religions tends to focus on internal religious reflections on the reality of religious plurality. It involves, as Alan Race has put it, "the endeavour to adumbrate some doctrine of other religions to evaluate the relationship between the Christian faith and the faith of other religions."[1] As such, it does not necessarily (even if desirably) involve actual engagement with other religions. However, such theological reflection inevitably arises in response to the encounter with the teachings, practices, and artefacts of other religions. One would thus expect beauty or aesthetics in general to be at least one element informing theological reflection.

I here suggest that the experience of beauty, or aesthetic appreciation of other religions, is closely related to theological preconception of the truth and value of those religions. The notion of beauty is not limited to purely aesthetic enjoyment, but involves any experience of the sublime, of transcendence which may become manifest in both pleasing and shocking or disorienting aesthetic forms. But the very openness to recognizing such transcendent beauty is based on theological views of revelation and its dissemination. I hope to illustrate this through the example of four Christian theologians who, in different epochs and contexts, have written powerfully of their experiences of beauty in other religions: Abbe Dubois, Henri de Lubac, Thomas Merton, and Jyoti Sahi.

Rejection of Beauty or Aesthetic Exclusivism

Until the early twentieth century, Christian views of other religions were largely shaped by a conception of the Church as the exclusive reservoir of revelation and means to salvation. Engagement with other religions thus also took the form of denunciation and demonstration of the superiority of Christianity. This is reflected in the attitudes and observations of Christian missionaries who lived in the midst of non-Christians and who were confronted on a daily basis with their teachings, practices, and artefacts. A powerful account of such attitudes may be found in the text *Hindu Manners, Customs and Ceremonies*, traditionally attributed to the French missionary Jean-Antoine Dubois (1765–1848), but currently thought to reflect the writing and re-writing of several Christian missionaries who lived and worked in India in the eighteenth and nineteenth centuries.[2] The text offers a wealth of information about social and ritual practices in South India and was for many decades one of the most detailed accounts of Hindu life and customs. The text, however, provides not only information but also clear and explicit judgment of the principles and practices observed. While the author (or authors) could muster some admiration for the elaborate detail of some Hindu temple architecture, when it came to the Hindu Gods, there is nothing but contempt for their representation and form, as reflected in this one of any number of descriptions:

> In vain are Hindu idols decked with rich ornaments; they are not rendered thereby less disagreeable in appearance. Their physiognomy is generally of frightful ugliness, which is carefully enhanced by daubing the images from time to time with a coating of dark paint. Some of the idols, thanks to the generous piety of rich votaries, have their eyes, mouth, and ears of gold or silver; but this makes them, if possibly, yet more hideous. The attitudes in which they are represented are either ridiculous, grotesque, or obscene. In short, everything is done to make them objects of disgust to any one not familiar with the sight of these strange monsters.[3]

Clearly, little effort is made to try to appreciate the aesthetic qualities of these images, even if only for believers. They are judged hideous, grotesque, obscene, and in no way comparable to the beauty of Christ and of Christianity. The alleged ugliness of their form is here clearly thought to confirm the falsehood of belief in these gods or idols. There is a faint admission in the last sentence of the possibility that beauty lies in the eyes of the beholder, and in the eyes of faith. But it is made clear that such appreciation is delusional and that there is nothing religiously or aesthetically significant about these idols. The book is not entirely critical of

Hinduism. The authors express some admiration for the caste system.[4] But there is no receptivity for the aesthetic qualities of religious objects or practices that might contradict the Christian faith.

Like other missionaries before and after him, Dubois adopted the simple lifestyle and clothing of Hindu sages. But this did not in any way sensitize him to the possibility of finding elements of truth and goodness in the Hindu tradition. As was the case with other missionaries, it was a way of rendering themselves, as well as the teachings of Christianity, amenable to Hindu tastes.

Though it is difficult and dangerous to generalize on the basis of only one example, it is probably fair to say that it was the theological denunciations of other religions that also barred Christians from appreciating the beauty or meaning of their artistic or symbolic expressions. Certain practices may have moved Christian observers. (Matteo Ricci, for example, was impressed with the ethical and social teachings of Confucius.) But a sharp distinction between cultural and religious practices allowed the exclusive religious truth claims to remain intact, or unaffected by cultural appreciation. Short of some recognition of God's Spirit at work outside Christianity, it thus seems difficult to attain some degree of aesthetic resonance with other religions, or to allow such experience to impact one's theological views.

Dependent Beauty or Aesthetic Inclusivism

In the course of the twentieth century, Christian attitudes toward the presence of truth and beauty in other religions gradually changed, mainly as a result of greater knowledge and deeper understanding of those religions. Access to the scriptures and the philosophical texts of other traditions revealed depths of spiritual and religious insight as well as similarities with Christianity hitherto unsuspected. This led to greater attention to and receptivity toward the religious and aesthetic expressions of other religions. The appropriation of religious forms in the process of inculturation

also led to a greater reflection on their original meaning and possible message for Christianity. And theologians became more vocal
about the presence of beauty in other religions.

In 1955, Henri de Lubac wrote a little-known book, *Aspects du
Bouddhisme*, Vol. 2: *Amida*. In his preface to the book, he expresses
his response to the images of Amida Buddha in the following moving terms:

> Rarely has human nostalgia taken form in a dream more
> pure. Rarely has man seemed to better experience his mis-
> ery and yet draw near to a religion of grace. Few symbols
> are as evocative of the supernatural world and its sovereign
> invasion than the Amida paintings of the "Descent" with
> their colossal Amida, luminous and serene, advancing in
> silence, Strength at once compassionate and implacable.[5]

While most French scholars of Buddhism at the beginning of the
twentieth century regarded Pure Land Buddhism as a popular and
therefore inferior form of Buddhism, theologians such as de Lubac and Karl Barth were intrigued by the similarities between this
type of Buddhism of grace and Christianity. In this description of
a painting of Amida, probably observed in the Musée Guimet in
Paris, de Lubac does more than describe what he sees. He is clearly
moved by the image and attempts to capture it in poetic, if not
spiritual terms. Immediately following this description of Amida,
however, de Lubac states:

> ...all of this, however, remains far from the Christian
> supernatural. Disengaged from the puerility of its fable,
> Amidism remains profoundly driven in the crepuscular
> thought and spirituality belonging to all "natural" reli-
> gion, as to all "natural" mysticism.[6]

These words bring the aesthetic experience squarely within the
fulfillment theology of the times. While there may be elements

of truth, goodness, and beauty in other religions, these are to be brought to completion or fulfillment in Christianity, the only true or supernatural religion. This attitude of inclusivism had become more widespread in the first half of the twentieth century. Though it may already be found in the writings of the Church fathers, who regarded certain philosophical teachings as *"preparatio evangelica,"* it became more prevalent in relation to other religions through such texts as J.N. Farquhar's *The Crown of Hinduism* (1912) and Pierre Johanns's *To Christ through the Vedanta* (1930). De Lubac was also close to Jules Monchanin, a French priest who, with the famous French Benedictine monk Henri Le Saux, attempted to establish a Benedictine Ashram in India based on a deep respect for the Indian spiritual tradition.

De Lubac's beautiful description of Amida thus reflects this theological current of greater openness to discovering elements of beauty and truth in other religions. For him, the universality of the Church meant that she should be able to encompass all forms of beauty or all types of artistic expression. "Why," he asks, "should she wish to make the rising sun show the colors of the sunset? As she is the only ark of salvation, within her immense nave she must give shelter to all varieties of humanity. She is the only banquet hall and the dishes she serves are the product of the whole of creation."[7] Whatever beauty is manifest in other religions is thus to be affirmed and taken up by Christianity. A prime example for him is the chapel of Charles de Foucault in El-Abiodh, where "From the flat roof the Angelus gives the call to prayer, and in the chapel an extra station in the Way of the Cross, a recess pointing toward Jerusalem as the mihrab of the mosques points towards Mecca, reminds all Abraham's children of the love shown by Christ in agony."[8]

The inclusivism of de Lubac expresses itself not only in the idea of the fulfillment of all beauty in Christianity, but also in the discernment of what is beautiful or pleasing or aesthetically moving. It is probably no coincidence that de Lubac found beauty in an image that resembles, at least thematically, the figure of Jesus Christ as savior. It would be difficult to imagine, for example, de Lubac or any other fulfillment theologian speaking in the same appreciative terms of, for example, Vairochana, or Vajrayogini, or Kali. Recognition of beauty in other religions is thus still clearly conditioned by and dependent on the familiar images and tropes of Christianity. And this beauty also finds its meaning and completion in Christ and in the "Christian supernatural." He states that "the beauty itself of the worship of Amida, and the depth derived from the Buddhist faith to which it remained faithful, only serve to put this teaching (of the universal transformation through the Incarnation of Jesus Christ) in a more shining light."[9] De Lubac thus maintained a distinction, prevalent in his day, between natural religions and the supernatural religion, Christianity. As such, the beauty of Amida both reveals itself and is overshadowed by the beauty of Christ. This is why one may speak of aesthetic inclusivism.

Autonomous Beauty and Aesthetic Pluralism

Increasing familiarity with the teachings and practices of other religions has led in the second half of the twentieth century to ever greater receptivity to the presence of beauty and truth in other religions and to the possibility of spiritual enrichment and growth. Monastics have played an important role in this process. Through inter-monastic dialogue and exchanges, Christian monks came to adopt, at times, certain Eastern meditative practices and to establish Zen gardens or practice tea ceremonies in Christian monasteries. These were seen not merely as derivative of Christianity, but as means to deepen and enhance the Christian experience. The experience of the beauty of Zen gardens may thus be regarded as autonomous, insofar as it did not immediately derive from analogous Christian aesthetics or teachings and as reflective of the belief that God's beauty may be refracted even in symbols, practices, and artefacts that are different from Christianity. To be sure, such beauty will tend to remain in continuity with basic Christian teachings and sensibilities. But it may also lead to aesthetic surprise or transformation, and to genuinely new insights and experiences. I believe that Thomas Merton's experience at Polonnaruwa may be an example of this.

This experience did not occur without context or preparation. Merton had for some time immersed himself in the study of other religions, in particular Taoism, Zen, and Tibetan Buddhism. In the course of studying these traditions and encountering monks from them, he increasingly came to believe in the deep unity of spiritual traditions, which he expressed in the following terms in a famous address to Hindu and Buddhist monks:

> The deepest level of communication is not communication, but communion. It is wordless. It is beyond words and it is beyond speech, and it is beyond concept. Not that we discover a new unity. We discover an older unity. My dear brothers, we are already one. But we imagine that we are not. And what we have to recover is our original unity. What we have to be is what we are.[10]

Whether Merton here refers to a common thirst for the divine or to a common humanity or to a common mystical experience is not entirely clear. However, his words do reflect a belief in the possibility of mutual understanding across religious traditions and in the validity of different religious paths. His *Asian Journal* also suggests a thirst for or openness to new experiences and for deep interreligious encounter. By the time Merton visited Asia, in 1968, the Vatican II document *Nostra Aetate* had also opened the door to greater recognition of other religions in their alterity and for genuine interreligious dialogue. The stage was thus set for his experience of the beauty of the Buddhist statues at Gal Vihara in Polonnaruwa, Sri Lanka. It is worth quoting the whole experience here:

> The path dips down to Gal Vihara: a wide, quiet, hollow, surrounded with trees. A low outcrop of rock, with a cave cut into it, and beside the cave a big seated Buddha on the left, a reclining Buddha on the right, and

Ananada, I guess, standing by the head of the reclining Buddha. In the cave, another seated Buddha. The vicar general, shying away from "paganism," hangs back and sits under a tree reading the guidebook. I am able to approach the Buddhas barefoot and undisturbed, my feet in wet grass, wet sand. Then the silence of the extraordinary faces. The great smiles. Huge and yet subtle. Filled with every possibility, questioning nothing, knowing everything, rejecting nothing, the peace not of emotional resignation but of Madhyamika, of sunyata, that has seen through every question without trying to discredit anyone or anything—*without refutation*—without establishing some other argument. For the doctrinaire, the mind that needs well-established positions, such peace, such silence can be frightening.

I was knocked over with a rush of relief and thankfulness at the obvious clarity of the figures, the clarity and fluidity of shape and line, the design of the monumental bodies composed into the rock shape and landscape figure, rock and tree. And the sweep of the bare rock sloping away on the other side of the hollow, where you can go back and see different aspects of the figures.

Looking at these figures I was suddenly, almost forcibly, jerked clean out of the habitual, half-tied vision of things, and an inner clearness, clarity, as if exploding from the rocks themselves, became evident and obvious. The queer evidence of the reclining figures, the smile, the sad smile of Ananada standing with arms folded (much more "imperative" than Da Vinci's Mona Lisa because completely simple and straightforward).

The thing about all this is that there is no puzzle, no problem, and really no "mystery." All problems are resolved and everything is clear, simply because what matters is clear. The rock, all matter, all life, is charged with dharmakaya...everything is emptiness and everything is compassion. *I don't know when in my life I have ever had such a sense of beauty and spiritual validity running together in one aesthetic illumination.* Surely, with Mahabalipuram and Polonnaruwa my Asian pilgrimage has come clear and purified itself. I mean, I know and have seen what I was obscurely looking for. I don't know what else remains but I have now seen and have pierced through the surface and have got beyond the shadow and the disguise. This is Asia in its purity, not covered over with garbage, Asian or European or American, and it is clear, pure, complete. It says everything; it needs nothing. And because it needs nothing it can afford to be silent, unnoticed, undiscovered. It does not need to be discovered. It is we, Asians included, who need to discover it.

The whole thing is very much a Zen garden, a span of bareness and openness and evidence and the great figures, motionless, yet with the lines in full movement, waves of vesture and bodily form, *a beautiful and holy vision.*[11]

Much has been made of this account of Merton's experience of the beauty of the Buddhist statues. Some have interpreted it as his experience of enlightenment, and some have seen it as an experience of conversion to Buddhism. Merton passed away a week after this experience, which gives it added pertinence, weight, and mystery.

A few things are striking about this experience in comparison with the two prior examples. First, he is clearly very familiar with the broader religious meaning of these images within the Buddhist context. There is not one reference to Christianity or to Christian themes in the description. The only comparison he makes is between Ananda and the Mona Lisa, and it is in favor of the former. His description and experience are entirely rendered in Buddhist terms. He also speaks of his "aesthetic illumination" as surpassing anything he had hitherto experienced. As such, Merton seems to be able to appreciate the beauty and majesty of the statues entirely on their own terms and to gain an experience of the sublime that is irreducible to any prior normative aesthetic or religious categories. This is why one may speak here of autonomous beauty or of a genuine experience of the alterity of the beauty of the other tradition.

This attitude toward the beauty of another religion naturally requires a framework in which other religions may indeed be understood and appreciated in their own terms. It has long been cultivated in the history of religions and in cultural anthropology as the proper way to study and understand other religions. In Christian theology of religions, it has generally come to be associated with theological pluralism, in which different religions are viewed as roughly equivalent reflections of the ultimate reality. It is not my intention here to dub Merton as a pluralist, since his writings are too complex for any facile categorization. However, his experience did presuppose an openness to finding distinctive truth and meaning in other religions, and thus a theology that recognized the possible presence of God or the manifestation of God's beauty in unique ways in other religious traditions. Merton did not live to relate this experience to his Christian faith. But his belief in the authenticity of different monastic traditions and in the unity of different spiritual paths allowed him to open himself up to an experience that was different from anything he had experienced before and that clearly had a transformative effect.

Beauty as Expression of Interreligious Dialogue

In the process of the inculturation of Christianity, Christian artists have long used the symbols and esthetic sensibilities of various cultures to express Christian teachings. These artistic expressions tended to remain very close to traditional Christian teachings, merely adapting them to local contexts without seeking to change or challenge them. Since the late twentieth century, however, Christian artists have gone further and used their art as a vehicle or means to interreligious dialogue. A famous example of this is the Indian Christian artist Jyoti Sahi. The son of an Indian father and a British mother, he studied art both in India and in England, and his work is a form of dialogue between Christianity and Hinduism. It not only seeks to "share my faith with people of other faiths," as Sahi puts it, but also to bring the meaning and depth of those other faiths into the awareness and perception of Christians. As a disciple of Bede Griffiths, he became deeply immersed in the spiritual teachings and practices of Hinduism and sought to express his understanding of Hindu wisdom in Christian images and his understanding of Christian wisdom in Hindu images. Beyond merely recognizing beauty and truth in other religions, Sahi thus attempts to integrate elements of the truth of Hinduism through Christian aesthetic expression. In a series of charcoal drawings, for example, he depicts various dimensions of Jesus' life and suffering through the use of yogic postures. Commenting on these images, Sahi states:

> These postures of the body attempt to find a spiritual reality embodied in Creation. For, although yoga is a physical practice, it is deeply connected with the imagination, or the way that we understand the body as a vessel or vehicle of the Spirit. In that sense, yoga has a cosmic dimension and is concerned with the transformation of Nature into a deeper experience of the spiritual force present in all of Creation. The body is thus not only something external: within the body there lies the world of the imagination. There is a profound link between soul and body, and the gestures of the body symbolize inner spiritual attitudes. It is in this way that we can understand an "inner landscape." Yogic postures can show us the body as a tree, a mountain, some animal like a snake or lion, or even as a seed. And the act of touching the earth can itself embody an inner humility—or kenosis—that honors the earth.[12]

The use of Hindu yogic imagery in Christian art thus draws attention to the neglect of the body in traditional Christian theology and art and to the relationship between the body and the spirit. Another famous and recurrent theme in Sahi's work involves the presentation of Jesus in the posture of the dancing Shiva, thus evoking a more creative and dynamic sense of Jesus Christ. With time, Sahi's art became increasingly infused with tribal and Dalit imagery, in which nature and the feminine play an important role. Commenting on his images of a tribal Madonna, he observes:

> Too often Christian imagery has focused on the mascu-
> line representation of the divine, leaving out the spiritual
> importance of the feminine figure. Indian art and cul-
> ture has tried to conceive of spiritual reality in terms that
> include both feminine and masculine characteristics.[13]

Here the beauty of the other religion becomes not merely a means to appreciate and further experience its truth, but a way to expand and deepen the understanding of one's own tradition. It allows artists immersed in the aesthetic and theological context of the other to appropriate certain symbols and themes and use them in order to bring about a greater openness toward the other tradition or traditions in Christian viewers, and to broaden their own aesthetic and spiritual imagination.

Though the recognition of beauty in the other thus requires some affirmation of divine revelation in other religions, beauty may also become a vehicle for advancing truth and understanding not only of the other religion, but also of one's own. Artists such as Jyoti Sahi, known as "the theologian with a brush," therefore play an important role in interreligious dialogue and comparative theology, or faith seeking understanding in dialogue with another religion.

Conclusion

The topic of beauty in theology of religions revolves around the question of whether one can, from a Christian theological point of view, acknowledge the existence of beauty in other religious traditions, and what the status is of that beauty in relation to the beauty of the gospel and of the Christian object of faith. Attention to beauty rather than truth or goodness might make some sense, both phenomenologically and theologically. Beauty may be regarded as one of the most pure and immediate forms of access to other religions. Observing the art and architecture of other religions or beautifully executed rituals may stir certain feelings or responses prior to any theoretical knowledge or theological reflection. As such, beauty may open the way to further theological reflection. And this may indeed happen, at least unconsciously.

However, on a theoretical and theological level, beauty in general and interreligious beauty in particular become much more difficult to thematize. Not only do the criteria of beauty tend to be culturally and at times religiously particular, but beauty functions in different ways in different religions, and the appreciation of the meaning of aesthetic expressions requires profound knowledge of the other tradition, as well as a theological license to explore the other tradition in such depth. This theological license within Christianity has focused primarily on questions of truth and salvific efficacy. Is there truth to be found in other religions, and what is the status of that truth in relation to the Christian claims to the unique salvific efficacy of Jesus Christ and of the Church?

The above discussion of Dubois, de Lubac, and Merton has made clear that aesthetic experiences of other religions are indeed deeply colored by theological presuppositions with regard to the status of those religions. For the Abbe Dubois, it was impossible to acknowledge any beauty in Hindu images, since these were deemed idolatrous and in direct opposition to the teachings of Christianity. Missionaries may have appreciated the beauty of certain cultural and religious forms that were not in contradiction to Christianity. But the explicit and very vocal judgment of Hindu images points to an aesthetic exclusivism directly consonant with theological exclusivism.

As Christianity became more open to other religions, theologians such as Henri de Lubac came to recognize beauty particularly in images that depicted certain similarities with Christianity or that could be taken up within Christianity and given Christian meaning. This also reflected the inclusivism of his day.

Only a few decades later, Thomas Merton had already developed a theological basis for acknowledging beauty in other religions in its own right, and for gaining aesthetic experiences that expanded his religious horizon. His experience of the beauty of the Buddhist statues arose from a sense of deep spiritual unity—one that, however, he does not explicate in Christocentric terms. The beauty of the images here is not derived from Christianity, but maintains a certain autonomy, which nevertheless may touch a Christian observer and open him or her up to a new experience.

Finally, the work of Jyoti Sahi represents the culmination of Christian openness toward the truth and beauty of other religions, where such beauty and truth are not only acknowledged, but also used to enrich and enhance Christian self-understanding and aesthetic experience and expression. To be sure, not all artistic expressions of other religions will become a source of inspiration for Christian artists. But the very possibility of exploring other traditions through the intimate connection between beauty and truth opens many new avenues for theological innovation and growth.

This sampling of different experiences of beauty in other religions thus suggests that in the interplay between truth and beauty, aesthetic experiences remain highly dependent on theological valuation of the other religion. This, however, does not preclude the possibility of aesthetic experiences in turn enriching theological understanding. One can only speculate about the ways in which Merton's experience might have informed his theological views. In opening the door to the recognition of truth in other religions, one may also gain aesthetic experiences that do not fit traditional criteria of beauty, but that may expand theological understanding.

Beauty, whether pleasing or terrible, has the effect of moving, uplifting, shocking, or transforming the observer. Profound aesthetic experiences in and of other religions may thus become a starting point for further exploration of the meaning and truth of particular symbols, images, and practices, not only for the other religion, but also for one's own. As such, beauty might come to play a more important role in Christian theology of religions and comparative theology alike.

Notes

1. Alan Race, *Christians and Religious Pluralism* (Maryknoll, NY: Orbis Books, 1983), 3.

2. In studying the original manuscript, the French researcher Sylvia Murr discovered the existence of a version of the manuscript, dated 1777 (many years prior to Dubois's arrival in India) and attributed to a certain Nicholas Jacques Desvaulx, an officer in the French army stationed in Pondicherry. Murr concludes that both Desvaulx and Dubois copied their own respective texts from a third and original "ur-text" that she attributes to the Jesuit Father Gaston-Laurent Coeurdoux (1691–1779), who worked as a missionary in Pondicherry. Murr published an annotated edition of the text accompanied by a study of the thought of Coeurdoux in two volumes: *L'Inde philosophique entre Bossuet et Voltaire:* Volume I: *Moeurs et coutumes des Indiens (1777),* and Volume II: *L'Indologie du père Coeurdoux. Stratégies, apologétique et scientificité* (Paris: École Française d'Extrême Orient, 1987).

3. Abbe Jean Antoine Dubois, *Hindu Manners, Customs, and Ceremonies* (Oxford: Oxford University Press, 1906), 581.

4. For example, the author states: "I am persuaded that it is simply and solely due to the distribution of the people into castes that India did not lapse into a state of barbarism, and that she preserved and perfected the arts and sciences of civilization whilst most other nations of the earth remained in a state of barbarism." Dubois, *Hindu Manners, Customs and Ceremonies,* 28.

5. In Henri de Lubac, *Amida* (Paris: Éditions du Seuil, 1955), 10. My translation.

6. *Idem.*

7. Henri de Lubac, *Catholicism* (London: Burns and Oates, 1950), 156.

8. Henri de Lubac, *Catholicism,* 154.

9. Henri de Lubac, *Amida*, 10.

10. Thomas Merton, *The Asian Journal of Thomas Merton*, ed. Naomi Burton, Brother Patrick Hart, and James Laughlin (New York: New Directions, 1973), 308.

11. Thomas Merton, *Asian Journal*, 235–36. My italics.

12. Jyoti Sahi, "Yoga and the Wounded Heart," *Religion and the Arts* 12 (2008): 54.

13. *Ibid.*, 68.

Works Cited

Dubois, Abbe Jean Antoine. *Hindu Manners, Customs and Ceremonies.* Oxford: Oxford University Press, 1906.

Lubac, Henri de. *Aspects du Bouddhisme*, vol. 2: *Amida*. Paris: Éditions du Seuil, 1954.

———. *Catholicism.* London: Burns and Oates, 1950.

Merton, Thomas. *The Asian Journal of Thomas Merton*, edited by Naomi Burton, Patrick Hart, and James Laughlin. New York: New Directions, 1973.

Murr, Sylvia, ed. *L'Inde philosophique entre Bossuet et Voltaire:* Vol. I: *Moeurs et coutumes Des Indiens (1777)*; Vol. II: *L'Indologie du Père Coeurdoux. Stratégies, apologétique et scientificité.* Paris: École Française d'Extrême Orient, 1987.

Race, Alan. *Christians and Religious Pluralism.* Maryknoll, NY: Orbis Books, 1983.

Sahi, Jyoti. "Yoga and the Wounded Heart." *Religion and the Arts* 12 (2008): 43–80.

Weil, Simone. *Gravity and Grace.* London and New York: Routledge, 2002.

Chapter Two

HIDDEN BEAUTY AND HOPE: THE FACE OF THE OTHER

Maria Clara Lucchetti Bingemer,
Pontifical Catholic University, Brazil

The Church is "essentially ecstatic, signifying a humble and expanding exstasis."

—CARDINAL LÉON-ÉTIENNE DUVAL[1]

According to the Argentine philosopher Juan Carlos Scannone, "neither the classic metaphysics of substance, nor the modern philosophy of the self-conscious subject adequately accounts for human personal identity insofar as it is personal (*ipse*). In other words, they don't give a conclusive answer to the question: Who?"[2] For this reason, some philosophical systems opt for a new paradigm: that of Otherness. This reflects an attempt to surmount the Cartesian axiom "I think," founded and centered in oneself. The intention is thus to discover that human beings are not definable solely by their cognitive and thinking capacity, but by their Otherness and intersubjectivity. Otherness, therefore, would constitute human personal identity.[3] However, such Otherness can be interpreted in ways that are not mutually exclusive. They could be "the Otherness of being—or of reality—with respect to the subject, of the body itself, of the Face of the Other, of the community of communication, of the ethic-religious we, of the voice of conscience, of phenomena saturated with benefaction, including religious manifestations of the sacred, etc."[4]

After defining some key concepts in Levinas's philosophy, we will, in this chapter, examine the journey of a very special witness of the twentieth century: the Trappist Christian de Chergé, prior of the community of Tibhirine, who was kidnapped and murdered in Algeria in 1996. For Christian and for de Chergé's community, beauty was found and contemplated in the Faces of the Muslims in whose country they lived as guests, hoping to dialogue and live together. We want to reflect on how, and in what manner, this beauty continued to be loved and respected—despite being a hidden beauty—when threats and persecution appeared.

Otherness and Difference: The Center of Levinas's Philosophy

The center of Levinas's philosophy is the epiphany manifested and revealed in the Face of the Other, who is poor and oppressed, and who questions violence. Levinas defines the other in two ways: the metaphysical other and the other as Face.

> The way in which the other presents himself, exceeding *the idea of the other in me*, we here name face. This *mode* does not consist in figuring as a theme under my gaze, in spreading itself forth as a set of qualities forming an image. The face of the Other at each moment destroys and overflows the plastic image it leaves me, the idea existing to my own measure and to the measure of its *ideatum*—the adequate idea. It does not manifest itself by these qualities, but καθ' αὐτό.[5] It *expresses itself.*[6]

Levinas clearly opts for responsibility for the other as the ethical basis for human society. And this society would be constructed from a transcendental perspective, which for him consists of the epiphany of the Face of the Other. It is only here that the relationship I–Other is established, leading to rational law and political structure as guarantees of liberty—which "presupposes" that each individual enters freely into relationships with others in such a way that the law and the structure are possible. But this relationship, this dialogue with the other, is characterized essentially by the absolute quality of the ethical relationship, which for Levinas is the relationship *"par excellence."*[7]

Thus, the philosopher, who is avowedly Lithuanian and Jewish, argues that any ethic that does not begin with the personal cannot be adequately transposed to the public level. The *other* and the *Face* are generic names, but in every moral encounter these names represent just one being—one Other, one Face. Nor can the name appear in the plural without losing its ethical stature, its moral meaning.[8] Collective concepts such as "the people" and "the community," in Levinas's understanding, do not go to the root of true ethics, which must always take place between "you and me."[9] And entering into this moral space means taking time away from daily work and from one's social position, as well as leaving aside mundane rules and conventions. To this ethical encounter of two—the other and I— one must come divested of one's own social apparatus, stripped of status, social distinctions, deficiencies, ranks or functions, being neither rich nor poor, elevated nor humble, powerful nor powerless—reduced to the naked essentiality of our common humanity.

In his essay *"La souffrance inutile"* ["Useless Suffering"], Levinas states that "intersubjectivity in its proper meaning is non-indifference to others."[10] It is a responsibility to others, but, before the reciprocity of such responsibility, it is inscribed in impersonal law. For this reason, the intersubjective perspective can survive, but it can also be lost in the political order of the city or in the law that establishes the reciprocal obligations of the citizens.[11]

Levinas holds that charity is impossible without justice, but that justice without charity becomes deformed.[12] Pope Benedict XVI, in his encyclical *Caritas in Veritate*, agreed with this position, but added that Christian charity goes further than symmetry with justice.[13] It incorporates the unlimited love of the Gospel in the Sermon on the Mount. However, he agreed that any charity that is not anchored in justice is not worthy of the name.

Thus, according to Levinas, the macro-ethical extension of moral responsibility in relation to the other goes beyond our defense against shared dangers. Accordingly, we want to keep in mind that, for Levinas, the overarching equivalent of moral responsibility is nothing less than justice—a quality of human existence that obviously requires the anticipation of global catastrophes as a preliminary condition. But moral responsibility can in no way be reduced to this. Neither can it be considered successful in this limited way, even if prevention might have been effective in some way.[14]

In view of what Levinas says about ethics, one must therefore be aware that ethics is not enough—especially when it is light and painless ethics, such as that which prevails today, and which certainly is not Levinasian ethics. From a theological point of view, we add to Levinas's ethical primordiality the need for mysticism—the experience of Mystery, of Transcendence—as a source of ethics. Only then does ethics cease to be an ethics of disaster prevention or of institutional safeguards and become an ethics of caring, of concern for the other, of being affected by what affects the other.[15]

If justice is understood as Levinas wished it to be, expanding and generalizing such a strictly selective responsibility, applied to the singular and unique other, then—as is true of this responsibility—justice must emerge not so much from the demands of the other as from an ethical impulse and from a concern with the ethical self, which assumes the responsibility of seeing that justice is done. In other words, within the conception that permeates all Levinasian work, moral responsibility is asymmetric and nonreciprocal. Therefore, it can be derived only from mysticism, which opens the subject toward the Whole.[16]

To do justice is to always demand more of oneself. Only when we know this will the desire for justice be unsusceptible to the most striking of dangers: that of self-satisfaction and of a conscience once and for all light, calm, and clean.[17]

The idea of justice is thus conceived at the moment of encounter between the experience of uniqueness (such as moral responsibility for the other) and the experience of the multiplicity of others (as in social life). It cannot dispense with either of these two elements, because if there were no memory of the uniqueness of the Face, there would be no idea of a generalized, "impersonal" justice. Morality is the school of justice. The infiniteness of moral responsibility, the limitlessness (even the silence!) of moral requirements, simply cannot be sustained when "the other" appears in the plural. The epiphany of the Face in its density and its "accusation" is indispensable for the existence of ethics and a commitment to justice.[18]

It is in its frailty and vulnerability that the Face of the Other is a constant temptation to murder.[19] Through its appearance as a naked, powerless, and needy Otherness—like the Biblical characters who personify the poor, the foreigner, the widow, and the orphan—the Face invites or even challenges the ego as it strives to achieve more happiness and power, seizing the other in his or her weakness. The naked and mortal Face seduces me, reducing me to myself and leading me to acts of violence and even to murder.[20]

And what is most intoxicating about this seduction is the fact that the violent ego realizes that it is in no way forbidden to manipulate others in their weakness.[21] According to Levinas, this is the heart of responsible, dialogical, and nonviolent ethics. In the vulnerability exposed in the Face of the Other, I discover myself as a potential murderer. I discover, at the same time, that the poverty of the other is a substantial strength, a radical resistance to my totalizing and reductionist cupidity. The Face of the Other thus appears as "opposition," insofar as it places itself in front of and "against" me, confronting me as a radical interdiction, as a resistance to all my obsessions.[22] This resistance, this force, this accusation raised against me in my violent potentiality, does not come from the free choice of the other but from his or her essential Otherness, in the destitution that proclaims itself as a protest against the violence of the ego.[23]

The Christian experience of God has this Otherness at its center. The difference of the Other is seeded through the whole of the Gospel of Jesus in the Face of the poor, the widow, the orphan, the woman, the pagan, the sick, and the leprous—also, and very frequently, the reconnaissance of the Face of the worshiped God in the Face of the God of the Other's faith and in the faith of the Other.

The experience of the Tibhirine monks can bestow significant light on this question and give it a special growth quality. Among them, the prior Christian de Chergé, a passionate and faithful Levinasian reader, reflects and brings a very moving process of recognition of the other as intrinsic value to be discerned, recognized, and loved.

Christian de Chergé and the Passion for Islam

Christian de Chergé was a Frenchman who entered the diocesan seminary of Paris and afterward felt the call to be a Trappist monk, a contemplative vocation that he chose to pursue in the heart of Algeria, a Muslim-majority country. When he uttered his last vows in the monastery, he said that the intimacy of that community went directly to his desire and to the deep sense of a consecration to the "communion of saints." This sense of intimacy and communion was something very important in his vocation, and it held deep meaning in the transformation of his original vocation into a universal prayer, which was made together with all the saints of North Africa and "all the saints hidden in Algerian countries, pagans, Jews, Christians or Muslims."[24]

Choosing to root his perpetual consecration in Algeria, de Chergé was fully aware that he was the guest of a people who welcomed him. He infinitely desired this dependence, as he understood and called himself a "beggar of love."[25] Nevertheless, he was also very aware of the perpetual insecurity and the great and kenotical divestiture that this call imposed on him. Writing to a friend, he said:

> The call I feel made me want to be a foreigner who has
> no more a home in this world in order to be able to go
> where God desires. But this same call consecrated myself

to live a vow of stability in this monastery, to be a living incarnation with all the inhabitants of this country, this City of God where all the frontiers of country, race and religion should one day disappear.[26]

After his election as prior, Christian became the anchor of this group, which would follow the prophetic intuitions of its presence in Islamic countries. For instance, he adopted a series of local habits in order to identify with the Muslims. During Ramadan, he fasted from morning to sunset, as did his neighbors, maintaining his normal work regimen and saying: "Eucharist is enough for me."[27] He also followed the Muslim tradition of taking off one's sandals before entering the chapel.[28] After coming ever closer to his brothers and sisters of Islam, he would create with others the movement "Lien de Paix" (Bond of Peace), which had as its goal the Mystic of the encounter.

Christian was a good reader of Levinas, and that contributed to his developing a mystique and a reflection in which Otherness and vulnerability, such essential categories in the Jewish philosophers' reflection, were strongly present.

We would like to reproduce here two texts written by Christian de Chergé. They reflect this Levinasian influence and demonstrate, in a luminous way, the intensity of his searching for and discovery of the hidden beauty of the other, which he allowed to inspire his life and monastic vocation.

To Pray with the Body and the Words of the Other

Among the prior's writings, there are many that testify to his passion for Islam and how he found beauty in this difference between his faith and the Other. Among those many texts, we first highlight one that we feel is especially significant. It describes a common prayer that de Chergé shares with a Muslim in the monastery chapel. The description is very discreet and somehow mysterious.

Nevertheless, it is quite evident that the experience is a common prayer by two mystics from different traditions.

There are three people that night in the chapel. Christian is one; the other is a Muslim who arrives afterward, and a third who arrives later and does not completely understand what is taking place.

NIGHT OF FIRE[29]

A quarter of an hour after Compline, back to the chapel....
Silence of the night, this beach at the coast of the Word,
where all words and noises of the day come to break.

Twilight of the night, under the shadow of a Presence entrusted to the custody of the trembling lamp of the sanctuary.

Prayer of surrender, prostrate, between the altar and the tabernacle: "Seek the LORD while He may be found; call to Him while He is near" said prophet Isaiah (liturgy of this day...).

And after, this other presence who comes close, sweetly, unusual.

You were there too, you too, very close to the same altar, knelt, prostrated brother.

Silence continues, during a long moment.

A whisper rises, coming from the depths, then enlarges, pulling up to some abyss, just as a peaceful and at the same time irresistible source: ALLAH! GOD! ALLAH AKBAR! "The great!" A sigh "God"! Again and again this sigh, as the one of a child sucking the breast who doesn't stop for a minute unless to resume the breath before asking again; the sigh of the one who knows that prayer is unappeasable, not sating by being there, turned to the Totally Other even being so small.

Silence. Then you turned to me: "Pray for me." Another silence, you waiting. We had just exchanged some words after your arrival, on Monday, with him, our common friend. You remain there. I need to risk words I will hardly hear.

Lord Unique and Almighty, Lord who sees us, You who unites everything under your sight, Lord of tenderness and mercy, God who is ours, fully.

Teach us to pray together, You, the only Master of prayer, You who attract first those who turn on to you: You, You, You....

From then on, our prayer in two voices. Arabic and French mix together, they meet mysteriously, they answer each other, they merge, they complement and combine. The Muslim invokes Christ. The Christian submits to God's plan over all the believers, and over one of them, the prophet Mohammed....

Afterward, one and the other search to penetrate together inside the Love who says God. Behold they are both in the storm....

"The waves assault me, order peace!" you say.

"Lord, save us, we perish!"

"Put your light in my heart, enlighten my way," you say.

"Put light in my eyes, light in my lips, light in my ears, light in my heart.... I am the light of the world. You are the light of the world, which shall not be hidden, as it must shine for me...."

The path becomes narrower, while the denser silence still opens a common path toward the shared love of this God.

You are the one who leaps. I welcome.

"I don't ask you for wealth; I don't ask for anything except the Love that comes from You, because nothing is lovable out of You, and nobody can love without You. I only want to love You in everything. Love is the source, the eye of religion. Love is the joyful consolation of faith."

Praise then overflows the place and the moment. It makes us go back in time to discover all the steps of the long adventure of God searching for humankind, since Abraham, the Friend.

And then he arrives, too. He was waiting for you, searching, surprised at not seeing you arrive for the evening meeting, to the prayer before the second meal of Ramadan that he took with you. He had just talked for a long time with some guests, answering your questions about the prayer "in the Spirit."

In the dark of the chapel, he didn't perceive at first glance anything else than a whisper. Intrigued, not daring to believe too much, he came and found us, here, together. He joined us. And the Word came to us immediately: "For where two or three have gathered together in My name, I AM there in their midst." What else can we ask?

Prayer becomes broader, less breathless. A complicity among three, more demanding for the interior ear which wishes itself available in each one's way, strange, baffling sometimes; the impression of wriggling in the sands! To allow each one's prayer to interplead us in the deepest of a silence without another voice, to recall ourselves during the flight, then to leap ourselves again in the direction of the other, suffused with a new echo. Note after note, the symphony is built in the fusion of those three different expressions of a same and unique fidelity, the one of the Spirit who is in God, who says "God!" Prayer against Satan's temptations, "the stoned"; afterward together, the "fatihá," the Magnificat (you repeat it, word after word), the Pater (you know it by heart) and, always and ever, the praise and thanksgiving.

Should we say we stopped? It was past 11 p.m.! Since 8 p.m. we were there, side by side...all this time, one moment, unbelievable! Exuberant joy, each one by his side, each one his way. Tomorrow, you will tell you wished to dance, after going around the buildings, four times, singing.

What if God Himself would laugh of the good trick He just played on centuries of imprecations among brothers called to pray to Him?

And he wanted, even then, to know how did you do it? You told him: "When I saw him there, alone, I felt it was necessary to do something. I was afraid and then I went... there was a force in me that pushed me...."

Before saying good-bye, this Monday, we talked of other things.

It was a little bit as if that burned still, and couldn't be said without being lost. "Fresh paintings" we do not touch, otherwise they will become all blurred.

You told me: "Everything is simple when God leads it." That is all.

N.B.: notes posted on paper on September 24th 1975. Until this day of birthday (September 21st 1976) I haven't met this brother of just one night. He exists. He tells me all the others.

This common prayer and this mystical moment, lived together by two men belonging to two different traditions, shows in a very moving way their belief in God and in the epiphany of the Other. From the differences that exist between them, the epiphany makes possible the humanly impossible: to pray to the God of the Other, to rejoice within the faith of the Other, and to experience a double ecstasy: that of going out of one's own tradition into the Other's tradition, and that of opening oneself up in order to be spiritually consoled by the Other's experience in the Other's tradition.

Levinas's influence is visible in Christian de Chergé's theology and spirituality, having impacted his conception of God and inspired his prayer and action. It even enlightens his reading of the Qur'an. In his homily of December 10, 1995, during Advent, when the threats of death were already very close to him and his monastery and community, he said:

As the definitive restoration of the Kingdom approaches, where we will understand at last all the "Why?" of our differences (Qur'an 5:48); now is the time of waiting for the other. And it is the time for MERCY. It is up to us to receive it with gratitude from the Very Other, as obscure witnesses of a difference, the one Jesus introduced coming to the world, light in our darkness. The Spirit of wisdom and force, of counsel and discernment, of knowledge and fear of the Lord presides over this difference, toward which he guides all the differences of "others" and my particular difference, while waiting for the Other; difference, my HOPE! Yes, truly, Lord, you are the Other we wait for![30]

The Other would come to Christian and his community in the form of martyrdom. Fr. Christophe Lebreton, novice master and the poet of the community, called their community a "community in epiclesis." He used this Eucharistic term of Catholic and Eastern liturgy to describe their situation: waiting for an almost certain death that would definitively "consecrate" them, while not leaving the monastery and the people to whom they were committed and devoted.[31]

Nevertheless, Christian refused to accept the title of martyr for the faith because he thought the term was charged with a form of integrism, of the conscience of being "pure," compared to others who are not. "Jesus purifies, in effect, but through love. To the one who is not pure, he still says: 'My friend.' The only possible martyrdom is the one of love.... Jesus' testimony in the face of death, his 'martyrdom' is 'the martyrdom of love, love for the human being, for all human beings. And the martyrdom of love includes forgiveness."[32]

The Face of the Other in the Hidden Beauty of Death

While the current-day terrorists' actions speak against Islam, the love of the prior for this religion and its members only grew, though not through an alienated, mystical feeling, projecting itself beyond historical conflicts. He also assumed the facts, knowing that God is not a stranger regarding human history. He accepted the risks of the present. Like his other religious brothers, he was there as an offering, without defense. This was to be where God wanted him to be.[33]

It was a situation in which fear was present. However, it was defeated by hope on a daily basis. A man of his time, Christian de Chergé was fully aware that faith, in times of secularization and even post-modernity, does not exclude doubt and questioning. While the martyrs of faith were hard on their judges, understanding themselves as "pure" in front of other "impure" ones who were responsible for his or her death, Jesus teaches that the only martyrdom is the one of love, of charity—even to the friend who betrays him, even to the one who is responsible for his death and whose feet he washed.

Jesus' martyrdom is full of love for all human beings, even the marginal, the thieves, the criminals, and the ones who act in darkness in the dead of night. This martyrdom includes forgiveness, the perfect gift, always unfinished because it is persistent in giving. Moreover, Christian reminded his monastic and religious community that this is what they did when they took their vows, delivering to God their lives and letting Him do with it what He wanted.

It is still this love that guides them. It is what makes them not take sides against others, or vice versa. Given a theological, spiritual, and political choice, they choose not an impossible neutrality, but the infinite and universal freedom of loving everyone, whoever they are. In addition, Christian offers this reminder:

> If I gave my life to Algerian people, I gave it also to the Emir S.A. (chief of the GIA). He will not take it up from myself, even if he decides to inflict on me the same treatment he gave to our Croatian friends. Moreover, in spite of that, I wish strongly that he will respect it, in the name of the love that God also inscribed in his human vocation. Jesus could not desire Judas' treason. Calling him "friend," he addresses the hidden love. He searches for his Father in this man. In addition, I even believe that He found him.[34]

The prior concludes by reminding his brothers that Christians are not the only ones to give this testimony and to live this martyrdom. In the history of the Algerian drama, there are many authentic martyrs of a simple and gracious love. Where there is this love, there is God. There the martyrdom of charity will happen, recognition of the Other in his/her divine transfiguration, the encounter with the hidden beauty of the Other.

It is this hope, this love, this innocence, this charity, this multiform and universal testimony (martyrdom) that gave and continues to give weight to the prior's and the whole community's testimony. The community lived in a state of epiclesis, waiting for what was to come. In addition, those men tried to find and feel beauty through this long and fearful waiting.

Christian's testament, surely one of the most important spiritual texts of the twentieth century, shows us that he expected until the end to meet and to see that hidden beauty of the Other, even when this otherness certainly was going to be the advent of his death. Even then, he could see this "Face" of the last moment with love and as a friend:

TESTAMENT OF
DOM CHRISTIAN DE CHERGÉ[35]
(opened on Pentecost Sunday, May 26, 1996)

FACING A GOODBYE...

If it should happen one day—and it could be today—that I become a victim of the terrorism which now seems ready to engulf all the foreigners living in Algeria, I would like my community, my Church and my family to remember that my life was GIVEN to God and to this country.

I ask them to accept the fact that the One Master of all life was not a stranger to this brutal departure.

I would ask them to pray for me: for how could I be found worthy of such an offering?

I ask them to associate this death with so many other equally violent ones which are forgotten through indifference or anonymity.

My life has no more value than any other. Nor any less value. In any case, it has not the innocence of childhood.

I have lived long enough to know that I am an accomplice in the evil which seems to prevail so terribly in the world, even in the evil which might blindly strike me down.

I should like, when the time comes, to have a moment of spiritual clarity which would allow me to beg forgiveness of God and of my fellow human beings, and at the same time forgive with all my heart the one who would strike me down.

I could not desire such a death. It seems to me important to state this.

I do not see, in fact, how I could rejoice if the people I love were indiscriminately accused of my murder.

It would be too high a price to pay for what will perhaps be called the "grace of martyrdom" to owe it to an Algerian, whoever he might be, especially if he says he is acting in fidelity to what he believes to be Islam.

I am aware of the scorn which can be heaped on the Algerians indiscriminately.

I am also aware of the caricatures of Islam which a certain Islamism fosters.

It is too easy to soothe one's conscience by identifying this religious way with the fundamentalist ideology of its extremists.

For me, Algeria and Islam are something different: it is a body and a soul.

I have proclaimed this often enough, I think, in the light of what I have received from it.

I so often find there that true strand of the Gospel which I learned at my mother's knee, my very first

Church, precisely in Algeria, and already inspired with respect for Muslim believers.

Obviously, my death will appear to confirm those who hastily judged me naive or idealistic.

"Let him tell us now what he thinks of his ideals!"

But these persons should know that finally my most avid curiosity will be set free.

This is what I shall be able to do, God willing: immerse my gaze in that of the Father to contemplate with him His children of Islam just as He sees them, all shining with the glory of Christ, the fruit of His Passion, filled with the Gift of the Spirit whose secret joy will always be to establish communion and restore the likeness, playing with the differences.

For this life lost, totally mine and totally theirs, I thank God, who seems to have willed it entirely for the sake of that JOY in everything and in spite of everything.

In this THANK YOU, which is said for everything in my life from now on, I certainly include you, friends of yesterday and today, and you, my friends of this place, along with my mother and father, my sisters and brothers and their families—you are the hundredfold granted as was promised!

And also you, my last-minute friend, who will not have known what you were doing:

Yes, I want this THANK YOU and this GOODBYE to be a "GOD BLESS" for you, too, because in God's Face I see yours.

May we meet again as happy thieves in Paradise, if it please God, the Father of us both.

AMEN! INSHALLAH!

> Algiers, 1st December 1993
> Tibhirine, 1st January 1994
> Christian +

Conclusion: *The Beauty of Communion and Solidarity until the End*

Dom Bernardo Olivera, the Abbot General of the Trappist order, says:

> The decision taken by the Atlas brothers is neither unique nor isolated. All those who belong to the Benedictine-Cistercian tradition made a vow of stability. It ties them until death to a community and to the place where this community lives. Many communities of our order have faced war and armed violence during those last years and had to reflect seriously about the meaning of this vow and make the crucial decision either to remain where they were or to leave.[36]

The seven brothers of Our Lady of Atlas simply offer the same testimony of love and faith as others have offered in the past. In each case, we face a grace given to a community, not only to an individual. In a Cenobite context, such as the Cistercian monastery, the fact of a life lived and given in community is particularly significant. This communitarian grace of martyrdom will also be a grace from and to the Church. This certainly adds to the beauty of this narrative. We have already seen the love of our brothers by the Church of Algeria and for their local Church of Algiers.[37] Their life and death are inscribed in the register of all those religious people, Christians or Muslims, who lived and gave their lives for God and for others.

The presence of death is not new for monks, says the Abbot General. On the contrary, death is traditionally a faithful and constant companion. The brothers write about this in a 1995 newsletter, at a moment when their common destiny is beginning to configure more and more clearly: "This companion took a more concrete view of direct threats, the close murders, certain visits.... This is offered to us as a test of truth, useful and not very comfortable."[38]

Experiencing that closeness, the community is freer than ever. When the GIA comes for his first visit, on Christmas Eve, the head of the group says: "You do not have a choice." "Yes, we have a choice," the Prior answers systematically, expressing in this way the gift he made "a priori" of his life, pronouncing the vows of his monastic consecration and his unfailing attachment to freedom for each being.[39]

What their community martyrdom shows—and the reason why their story touches us so deeply—is that, in the end, even in silence and invisibility, the fire continues to burn. This fire enlightens and shows the beauty that was hidden and now shines powerfully. It is the fire of love. That fire challenges the ocean of weakness and compromises in which we live.[40]

Notes

1. "L'Eglise est donc 'extatique à elle-même; elle est une exstase humble et dilatante,'" as cited in: Raymond Facélina, *Théologie en situation: Une communauté chrétienne dans le Tiers-Monde*, Algérie 1962–1974: étude pour le 5e colloque du Cerdic, Strasbourg, 7–8 juin 1974 (Strasbourg: Cerdic, 1974), 280, referencing Léon-Etienne Duval, "L'Espérance de l'Eglise," Conférence a l'Urash, Algaer, 28 mars 1971.

2. Juan Carlos Scannone, "Identidad personal, alteridad interpersonal y relación religiosa: Aporte filosófico," *Stromata* 58 (2002): 249–62, n. 3–4.

3. The reader is referred to the philosophies of Paul Ricoeur, who proposes the recognition of oneself as another, and of Emmanuel Levinas, who constructed his whole philosophical system upon an ethics derived from the epiphany of the Face of the Other.

4. Juan Carlos Scannone, op cit.

5. Greek expression meaning to express by himself; *"per se"* in Latin.

6. Emmanuel Levinas, *Totalité et infini: Essai sur l'extériorité* (La Haye: Martinus Nijhoff, 1971 [1st ed. 1961], 38). (English ed.: *Totality and Infinity: An Essay on Exteriority*, trans. Alphonso Lingis. Pittsburgh, PA: Duquesne University Press, 1969, 50–51.)

7. Emmanuel Levinas, *Liberté et commandement* (Paris: Livre de Poche, 1999), 267–70.

8. Levinas, *Totalité et infini*, 46. English ed.: 73–74.

9. Martin Buber, *Eu e tu* [*I and Thou*] (São Paulo, Brazil: Centauro, 2008). See also all of Levinas's work, which has many points of contact with that of Buber.

10. Levinas, *La souffrance inutile: Entre nous. Essais sur le penser-à-l'autre* (Paris: Grasset, 1991), 119. Translated from the original. (An English translation of the entire essay is found in Richard A. Cohen, "Useless Suffering," in *The Provocation of Levinas*, ed. R. Bernasconi and D. Wood [London and New York: Routledge, 1988], 156–67, here at 165.)

11. See Zygmunt Bauman, *Postmodernity and Its Discontents* (New York: New York University Press, 1997), 47.

12. Ibid., 49.

13. Pope Benedict XVI, *Charity in Truth*, Encyclical of June 29, 2009, 6–7.

14. Bauman, *Postmodernity and Its Discontents*, 56.

15. See the thought, and especially the ethical behavior, of persons such as Simone Weil, Etty Hillesum, and others.

16. Bauman, *Postmodernity and Its Discontents*, 62.

17. Ibid., 69.

18. Ibid., 51.

19. Emmanuel Levinas, *Éthique et infini: Dialogues avec Philippe Nemo* (Paris: Fayard-Radio France, 1983), 90. (English ed.: *Ethics and Infinity*. Pittsburgh, PA: Duquesne University Press, 1995.)

20. Emmanuel Levinas, *De Dieu qui vient à l'idée* (Paris: Vrin, 1982), 244–45. (English ed.: *Of God Who Comes to Mind*. Stanford, CA: Stanford University Press, 1998.)

21. Emmanuel Levinas, "Éthique et philosophie première. La proximité de l'autre," *Phréatique* 39 (1986): 124, n. 39.

22. Emmanuel Levinas, *En découvrant l'existence avec Husserl et Heidegger* (Paris: Vrin, 2002), 173. (English ed.: *Discovering Existence with Husserl and Heidegger*. Evanston, IL: Northwestern University Press, 1998.)

23. Cf. Emmanuel Levinas, *À l'heure des nations* (Montpellier: Fata Morgana, 1987), 141. (English ed.: *In the Time of Nations*. London: Bloomsbury Academic, 2007.)

24. Marie-Christine Ray, *Christian de Chergé: Prieur de Tibhirine* (Paris: Bayard-Centurion, 1998), 82–84.

25. John W. Kiser, *The Monks of Tibhirine: Faith, Love and Terror in Algeria* (New York: St. Martin's Griffin, 2002), 39.

26. Ibid., 49.

27. Marie-Christine Ray, op cit., 105.

28. John W. Kiser, *Passion pour l'Algérie: Les moines de Tibhirine* (Namur, Belgium: La Procure, n.d.), 85.

29. Christian de Chergé, *L'invincible espérance*, Textes recueillis et présentés par Bruno Chenu (Paris: Bayard, 2010), 33–38. Our translation.

30. Christian de Chergé, *L'Autre que nous attendons: Homélies de Père Christian de Chergé, 1970–1996* (Godewaersvelde: Éditions de Bellefontaine, 2009). Collection *Les cahiers de Tibhirine*. Série Paroles; 2, épigraphe de tout le volume, x.

31. <http://www.newadvent.org/cathen/05502a.htm> accessed March 22, 2017: *Epiklesis* (Latin *invocatio*) is the name of a prayer that occurs in all Eastern liturgies (and originally in Western liturgies as well) after the words of Institution, in which the celebrant prays that God may send down His Holy Spirit to change this bread and wine into the Body and Blood of His Son. The epiclesis (also spelled epiklesis; from the ancient Greek: ἐπίκλησις "invocation" or "calling down from on high") is the part of the Anaphora (Eucharistic Prayer) through which the priest invokes the Holy Spirit (or the power of His blessing) upon the Eucharistic bread and wine.

32. Christine Ray, *Christian de Chergé*, 193.

33. Christian de Chergé, *L'Autre que nous attendons*, 512.

34. Ibid., 419–20.

35. <https://www.americamagazine.org/content/all-things/dom-christians-testament> accessed July 6, 2017.

36. Bernardo Olivera, *How Far to Follow? The Martyrs of Atlas* (Petersham, MA: St. Bede's Publications, 1997), 16.

37. Ibid., 21.

38. Bruno Chenu, *Sept vies pour Dieu et l'Algérie* (Paris: Bayard, 1996), letter of November 21, 1995, 21. Quoted by Charles Henning, *Petite vie des moines de Tibhirine* (Paris: DDB, 2006), 51.

39. Charles Henning, op cit., 44. The monks, following Fr. Christian's suggestions, meditated on the writings of Etty Hillesum, which hit them with an incredible force: "You know I have the power to make

you die," says the executioner. And the martyr has this response: "You know I have the power of being killed."

40. Bruno Frappat, "27 mars 1996, l'enlèvement des moines de Tibhirine." *La Croix*, May 29, 1996 <http://www.la-croix.com/Religion/Monde/27-mars-1996-enlevement-moines-Tihirine-2016-03-27-1200749232> accessed July 6, 2017.

Works Cited

Bauman, Zygmunt. *Postmodernity and Its Discontents*. New York: New York University Press, 1997.

Buber, Martin. *Eu e tu*. São Paulo, Brazil: Centauro, 2008. (English ed.: Greenwich, CT: Touchstone, 1971.)

Chenu, Bruno. *Sept vies pour Dieu et l'Algérie*. Paris: Bayard, 1996.

Chergé, Christian de. *L'Autre que nous attendons: Homélies de Père Christian de Chergé, 1970–1996*. Godewaersvelde: Éditions de Belle-fontaine, 2009.

———. *L'invincible espérance*. Textes recueillis et présentés par Bruno Chenu. Paris: Bayard, 2010.

Frappat, Bruno. "27 mars 1996, l'enlèvement des moines de Tibhirine." *La Croix*, May 29, 1996. <http://www.la-croix.com/Religion/Monde/27-mars-1996-enlevement-moines-Tibhirine-2016-03-27-1200749232>

Henning, Charles. *Petite vie des moines de Tibhirine*. Paris: DDB, 2006.

Kiser, Joseph W. *The Monks of Tibhirine: Faith, Love and Terror in Algeria*. New York: St. Martin's Griffin, 2002. (French ed.: *Passion pour l'Algérie: Les moines de Tibhirine*. Namur, Belgium: La Procure, n.d.)

Levinas, Emmanuel. *À l'heure des nations*. Montpellier: Fata Morgana, 1987. (English ed.: *In the Time of Nations*. London: Bloomsbury Academic, 2007).

———. *De Dieu qui vient à l'idée*. Paris: Vrin, 1982. (English ed.: *Of God Who Comes to Mind*. Stanford, CA: Stanford University Press, 1998.)

———. *En découvrant l'existence avec Husserl et Heidegger*. Paris: Vrin, 2002. (English ed.: *Discovering Existence with Husserl and Heidegger*. Evanston, IL: Northwestern University Press, 1998.)

————. *Éthique et infini: Dialogues avec Philippe Nemo.* Paris: Fayard-Radio France, 1983. (English ed.: *Ethics and Infinity.* Pittsburgh, PA: Duquesne University Press, 1995.)

————. "Éthique et philosophie première: La proximité de l'autre." *Phréatique* 39 (1986).

————. *Liberté et commandement.* Paris: Livre de Poche, 1999.

————. *La souffrance inutile: Entre nous. Essais sur le penser-à-l'autre* (Paris: Grasset, 1991), 100–112. (English ed.: Richard A. Cohen, "Useless Suffering," in *The Provocation of Levinas*, ed. R. Bernasconi and D. Wood [London and New York: Routledge, 1988)\], 156–67.)

————. *Totalité et infini: Essai sur L'extériorité.* La Haye: Martinus Nijhoff, 1971. (English ed.: *Totality and Infinity: An Essay on Exteriority*, translated by Alphonso Lingis. Pittsburgh, PA: Duquesne University Press, 1969.)

Olivera, Bernardo. *How Far to Follow? The Martyrs of Atlas.* Petersham, MA: St. Bede's Publications, 1997.

Ray, Marie-Christine. *Christian de Chergé: Prieur de Tibhirine.* Paris: Bayard-Centurion, 1998.

Scannone, Juan Carlos. "Identidad personal, alteridad interpersonal y relación religiosa: Aporte filosófico." *Stromata* 58 (2002): 249–62.

Chapter Three

TRAGIC BEAUTY: THE CRY OF THE SUFFERING AND INTERFAITH AESTHETICS

Peter Casarella, University of Notre Dame

When I seek to find beauty in the Other, I do so as one who has taken to heart what *Nostra Aetate* says regarding the "what is true and holy" in faiths other than Christianity and "the high regard for the manner of life and conduct [as well as] the precepts and doctrines" of these faiths.[1] But my own cultural background also contributes to what I am looking to affirm and what I am able to perceive through these desires for an authentic encounter with the beauty of another. Joseph (then-Cardinal) Ratzinger maintained that interreligious encounters are *ipso facto* intercultural encounters.[2] In other words, he asserted that there is a dimension of interculturality at the base of every genuine interreligious encounter.[3] By contrast, dialogue with an adherent to another religion that programmatically ignores culture presumes (or at least introduces the notion) that religions in our world today are somehow uprooted from the very soil in which they have been planted. With that false assumption, we would also be inventing the artificial and secularizing construct that global faiths are culturally naked and capable of being transferred from one culture to another, while somehow remaining indifferent to the fact or process of translation. Interfaith encounters therefore include an intercultural dimension. It is better to bring that element to the fore (even if it is difficult—perhaps even impossible—to isolate in a pristine manner) rather than to ignore or sidestep its presence.

The question of beauty seems, at first glance, inopportune. Even before we in the West were convicted by the image of a drowned Syrian boy washed ashore on a Turkish beach, we already knew that globalization is increasingly marked by mass migrations of peoples from their own land, or what Homi Bhabha calls the "poetics of exile, [i.e.,] the grim prose of political and economic refugees."[4] This discourse of people and cultures in motion is also "theopoetic."[5] The religious poetics of mass migration does not uplift the soul to new heights but moves and shapes it in other important ways.[6] The believer is called to remember the plight of nomads who maintained or tested their faith in other wildernesses and conditions of oppression.[7] In terms of its genre, the theopoetics of mass migration is akin to the Biblical genre of prophetic lamentations cried out in the name of the people of God: "for he has not despised or abhorred the affliction of the afflicted; and he has not hid his face from him, but has heard, when he cried to him."[8] Just as (in the words of Gustavo Gutiérrez) "the world of justice finds its full meaning and source in the freely given love of God," so too does the discipline of theopoetics, considered in terms of an openness to interfaith dialogue, need to focus on the enveloping atmosphere of gratuitous beauty as it is intersected by the cries, images, and laments of those who beckon for justice.[9]

In this essay I explore a Latino/a lens for finding beauty in the Other. Specifically, I interrogate the notion of "tragic beauty" as developed in conversation with fellow Latino/a theologians.[10] What is "tragic beauty"? Let us first consider a moving and well-articulated testimony. Alex Nava, a Latino scholar of religion at the University of Arizona at Tucson, recounts his experience of being haunted by the faces of undocumented immigrants to whom he brought water.[11] In the desert a bottle of water is only a stop-gap on the often-deadly journey. Nava is aware that the life of the pilgrims he encountered one day might very well have been extinguished the next day by the scorching heat of the desert. For Nava, the natural beauty *and* hidden fecundity of the landscape serve as a foil to the real carnage that remains just as clearly in view. The simultaneous and equally moving epiphanies of beauty and mortality haunt Nava. There is no time in the desert to be engaged in dialogue with other religions. The dialogue is still with God, and it concerns one's very survival, one's passage through the desert.

What kind of beauty does one perceive here? Do we even have the luxury of introducing the category of beauty in the face of the parched throats of the desert nomads facing the real possibility of their own extermination? We need to start by re-orienting ourselves with respect to the domain of aesthetics and understanding how the discipline of aesthetics is being received today. In much of modern philosophy, for example, the domain of aesthetics is principally the domain of sense perception. Immanuel Kant plays an important role in this development. In the face of palpable innocent suffering, however, an empathetic human being cannot detach himself or herself subjectively by means of a Kantian aesthetics of disinterestedness.[12] For Kant, beautiful nature gives rise to a sensibility of one's moral destiny, a sensibility that in his view does not arise naturally from the beautiful work of art.[13] Kant tends to bifurcate the purposiveness of the ethical standpoint from the non-purposiveness of aesthetic wonder.

The tragic juxtaposition in the desert of radiant flowers and desiccated corpses feeds neither Kantian moral purposiveness nor the all-embracing Kantian category of aesthetic genius. On the contrary, the perception in the world of a fragment of something like beauty is by its very nature *a beckoning* to involvement. That fragment is not the flower and certainly not the corpse, but the event whereby flower and corpse are together assimilated into consciousness. It is at once a call to rectify the socio-ecological order that is only hinted at by the contrastive experience of viewing life and death in a single glance.[14] The perception of tragic beauty thus unveils a moral conscience that invites participation in the concrete task of social justice. Here Kant's initial insight into the moral purposiveness of natural beauty was not wholly incorrect, because the call to liberating praxis is at the same time a yearning for *more than* a social sense of belonging.

This essay has three parts. In the first part I develop an interpretation of the concept of tragic beauty in Latino/a theological aesthetics. In the second, shorter part, I demonstrate the consonance of this view, which is drawn from Latino/a theology, with other discourses of tragic beauty in the global South. In the third part, I offer a constructive way to think about the relationship between tragic beauty and interfaith aesthetics. This third part will represent my positive contribution to our unfolding of the new task of "finding beauty in the Other."[15] The second section thus corresponds to the "World Church" focus of our doctoral concentration at Notre Dame, and the third part integrates this reflection with the "World Religions" focus of the same area. In this process, the positive contribution that Latino/a theology can make to both disciplines will be broached. I conclude with some brief reflections on this theme.

1. Tragic Beauty in Latino/a Theological Aesthetics

First of all, the notion of Latino/a theopoetics needs further clarification. Latino/a theology has, since its inception, focused on articulating not only concrete acts of devotion or distinct religious symbols but the integration of symbolic reasoning into the task of theology itself. The integration does not subsume theology into a "literary" or "poetic" straitjacket but authentically adapts the exigencies and rigor of faith seeking understanding to the creativity of the Latino/a community. As Sixto García has written:

> The idea of a Hispanic theologian as a poet of his or her community may easily invoke the wrong images: a Hispanic theologian as Walt Whitman, Robert Frost, or Antonio Machado of a community.... For the Hispanic mind, especially the religious-theological mind, [he or she] performs [the task of theology] in deep contact with myths, stories, traditions, and nature, and this contact, this dialogue, requires a poetic framework in its theolog-

ical formulations. In expressing the Trinitarian concept of *perichoresis*, for example, the Hispanic theologian must formulate it through the analogies of family love, of nature's interpenetration of being, of the metaphors of conjugal intimacies, of the beauty of human conversation and dialogue, using the vocabulary and story frameworks known to and constitutive of the tradition and heritage of his or her particular community.[16]

For Latino/a theologians, theological reason—the reason of faith—is symbolic. It is not a question, as in the hermeneutics of Paul Ricoeur, of the symbol giving rise to thought. That model, however rich in its own mode of reflectivity, can dissipate the distinctively Latino/a contribution into a way station on the path to a general theory of hermeneutics devoid of any specific cultural content. The relationship between symbolic knowing and rational reflection is a two-way street. Hence, theopoetics is also not a complete reversal of the relationship between the non-discursive and stable self-presentation of an image on the one hand, and the aniconic, dialectical movement of rational reflection. The use of metaphor *and* analogy in Latino/a theopoetics poses the question of the discourse of gratuitousness and prophecy in a new key. The Latino/a theologian "reads" the images in nature and culture through a popular lens, viz. through the eyes of the people of God.[17] The awakening of the soul of a people through wonder and awe is therefore a key step in the development of a Latino/a hermeneutics of nature and culture.[18]

The Latino/a lens on beauty is one that emphasizes the unitive revelatory experience of participation rather than the post-Kantian stance of disinterested perceptual contemplation.[19] The work of art here can be a cultural monument or an event of popular religion. What matters is that we are not talking about art for art's sake. We are not attempting to abstract in an artificial manner what is artistic from its religious or cultural substrate.[20] In fact, we are talking about participating in a surprising new reality, a new event of being. García-Rivera uses the example of the Vietnam Veterans

Memorial in Washington, D.C. It was already a revelation of sorts
when the civil authorities in the nation's capital granted this commission to a 21-year-old child of exiles from Communist China
who, at the time of its shocking disclosure, was only a fledgling
architecture student at Yale University. The young Maya Lin beat
out her own professors of architecture in this competition! Not
surprisingly, the unKantian Latino/a lens also comes into play here.
The memorial does not adhere to traditional notions of grandiose
monuments to veterans. It is possible that Lin's experience of seeing the unassuming listing of the names of the fallen alumni at
the entrance to the Yale Dining Hall may have played a role in her
unorthodox conception.

In any case, the monument in the nation's capital unsuspect-
ingly creates a personal relationship between the viewer and the
fallen. Touching a sheer black wall inscribed with the names of
the fallen soldiers is an *interested* form of aesthetic-religious contemplation.[21] "Such touch," writes García-Rivera, "is more than
mere sensuality. It is a kind of healing, a unitive experience that
makes the soul whole."[22] There are parallels here to the experience
of touch in popular religion. The same dynamic is in play when a
Peruvian-American (or any person, for that matter) clutches as an
act of faith a holy card of San Martín de Porres.[23] As a work of art,
the holy card is mass produced, almost kitsch. But the fact that
it does not belong to high culture only makes the unitary revelatory experience more authentic. This is precisely why Pope Paul VI,
in bringing the term *via pulchritudinis* ("way of beauty") into the
magisterium of the Catholic Church, offered this way of direct engagement with sensual realities as an essential complement to the
dissecting *via veritatis* ("way of truth") of the academics.[24]

Let us consider another concrete example of theopoetics in
a tragic key. In Latino/a theology, the memory of the passion of
Christ, as it is reenacted in the passion plays on Good Friday, is the
key to unlocking the mystery of suffering.[25] How are human tragedies reconciled by the mystery of grace? There is no easy answer
here, no *deus ex machina*. Traditional theological categories are not

unwelcome here, but they cannot be repeated without looking to the intercultural and interreligious tasks at hand. Perhaps it is appropriate to turn to a more classical source on tragedy and grace, one that in its own way suggests an opening to interculturality. Joseph Ratzinger, in a key essay on the very notion of a Christian conscience, makes the following comment on the acquittal of Orestes for the murder of his mother in Aeschylus's *Oresteia*. The play thematizes a pre-Christian response to the restoration of order by the gods, to the overcoming of a system of blood vengeance through a new ethic of political justice:

> The myth, while representing the transition from a system of blood vengeance to the right order of community, signifies much more than just that. Hans Urs Von Balthasar expressed this "more" as follows: "... Calming grace always assists in the establishing of justice, not the old graceless justice of the Erinyes period, but that which is full of grace. ..." This myth speaks to us of the human longing that conscience's objectively just indictment and the attendant destructive, interior distress it causes in [the human person], not be the last word. It thus speaks of an authority of grace, a power of expiation which allows the guilt to vanish and makes truth at last truly redemptive. It is the longing for a truth which doesn't just make demands of us but also transforms us through expiation and pardon. Through these, as Aeschylus puts it, "guilt is washed away" and our being is transformed from within, beyond our own capability. This is the real innovation of Christianity.[26]

The transformation through expiation and pardon points in an open-ended way to a higher truth, one that is not merely political. At this juncture, we are already at the point at which we view the intersecting of the intercultural and the inter-religious. The publicly performed symbolic drama of the passion play speaks to the same washing away of guilt presaged by Aeschylus. Mythical and symbolical forms incarnate a new reality that appears in the midst of everyday experience and makes possible a new order for personal and social life.[27]

The religious imagery here might suggest a posture of self-denunciation or even fatalism. How does such an overtly tragic consciousness overcome futility? The Latino/a experience of tragic beauty, for example, is not the same as the Nietzschean *amor fati*.[28] When Nietzsche speaks about a love of fate, he is talking about a passive and lonely submission to a mystery that is inscribed into an elusive order of nature. Latino/as are caricaturized as fatalist, but our expressive mode of aesthetic participation is neither a submission to fate nor the agonal struggle of a Nietzschean superman. Like the Nietzschean attitude, it is ultimately affirmative in a redemptive key. The full disclosure of the dynamics of tragic beauty also reveals itself to be a joyful and highly communal affair. Latino/a theopoetics is unique in the context of other theories of tragic beauty (e.g., the "star-crossed lovers" of *Romeo and Juliet*) in terms of its conscious desire to redeem fatalism *dolorosamente* ("while still in pain"). This hope for the reversal of structural sin through new structures of gratuity and hospitality is the opposite of the postmodern retrieval of the *amor fati*. It is more in the spirit of *la agonía del cristianismo* ("the agony of Christianity") or what John MacKay, the early-twentieth-century Scottish Presbyterian missionary to Latin America and student of Miguel de Unamuno, called *The Other Spanish Christ*.[29]

The dynamics of being offered a hidden cleansing from within in a truly modest and human manner but by a power that lies beyond our own capacity for self-correction still has a rather precise analogue in Christian piety. For both Latin Americans and U.S. Latino/as, Mary, who grieves at the foot of the cross,

> becomes the sign of the Spirit of holiness and healing for suffering and marginalized Hispanic faith communities. She points away from herself to the Spirit, who has made her its privileged place of indwelling in salvation history.[30]

In the words of Clodovis Boff, "with and like her Son, Mary is the conquered-conqueror."[31] She opens up in this pericope a "spirituality of failure (*espiritualidade do fracasso*)."[32] It is for many non-Latino/ as a highly unusual and not terribly Anglophone understanding of failure, because the emergence of the Spirit of life takes place precisely here in the midst of the seeming breakdown of a normal life.

García-Rivera calls this new dynamic of tragic beauty (drawing in a cross-cultural way upon Jonathan Edwards) *commercium ad-mirabile*, a wondrous exchange between God and humanity that has two distinct dimensions.[33] It is *ad-mirabile* because we are drawn to wonder not just by falling into a dreamy state of oblivion but through a dual form of memorializing engagement. Passively, the wonder of the exchange is something that we look *at*. We absorb what we see in order to determine its objectivity, its status as full of grace. Actively, however, we are also looking "through." García-Rivera summarizes: "Together we have the admirable process that is the key, I believe, to an interfaith [dialogue, by] 'looking at by looking through.'"[34] Only by contemplating interfaith realities through this double lens can "that which is loved by another become ours to love as well."[35]

2. Tragic Beauty in Global Catholicism

Latino/a theopoetics arises from the everyday experiences of the faithful who live in the United States. It speaks to the daily struggle of the 50 percent of Christians around the globe who speak Spanish. It is equally a witness to and a point of departure for comprehending global Catholicism today. Many of the key features of Latino/a theopoetics resonate with other forms of theological aesthetics that are being developed in the global South. Elsewhere, at the original conference on "Finding Beauty in the Other" and in this volume, the contributions on Africa have placed a certain amount of emphasis on the practical-moral dimensions (African *phronesis*, if you will) of African theological aesthetics.[36] Teresia

Hinga has rightly lifted up for our consideration the work of Mercy Oduyoye, a Methodist exegete and theologian from Ghana who spoke about the communitarian and feminist metaphor of the weaving of the Kente cloth, and Jean-Marc Ela, a sociologist and priest from Cameroon.[37] The other panelists highlighted similar approaches: the cultural analysis of the early missionaries (Paul Kollman), the disciplines of goodness in the work of reconciliation (e.g., Emmanuel Katongole, speaking on Marguerite Barankitse and her initiative at building a new home for child refugees of war at Maison Shalom), and the relationship of morality and aesthetics in the Igbo symbol of the eagle (Paulinus Odozor). There are many convergences to explore here, but I would also add, as Martin Nkafu has noted, that there is a vital force in African culture and even a vitalogical aesthetics that parallels the strong sense of symbolic *realism* and the doctrine of ontological participation in the rhythms of being that undergirds Latino/a theopoetics.[38]

Another family of voices from the global South that needs to be heeded is that of the Catholic theologians from the Philippines. Like Latino/a theologians, theologians from the Philippines have a long and even partly Hispanic popular tradition of celebrating the "Payson," i.e., the death and resurrection of the human Jesus. Like Latino/a theologians, they consider popular religion in the context of the struggle of the people. Eleazar Fernandez links this celebration of a popular devotion to the spirit of resistance that, at least in part, inspired the Revolution of 1896 against Spain, as well as the People's Power Revolution of 1986.[39] Agnes Brazal offers an analysis of theological aesthetics that looks not only at popular religion as "weapons of the weak" (a category popularized through the work of the Yale anthropologist James Scott) but also as forms of resistance against hegemonic power.[40] Gemma Cruz's *An Intercultural Theology of Migration* makes similar claims about the prayer services, service activities, and para-liturgies of resistance of the Filipina domestic helpers who are treated unjustly in Hong Kong.[41]

Finally, I would like to note the similarity between the Latino/a intercultural methodology and the threefold dialogue with Asian culture, the poor, and other religions that was introduced by the Federated Asian Bishops' Conference (FABC) in the 1970s.[42] This approach offered a wholistic method for inculturation, integral human development, and evangelization that can be easily transferred into other domains of analysis and pastoral practice. In subsequent meetings of the FABC, the principle of the triple dialogue was affirmed and further elaborated in terms of a dialogical model of the Church:

> The dialogue approach revolves around three key poles: local Church, dialogue, and the Asian peoples and their realities. Almost simplistically, it can be represented in a schema:
>
> Local Church <<< DIALOGUE >>> Asia's Cultures, Asia's Religions
> (subject)   (approach)
>
> One must point out that the arrows on either side of the word *dialogue* move in two directions. Certainly, this indicates that this dialogical approach is always a two-fold process of dynamic interaction. There is always mutual reinforcement; this means that while the Church influences the people, their cultures and religions, the Church herself is concomitantly being shaped and molded. In a word, the dynamic of inculturation is always at work.[43]

The Asian triple dialogue transcends the idea of three *separate* dialogue partners for the Church: the poor, Asian culture, and non-Christians. It demonstrates that listening to the poor, learning from other faith traditions, and attending to the problem of inculturation are all cut of the same cloth. The triple dialogue also confirms that dialogue needs a vision of the whole that is greater than its parts. One cannot honestly enter into dialogue with the goal of simply addressing just one dimension of someone's otherness. We turn now to the interrogation of the religious Other while keeping this wholistic model in mind.

3. Tragic Beauty and Interfaith Aesthetics

Before his untimely death in 2010, Alex García-Rivera wrote extensively about the Latino/a experience of art and beauty. I last saw him
at a conference that he arranged in 2008 with Ron Nakasone at the
Jesuit School of Theology at Berkeley. The conference was provoca-
tively titled "Beauty: The Color of Truth." García-Rivera's essay on
interfaith aesthetics reflects the fruits of the friendship with Nakasone and the true power of a mutual learning process.[44] In the essay
he explores the dialogue between Eastern and Western religious
aesthetics by focusing on a sixteenth-century Korean tea bowl. The
tea bowl embodies a Buddhist aesthetic of non-duality while not
abstracting from the reality of a people. In contrast to Western
distinctions between arts and crafts or between non-dogmatic
spirituality and religious doctrine and observance, the spirituality
of the tea bowl lies in the self-presentation of the entirety. Before
the split between subjective perception of beauty and beauty in
itself, the tea bowl *is*. Here I am reminded of Heidegger's reflections upon viewing *The Shoes* by Vincent van Gogh.[45] Heidegger
knew well that the French peasants who owned these shoes wore
them for their sheer utility and hardly needed to reflect upon that
fact in order to affirm it. It is nonetheless the case that the painting
of Van Gogh causes one to reflect upon the fact that "in the shoes
vibrates the silence call of the earth, its quiet gift of the ripening
grain and its unexplained self-refusal in the fallow desolation of the
wintry field."[46] The painting spoke a truth about the shoes that was
not otherwise present to view.[47] A similar insight arises with the
tea bowl. "A true awareness of beauty," writes Yanagi Soetsu, the
founder of Mingei aesthetics of the beauty of everyday craftsman-
ship, "is to be found where beauty watches beauty."[48]

García-Rivera applies this non-dualist aesthetic of Korean Buddhism to the analysis of a pointillist depiction of a starry night by
a religious painter from California. Through the revival of Poin-
tillism, the Western painter also tries to thematize the question
of revealing and concealing. In this exchange, we encounter the

difference between Buddhist non-duality and the Christian doctrine of grasping the interconnectedness of all things through the
lens of the revelation of an Incarnate God. What kind of "beauty"
is disclosed in this dialogical exercise? Not Western, not Eastern.
Not a spirituality without religion, not a religion with an interfaith
dimension or spirituality.

What lies in the "space" between the tea bowl and the view
of *Starlight* from Big Sur as depicted by a Camaldolese monk, Fr.
Arthur Poulin? The tragic dimension to this experience lies in the
unsaid, the hard task of not placing labels on what cannot be readily
translated into discourse. This unsaid (and to some degree unsayable) middle space is what García-Rivera evokes as *ad-mirabile*.
García-Rivera says that the *ad-mirabile* is the coincidence of opposites of the passive act of "looking at" with the active perception that
"looks through." Interfaith aesthetics looks at by looking through.
Passively, there remains a doctrinal difference between non-duality
and the hypostatic union. Actively, we perceive a way to look beyond this difference to a common, non-discursive faith, a faith that
the sudden appearance of reality as beautiful in its entirety is basic
to grasping life, especially in its most tragic dimensions.

Latino interfaith aesthetics is a new area of research and dialogical practice. It needs to be brought into dialogue with other
approaches. I would suggest that the approach taken in Francis
Clooney's *His Hiding Place Is Darkness* is very suggestive in this
regard, for it also brings together the inter-religious task of theological aesthetics with a wise reflection on the process of questioning
in the very midst of being gripped by a religious passion:

> *His Hiding Place Is Darkness* does not block the return
> to the great questions; it simply highlights the danger in
> going back with amnesia to ordinary ways of theology;
> it pleas for slow learning that sacrifices efficiency for the
> sake of deeper currents of encounter. In writing of God
> in more formal doctrinal and systematic terms, theolo-
> gians must write in the shadow of the images, the poetry,

and the drama of a beloved who may still hide even
when everything should be most certain, definitively decided.... In this situation, the best theological words are
those which are tattered, incomplete, and humble before
the silences of the beloved.[49]

Clooney's approach to Hindu-Christian dialogue interrogates the
beauty of the Other by looking at and looking through. He deftly
brings to the fore "The surfeit of speech on divine love dramatized
in two traditions."[50] Clooney thereby highlights the longing for an
absent Other in a non-Romantic and theodramatic way. His approach is just as theopoetic as Latino interfaith aesthetics, for both
approaches highlight and problematize the troublesome challenge
of glimpsing the flash of beauty. Finally, the point of divergence
between Clooney's theopoetics and that of Latino/a theologians is
the ongoing conversation with the language and everyday practices
of the people of God. Clooney's method is one of looking carefully
at a stable text, but the Latino/a approach also looks to *testigos* or
witnesses of faith.[51] We turn now to a poignant example of the
aesthetics of witnessing.

IV. Conclusion

Latino/a theology has reflected for several decades on finding
beauty in the Other. This essay only tries to develop the interfaith
dimension in terms that are palatable to a discipline that attends to
both global Catholicism and the contemporary global challenge of
interfaith encounter. It is fitting to conclude not with a conceptual
synthesis but with an example of an extraordinary witness to this
daunting task. Again, the Latino/a lens will be applied to the task
of interpretation, even though the witness himself is a Frenchman
who lived and died in Algeria.

Christian de Chergé, one of the slain monks of Tibhirine, wrote
a testament in Paris before returning to Algiers, where he was then

beheaded in what appeared to be an act of Islamic terrorism.[52] The testament is written in the form of a letter to the assassin that he anticipated he would one day meet. There are clear overtones of the philosophy of Emmanuel Levinas in his final exhortation, but there is no formal pretense of interpreting the philosopher. His goal is to bear witness to the fate that he has been told by countless authorities he will endure if he does not flee his residence in Algeria. The monastic virtue of stability is no small part of his decision to stay there. In the testament itself, he offers thanks and says goodbye, and in the process speaks of the two happy thieves encountering one another face-to-face within the visage of God:

> Oui, pour toi aussi je le veux ce MERCI, et cet "À-DIEU" envisagé de toi. Et qu'il nous soit donné de nous retrouver, larrons heureux, en paradis, s'il plaît à Dieu, notre Père à tous deux.

> Yes, I want this THANK YOU and this GOODBYE to be a "GOD-BLESS" for you, too, because in God's face I see yours. May we meet again as happy thieves in Paradise, if it please God, the Father of us both.[53]

It is interesting to think about this *À-dieu envisagé de toi* in the context of the bodies of the undocumented dying in the Arizona desert. The phrase is purely Levinasian but has ramifications that extend far and wide. The pilgrims witnessed by Nava say *A-dios* to their families in the hope of a new life north of the border. They know that they must pass through hell in order to arrive at their destination. What do they envisage when they speak this *A-dios*? This word itself invites us to "look at by looking through." For example, in writing about a debate between Heidegger and Levinas on the meaning of death, Jacques Derrida offers three explanations of *A-dieu*: (1) a salutation or benediction at the moment of meeting (i.e., "Hello!"); (2) a salutation or benediction at the moment of departure, which could be a departure of death; and (3) "the *a-dieu*, for God or before God and before anything else or any relation to the other, in every other adieu."[54] Keep in mind that *Adios* is not commonly used as a salutation, but as a farewell is also not nearly as final as the French *Adieu*. In terms of the ontology of the translated passage, Latino/as are less likely to see their departure for a foreign land as a definitive break with family, nation, or life itself. Even if the Latino/a pilgrim is taking a greater risk, the ambiguity of the farewell crosses the borders of discourses and lands. Both sayings (*A-dieu*, *A-dios*) maintain this triple meaning—greeting, departing, and commending the pilgrim to being accompanied by God.

Finding beauty in the Other is a reiterative process, one filled with multiple salutations and leave-takings. In concluding, we are thus left with more questions than answers. What kind of *A-dios* did Nava speak after he offered them a bottle of water? I imagine that he commended them to go with God through the suffering of hell, knowing that there may not be a return to country, family, or life at all. Did he envisage seeing them before the face of God as happy thieves in the manner of Christian de Chergé? I ask these questions without offering answers. They are not questions with fixed answers. Yet they seem to me to be the very questions that we must pose to ourselves if we are to open ourselves to discovering the tragic beauty of the other today.

Notes

1. *Nostra Aetate*, Declaration on the Relation of the Church to Non-Christian Religions, October 28, 1965, as cited in *Vatican Council II*, ed. Austin Flannery, O.P. (Northpoint, NY: Costello, 1988, rev. ed.), 739.
2. Joseph Ratzinger, "Christ, Faith, and the Challenge of Cultures: Address to the Presidents of the Asian Bishops' Conference," speech made during a March 2–5, 1993, meeting in Hong Kong.
3. See Joseph Cardinal Ratzinger, *Truth and Tolerance: Christian Belief and World Religions* (San Francisco, CA: Ignatius Press, 2004), 64; and Peter Casarella, "Culture and Conscience in the Thought of Jo-

seph Ratzinger/Pope Benedict XVI," in *Explorations in the Theology of Benedict XVI*, ed. John C. Cavadini (Notre Dame, IN: University of Notre Dame Press, 2012), 63–86.

4. Homi Bhabha, *The Location of Culture* (London: Routledge, 1994), 7.

5. On the manifold senses of "theopoetics," see my Foreword to Anne M. Carpenter, *Theopoetics: Hans Urs von Balthasar on the Risk of Art and Being* (Notre Dame, IN: University of Notre Dame Press, 2015). I am also currently preparing a co-authored volume for the Catholic University of America Press with Maria Clara Luchetti Bingemer on the intercultural dimensions of theopoetics titled *Living Waters for Parched Hearts*.

6. The relationship between beauty and justice is a familiar theme within certain forms of Latino/a theology. See, for example, Michelle A. González, *Sor Juana: Beauty and Justice in the Americas* (Maryknoll, NY: Orbis Books, 2003), a key early text on this topic.

7. Paul Celan is a notoriously complex figure but can be viewed as a deeply religious poet who thematizes the modern plight of exile. For a brief reflection on this theme, see Shoshana Olidort, "Paul Celan: A Poet in Exile," *My Jewish Learning*, available online at <http://www.myjewishlearning.com/article/paul-celan/>, accessed September 13, 2017.

8. Psalm 22:25. Cf. Gustavo Gutiérrez, *On Job: God-Talk and the Suffering of the Innocent* (Maryknoll, NY: Orbis Books, 1987), 99.

9. Gustavo Gutiérrez, *On Job*, 96.

10. There are certain parallels between "tragic beauty" and what Kristen Drahos has perspicaciously termed "dark beauty," but also important divergences. See Kristen M. Drahos, "Dark Beauty: Towards a Catholic Theological Aesthetic," Ph.D. dissertation, University of Notre Dame, 2016.

11. Alex Nava, "On Tragic Beauty," in *New Horizons in Hispanic/Latino(a) Theology*, ed. Benjamín Valentín (Cleveland, OH: Pilgrim Press, 2003), 181–200.

12. On this issue, I still find instructive Hans-Georg Gadamer, *Truth and Method* (New York: Crossroad, 1985), 39–73.

13. Hans-Georg Gadamer, *Truth and Method*, 46–47.

14. See Alejandro García-Rivera's discussion of "being as foregrounding" in *The Community of the Beautiful: A Theological Aesthetics* (Collegeville, MN: Liturgical Press, 1999), 168–70.

15. In the Introduction to this volume, Mun'im Sirry and I argued for a certain priority of the process over the product in the search for the beauty of the other. This is an important point. In reading the original draft of this paper, some of the respondents asked about my relationship to process theology. Process theology does not figure into this essay, but the analogy of the creative process of the making of a work of art is a central leitmotif in the theopoetics being adumbrated. While the term *theopoetics* has become assimilated to process theology in many circles, that identification is hardly necessary for the argument being made here.

16. Sixto J. García, "A Hispanic Approach to Trinitarian Theology: The Dynamics of Celebration, Reflection, and Praxis," in *We Are a People! Initiatives in Hispanic American Theology*, ed. Roberto S. Goizueta (Philadelphia, PA: Fortress, 1992), 107–32, here at 115, 116–17.

17. The word "popular" in English carries connotations of commercialization. *Lo popular*, on the other hand, is a discourse that inherently resists commodification. I speak about the issue of commodification in Peter J. Casarella, "The Painted Word," *Journal of Hispanic/Latino Theology* 6, no. 2 (November 1998): 18–42.

18. Cecilia González-Andrieu, *The Bridge to Wonder: Art as a Gospel of Beauty* (Waco, TX: Baylor University Press, 2012).

19. This is the language used by Alejandro García-Rivera, citing Nicholas Wolterstorff: "On a New List of Aesthetic Categories," in *Theological Aesthetics after von Balthasar*, ed. Oleg Bychkov and James Fodor (London and New York: Routledge, 2016), 173–74. See also Nicholas Wolterstorff, "Beyond Beauty and the Aesthetic in the Engagement of Religion and Art," in *Theological Aesthetics after von Balthasar*, 119–34.

20. For an analysis of the distinction and relation between art and religion in Latino/a experience, see Peter Casarella, "Art and the U.S. Latina and Latino Religious Experience," in *Introduction to the U.S. Latina and Latino Religious Experience*, ed. Hector Avalos (Boston: Brill, 2004), 143–69.

21. Alejandro García-Rivera, "On a New List of Aesthetic Categories," 174.

22. Ibid.

23. Ibid., 178–79.

24. Pope Paul VI said: "There is another way, a way open to all, even to people of humble condition, which we call the way of beauty;

to this path leads that treasure, the marvelous and most beautiful doctrine of Mary and the Holy Spirit, in which the investigations of this Marian Congress ought to delve." Paul VI, address to Marian Congress, May 16, 1975. See also the essay by Francis Clooney, S.J., in this volume.

25. Sixto J. García, "A Hispanic Approach to Trinitarian Theology," 124.

26. Joseph Ratzinger, "Conscience and Truth," in *On Conscience: Two Essays* (San Francisco, CA: Ignatius Press, 2007), 12. This translation was altered to be gender-inclusive.

27. Cf. Emmanuel M. Katongole and Jonathan Wilson-Hartgrove, *Mirror to the Church: Resurrecting Faith after the Genocide in Rwanda* (Grand Rapids, MI: Zondervan, 2009).

28. Friedrich Nietzsche, *The Gay Science*, IV, Aphorism, #276 (New York: Vintage, 1974), 223: "I want to learn more and more to see as beautiful what is necessary in things; then I shall be one of those who make things beautiful. *Amor fati*: let that be my love henceforth! I do not want to wage war against what is ugly. I do not want to accuse; I do not even want to accuse those who accuse. Looking away shall be my only negation. And all in all and on the whole: some day I wish to be only a Yes-sayer."

29. See Miguel de Unamuno, *La agonía del cristianismo* (Buenos Aires: Editorial Losada S.A., 1938; first ed. 1924), and John A. Mackay, *The Other Spanish Christ: A Study in the Spiritual History of Spain and Latin America* (Eugene, OR: Wipf and Stock, 2001; first ed. 1932).

30. Sixto J. García, "A Hispanic Approach to Trinitarian Theology," 122–23.

31. Clodovis Boff, *Mariología social. O significado da Virgem para a sociedade* (Paulus: São Paulo, 2006), 445.

32. Ibid. On Mary's solidarity with the indigenous who chew coca leaves, see Gustavo Gutiérrez, *The God of Life* (Maryknoll, NY: Orbis Books, 1991), 178–79.

33. Alex García-Rivera, "Interfaith Aesthetics," 190.

34. Ibid.

35. Ibid., 190–91.

36. These remarks were developed in conversation with two other conference presenters, Emmanuel Katongole and Paul Kollman, whose contributions are sadly not included in this publication. The original form of the remarks was maintained here for the sake of continuity

with the spontaneity of the original discussion. Odozor's contribution can be found in this volume. For a Latino/a counterpart to the question of faith and ethics, one might consider Christopher Tirres, *The Aesthetics and Ethics of Faith: A Dialogue between Liberationist and Pragmatic Thought* (Oxford: Oxford University Press, 2014).

37. See the contribution by Teresia Hinga in this volume.
38. Martin Nkafu, "Vitalogia: Espressione del pensiero africano," in *Aprire la filosofia all'intercultura*, ed. Martin Nkafu (Bologna: Editrice Missionera Italiana, 2003), 117–18.
39. Eleazar S. Fernandez, *Toward a Theology of Struggle* (Maryknoll, NY: Orbis Books, 1994).
40. See Agnes Brazal, "Power-Beauty and Prophetic Resistance: A Postcolonial Approach," in *Witnessing: Prophecy, Politics, and Wisdom*, ed. Maria Clara Bingemer and Peter Casarella (Maryknoll, NY: Orbis Books, 2014), 60–67.
41. Gemma Cruz, *An Intercultural Theology of Migration: Pilgrims in the Wilderness* (Leiden and Boston: Brill, 2010), 93–101.
42. James H. Kroeger, M.M. "The Faith-Culture Dialogue in Asia: Ten FABC Insights on Inculturation," available online at <http://cca.org.hk/home/ctc/ctc08-03/10_james_kroeger93.pdf>, accessed September 12, 2017.
43. Ibid.
44. Alejandro García-Rivera, "Interfaith Aesthetics: Where Theology and Spirituality Meet," in *Exploring Christian Theology*, ed. Bruce H. Lescher and Elizabeth Liebert (New York: Paulist Press, 2006), 178–95.
45. Martin Heidegger, "The Origin of the Work of Art," in *Poetry, Language, Thought* (New York: Harper & Row, 1971), 15–87.
46. "The Origin of the Work of Art," 34.
47. On some parallels between Heidegger's poetics and the visual aesthetics of Zen, see Runette Kruger, "The (Extra) Oordinary (Con) Texts of Beauty and Be-ing," *South African Journal of Art History* 25, number 1 (2009): 137–40, available online at <https://www.academia.edu/1900250/The_extra_ordinary_con_texts_of_beauty_and_be-ing>. accessed September 12, 2017.
48. Muneyoshi Yanagi and Bernard Leach, *The Unknown Craftsman: A Japanese Insight into Beauty* (rev. ed., Tokyo: Kodansha International, 1989), 152.

49. Francis X. Clooney, S.J., *His Hiding Place Is Darkness: A Hindu-Catholic Theopoetics of Divine Absence* (Stanford, CA: Stanford University Press, 2014), 127.
50. *His Hiding Place Is Darkness*, 16–48, here at 47.
51. Cf. Peter Casarella, "Conversion and Witnessing: Intercultural Renewal in a World Church," *Proceedings of the Catholic Theological Society of America* 68 (2013): 1–17.
52. It is not clear whether the act was performed by Muslim terrorists or by the Algerian government, which then made it seem like an act of terrorism.
53. The testament can be found online at <https://www.firstthings.com/article/1996/08/last-testament>.
54. Jacques Derrida, *The Gift of Death* (Chicago: University of Chicago Press, 1995), 47.

Works Cited

Bhabha, Homi. *The Location of Culture*. London: Routledge, 1994.

Boff, Clodovis. *Mariología social. O Significado da virgem para a sociedade*. Paulus: São Paulo, 2006.

Brazal, Agnes. "Power-Beauty and Prophetic Resistance: A Postcolonial Approach." In *Witnessing: Prophecy, Politics, and Wisdom*, edited by Maria Clara Bingemer and Peter Casarella. Maryknoll, NY: Orbis Books, 2014.

Carpenter, Anne M. *Theopoetics: Hans Urs von Balthasar on the Risk of Art and Being*. Notre Dame, IN: University of Notre Dame Press, 2015.

Casarella, Peter. "Art and the U.S. Latina and Latino Religious Experience." In *Introduction to the U.S. Latina and Latino Religious Experience*, edited by Hector Avalos, 143–69. Boston: Brill, 2004.

———. "Conversion and Witnessing: Intercultural Renewal in a World Church." *Proceedings of the Catholic Theological Society of America* 68 (2013): 1–17.

———. "Culture and Conscience in the Thought of Joseph Ratzinger/Pope Benedict XVI." In *Explorations in the Theology of Benedict*

XVI, edited by John C. Cavadini. Notre Dame, IN: University of Notre Dame Press, 2012.

———. "The Painted Word." *Journal of Hispanic/Latino Theology* 6, no. 2 (November 1998): 18–42.

Clooney, Francis X., S.J. *His Hiding Place Is Darkness: A Hindu-Catholic Theopoetics of Divine Absence.* Stanford, CA: Stanford University Press, 2014.

Cruz, Gemma. *An Intercultural Theology of Migration: Pilgrims in the Wilderness.* Leiden and Boston: Brill, 2010.

Derrida, Jacques. *The Gift of Death.* Chicago: University of Chicago Press, 1995.

Fernandez, Eleazar S. *Toward a Theology of Struggle.* Maryknoll, NY: Orbis Books, 1994.

Gadamer, Hans-Georg. *Truth and Method.* New York: Crossroad, 1985.

García, Sixto J. "A Hispanic Approach to Trinitarian Theology: The Dynamics of Celebration, Reflection, and Praxis." In *We Are a People! Initiatives in Hispanic American Theology*, edited by Roberto S. Goizueta, 107–32. Philadelphia, PA: Fortress Press, 1992.

García-Rivera, Alejandro. *The Community of the Beautiful: A Theological Aesthetics.* Collegeville, MN: Liturgical Press, 1999.

———. "Interfaith Aesthetics: Where Theology and Spirituality Meet." In *Exploring Christian Theology*, edited by Bruce H. Lescher and Elizabeth Liebert, 178–95. New York: Paulist Press, 2006.

González, Michelle A. *Sor Juana: Beauty and Justice in the Americas.* Maryknoll, NY: Orbis Books, 2003.

González-Andrieu, Cecilia. *The Bridge to Wonder: Art as a Gospel of Beauty.* Waco, TX: Baylor University Press, 2012.

Gutiérrez, Gustavo. *The God of Life.* Maryknoll, NY: Orbis Books, 1991.

———. *On Job: God-Talk and the Suffering of the Innocent.* Maryknoll, NY: Orbis Books, 1987.

Heidegger, Martin. "The Origin of the Work of Art." In *Poetry, Language, Thought.* New York: Harper & Row, 1971.

Katongole, Emmanuel M., and Jonathan Wilson-Hartgrove. *Mirror to the Church: Resurrecting Faith after the Genocide in Rwanda.* Grand Rapids, MI: Zondervan, 2009.

Nava, Alex. "On Tragic Beauty." In *New Horizons in Hispanic/Latino(a) Theology*, edited by Benjamín Valentín. Cleveland: Pilgrim Press, 2003.

Nkafu, Martin. "Vitalogia: Espressione del pensiero africano." In *Aprire la filosofia all'intercultura*, edited by Martin Nkafu. Bologna: Editrice Missionera Italiana, 2003.

Ratzinger, Joseph Cardinal. "Conscience and Truth." In *On Conscience: Two Essays*. San Francisco, CA: Ignatius Press, 2007.

———. *Truth and Tolerance: Christian Belief and World Religions*. San Francisco, CA: Ignatius Press, 2004.

Tirres, Christopher. *The Aesthetics and Ethics of Faith: A Dialogue between Liberationist and Pragmatic Thought*. Oxford: Oxford University Press, 2014.

Yanagi, Muneyoshi, and Bernard Leach. *The Unknown Craftsman: A Japanese Insight into Beauty*. Rev. ed. Tokyo: Kodansha International, 1989.

Chapter Four

THE BEAUTY OF LOVE AND FORGIVENESS?[1]

Lawrence E. Sullivan, University of Notre Dame

Four Views and a Question

I want to look at "Finding Beauty in the Other" from four points
of view, each of which I will exemplify with cases. I have a particular question to ask of these case examples: What role do love and
forgiveness play in finding beauty in the "Other"?

Imaginal Exercise

Before outlining the four points of view, I would like to pause for a
moment. My account is mostly an academic one, but it is also centered on questions and stories deeply personal to me, which I feel the
subject calls for. Therefore, before starting my reflections, I'll slow
down our brief time together by allowing you also to look inward. I
invite you also to locate experiences of love and forgiveness of your
own and let them serve as benchmarks during my reflections. Would
you please close your eyes, take a comfortable position, and become
aware of your breathing? I'll pause between each of my sentences, to
let you pace your reflections. Take some nice, even breaths. Become
aware of your breathing. Leave off developing any chain of argument
and just become aware of your own presence in this room, relaxed
in your chair, aware of whatever sounds there may be in the background but letting them pass through without disturbing you.

For this first minute, allow to come to your mind an experience of love in your life. Don't wait for the most important experience. There's no need for triage here. Whatever comes to mind is good. And, in an Ignatian sense, let this experience compose a place around it. Picture where this experience of love is happening. Enter into this place with your imagination; become a presence there. Take a good look around and notice where you are and who is here. Look on the faces of those here in this place of your experience of love. What draws your attention? What in this place attracts your mind's eye? Is there something beautiful here, someone beautiful here who catches your eye? Take notice of your own reactions and your feelings as you regard this scene and these figures.

Allow me to pull you away from here and direct your thoughts to another experience, an experience of forgiveness in your life. Again, this need not be an encyclopedic review of all your experiences of forgiveness. Simply enter the scenario that first presents itself to your memory. Where are you and who is here? Can you see faces? Is there something beautiful in this scenario that draws your attention? Note what that may be and what response that may evoke within you.

The Value of Personal Experience

I thank you for taking on this brief imaginal exercise to open up space for a personal benchmark of the fundamental experiences of love and forgiveness, which I now want to address. I open up this space for your personal experience because, from one philosophical point of view at least, love and forgiveness do not exist in the abstract, as is perhaps true also of pain. These are virtues or powers or faculties that are embodied. And their scale of existence is not therefore cumulative or collective; rather, they exist on their greatest scale and in their most pressing reality in the experience of the individuals who embody them—in us. So here we are, returned to full attention as participant observers of the world we are in, the "world" significantly constituted in us, our perceptions, our awareness.

I said at the outset of my remarks that I want to ask about the role of love and forgiveness in the process of "Finding Beauty in the Other," a process of discovering beauty that can be viewed in four ways.

THE FIRST POINT OF VIEW is to look upon finding beauty as a process of elimination. Can we weed out what is not beautiful—can we remove what is ugly—and find the beautiful in what remains? Can we find beauty in the "other" by somehow taking away what is repulsive? How might love and forgiveness be involved in that process of eliminating what is hideous in the "Other"?

THE SECOND POINT OF VIEW looks on beauty and unattractiveness in a way that fuses the two opposites together—for example, by revealing their underlying unity. Thus, the second path could somehow find Otherness itself—in its unassimilable strangeness, say—to be a form of beauty.

A THIRD APPROACH would be where love and forgiveness transmute what is ugly in a way that renders beautiful that which is unattractive.

THE FOURTH AND LAST POINT OF VIEW will be my own point of view. That's a teaser.

The First Approach: The Process of Elimination

NOW TO SOME CASE ILLUSTRATIONS. The first approach, the process of elimination, has been adumbrated in earlier presentations in this conference. I think, for example, of Gabriel Reynolds's paper on "the punishments." They depict scenarios of destruction that exterminate what is appalling, atrocious, and morally despicable, to leave behind a more admirable world marked by the beauty of the virtuous.

The process of elimination has been hard at work in religious traditions for millennia, through scenarios of apocalyptic cataclysm, for instance. Myths of origin also regularly depict the destruction of primordial worlds marred by abhorrent behavior and monstrous beings. So do religio-historical accounts. Think of the cleansing flood of Noah's day, for instance, or the elimination of Pharaoh's chariots and charioteers in the cleansing destruction of the Red Sea. And this process of elimination features dramatically in religions beyond the Abrahamic traditions: in the significant scenarios of what the Japanese called *mappo* and the Chinese called *mò fǎ*, the final age of the Dharma, dramatized in the writings and art of Buddhism; and in the apocalyptic end of the world, manifest in the *Mahabharata* on a scale that is literally epic.

AMONG SOUTH AMERICAN INDIGENOUS PEOPLES, where I have a special interest that I detailed in my book *Icanchu's Drum*, Guaraní peoples ardently sought the Land Without Evil, *Ywy Marae'y*, in their remarkable migrations across wide swaths of the continent. The Guaraní dance-pilgrimages were compelled by their religious hopes for freedom and lightness of being, and driven as well by the desire to be rid of the heavy circumstances of colonization, oppression, and the microbial shock waves of disease. For generations, not only in the Jesuit reductions in Paraguay and Argentina in the seventeenth and eighteenth centuries, but across the continent in times long before and after that, they sought what they described as a beautiful condition free of evil, ugliness, and disease. Their ritual line dances were meant to transport them physically to the final paradise, lifted into *Ywy Marae'ey* while in continuous motion, as happened in mythical times to the spiraling stars of the Milky Way.

Gabriel Reynolds suggested that the scenarios of punishment and apocalyptic cosmic destruction may be best seen as moral exhortations to live a more beautiful life—a very insightful point. Nonetheless, there are religious communities that have taken these scenarios literally and not simply as moral exhortations, and beauty can play a role in their reckoning. Consider, for example, the Indiana prophet Jim Jones, who in November 1978 led more than 900 members of the People's Temple that he established in Guyana to their deaths by drinking cyanide-laced beverages. Over 300 of the dead were minor children. Jones's death tape, as it is called, records the final hours of their lives and is full of invocations of beauty: "let's make this a beautiful day," "you are beautiful people," "the beauty of this place." Similarly, I served on the panel convoked by President Bill Clinton that investigated the events surrounding the death of the prophet David Koresh and his Branch Davidian followers in Waco, Texas. The beauty of the remnant that was to remain, including the children whom Koresh fathered with various women in the community, was one of the drivers toward the eschatological culmination of time. As it turned out, the ending came in a conflagration of the community residence and the death of 80 people, including 22 minors, inside the Mount Carmel compound in Waco on April 19, 1993. Aside from moral exhortation, some processes of elimination as a path to beauty are taken literally.

SHAME. I have been talking about this first point of view, a process of elimination in which ugly dross is burned away to leave behind what is luminous and beautiful—a strategy that includes cleansing cataclysm and apocalypse. A less violent process of elimination is shame. Leon Kass, the physician and philosopher from the University of Chicago, relies on Erwin Straus, a neurologist and philosopher, to make strong arguments about shame in his book *Toward a More Natural Science: Biology and Human Affairs.*[2] Both Kass and Straus rely in turn on Kurt Riezler, a German diplomat and philosopher. You'll note that philosophers who have day jobs allow themselves to make creative points, perhaps buoyed by pay scales from professions other than philosophy. Kass, Straus, and Riezler considered shame a robust human faculty. Kass defines shame as "a faculty of the soul" that allows human beings to perceive and then cover over what is ugly or repulsive, and hide it from oneself and others. Think of that: shame, a robust faculty of the soul.

Having announced it as a spiritual faculty, Kass hastens to remain a physician and observes that shame has physiological aspects. He discusses blushing extensively to show that, like beauty—which is

shame's twin and has been philosophically regarded as such throughout history—shame has, in the end, a physiological basis. Shame is
based in the body. Shame is the body self-aware, in the presence of
others; the body socially present to itself. Shame especially evinces,
then, the self-possession of a psychosocial perception of myself, aware
of being in your presence precisely when you are aware of being in
my presence as well as in the presence of others at the same time.
Shame reflects a "hall of mirrors" awareness whereby everyone sees
one another seeing one another. Or as the Blues Master says, "I know
that you know that they know…you treated me no good." Thus,
shame occurs in this hyper-reflexive context. As such, Kass says that
shame, in regard to both outward beauty and morally upstanding
beauty—"looking good" in all the senses of that expression—is both
preventive and post-operative. In other words, shame steers you down
the channels of virtue, but if you should breach those constraints and
do something shameful, shame will steer you back toward recovery,
remediation, and reconciliation. So let's keep in mind that a process
of elimination—up to and including the process of shame—can direct us toward what is beautiful.

The Second Approach: Uniting Ugliness and Beauty

Let's look now at the second approach to finding beauty in the
Other, wherein what is ugly is embraced, in its very otherness and
unsettling strangeness, as something beautiful and attractive.

Georges Rouault's *Miserere*

I want to turn to the French artist Georges Rouault and his
enormous lifelong *oeuvre* called the *Miserere*, often translated as
"Suffering," begun in 1916 in France, during the thundering culmi-
nations of trench warfare in World War I. Rouault's publisher had
suggested at the time that the artist create 65 etchings, a series that
he began in 1916 and completed more than a decade later, in 1927.

However, the etchings were not published until 1944, toward the end of World War II, because Rouault began to elaborate on those original etchings in a long continuum of artistic transformations that stretched throughout the excruciating periods of social suffering in Depression-era and World War II Europe. Rouault brought to bear on these works all the multiple artistic techniques and coloring schemes of his career. In the course of working on them he created many versions, transformations, and printings. The entire collected series was finally published in 1948, after the devastation of World War II. *Miserere* thus reflects a lifetime of artistic meditation on the realities of human suffering, seen through the lens of the Passion of Jesus. I am reminded of Pope Benedict XVI's description of what he calls "the wound" that penetrates so much of Christian art, the gash that exists between the beauty of Christ the Comely Bridegroom and the beauty of Christ the Suffering Servant, in whom there is no comeliness. It is there in that wound, the unhealed space between irreconcilable poles of the beauty of humanity and the repulsiveness of suffering at one another's hands, that Rouault inserts himself for the lifetime of his artistry.

In the first layer of this complex work, Rouault draws heavy, dark-ink outlines that he will later photographically transpose onto other media as a basis for his etchings on metal, for example. His ink drawings imitate the lead—the dross, the base metal—that outlines the figures in stained-glass windows. As a boy of fourteen and later, before he became an artist, Rouault was apprenticed as a stained-glass worker. The ontogeny of *Miserere* as a work of art will recapitulate the phylogeny of his own evolution as an artist. The transmutation of base metal into light through stained glass lies at the foundation of his artistic formation and understanding. Rouault creates the figure of Christ in these very heavily marked, lead-dark outlines. The 65 scenes of Christ's Passion and Agony, the Via Crucis, become the inexpungable base for all the reflections and embellishments that follow. Throughout his artistic lifetime, from 1916 to 1948, he begins to color in these dark outlines, and an amazing transformation takes place. He uses the palette of colors from stained glass, something that he receives in the French Gothic inheritance of Sainte-Chapelle and Chartres, which contain a whole theology of light and glass developed from the twelfth century forward. As you may recall, in the Sainte-Chapelle, Saint Louis IX's personal residential chapel built to contain the relic of the crown of thorns brought from the Crusades, there is an oculus of thick, clear glass in the easternmost window, the window depicting the Passion. On the day of the spring equinox in the Easter season, that oculus magnifies a single ray of dawn-light and sends it into the center of the chapel, a microcosm of the space-time of creation, which is made evident in the depictions fashioned in the stained-glass panels that line all the walls of the building. Those panels portray the episodes of salvation history through time, from the days of creation through the times of the Biblical kings and prophets to the time of Christ and the early church. The ray of light from the Easter dawn travels through the body of space-time in the church, a microcosm of the world, and strikes the nimbus of Christ the apocalyptic Judge at the end of time, encircling his head with a perfectly round golden halo to mark the end of time. Through Jesus' Passion, the light of grace flows through all time and space, from the creation of the world, brought into being with that opening annunciation, "let there be light," to the final Judgment.

Rouault brings this exquisitely beauteous theology of grace-filled light, colorfully refracted through the stained-glass colors of space and time, to the Passion of Jesus, in whom, as Scripture says, "there is no comeliness," no beauty at all. Over the course of Rouault's lifetime the Passion, the paradigm of dark suffering that lies at the base of the *Miserere* and in some measure of all mortal life, becomes tinted with the beauty of color, in myriad variations. Increasingly, the atrocious deadly wounds of Christ take on the tones and hues of stained-glass colors. Eventually Rouault has the welts and bruises take on a clownish aspect—he paints them as the face paint of a clown. Christ becomes a fool for our sake, and "suffering" has a face. In his own way, Rouault develops a redemptive theology of the face—something that the Belgian theologian

Alphonse de Waelhens, the French-Lithuanian philosopher Emmanuel Levinas, and the French theologian Jean-Luc Marion will later develop in significant ways.

As Jean-Paul Sartre pointed out in his *Esquisse d'une théorie des émotions*,[3] the face is a cosmological instrument that is always a disguise—it reveals and covers over at the same time. A face can lie, and also, by giving away the truth, it can betray one's lying words. The face is inherently ambivalent and is always therefore "othering." So Rouault raises the question: When do you ever get beneath the face; or are we always presenting one or another guise to each other? Are we humans never so much ourselves as when we are *acting* an "Other"? Is this not what Jesus foolishly does: a divine being become totally "Other" by becoming fully human—taking on himself the sins of us all so that by his stripes we, in turn, are healed, "othered" in turn? Rouault clearly thinks so: over time the *Miserere* reveals Christ the Suffering Fool, even dressing him in a clown hat and harlequin outfit. And, in terms of the question posed at the beginning, does not this particular act of healing, accomplished through the love and forgiveness revealed in Jesus' Passion, close "the wound," the gap between what is ugly and beautiful, enabling us to find beauty in all "Others"? In the event of Jesus' Passion, which he undergoes out of love for the forgiveness of sins, an atrocious and ugly act is revealed to be beautiful, taking on the living colors that evolve over the slow-motion course of Rouault's artistic lifetime.

The Third Approach: Transmuting What Is Ugly

Let us move to consider a third way, important to me, in which love and forgiveness help us find beauty in the Other by transmuting what is ugly. Such re-envisioning of ugliness as a sign of lovable humanity has long been a religious concern found abundantly throughout world mythologies, as analyzed, for example, by Georges Dumézil and Claude Lévi-Strauss. For quick reference, think of the Pueblo account of the Ash-boy or the many variations of the Cinderella tale found in Indo-European literature. These mythic tropes illustrate how, with a proper change in understanding, another way of looking at reality, the true nature of those dumped into unattractive circumstances can be revealed to show their essential beauty.

Examining this approach involves some autobiography and a half-dozen thumbnail sketches to illustrate their range and variety, but also to demonstrate their shared point of view. I was a professor here at Notre Dame for eight years in the departments of theology and anthropology, and in the Kroch and Kellogg Institutes as well. During that time, I was invited to join the Board of Trustees of the Fetzer Institute, a global foundation based in Michigan; and, toward the end of my time at Notre Dame, I was invited to become the President and CEO of the Fetzer Institute, a position I held for a number of years.

The Fetzer mission attracted me: "to foster awareness of the power of love and forgiveness in the emerging global community." Rather than abstractly define love and forgiveness ahead of time, we decided—for the same philosophical reasons mentioned above, about love and forgiveness being embodied powers—to raise up living exemplars whom advisors we gathered into councils pointed to as outstanding embodiments of love and forgiveness. We then tried to learn more about love and forgiveness from the lives of the individuals who were admired for embodying these virtues. Obviously, proceeding in this way called for latitude regarding what our advisors might regard as loving and forgiving. The advisors were leaders drawn from every possible walk of life—from lawyers, labor leaders, and doctors to engineers, scientists, Olympic athletes, and more. We felt that this way of benchmarking love and forgiveness in the lived experience of our advisors and exemplars was a sure-footed way toward our goal of fostering awareness of the power of love and forgiveness in the emerging global community. We eventually identified 200 different exemplars of love and forgiveness from scores of countries, examining them for the purpose of learning from them and also of drawing motivation from their life-transforming examples. In the course of the work, our "fostering awareness" sometimes took the form of documenting these lives in films or televised interviews, so that they became like 200 beautiful icons embodying love and forgiveness. I only want to mention a few of them to give you the flavor of their variety and to address how we might "find Beauty in the Other" by contemplating our human circumstances when they are transformed by love and forgiveness.

Post-Conflict Resolution in Bosnia-Herzegovina

I begin with an example from postwar Bosnia-Herzegovina, where we collaborated with the Post-Conflict Resolution Center on a project called "Ordinary Heroes." During the tumultuous, horrific ethnic conflicts in Bosnia-Herzegovina, ordinary people did step forward in impossibly difficult circumstances to love the Other—the ethnic other, the religious other. What motivated them to find beauty in the "Other" in such atrocious circumstances? Our project investigated the cases. One story, for example, was documented in a film series that has now been televised throughout the Balkan region and has been made the subject of workshops for youth. The story is about a gas station attendant, a Muslim Bosnian, who was captured and brought to a concentration camp. He managed, miraculously, to escape in the middle of the night, but he had been terribly beaten, and he desperately needed a place to hide from those chasing him. He scrambled his way to an unknown stranger's door and knocked on it. Mina, a Christian woman who is now 80, looked him over. She did not know him but immediately sized up his plight. He didn't "look good," in the words of Leon Kass. Having been shamefully beaten, he was disfigured and discolored from his bruises, like Rouault's clown. In him there was no comeliness. With no time to hesitate, and at great risk to herself, Mina took him in and hid him. We have her account and his account of this gratuitous act of love.

Salih, another Muslim man who had been interned in the Bat-kovic Concentration Camp, thought he was being frog-marched to his death at a military checkpoint. When he looked up, however, he saw a man named Đorđe, a Christian who had been his class-mate when they were younger and who had somehow infiltrated the prison to have Salih released into his company. It turns out that Đorđe returned time and again to places where prisoners were de-tained to effect the release of people who were not Christians, who were Muslims and who were from ethnic groups different from his own. The "Ordinary Heroes" project tried simply to record these acts of love and, throughout the post-conflict process of reconcili-ation, record also the related acts of forgiveness. The project has subsequently been recognized by the United Nations Alliance of Civilizations, receiving an award from U.N. Secretary General Ban Ki-moon as the most innovative grassroots project carried on by a non-profit organization. Because of the love embodied in in-dividual cases, and also eventually embodied in the post-conflict reconciliation and forgiveness that has since been extended, the brutality and the ugliness could not extinguish the power to find beauty in the "Other," a realization that can lend us hope and cour-age to do likewise.

The Afghan Institute of Learning

For a second example, let me mention Sakena Yacoobi, an Af-ghan woman who had come to the United States as a graduate student in Detroit. I asked her to join an advisory council at the Fetzer Institute to help point us toward exemplars of love and for-giveness. Sakena's own story would qualify as such an example. Her father had made it possible for her to leave war-torn Afghanistan to peacefully undertake her graduate studies in Michigan in the 1990s. But when she saw what was happening at home under the Taliban at that time, when she saw how impossible it was becoming for girls and women to attain an education, she decided to return to Afghanistan and try to do something about it. Initially, she formed underground cells of women educators teaching girls and other women in dangerous circumstances and in hiding. Teachers suffered; some were killed and others were rejected by their families. Eventually Sakena blended the different cells into a network called the Afghan Institute of Learning, which teaches the full range of subjects, including math and sciences. Her institute now educates some 400,000 girls and women each year and has educated some 10 million women across Afghanistan and Pakistan. I witnessed a conversation between Sakena—a Muslim from Herat—and a U.S. marine officer who had deployed multiple times in Afghanistan. After listening to her story, which the soldier openly admired, he said, "May I ask you a very personal question?" She said, "Please, ask me anything." He asked, "I'm sorry to be so blunt, but why aren't you dead?" She took in his question and answered right away with a straight face: "On the one hand, I've always been a loving person, and I embrace everyone I find." Then she added, with a twinkle in her eye, "On the other hand, I have also learned to change cars en route to my destinations, avoid taking the same routes, and other precautions," which she went on to describe. That answer made good sense to the marine officer, and they engaged in an appreciative conversation. All of which is to say that Sakena is very grounded in the practical realities of her dangerous world. She is cognizant of the ugliness in the world around her, but, taking as her guide the love described by the Islamic mystical poet Rumi, she is determined to love the beauty that she finds in the hearts and minds of her conflicted world, a love ultimately rooted in the divine creator's love for creation.

Persevering for Participative Design in South Asia

A third example is Kirtee Shah, a high-level Indian architect who embraces people who have no home and no means to provide themselves with one. Kirtee chaired our Design Council. He is a devoted Jain who sees to it that worthy homes are built in the neediest urban settings afflicted by poverty—locales destructively affected by insufficient support from civil society, especially communities ravaged by the wantonness of human conflict as well as by such unforeseen natural disasters as earthquakes and tidal waves. Sitting here in this lovely university, it takes a mighty labor of imagination to picture how difficult these nearly intractable problems can be. Jesus himself says in the Gospel, "The poor you will always have with you." The home is the primary built space; living without a home pitches people into dehumanizing conditions, in the eyes of others and in their own self-estimations. Kirtee's successful approach to housing the poor en masse is grounded in his discovery of beauty in the homeless, the un-sheltered "Other" who suffer in dehumanizing circumstances, mired in bureaucratic indifference and ineptitude, without leverage or advocates to pull them through.

Kirtee is the Chairman of KSA Design Planning Services Ltd. and also the founder of the Ahmedabad Study Action Group (ASAG), a remarkable nonprofit foundation that he has directed for 35 years. Kirtee is phenomenally persistent. He perseveres no matter how strong the headwinds. That toughness can give pause to people in authority when he very insistently presses them to use their positions for the good of those in need. But Kirtee's perseverance is also coupled with an abiding confidence in the capacity of human beings to do good, for themselves and others, no matter how dire their circumstances. He finds beauty, strength, and self-reliance in those "Others," the masses who are suffering from homelessness, oppression as minorities, and forced migration as refugees of conflict or natural disaster.

By pointing to the beauty and capacity that they have within themselves, Kirtee awakens people's confidence and resourcefulness and empowers those who are suffering abject poverty and official powerlessness. He then presses them to find their "inner architect." He urges them to love and forgive their neighbors so that they overcome the fierce scrapping over scarce resources—a ferocious competition for survival into which they are cast by dint of disaster—and pool their creative powers in order to put them at the service of their neighbors in need. By empowering those in need to creatively address their own plight and that of their neighbors, a process that he calls "participative design," Kirtee has catalyzed very creative large-scale solutions to homelessness in places and times where few other professional architects are willing or able to be available—for example, in Sri Lanka, northern Nigeria, and areas of Indonesia. Kirtee has applied this large-scale philosophy of providing shelter and facilities for many tens of thousands in his capacity as president of the Habitat International Coalition, which is the world's largest coalition of Habitat Professionals addressing housing rights and sustainable urban development for those most in need. Among other initiatives, Kirtee was the founding President of India Habitat Forum (INHAF) and co-founder of the Ashoka Innovator, which now operates in 45 countries.

Open House in Israel

A fourth example comes from Israel and is called the Open House Movement. Yehezkel Landau, a Jewish rabbi who served on our World Religions Advisory Council, and his wife, Dalia, were one day seated in their home in Israel when suddenly there was a knock at the door. The unknown stranger in the entryway explained, "This home once belonged to my family [the Al-Kharyri family]. We are Palestinians, but our family was displaced from this home at the time of the establishment of the state of Israel. We would love the chance, if possible, to revisit the house and our memories." Rabbi Yehezkel invited them in. As the hosts heard their visitors' story, Dalia, who had grown up in that family home of Bulgarian refugees during her childhood, felt deeply troubled on learning that the Al-Kharyri family was forcibly evacuated from the house in 1948. Yehezkel felt personally ashamed. He was not making a geopolitical statement but describing his own feeling of shame on hearing the history of this displaced Arab family's connection to his Jewish home. Think back to Leon Kass's description of shame as "a robust faculty of the soul," rooted even in physiology of the blushing body, active instinctively when discovering something ugly. Kass contended that shame is that rush of self-awareness when an underlying ugliness—something that does not "look good" in the moral sense—discloses itself in the presence of another who also sees the source of your shame in the same hyper-reflexive mirroring glance shared by both you and the "other" who is present.

So Rabbi Yehezkel and his then-wife Dalia Ashkenazi transformed their home into a house of dialogue for Israelis and Palestinians, setting it up so that the house could be jointly owned and shared by Israelis and Palestinians together: an Open House. For the past 25 years, the Open House has been a "laboratory for reconciliation" where the most remarkable things have happened while finding beauty in the "Other." The path of discovery passing through the Open House has often been problem-centered and difficult, but by now has been travelled by thousands of Jews and Arabs fueled by the love and forgiveness extended to one another along the way. Rabbi Yehezkel Landau took these lessons to the Hartford Seminary in Connecticut, where he held the Chair in Abrahamic Partnerships for 14 years before moving recently to Boston University.

Forgiveness in Gulu, Uganda

The fifth example is Angelina Atyam, a mother and midwife from Gulu in northern Uganda, who served on our Advisory Council for the Governing Professions. In 1996, her 14-year-old daughter was abducted from a boarding school, along with 139 other children, by the Lord's Resistance Army (LRA), an anti-government guerilla force led by the warlord Joseph Kony. Although many children were eventually freed, Angelina's child, named Charlotte, was held captive along with others for eight years. As you can imagine, Angelina's story is long and is complicated by many fraught decisions and events. She formed the Concerned Parents Association (CPA) and campaigned vigorously for the children's freedom across all of northern Uganda and in the halls of government. Eight months later her outspoken activism won her the offer from the guerillas of freeing Charlotte if she would, in exchange, leave off her public relations campaign. To the shock of some family and friends, she turned down the chance to have her own child released unless all the children of the other CPA parents were also returned. Kony's group keeps young female captors as sex slaves and, like other marauding guerilla bands, tries to gain national or international attention by compelling the male child-soldiers whom they have pressed into their service to commit initiatory ritual-like atrocities in an attempt both to terrorize local populations and make it impossible for the recruits to return home to civil society. A common brutal initiatory act has been to disfigure, or even slice off, the faces of people in the villages from which they come, the faces of relatives and friends. After committing such acts, returning home is virtually unthinkable, and the young perpetrators become permanent outlaws trapped under the control of their commanders.

Long before Charlotte was freed, at age 23, with her two children, Angelina had come to a strong realization while saying the Lord's Prayer. Reciting the phrase "forgive us our trespasses as we forgive those who trespass against us," she choked over the realization that "I am so far from that!" Among subsequent thoughts and actions that contributed to her transformation, she decided to attend the funeral of one of the LRA guerilla leaders, journeying to his home village to offer comfort to the disconsolate mother and weeping alongside that mother over the death of her son, the vicious young killer who had destroyed so many lives and, in the course of doing so, had effectively destroyed the goodness of his own life as well.

Angelina began a movement to extend forgiveness and effect reconciliation—without which, she pointed out, there would be no future to hope for. As she did this she did not hide from the brutal realities and even exposed them. For her efforts at petitioning the U.N. General Assembly to intervene, she become the co-recipient of the 1998 U.N. Human Rights Prize. And she brought to light in excruciating detail the ongoing atrocities being committed against old and young alike at Ngai in Apac District in an address before the U.N. Security Council on October 23, 2002. At the same time, arguing that there are no winners in war, whose divisions and agonies are self-perpetuating, Angelina is pressing for a national process of forgiveness and reconciliation as the best path forward to a fruitful future of peace.

Angelina, and many of her fellow Ugandans who have been moved by her convictions to join her, are human beings who are finding beauty in the "Other." In the course of doing so, they themselves shine radiantly beautiful in the cruelest of human circumstances. With the help of Professor Daniel Philpott of the University of Notre Dame, the Oscar-nominated film team of Jason Cohen and Thomas Christopher produced a brief documentary about Angelina Atyam and others associated with her movement for forgiveness and reconciliation in northern Uganda. Sitting with Angelina, I am astounded and moved beyond measure to wonder at the kind of power she has to transform a vicious situation into something more—dare we use the word?—beautiful. Angelina herself attributes that power to forgive others not to herself but to the divine grace of "Our Father, who art in heaven."

On Death Row in San Quentin

A sixth case comes from San Quentin, California's oldest prison, just north of San Francisco, which houses the state's only death row for male prisoners. The Condemned Unit at San Quentin is the largest death row in the western hemisphere, holding some 700 inmates. What they have done is not beautiful; neither is their own fate after conviction by a jury. Prisoners sentenced to death were at one time hanged at San Quentin or were executed in its still-existing gas chamber. Since 1996, they have been put to death there by lethal injection.

Jacques Verduin, who works with these death row prisoners, is founder and director of GRIP, "Guiding Rage into Power," and was introduced to Fetzer by our Law Council. The Insight-Out process that Jacques founded and directed within the GRIP program at San Quentin for 20 years became a focus of our Fetzer strategic planning gathering in Assisi, Italy. GRIP, as described on its website, is a year-long program guided by Verduin that enables prisoners to "turn the stigma of being a violent offender into a badge of being a non-violent Peacekeeper." Through GRIP the men transform their own behavior and acquire skills to become agents of change who can help defuse the conflicts around them. Within the GRIP program (which includes some non-death-row-inmates, the Insight-Out process guides incarcerated men on a healing journey, at first deeply within themselves and then eventually outside of prison, to serve others and to give back to communities from whom they had once taken. Insight-Out aims to help prisoners "become free from prison before they leave prison." By accomplishing these inner and outer goals, Jacques's Insight-Out process also aims to reform a prison system that is engulfing more and more people across the United States and the world.

As Verduin puts it on the Insight-Out website: "Only in directly supporting our prisoners in transforming themselves can we transform our prison system as well. Working firmly outside the 'us and them' fallacy... engaged citizens who include law enforcement, victims, prisoner and at-risk youth can consider ourselves stakeholders in the prison environment... to restore and secure our communities by playing a role in how we do prisons—and how we do not." In that way incarceration can move beyond punishment to rehabilitation, affording prisoners the chance to learn to "take responsibility and honor their victims, heal the pain they lashed out from and learn the skills that give them a second chance."

Jacques finds beauty in these incarcerated Others and, through a careful process rooted in love and forgiveness, he invites them to examine themselves to ferret out the sources of their ugly and harmful rage, yes, but also to discover the beauty that they can love as a seed within themselves and which can flower to become the basis for a new, revitalized existence. Fetzer subsequently produced a brief film created during the Insight-Out process by the incarcerated inmates themselves, which is available on YouTube. Positioning himself in front of a white board to tote up their answers, Jacques asks a group, "How many minutes did it take for you to commit the act that put you in here?" And "How much time have you spent here in prison as a result?" The eleven men total up 18 minutes of rage in their lives that led them to serve 277 years in prison. Jacques guides the prisoners "in reflections on their scars and on the scars they have inflicted on others with the goal of learning how to stop their own violence and teach nonviolence to others." In 2013 The Fetzer Advisory Council on NGOs awarded Insight-Out its first-place Award for Notable Nonprofit as the NGO that best fosters love and forgiveness, as judged by the online votes of some 30,000 public voters from 89 countries.

Saving Others on 9/11

As a final example, the circumstance of our meeting here on the campus of the University of Notre Dame, home of the Fighting Irish, over September 11, calls to mind the case of Welles Crowther. As a Boston College student-athlete, Welles played Division 1 lacrosse at BC while completing a major in economics. Our Fetzer Advisory Council on Sport put Welles forward as an outstanding exemplar of love in action. We can use two markers to follow his story. First, Welles always wanted to be a firefighter. As a 16-year-old in Nyack, New York, Welles joined his father to become a volunteer firefighter and trained with the Empire Hook and Ladder Company. Second, whether on the field or off it, Welles always wore or carried a version of the red bandanna his father had given him when he was six years old. After graduating with honors in economics from BC, where he was known for wearing a red bandanna under his helmet, Welles went into investment banking and became an equities trader for Sandler O'Neill and Partners on the 104th floor of the Twin Towers of the World Trade Center in New York City. Though enjoying professional success in his field at age 24, he was considering moving from equities trading to joining the New York Fire Department. When disaster struck the Twin Towers on September 11, 2001, Welles had been training for eight years to work inside buildings beset by smoke and fire.

Already on 9/11 news reporters began hearing from multiple survivors that they had been guided from upper floors through descending stairwells to safety by "a man with a red bandanna." The full story was pieced together from as many as twenty-two survivors afterward and reported in an ESPN piece for *Outside the Lines*. When all hell broke loose, Welles was on his office floor, the 104th, above the plane that hit the building at 9:03 A.M. Able to orient himself in the chaos, Welles made his way through the fiery floors where the planes hit, from floor 86 to floor 78, where he called his mother at 9:12 to let her know that he was "OK." There, in that sky lobby, he encountered a group huddled near an elevator, including some who were badly injured. With the red bandanna around his head to block smoke from entering his nose and mouth, Welles heaved into sight, carrying a young woman on his back, and directed Ling Young, who was badly burned and blinded by the blood on her glasses, toward the stairs. Ling Young worked in the New York Tax Office and lived to tell this story. Welles said, in an authoritative voice, to follow him. He led people through the smoke and fire, tamping out the flames when necessary, down seventeen flights to safety.

Then he returned to the 78th floor to lead and carry down others. Welles did this multiple times until he could return no more. He's an experienced guy who knows, "I better get out of this building," and he knows the way out, but he goes back up. Judy Wein, who worked on the 103rd floor with the AON Corporation, said on CNN—as reported by Greg Botelho and Maria Hinojosa in "The Man with the Red Bandanna"—"if he had not come back I wouldn't have made it. People can live 100 years and not have the compassion, the wherewithal to do what he did." His body was found six months later in the South Tower Lobby in the company of other New York City firefighters and emergency responders. The New York Fire Department posthumously made him a member of the department. In Assisi, we held a "Red Bandanna Run" to commemorate Welles, and we helped create the Red Bandanna Project for character development in classrooms, sports teams, camps, and youth programs to reflect on the transformative power of the love that Welles embodied for "Others," complete strangers.

Transmuting Ugliness

Each one of these cases stands on its own. Taken together, however, these examples suggest that individuals who embody love and forgiveness can prove themselves capable of embracing situations that are repulsive—atrocious in the literal sense—like Saint Francis of Assisi kissing the wounds of a leper. In a manner worth fathoming, their love and forgiveness have infused the ugliness and transmuted what is thoroughly unattractive into something we can behold and contemplate, to our shock, as a context where beauty can be found after all.

The Fourth Approach:
Human Call to Reimagine the World in Beauty

THE LAST POINT OF VIEW IS MY OWN, though it derives special support from three colleagues of mine over the years who have helped me consider this approach. One is Ioan Culianu, whom some of you may have known. He was assassinated at the age of 40—we were both 40 at that time. He was a professor, a colleague, at the University of Chicago, and he was shot in the back of the neck while in the third-floor men's room. Years before that, Ioan escaped from Romania to Italy where for a while he was interned in a refugee camp outside Rome. He became a scholar of comparative religious history at the Catholic University of Milan and at the Sorbonne in Paris, and he was especially interested in notions of love as they related to optics and theories of light in Islamic and Jewish thinking, as these came eventually to undergird Western European thinking during the Renaissance. Ioan was also a historian of science who was fascinated by the interplay between optics of light and understandings of love.

The second colleague, who also enjoyed a fruitful relationship with Ioan, is Moshe Idel, a Jewish scholar of Kabbalah who migrated from Romania to Israel. In *Le porte della giustizia*,[4] for example, Idel traces and comments at book length on many similar Jewish ideas about light and love and their related histories to Christian and Islamic expressions in the context of presenting a late-thirteenth-century text that he attributes to Natan ben Sa'adya Har'ar, a resident of Messina in Sicily and a disciple of Abulafia.

The third colleague I want to reference is Abdelhamid I. "Bashi" Sabra of Harvard, an Egyptian. Bashi had written his Ph.D. on theories of light in Newton and Descartes, but eventually spent most of his career focusing on the history of Islamic sciences, especially the optics of Ibn al-Haytham, the astrologer in the Abbasid Caliphate. The big debate in optics is whether we are we receiving impressions from objects, the way Aristotle thought, on our retinas, or we are projecting outward our experiences, perceptions, and understandings, like rays, onto objects. Sabra wisely helped me to see how both parts of that dialectical exchange have a say in the process of human seeing.

Love and Forgiveness and the Human Vocation to Find Beauty

Let me cut to the chase: love and forgiveness allow us to live in the world and behold it as "participative designers," participants whose observations make a difference to the world we know. We receive impressions from the material world, but we also project our perceptions and infuse our creative and imaginal discoveries into the social world, living cosmos, and material universe. When we take in "other" objects, people, and events in these rich, creative, interactively creative ways, they are not untouched by who we are, and in the act of discovering and "seeing" them, we do not leave them unchanged.

Love and forgiveness, along with other "robust human faculties" such as shame and the perception of beauty, therefore constitute what Herman Wouk once called "a second big bang." Through human perceptions and knowledge, increasingly aided by instruments that extend our human intelligence and sensibilities through such optical accessories as Xandra telescopes or electron microscopes, for example, the entire world is being taken in and re-created as a known world through human experience and understanding, from the macrocosms of outer space to the inner microcosms of neurons and nanochemistry.

Though only a speck in the ocean of time, the qualitative shift brought about in the cosmos because of our unique and significant transformative human contribution to the universe should not be underestimated. It may have taken eons to set the cosmic stage, but in a fundamental reckoning that constitutes the meaning of the human role in the universe, the world that arises in this shift, the world that appears in human understanding, is not the same as the world that pre-existed it. After that shift, all realities can be taken in through the dispositions to love and forgive what we see, and through all the other human faculties as well. The universe is reflexively infused with human intelligence and other faculties, including moral dispositions. In the process of taking in the world and its realities, human perception and the human dispositions to love and forgive transform the realities and events that do not on their first face "look good" because, at the least, they appear random and indifferent—or even brutal, atrocious, and inhumane. Through love and forgiveness, as we have seen in concrete cases, this ugliness and brutishness can be somehow transformed or reset in contexts where we find beauty in the "Other," a judgment that, in any case, only human beings are able and entitled to make on account of their own perceptive role in the cosmos.

Effecting transformations of this kind may be the highest calling of humanity, a call that attunes us to the light of grace as it is understood in different religious traditions, howsoever variously "grace"—or beauty—be understood. Fulfilling our human vocation may require us to regard one another—and the world itself —with love and forgiveness, even going so far as to look upon human suffering and its roots, whether they be social or natural, with that transformative vision, as Rouault did and Voltaire refused to do. Perhaps only when we look through the lens of love and forgiveness can we be sure to find beauty in any "Other"—friend, stranger, foe, cosmos.

Notes

1. The editors transcribed and edited only lightly the talk that Sullivan gave at the conference in 2015 with the hope of preserving something of its dynamic quality. As a result, the direct references to the participants in that audience are intentionally left in the written text.
2. Leon Kass, *Toward a More Natural Science: Biology and Human Affairs* (New York: Free Press, 1985).
3. Jean-Paul Sartre, *Esquisse d'une théorie des émotions* (Paris: Hermann, 1948).
4. Moshe Idel, *Le porte della giustizia* (Milano: Adelphi, 2001).

Works Cited

Idel, Moshe. *Le porte della giustizia*. Milano: Adelphi, 2001.
Kass, Leon. *Toward a More Natural Science: Biology and Human Affairs.* New York: Free Press, 1985.
Sartre, Jean-Paul. *Esquisse d'une théorie des émotions*. Paris: Hermann, 1948.

Part II

BEAUTY AND ISLAM

Chapter Five

DIVINE MERCY IN THE QUR'ĀN[1]

Gabriel Said Reynolds, University of Notre Dame

Four different passages in the Qur'ān speak of God's "good" or "beautiful names" (*al-asmā' al-ḥusnā*):

> To Allah belong the Beautiful Names, so supplicate Him by them, and abandon those who commit sacrilege in His names. Soon they shall be requited for what they used to do. (Q 7:180)

> *Say*, "Invoke 'Allah' or invoke 'the compassionate [*al-raḥmān*].' Whichever [of His Names] you may invoke, to Him belong the Beautiful Names." *Be neither* loud in *your* prayer, nor murmur it, but *follow* a middle course between these. (Q 17:110)

> Allah—there is no god except Him—to Him belong the Beautiful Names. (Q 20:8)

> He is Allah, the Creator, the Maker, the Former. To Him belong the Beautiful Names. Whatever there is in the heavens glorifies Him and [whatever there is in] the earth, and He is the All-mighty, the All-wise. (Q 59:24)[2]

According to an idea found in the hadith but not in the Qur'ān, these "beautiful" names number 99.[3] In the course of Islamic tradition, different lists of God's beautiful names were compiled.[4] Most of these lists include some names for God (such as *al-'adl*, "the just," or *al-māni'*, "the withholder") that are not found in the Qur'ān, and exclude other names for God that are found in the Qur'ān.[5] Some classical Muslim scholars, including most Mu'tazilites, accepted the principle that a name could be assigned to God that He does not use for Himself in the Qur'ān. Others, including most of the Ash'arites (notably excluding al-Bāqillānī [d. 1014]), disagreed, although they allowed for names for God attested in the hadith.[6]

The first 13 of God's "beautiful" names in the most commonly cited traditional list thereof come from Q 59:22–24 (the last verse of which is cited above). Following "He is God and there is no god other than Him" ("God" is conceived of as a "name" in this list), the next two names are *"al-raḥmān"* and *"al-raḥīm"*: "the compassionate," "the merciful."[7] In other words, the notion of divine compassion or mercy is prominent in Islamic traditions on God's "beautiful" names. It is also central to the Islamic conception of God more generally.

The importance of mercy to the Islamic concept of God is frequently emphasized by Muslim scholars. The twentieth-century Indian politician and scholar Abū l-Kalām Āzād (d. 1958) writes that God is called both *al-raḥmān* and *al-raḥīm* "because the Koran wants to stamp [*raḥma*; 'mercy'] on man's memory as the most obvious and conspicuous attribute in the idea of God, it wants to express that God is entirely [mercy]."[8] Abū l-Ḥasan 'Alī Nadwī (d. 1999), another influential twentieth-century Indian scholar, comments in his work *Guidance from the Holy Koran*: "Mercy is Allah's favorite attribute."[9] In an address on Q 55 (entitled *al-Raḥmān*, "the compassionate"), the American Muslim preacher Hamza Yusuf declares: "The essential nature of God is Merciful, it's not Majestic. He is Majestic and Beautiful, but the quality that He wants to reveal to man is first and foremost Mercy."[10]

Many non-Muslims, too, have commented on the place of mercy in the Islamic conception of God. In his papal bull *Misericordiae Vultus*, which announced a Jubilee year in the Catholic Church (from December 8, 2015, to November 20, 2016) dedicated to the theme of mercy, Pope Francis writes:

> There is an aspect of mercy that goes beyond the confines
> of the Church. It relates us to Judaism and Islam, both
> of which consider mercy to be one of God's most im-
> portant attributes.... Among the privileged names that
> Islam attributes to the Creator are "Merciful and Kind."
> This invocation is often on the lips of faithful Muslims
> who feel themselves accompanied and sustained by
> mercy in their daily weakness. They too believe that no
> one can place a limit on divine mercy because its doors
> are always open.[11]

Of particular note here is Francis's conclusion in the final sentence
that both Christians and Muslims ("They *too* believe") hold God's
mercy to be without limits. In articulating this idea, Pope Francis
is understandably concerned with religious dialogue, with finding
common ground between Muslims and Christians. Yet according
to the Islamic understanding, is God's mercy in fact limitless?

The present paper is dedicated to exploring further the roots
of the Islamic idea of divine mercy in the Qur'ān. We will see
that while the Qur'ān indeed emphasizes God's mercy, it does not
make His mercy universal. The God of the Qur'ān is not merciful
to wrongdoers, and He is not merciful to those who deny Him, or
who deny His prophets. To such as these, the God of the Qur'ān is
wrathful, even vengeful. The mercy of the Qur'ān's God does not
lie in loving or forgiving wrongdoers or unbelievers. Instead it lies
principally in the signs that He gives them in nature, and through
the ministry of the prophets.

Mercy and Vengeance in the Qur'ān

The theme of divine mercy is prominent in the Qur'ān. As Harris Birkeland has pointed out, in certain Suras the Qur'ān speaks
principally of God's mercy or guidance with no reference to divine
judgment.[12] The importance of mercy to the Qur'ān's conception

of God is evident from the vocabulary it uses to describe Him. The Qur'ān frequently speaks of God as *raḥīm* ("merciful"; 115 times, not counting the invocation, known as the *basmala*, which opens every Sura except for Sura 9), *ghafūr* ("forgiving"; 91 times), *tawwāb* ("clement"; 9 times), and *ra'ūf* ("kind"; 9 times). Very often these terms appear as rhyme words at the end of verses, but this can hardly be thought of as invalidating their importance.[13] As Jacques Jomier points out, on four occasions the Qur'ān names God "the most merciful of the merciful" (*arḥam al-rāḥimīn*).[14]

The Qur'ān frequently refers to God not only as *allāh* but also as *al-raḥmān*, a term generally associated with mercy because of the root (*r.ḥ.m.*), which it shares with *al-raḥīm* (which makes it difficult to translate the pair *al-raḥmān al-raḥim*; above I have rendered this as "the compassionate, the merciful").[15] As Arne Ambros points out, however, the name *al-raḥmān* is used for God in a number of verses in which God is not merciful at all.[16] This is the case with Q 19:45, which has Abraham telling his (pagan) father, "I am indeed afraid that a punishment from [*al-raḥmān*] will befall you, and you will become Satan's accomplice," and 21:42, which has God command the prophet: "*Say, 'Who can guard you, day and night, against* [the punishment of] [*al-raḥmān*]," (see also 36:11, 23; 50:33; 67:20). Such verses suggest that *al-raḥmān* is used simply as a proper name in the Qur'ān. The choice of the Qur'ān's author to use this name is undoubtedly connected to the use of cognate forms thereof (for example, *raḥmānān* in South Arabian Sabaean) by earlier Arabian monotheists in the centuries leading up to Islam.[17] It could be wrong, therefore, to insist that the Qur'ān's author meant to emphasize God's mercy by choosing to use the name *al-raḥmān* for God.[18]

In any case, it is important to add that the God of the Qur'ān is not only merciful. On four occasions the Qur'ān speaks of God as "vengeful" (*dhū intiqām*; Q 3:4; 5:95; 14:47; 39:37). The God of the Qur'ān is not slow to judge, but "quick to judge" (*sarī' al-ḥisāb*; 16 times), and He is "severe in punishment" (*shadīd al-'iqāb*; 28 times). The Qur'ān speaks frequently of God's wrath (*ghaḍab*). The first chapter in the Qur'ān has the believers pray that they will not be guided in the path of those who have incurred God's wrath (*al-maghḍūbi ʿalayhim*; Q 1:7). The God of the Qur'ān is frequently said to be wrathful, in particular toward the Jews (see, e.g., Q 2:61, 90–91; 3:112; 5:60; 7:150, 152; 20:86; 58:14; 60:13), a people whom He has cursed (Q 2:88; 5:60).[19] Yet God's wrath is not limited to the Jews. He is wrathful against those who commit murder (Q 4:93), against the polytheists (Q 7:71; 16:106; 48:6), against the hypocrites (Q 48:6), against those who turn their backs in battle (8:16), and against adulterers (Q 24:90). Qur'ān 40:10 even speaks of the "loathing" (*maqt*) of God when it reports that on the Day of Judgment the unbelievers will be told: "Surely Allah's loathing is greater than your outrage towards yourselves, as you were invited to faith, but you disbelieved."[20]

Thus the Qur'ān emphasizes both God's mercy *and* His vengeance. At times it juxtaposes these two qualities in the same verse, as when it has God declare:

> And appoint goodness for us in this world and the Hereafter, for indeed we have come back to You. Said He, "I visit My punishment on whomever I wish, but My mercy embraces all things. Soon I shall appoint it for those who are Godwary and give the zakat and those who believe in Our signs." (Q 7:156)

Fazlur Rahman, in his influential work *Major Themes of the Qur'ān*, refers to this verse to support his argument that the Qur'ān's God is fundamentally merciful. Rahman, however, cites only the line "My mercy comprehends all (*raḥmatī wasiʿat kulla shayʾ*)."[21] In fact, the question of God's mercy in the Qur'ān is more complicated than Rahman lets on. What the Qur'ān actually gives us in this verse is not a clear statement on mercy but a theological paradox. On the one hand, God punishes whomever he wishes. On the other, His mercy "embraces all things." In order to understand this paradox, and the Qur'ānic position on divine mercy generally, a closer examination of the references in the Qur'ān to divine mercy is in order.

Types of Divine Mercy in the Qur'ān: Nature

In his work *God, Muḥammad and the Unbelievers: A Qur'anic Study*, David Marshall argues convincingly that there are three elements to divine mercy in the Qur'ān: (1) creation/nature, (2) revelation or the ministry of prophets, and (3) the forgiveness of sins.[22] I will follow his categories in the following discussion, beginning with God's mercy in creation/nature.

The Qur'ān presents the very creation of humans as an act of God's mercy.[23] In Sura 16 the Qur'ān declares: "Allah has brought you forth from the bellies of your mothers while you did not know anything. He made for you hearing, eyesight, and hearts so that you may give thanks" (Q 16:78). In this verse the Qur'ān implies that humans should not take for granted their ability to see, or to hear, or to feel emotions (if this is how we should understand the reference to hearts). These are all gifts from God that He was not obliged to give to humans. They should acknowledge such things as a manifestation of divine mercy and, in response, be grateful.

Elsewhere the Qur'ān insists that in fact humans tend *not* to be grateful for these gifts: "Say, 'It is He who created you, and made for you hearing, eyesight, and hearts. Little do you thank'" (Q 67:23), or again, "Then He proportioned him and breathed into him of His Spirit, and made for you hearing, sight, and hearts. Little do you thank" (Q 32:9; cf. also 23:78).

Sura 76 suggests that the creation of humans is a test, and continues by describing the punishment for those who fail the test and the rewards for those who pass it:

> We indeed created man from the drop of a mixed fluid so that We may put him to test, so We endowed him with hearing and sight. We have indeed guided him to the way, be he grateful or ungrateful. We have indeed prepared for the faithless chains, iron collars and a blaze. Indeed, the pious will drink from a cup seasoned with

kāfūr, a spring where Allah's servants will drink, making
it gush forth as they please. (Q 76:2–6)

Thus we begin to appreciate that creation in the Qur'ān is not *only*
an act of mercy or grace. The gifts of hearing and sight, we might
say, come with strings attached. God has given humans these faculties, but He expects something in response. He expects humans
to recognize that these gifts come from Him and to be grateful in
return. Those who fail to do so will be punished. Those who do so
will be rewarded. Thus mercy is connected to judgment.

In other passages, the Qur'ān insists that God's mercy is not
only found in the creation of human faculties (seeing, hearing, etc.)
but also in the creation of those things in nature that are useful to
humans. In Sura 7 the Qur'ān describes the rain that gives life to
the land as a mercy:

> It is He who sends forth the winds as harbingers of His
> mercy. When they bear [rain-] laden clouds, We drive
> them toward a dead land and send down water on it,
> and with it We bring forth all kinds of crops. Thus
> shall We raise the dead; maybe you will take admoni-
> tion. (Q 7:57)

In this passage the Qur'ān uses the example of rain not only to
illustrate the goodness of God in nature, but also to make an argument about the resurrection: just as a dead land comes to life, so
too will dead bodies come to life. At the end of the verse it seems
to call on its audience to reflect on these things ("maybe you will
take admonition").

Elsewhere the Qur'ān asks its audience to reflect on their food:

> Let man consider his food: We pour down plenteous
> water [from the sky], then We split the earth making
> fissures in it and make the grain grow in it, as well as
> vines and vegetables, olives and date palms, and densely-

planted gardens, fruits and pastures, as a sustenance for
you and your livestock. (Q 80:24–32)[24]

Many other passages that describe nature in a similar way might
be cited.[25]

As with its references to the creation of the human faculties of
hearing and sight, the Qur'ān presents the creation of useful things
in nature as a sort of test. The God of the Qur'ān expects that humans will reflect on the world around them, recognize those things
that are useful to them as manifestations of divine mercy, and express gratitude to God in response. It is telling that Qur'ān 80:24
begins with the command, "Let man consider his food." Humans
are not simply to eat; they are to think about what they are eating.

Again, one has the sense that creation in the Qur'ān is not a
simple gift to humanity. It is a test. Not surprisingly, we find that
this passage, too, is followed by a description of divine judgment:

> So when the deafening Cry comes—the day when a
> man will evade his brother, his mother and his father,
> his spouse and his sons—each of them will have a task
> to keep him preoccupied on that day. Some faces will be
> bright on that day, laughing and joyous, and some faces
> on that day will be covered with dust, overcast with
> gloom. It is they who are the faithless, the vicious. (Q
> 80:33–42; cf. 16:79–84)

In Sura 20 the Qur'ān describes the things of nature as signs (*āyāt*)
that should cause humans to reflect and believe in God:

> He, who made the earth for you a cradle and threaded
> for you therein ways, and sent down water from the sky
> and We brought forth with it various kinds of vegetation,
> [saying] "Eat and pasture your cattle. There are indeed
> signs in that for those who have sense." (Q 20:53–54)

Such passages might be compared to the perspective of Paul in his letter to the Romans in which he insists that both the existence and the power of God are evident to all from nature: "Ever since the creation of the world his invisible nature, namely, his eternal power and deity, has been clearly perceived in the things that have been made" (Rom 1:20).

Like Paul, the Qur'ān makes it clear that the good things of nature should be evident to everyone. Some people, however, recognize these blessings, and some do not. This scenario is played out in a long passage on nature in Sura 16 (16:79–81) that concludes with the declaration:

> It is Allah who made for you the shade from what He has created, and made for you retreats in the mountains, and made for you garments that protect you from heat, and garments that protect you from your [mutual] violence. That is how He completes His blessing upon you so that you may submit [to Him]. (Q 16:81)

The Qur'ān declares that humans, upon recognizing the good things in nature, should "submit" (*tuslimūn*) to God. The following two verses note that some people ultimately do not: "But if they turn their backs [on *you*], your [sing.] duty is only to communicate in clear terms. They recognize the blessing of Allah and then deny it, and most of them are faithless" (Q 16:82–83).

One might also compare these passages to the declaration of Jesus in the Gospel of Matthew, according to which God shares the blessings of nature with both the good and the evil:

> But I say to you, Love your enemies and pray for those who persecute you, so that you may be sons of your Father who is in heaven; for he makes his sun rise on the evil and on the good, and sends rain on the just and on the unjust. (Mat 5:44–45)

Jesus in Matthew is concerned with the human response to the mercy of God in nature. Jesus exhorts his followers to love their enemies by insisting that in so doing they will follow the example of God who blesses even the evil, and the unjust, with the good things of nature. As God has blessed even the wrongdoers, so humans should love even their enemies. The Qur'ān does not draw this moral lesson. Instead, the Qur'ān calls attention to the blessings of nature in order to convince its audience to believe.

Here we have an important insight into the fundamental nature of Qur'ānic rhetoric: the Qur'ān is not as concerned with unveiling the nature of God as it is with evoking a human response. As Fazlur Rahman puts it, "The Qur'ān is a document that is squarely aimed at man."[26]

Types of Divine Mercy in the Qur'ān: The Ministry of Prophets

A second element of divine mercy according to the Qur'ān is found in the sending of prophets. God sends the prophet as a "warner" (Ar. *nadhīr*) and a "herald of good news" (*bashīr*) to humanity in order that humans might escape divine destruction on earth and ultimately go to heaven instead of hell. In Sura 22 we read:

> To how many a town did I give respite while it was doing wrong! Then I seized it, and toward Me is the destination. *Say,* "O mankind! I am only a manifest warner to you!" As for those who have faith and do righteous deeds, for them will be forgiveness and a noble provision. But as for those who contend with Our signs, seeking to frustrate [their purpose], they shall be the inmates of hell. (Q 22:48–51; cf. 2:119)

Before He destroys unbelieving and wrongdoing peoples, God warns them, thereby giving them a chance to repent. The end of

Qur'ān 17:15 has God declare: "We do not punish [any community] until We have sent [it] an apostle." From the Qur'ān's perspective, this warning given by prophets is itself an expression of divine mercy. Thus we understand why the Qur'ān speaks of its own prophet as a "mercy" given to people in Sura 21, where God declares: "We did not send you but as a mercy to all the nations" (Q 21:107).

Moreover, from this perspective one can see how the Qur'ānic rhetoric on divine punishment (including both God's destruction of human civilizations on earth and His condemnation of humans to hell) can be seen as an expression of divine mercy. God, one might say, was not obliged to send prophets to warn humans of divine punishment. He could have left them alone to figure things out for themselves (on the basis of the signs in nature). He chose, however, to help them by sending prophets to warn them of the dire consequences of a wrong decision.

It is from this perspective that we might understand why the Qur'ān frequently relates accounts—commonly referred to as "punishment stories" (a translation from a term coined in German: *Straflegenden*)—in which God destroys nations that reject a prophet. These punishment stories are concentrated in a number of Suras—7, 11, 26, 37, and 54 (but see also Q 71 for another version of the Noah story)—all of which are traditionally classified as "Meccan" (although these accounts are also mentioned in two so-called Medinan Suras: Q 9:70; 22:42–44).[27] Some but not all of these accounts involve Biblical characters such as Noah, Lot, and Moses (the punishment stories of Q 37:75–148 notably include only Biblical characters).

It is interesting to note that these characters in the Qur'ān retain certain characteristics of their Biblical narratives. The Qur'ān does not, for example, have the people of Noah destroyed by fire or wind instead of water, or the people of Lot destroyed by water, or Pharaoh and his chariots cast out into the desert and not thrown into the sea. Yet the role of Biblical narratives in shaping the Qur'ānic punishment stories is ornamental. The Qur'ān uses certain distinctive features of those Biblical narratives—perhaps because they were so well known that it could not do otherwise. However, those Biblical narratives themselves are completely transformed to fit the standard model of the punishment stories. For the Qur'ān is not concerned with teaching its audience how the stories of Noah, Lot, and Moses fit into a grand historical narrative. Rather, it is concerned with making a religious argument to the people of its own time by asking the question *ubi sunt qui ante nos fuerunt* ("where have those who were before us gone?").

Precisely because the Qur'ān does not fit these characters into a historical narrative, it is able to integrate into the punishment stories other characters unknown to the Bible, including Hūd, Ṣāliḥ, and Shu'ayb, characters who presumably came from pre-Qur'ānic Arabian lore. These characters, too, are poured into the same prophetic mold. All of these stories, whether they involve Biblical or non-Biblical characters, involve the same scenario. To show the cyclic nature of these accounts, I will cite here excerpts from six punishment stories, according to the three principal stages of these accounts as they appear in Sura 7.

1. The Prophet Preaches to His People

> "[Noah] said, 'O my people, worship Allah! You have no other god besides Him. Indeed I fear for you the punishment of a tremendous day'" (Q 7:59).

> "[Hūd] said, 'O my people, worship Allah! You have no other god besides Him. Will you not then be wary [of Him]?'" (Q 7:65).

> "[Ṣāliḥ] said, 'O my people, worship Allah! You have no other god besides Him. There has certainly come to you a manifest proof from your Lord. This she-camel of Allah is a sign for you'" (7:73).

"[Lot] said to his people, 'What! Do you commit an outrage none in the world ever committed before you?!'" (7:80).

"[Shu'ayb] said, 'O my people, worship Allah! You have no other god besides Him. There has certainly come to you a manifest proof from your Lord. Observe fully the measure and the balance, and do not cheat the people of their goods, and do not cause corruption on the earth after its restoration'" (Q 7:85).

"And Moses said, 'O Pharaoh, I am indeed an apostle from the Lord of all the worlds. It behooves me to say nothing about Allah except the truth. I certainly bring you a clear proof from your Lord. So let the Children of Israel go with me'" (Q 7:104–5).

2. The People Reject the Prophet

"The elite of [Noah's] people said, 'Indeed we see you in manifest error'" (Q 7:60).

"The elite of [Hūd's] people who were faithless said, 'Indeed we see you to be in folly, and indeed we consider you to be a liar'" (Q 7:66).

"So they hamstrung the She-camel and defied the command of their Lord, and they said, 'O Ṣāliḥ, bring us what you threaten us with, if you are one of the apostles'" (Q 7:77).

"But the only answer of [Lot's] people was that they said, 'Expel them from your town! They are indeed a puritanical lot'" (Q 7:82).

"The elite of his people who were arrogant said, 'O Shu'ayb, we will surely expel you and the faithful who are with you from our town, or else you shall revert to our creed.' He said, 'What! Even if we should be unwilling?!'" (Q 7:88).

"[Pharaoh] said, 'If you have brought a sign, produce it, should you be truthful'" (Q 7:106).

3. God Destroys the Unbelievers

"So We delivered him and those who were with him in the ark, and We drowned those who denied Our signs. Indeed they were a blind lot" (Q 7:64).

"Then We delivered Hūd and those who were with him by a mercy from Us, and We rooted out those who denied Our signs and were not faithful" (Q 7:72).

"Thereupon the earthquake seized them and they lay lifeless prostrate in their homes. So he abandoned them [to their fate], and said, 'O my people! Certainly I communicated to you the message of my Lord, and I was your well-wisher, but you did not like well-wishers'" (Q 7:78–79).

"Thereupon We delivered him and his family, except his wife; she was one of those who remained behind. Then We poured down upon them a rain [of stones]. So observe how was the fate of the guilty!" (Q 7:83–84).

"So the earthquake seized them and they lay lifeless prostrate in their homes. Those who impugned Shu'ayb became as if they had never lived there. Those who impugned Shu'ayb were themselves the losers" (Q 7:91–92).

"So We took vengeance on [Pharaoh's people] and
drowned them in the sea, for they denied Our signs and
were oblivious to them" (Q 7:136).

The way in which the Qur'ān tells these stories of warning, disbelief, and destruction one after another tells us something about its
fundamental concern. The Qur'ān seeks to warn *its own* audience
and thereby to convince them to believe in its God and its prophet,
Muhammad. Thus, in the Qur'ān, the prophets of the past *are
prophets of the present*. One scholar has gone so far as to speak of
"monoprophetism" in the Qur'ān.[28]

The point of these stories, in any case, is that upon hearing them,
the Qur'ān's audience will make a better choice than that of those
who choose not to believe in the prophet sent to them. It means
to inspire fear of God. One might think of how, in the Gospel of
Matthew, Jesus tells us, "Do not be afraid of those who kill the
body but cannot kill the soul. Rather, be afraid of the One who
can destroy both soul and body in hell" (Mat 10:28). Similarly, in
Surat al-Baqara the Qur'ān, referring to wrongdoers, declares: "So
do not fear them, but fear Me" (Q 2:150).

It is interesting to note, for our purposes, that the prophets not
only warn their people of a calamity; they also invite their people to
look back at how earlier generations were destroyed and how the present generation now stands in their place. Thus in Sura 7 the Qur'ān
has Hūd refer to the destruction of the people of Noah, saying:

> Do you consider it odd that there should come to you a
> reminder from your Lord through a man from among
> yourselves, so that he may warn you? Remember when
> He made you successors after the people of Noah, and
> increased you vastly in creation. So remember Allah's
> bounties so that you may be felicitous. (7:69)

When the people of Hūd, 'Ād, ignore him and are consequently destroyed, the Qur'ān has Ṣāliḥ use them as an example. He declares:

Remember when He made you successors after [the people of] 'Ād, and settled you in the land: you build palaces
in its plains, and hew houses out of the mountains. So
remember Allah's bounties, and do not act wickedly on
the earth, causing corruption. (Q 7:74)

Thus, just as Hūd and Ṣāliḥ point to the fate of earlier peoples
in order to convince their own people to believe, so the Qur'ān's
Prophet does the same. Muḥammad, one might say, is the latest of
the prophets of the punishment stories. In this light we can understand why the Qur'ān so often refers to its own Prophet as a warner,
nadhīr (a term that appears 44 times in the Qur'ān).[29]

This suggestion does not take us very far from the way in
which classical Muslim theologians thought of divine grace, or
luṭf. For the (Basran) Mu'tazilī Qāḍī 'Abd al-Jabbār (d. 415/1025),
God is actually obliged by His just nature to help humans fulfill
the commands or the law that He has imposed on them.[30] 'Abd
al-Jabbār—who dedicates an entire volume (13) of his encyclopedic theological work *al-Mūghnī* to this question—defines *luṭf*
as "anything that moves a man to choose obedience or makes
it easier for him to choose so."[31] And among these things are
"health, wisdom, the use of reason, prophecy, and the provision
of holy books."[32] The point of *luṭf* is that it helps humans to
make the right choice without compelling them. Thus even the
threat of hell, or *al-wa'īd*, is a sort of grace. To this effect 'Abd
al-Jabbār writes:

As for the threat of hell, it is a favor (*luṭf*) to humans
tasked with obedience from God Most High, as is the
repeating of it in the book of God Most High, and as are
the statements with mention of the exhorting servants,
blaming them, and reproaching them, in the rest of the
Book, in the ways that they appear in the Qur'ān. This
is a favor (*luṭf*) and a goodness.[33]

The aforementioned Indian scholar Abū l-Ḥasan 'Alī Nadwī, in his work *Guidance from the Holy Qur'ān*, similarly describes the ministry of prophets as an expression of divine mercy in comments he makes on Sura 7:43. Here the Qur'ān has the blessed who have been rewarded with paradise declare: "All praise belongs to Allah, who guided us to this. Had not Allah guided us, we would have never been guided. Our Lord's apostles had certainly brought the truth" (Q 7:43). Nadwī comments that those who are admitted to paradise "could not attain this coveted place by dint of their own intelligence, academic accomplishment or personal effort. It was Allah's mercy and guidance that led them to their destination."[34] Nadwī continues by explaining that divine guidance takes place above all through the ministry of prophets:

> A further truth is also clarified whereby Allah does not descend to the earth to guide each and every human being. Nor does he take anyone's hand in His in order to show him the way to Paradise. Instead, He has devised certain ways for man's guidance. Of these the most prominent is His arrangement of sending down His Messengers who come with the truth.[35]

Nadwī believes that without the ministry of prophets, humans would not have been able to figure things out for themselves. As he puts it: "Had they not come with the truth, man would have been lost in error. He would have certainly landed in a place other than Paradise."[36]

The notion of the ministry of prophets as an expression of divine mercy might even be reflected in Qur'ān 96:1–5, a passage traditionally seen as the first revelation that the angel Gabriel brought to the Prophet Muḥammad:

> Read in the Name of your Lord who created; created man from a clinging mass. Read, and your Lord is the

most generous, who taught by the pen, taught man what
he did not know. (Q 96:1–5)[37]

Although it is not clear what is meant by God "teaching by the pen"
(v. 4), the last verse in this passage seems to allude to the sending of
revelation when it insists that God has taught humans things they
"did not know." In other words, God realized that humans were
not able to reason their way to righteousness and belief (even with
the help of divine signs in nature). They needed to hear the divine
message, which God mercifully provided.[38]

Types of Divine Mercy in the Qur'ān: Forgiveness

Finally, the Qur'ān speaks repeatedly of God's forgiveness of re-
pentant sinners or unbelievers as an expression of His mercy. In
Sura 5 the Qur'ān implores the Jews and Christians to repent of
their erroneous ways and trust in God's clemency: "Will they not
repent to Allah and plead to Him for forgiveness? Yet Allah is
all-forgiving, all-merciful" (Q 5:74).[39] The connection of forgiveness to repentance is found again in Sura 40—a Sura known
under the title "Forgiver" (*ghāfir*). Here the Qur'ān describes God
as "Forgiver of sins and acceptor of repentance, severe in retribution, all-bountiful" (Q 40:3).

Several verses later we find the angels surrounding the throne,
interceding for humans. When we hear them pray, however, they
do not ask that God forgive *all* humans. They ask that He forgive
those who repent and follow God:

> Those who bear the Throne and those who are around it
> celebrate the praise of their Lord and have faith in Him,
> and they plead for forgiveness for the faithful: "Our
> Lord! You embrace all things in Your mercy and knowl-
> edge. So forgive those who repent and follow Your way
> and save them from the punishment of hell." (Q 40:8)

Other passages of the Qur'ān help us define the limits of divine forgiveness more precisely. While the God of the Qur'ān will forgive penitent believers (those who "follow [God's] way"), He will not forgive unbelievers. This much is evident from certain passages concerned with the hypocrites (*al-munāfiqūn*), those who pretend to be believers in God and His messenger but are secretly unbelievers. In Q 63:6, the Qur'ān insists that believers should not ask for the forgiveness of such people because God will never forgive them: "It is the same for them whether *you* plead for forgiveness for them, or do not plead for forgiveness for them: Allah will never forgive them. Indeed, Allah does not guide the transgressing lot."[40] In a second passage concerned with the hypocrites, the Qur'ān uses hyperbolic language in insisting that God will not forgive them even if the Prophet himself intercedes on their behalf:

> Whether you plead forgiveness for them or do not plead forgiveness for them, even if you plead forgiveness for them seventy times, Allah will never forgive them because they defied Allah and His Apostle; and Allah does not guide the transgressing lot. (Q 9:80)

This passage seems to have an echo of the Gospels. In Matthew 18 we find the following dialogue:

> Then Peter came up and said to him, "Lord, how often shall my brother sin against me, and I forgive him? As many as seven times?"
> Jesus said to him, "I do not say to you seven times, but seventy times seven." (Mat 18:21–22)

There may not be a direct relationship between Qur'ān 9:80 and Matthew 18:21–22. The Qur'ān is concerned with whether God will forgive an unbeliever, while in Matthew the question is whether believers should forgive those who sin against them. However, it seems likely that the Qur'ān means to respond indirectly to this

Gospel passage, or perhaps more likely to a version of this Gospel passage transmitted orally (why else, one might ask, would the Qur'ān's author decide on the number "seventy"?).[41]

In this regard we might see more clearly the point that the Qur'ān means to make about the limits of God's forgiveness. God does not forgive unbelievers (the phrase rendered "defied Allah and His apostle" in Q 9:80 is *kafarū bi-llāhi wa-rasūlihi*, or "disbelieved in God and His messenger"). To this effect Marshall writes: "In all this the underlying logic is that God is merciful to those to whom his justice permits him to be merciful, and by definition the unbeliever is excluded from this category."[42]

Among unbelievers, the Qur'ān shows a particular concern for those guilty of worshipping beings other than Allah. In the New Testament we read of an unforgivable sin, "blasphemy against the Holy Spirit."[43] In the Qur'ān we also read of an unforgivable sin, but that sin is polytheism, or associating something else with God (in Arabic, *shirk*). In two different passages in the same Sura, we read that God will never forgive this sin:

> Indeed, Allah does not forgive that a partner should be ascribed to Him, but He forgives anything besides that to whomever He wishes. Whoever ascribes partners (*yushrik*) to Allah has indeed fabricated [a lie] in great sinfulness. (Q 4:48; cf. 4:116)

It is perhaps no surprise, then, to find Jesus in the Qur'ān condemning those guilty of this sin to hell. In Sura 5 he declares: "Indeed, whoever ascribes partners to Allah, Allah will forbid him [entry into] paradise and his refuge will be the Fire, and the wrongdoers will not have any helpers" (Q 5:72).[44]

It is also no surprise to find the Qur'ān's insistence that believers not pray for the forgiveness of unbelievers.[45] There is no point in praying for unbelievers, according to the Qur'ān, since God has already made it clear that He will not forgive them. Indeed, to do so would be a sort of insolence, an implicit rejection of God's decree.

It is true that the Qur'ān includes an account of Abraham praying for his unbelieving father's forgiveness. In Sura 19 Abraham declares to his father:

> Peace be to you! I shall plead with my Lord to forgive you. He is indeed gracious to me. I dissociate myself from you and whatever you invoke besides Allah. I will supplicate my Lord. Hopefully, I will not be unblessed in supplicating my Lord. (Q 19:47–48; cf. Q 14:41; 60:4)[46]

In Sura 9, however, the Qur'ān strictly forbids believers from praying for unbelievers and—as though countering a possible objection—it explains away Abraham's prayer for his father:

> The Prophet and the faithful may not plead for the forgiveness of the polytheists, even if they should be [their] relatives, after it has become clear to them that they will be the inmates of hell. Abraham's pleading forgiveness for his father was only to fulfill a promise he had made him. So when it became clear to him that he was an enemy of God, he repudiated him. Indeed, Abraham was most plaintive and forbearing. (Q 9:113–14)

The medieval Muslim scholar al-Wāḥidī (d. 1075) relates a poignant story (on the authority of Ibn Mas'ūd) about the Prophet Muḥammad's grief for his mother (who died an unbeliever) that explains when and why God revealed this passage:

> The Messenger of Allah went out one day to look at the graveyards and we went out with him. He ordered us to sit and then proceeded across until he stopped at one particular grave. He spoke to it for a long time and then the Messenger of Allah wept loudly and we wept for his weeping. After a while, he came toward us and was met by 'Umar ibn al-Khattab who asked him: "O Messenger

of Allah, what has made you cry, for we also cried and
we were also scared?" He came toward us, sat with us
and then said: "My weeping made you scared?" We said:
"Yes, O Messenger of Allah!" He said: "The grave you
saw me talking to is the grave of Aminah bint Wahb. I
sought permission from my Lord to visit her and He allowed me to do so. Then, I asked His permission to pray
for her forgiveness and He did not grant it. The words of
Allah... were revealed and I was seized by the tenderness
which a son has toward his mother. This is the reason
why I wept."[47]

According to the Qur'ān, unbelievers are beyond the bounds of
divine forgiveness. Accordingly, we find the God of the Qur'ān
elsewhere stating simply that He does not love the unbelievers. Q
2:276 declares: "Allah does not love any sinful ingrate" (the word
for "ingrate" is *kāfir*, "unbeliever"). Q 3:32 is similar: "Allah does
not love the faithless" (cf. Q 30:45).[48] Q 40:10 (cited above) implies
that God *hates* the faithless.

Yet these are not the only categories of people whom God does
not love. God does not love the wrongdoers (*al-ẓālimūn*; Q 3:57,
140; 42:40), the transgressors (*al-muʿtadūn*; Q 2:190; 5:87; 7:55),
the arrogant (*al-mustakbirūn*; *al-mukhtālūn*; Q 4:36; 16:23; 31:18;
57:23), the proud (*al-fakhūrūn*; Q 4:36; 31:18; 57:23), the wasteful (*al-
musrifūn*; Q 6:141; 7:31), the treacherous (Q 8:58; 22:38), the corrupt
(*al-mufsidūn*; 5:64; 28:77), or the boastful (*al-fariḥūn*; Q 28:76). In
the Qur'ān, all of these categories, which we might group together
under the notion of sinfulness, place humans in a position of opposition to God similar to unbelief.

Thus we seem to have another insight on the limits of God's
forgiveness. We have seen above that God will forgive believers
who repent of their sins, and that He will not forgive unbelievers.
The repeated Qur'ānic assertions that God does not love sinners
suggests that He will also not forgive believers who do *not* repent of
their sins. Such wrongdoers, too, seem to be beyond the bounds of

divine mercy. This seems to be the implication of Q 4:17–18, which makes human penitence a condition of divine forgiveness:

> [Acceptance of] repentance by Allah is only for those who commit evil out of ignorance and then repent promptly. It is such whose repentance Allah will accept, and Allah is all-knowing, all-wise. But [acceptance of] repentance is not for those who go on committing misdeeds: when death approaches any of them, he says, "I repent now." Nor is it for those who die while they are faithless. For such We have prepared a painful punishment. (Q 4:17–18)

The conditions of divine forgiveness are clear in this passage. God will forgive those who "commit evil out of ignorance and then repent."[49] He will not forgive those who die as unbelievers (the "faithless"). He will not even forgive those who repent on their deathbeds (something in tension with the traditional reports that Muḥammad implored his uncle Abū Ṭālib to convert on his deathbed).[50] The Qur'ān illustrates this latter point with a passage in which Pharaoh repents and believes at the moment of his death but is still not forgiven (Q 10:90–92). According to a popular tradition, the angel Gabriel stuffed mud in the mouth of Pharaoh to make sure that God would not hear his declaration of repentance and belief.[51]

Something similar might be said of a declaration made by Abraham in Q 15:56. In a passage related to the story of the three mysterious visitors in Genesis 18, the Qur'ān describes how certain messengers came to give Abraham good news of a son (Isaac) in his old age. After describing their annunciation of a son, the Qur'ān continues: "They said, 'We bring you good news in truth; so do not be despondent' (Q 15:55). [Abraham] said, 'Who despairs of his Lord's mercy except the astray?!'" (56).[52]

The point of Abraham's declaration, it seems, is that those who are "astray" *should* despair of God's mercy. This point is made clear by what happens next in Qur'ān 15: the "visitors" to Abraham continue on to the people of Lot, "a guilty people" (Q 15:58), and destroy them.

Theological Debates

To many Muslim observers, however, the state of the sinful believer in the Qur'ān remained ambiguous. The God of the Qur'ān, as we have seen, does not love sinners and will only forgive them when they repent. This, however, left Muslim theologians with an eschatological enigma. Are not all believers guilty of some sins? Certainly *everyone* cannot be doomed, since the Qur'ān also promises paradise to the believers. So how much sin is too much sin? The present chapter is not principally concerned with the later unfolding of Islamic theology, and I will not attempt to answer this question in detail. I would, however, like to illustrate briefly how the Qur'ānic material on forgiveness shaped later Islamic eschatology.

Muslim theologians tended to divide sins between major sins (*kabā'ir*) and minor sins (*ṣaghā'ir*). In the classic work on the subject, Muḥammad Shams al-Dīn al-Dhahabī (d. 1348) identified 70 major sins, the first of which is "unbelief" itself.[53] In part based on Q 53:31–32, most Muslim theologians agreed at least that God might forgive believers guilty only of minor sins and admit them into paradise. It was the status of sinners guilty of major sins that caused them trouble.

Classical Muslim scholars debated fiercely the question of whether Muslims guilty of major sins, but who continue to declare their faith in Islam, fall into the category of unbelief (*kufr*). The Muslim sect known as the Khārijites seems to have asserted that they did (although the precise categories of *kabā'ir* and *ṣaghā'ir* were not yet defined in the early days of the Khārijites). The theological movement known as the Murji'a unambiguously affirmed that such sinners are still believers and insisted that it was God's right to forgive or punish them as He wills in the afterlife. Another prominent theological school, the Mu'tazila, held to what they called the "intermediate position" (*al-manzila bayna al-manzila-tayn*) between the Khārijites and the Murji'a, insisting that such sinners can neither be called unbelievers nor believers (although they affirmed that these sinners would be punished in hell).

The Ash'ariyya, who would become the standard school of Sunnī theology, embraced a position closer to the Murji'a: grave sinners were not unbelievers and could still be saved by the mercy of God. As long as these sinners are "people of the Qibla" (that is, Muslims who pray in the direction of Mecca), they remain "believers" no matter how great their sin. This position is articulated, for example, in the Creed of al-Ash'arī (d. 935), the founder and namesake of the school (and a former Mu'tazilī). Orthodox Muslims, he writes, "do not declare any of the people of the Qibla an unbeliever because of a sin which he commits, such as adultery, theft and similar great sins."[54]

Elsewhere in this creed we read how al-Ash'arī works out the question of God's judgment for a believer guilty of major sins:

> They do not bear witness of Hell (being certain) for any great sinner, nor do they say that Paradise (is certain) for any monotheist, until it comes about that God has placed them where He willed. They say that the affair of these (people) belongs to God; if He wills, He punishes them, and if He wills, He forgives them.[55]

A similarly agnostic position on the fate of the sinful believer is found in the creed of another Sunnī thinker, al-Ash'arī's contemporary, al-Ṭaḥāwī (d. 933). He writes:

> We hope for Paradise for the believers who do good, but we are not certain of it, and do not bear witness to them (as having attained it). We seek forgiveness for their evil deeds and we fear for them, but we do not despair of them. Certainty (of Paradise) and despair both turn people away from the religion, and the way of truth for the people of the Qibla lies between them.[56]

One can imagine that this theological position was constructed in part to avoid disorder (*fitna*) in Islamic societies. It should not be forgotten that according to Islamic doctrine unbelievers are not simply to be spurned or reviled. Muslims have a duty to fight against unbelievers. Al-Ash'arī himself writes that Muslims "affirm the duty of Jihād against the polytheists from the time of God's sending of His Prophet until the last band which fights the Dajjāl [the anti-Christ] and after that."[57] If all gravely sinful Muslims were suddenly to fall within the category of unbelief, the possibilities for civil strife would be endless. In fact the early history of the Khārijites was marked by violence and bloodshed.[58] That Ash'arī was concerned about avoiding such a situation is also evident from his position that faithful Muslims should not rebel against an unrighteous ruler.[59]

The creedal statements of al-Ash'arī and al-Ṭaḥāwī also follow from a widespread hadith (on the authority of Abū Hurayra) that explains exactly how sinful Muslims will be saved. According to this hadith, a bridge will be set up above the fires of hell on the Day of Judgment, a bridge that all souls will be compelled to cross.[60] Hooks on the bridge will draw both unbelievers and sinful believers down into hell as they try to pass by. However, angels will dive into the fire of hell to save sinful Muslims:

> Some people will be ruined because of their evil deeds, and some will be cut into pieces and fall down in Hell, but will be saved afterwards, when Allah has finished the judgments among His slaves, and intends to take out of the Fire whoever He wishes to take out from among those who used to testify that none had the right to be worshipped but Allah. We will order the angels to take them out and the angels will know them by the mark of the traces of prostration (on their foreheads), for Allah banned the fire to consume the traces of prostration on the body of Adam's son.[61]

Like the declarations of al-Ash'arī and al-Ṭaḥāwī, this hadith leaves the question of exactly which, or how many, sinful believers will be saved to the inscrutable will of God. Certain Muslim theologians, however, took the position that *all* Muslims will be saved from hell. The famous Ash'arī theologian (and philosopher and mystic) al-Ghazālī (d. 1111) writes: "Monotheists will be taken out of Hell after punishment. By the grace of God no monotheist will remain in Gehenna and no monotheist will be everlastingly in Hell."[62] Still more extreme was a tradition associated with a companion of the Prophet named 'Abdallāh b. 'Amr b. al-'Āṣ (d. 685), who is said to have concluded that all people, including unbelievers, will eventually be saved: "A day will come when the gates of hell will be closed and no longer will anyone be inside."[63] The notion that the fires of hell are therapeutic, and that eventually all beings (including the devil!) will be saved from hell (a teaching known as *apokatastasis* and associated—wrongly or rightly—with Origen [d. 254] in the early Church), would ultimately be argued by the Damascene scholar Ibn Taymiyya (d. 1328) and his disciple Ibn Qayyim al-Jawziyya (d. 1350).[64]

While their argument is largely based on hadith,[65] Ibn Taymiyya also points to a relevant Qur'ānic passage:

> As for the wretched, they shall be in the Fire: their lot
> therein will be groaning and wailing. They will remain
> in it for as long as the heavens and the earth endure—
> except what *your* Lord may wish; indeed your Lord does
> whatever He desires. (Q 11:106–7)[66]

The phrase "except what your Lord may wish" in this passage led Ibn Taymiyya and Ibn Qayyim al-Jawziyya to argue that God, if He wills, may save all of those who are condemned to hell. This phrase indeed suggests that God's will trumps any human notion of justice. The Mu'tazilī exegete al-Zamakhsharī (d. 1144) accordingly labored to explain it away.[67]

Another theological problem surrounded the possibility that God actively plots against unbelievers, wrongdoers, and hypocrites to keep them from belief and repentance.[68] At one point the Qur'ān asks rhetorically: "Do they feel secure from Allah's devising (*makr*)? No one feels secure from Allah's devising except the people who are losers" (Q 7:99; on God scheming, or devising, see also Q 3:54; 8:30; 11:21). In the very next verse the Qur'ān has God threaten His audience with the "sealing" of their hearts: "Does it not dawn upon those who inherited the earth after its [former] inhabitants that if We wish We will punish them for their sins and set a seal on their hearts so they would not hear?" (Q 7:100).[69]

The God of the Qur'ān does not simply leave the unbelievers to wander in error. He actively leads them further astray (4:88, 143; 7:186; 1:33; 30:29; 39:23, 36; 40:33; 42:46). He causes hypocrisy to enter the hearts of those who disregard Him (Q 9:76–77), and He increases the sickness in the hearts of those who seek to deceive him (Q 2:10). The God of the Qur'ān, in other words, is not only a God of mercy. He is also a God of vengeance.

Conclusion

Yet how can God be both merciful and vengeful? The author of the Qur'ān clearly thought that these two things could go together, as he often mentions God's mercy and God's vengeance together. Q 5:98 declares: "Know that Allah is severe in retribution, and that Allah is all-forgiving, all-merciful." In Sura 7, after an account that has God punish a people who violate the Sabbath by turning them into monkeys, the Qur'ān declares:

> And when your Lord proclaimed that He would surely send against them, until the Day of Resurrection, those who would inflict a terrible punishment on them. Your Lord is indeed swift in retribution, and indeed He is all-forgiving, all-merciful. (Q 7:167)[70]

Indeed, we find that some of the most impressive declarations regarding the mercy of God are accompanied by references to divine judgment. In Q 6:12, and again in 6:54, the Qur'ān explains that God "has made mercy incumbent upon Himself." In both cases, however, this declaration is not unequivocal. In 6:12 the Qur'ān declares:

> Say, "To whom belongs whatever is in the heavens and the earth?" Say, "To Allah. He has made mercy incumbent upon Himself. He will surely gather you on the Day of Resurrection, in which there is no doubt. Those who have ruined their souls will not have faith." (Q 6:12)[71]

The declaration that God "has made mercy incumbent upon Himself" is sandwiched between two other declarations: first, that God possesses everything in heaven and earth; and second, that God will gather everyone together (presumably, to judge them) on the Day of Resurrection. In Q 6:54, the Qur'ān explains that God's mercy is only for those who commit evil out of ignorance and subsequently repent.[72]

All of this leads us to the conclusion of Johan Bouman: "God waits for humans to first fulfill certain specific conditions, before forgiveness will be shared with him."[73] God's forgiveness, in other words, is a reward and not a grace (cf. also Q 5:9; 29:7).

To David Marshall, the Qur'ān's vision of divine mercy involves a certain paradox:

> It might appear incoherent to affirm both a universality in God's mercy and also its non-applicability to the unbeliever. This apparent incoherence in my argument is, however, a reflection of the paradoxical position in which the Qur'ān sees the unbeliever as standing during this life. Considered as a part of the human race as a whole, the unbeliever benefits from the universal expressions of the divine mercy mentioned above; considered as an unbeliever, he is the object of the divine wrath.[74]

The resolution to this paradox is to think differently about "universal expressions of the divine mercy," namely creation/nature and the ministry of the prophets (the first two of Marshall's categories). A close reading of the Qur'ān suggests that these things are provisional. God gives the blessings of nature to humans *in order that* they might reflect on those blessings and believe. On creation, Toshihiko Izutsu writes: "The Koran may be regarded in a certain sense as a grand hymn in honor of Divine Creation. At any rate, the whole Koran is literally impregnated with the thought of Creation and a feeling of profound admiration for it."[75] Izutsu's description of the presentation of creation in the Qur'ān, while moving, does not fully capture the Qur'ān's interest in speaking of creation. The Qur'ān points to creation not simply to itemize its marvels, or to give glory to the creator. The Qur'ān points to creation in order to evoke a human response. Creation is a sign (*āya*).[76] Humans are meant to observe it and respond by submitting to the creator. The Qur'ān is not a "hymn in honor of Divine Creation." It refers to creation always and only for the sake of its larger argument about obedience to God (and His prophet). Elsewhere Izutsu seems to capture this idea when he writes:

> Just as a waymark must not cause a traveler to rivet his eyes on itself, but direct him towards a certain place which is the real destination of his travel, so every natural phenomenon, instead of absorbing our attention, *as a natural phenomenon*, and transfixing it immovably to itself, should act always in such a way that our attention be directed towards something beyond it.[77]

Similarly, God sends prophets to humans *in order that* humans might listen to them and have faith. In Sura 7 the Qur'ān describes the revelation that the Prophet has brought as a mercy, but tellingly it makes this revelation a mercy *only* for those who have faith: "Certainly We have brought them a Book which We have elaborated with knowledge, as guidance and mercy for a people who have faith" (Q 7:52).[78] The authors of *Tafsīr Jalālayn* define mercy (*raḥma*) as "to want what is good for those who deserve it."[79] Their definition indeed hits the mark.

Thus the God of the Qur'ān is "the compassionate, the merciful," principally because of the opportunities that He provides for humans to repent and believe. He has made humans capable of reflecting on the signs in nature, and He has sent to humans further signs through the prophets.[80]

Now that these things are done, God's compassion and mercy are offered only to those who have made the right choice. These He will guide on a straight path. The others He will lead astray.

Notes

1. I would like to express my gratitude to all those who participated in the academia.edu session on this paper, especially Raashid Goyal, who offered many helpful observations. All errors are my own.

2. In the present article I generally cite the Qur'ān translation of Ali Quli Qara'i: *The Qur'an with Phrase-by-Phrase English Translation* (New York: Tahrike Taarsile Qur'ān, 2007). Here I have modified Quli Qara'i's translation by rendering *ḥusnā* as "Beautiful" (he has, instead, "Best"). The term *al-ḥusnā* (the feminine form of the superlative *al-aḥsan*, from the root *ḥ.s.n.*) can imply both "best" and "most beautiful." Thus *al-asmā' al-ḥusnā* is translated into French by Régis Blachère as "les noms les plus beaux." Régis Blachère, *Le Coran* (Paris: Maisonneuve, 1957).

3. A hadith attributed to Abū Hurayra and preserved in a number of different collections has the Prophet say, "Allah has ninety-nine names, one hundred less one, and whoever counts them...will enter Paradise." Bukhārī, *Ṣaḥīḥ*, 54, *K. al-Shurūṭ*, "*Bāb mā yajūz min al-ishtirāṭ*." For the Arabic text and English translation, see *Saḥīḥ Bukhārī*, trans. Muhammad Muhsin Khan (Riyadh: Dar-us-Salam, 1997), 3:540. See also ibid., 80, *K. al-Daʿwāt*, "*Bāb li-llāh miʾatu ismin ghayra wāḥid*." This same hadith is also found in the collections of Tirmidhī (*K. al-Daʿwāt ʿan rasūl Allāh*) and Ibn Māja (*K. al-Duʿāʾ*), always on the authority of Abū Hurayra.

4. For one example see the hadith, also attributed to Abū Hurayra, in *Jāmiʿ al-Tirmidhī*, 48, *K. al-Daʿwāt ʿan rasūl Allāh*. For the Ara-

bic text and English translation see *Jāmi' al-Tirmidhī*, trans. Abu Khaliyl (Riyadh: Maktaba Dar-us-Salam, 2007), 6:221–24. For a complete listing and discussion of the traditional lists see D. Gimaret, *Les noms divins en Islam* (Paris: Cerf, 1988), 51–68. Some Muslim theologians refused to call God by certain names that, on the contrary, *are* used for Him in the Qur'ān since, they argued, the meaning of such a term had changed through time (this is the case, for example, with *wakīl*, which is used for God in Q 3:173). On this see Gimaret, 41.

5. A discussion of the development of the "beautiful names" of God in Islam is also found in D. Rahbar, *God of Justice: A Study in the Ethical Doctrine of the Qur'ān* (Leiden: Brill, 1960), 8–18. Rahbar is critical of the idea that an Islamic theology of God could be developed on the basis of these lists of divine names. He notes, among other things, that these names tend to include pairs of opposites, e.g., *al-Ḍārr* and *al-Nāfi'* ("the one who harms" and "the one who benefits"), *al-Muṭī* and *al-Māni'* ("the giver" and "the withholder"), or *al-Hādī* and *al-Muḍill* ("the one who guides" and "the one who leads astray"). From Rahbar's perspective, these pairs suggest that a focus on these names—which, according to Rahbar, have an origin in mystical, Ṣūfī devotions—could lead one to the conclusion that there is mysteriousness, if not incoherence or arbitrariness, in the Islamic conception of God. However, inasmuch as most of these names are Qur'ānic, they do reflect a genuine feature of the Qur'ān's representation of God—for example, an insistence that He is responsible for both good and evil (a conclusion that certain currents of Islamic theology, notably the Mu'tazila, would resist).

6. See Gimaret, 55–62. A list attributed to the traditionalist Sufyān b. 'Uyayna (d. 195/810) includes 99 names found exclusively in the Qur'an. See Gimaret, 69–71.

7. This combination, also found in Q 1:1, recalls the divine invocation known as the *basmala* (*bi-smi llāhi l-raḥmāni l-raḥīm*), which precedes all of the Qur'ān's Suras except for Sura 9. For the full list see Gimaret, 56.

8. Abū l-Kalām Āzād, *Tarjumān al-Qur'ān*; translation taken from J.M.S. Baljon, *Modern Muslim Koran Interpretation (1880–1960)* (Leiden: Brill, 1961), 59.

9. Abū l-Ḥasan 'Alī Nadwī, *Guidance from the Holy Koran*, trans. Abdur Raheem Kidwai (Markfield: The Islamic Foundation, 2005), 189. This comment occurs in the midst of Nadwī's discussion of Q 21:107, which describes the Qur'ān's prophet as a "mercy unto people."

10. See <https://www.youtube.com/watch?v=k9MZHuZO7kk>, accessed January 26, 2017.

11. *Misericordiae Vultus*, para. 23.

12. In his work *The Lord Guideth: Studies in Primitive Islam* (Oslo: Aschehoug, 1956), Harris Birkeland makes this case for Suras 93, 94, 108, 105, and 106, which (he argues) represent the earliest proclamations of Muḥammad. Birkeland thus holds that at first Muḥammad had an idea of divine guidance bereft of any idea of divine judgment. God was guide, not judge: "The experience which became decisive for Muhammed's whole future activity must have been the recognition of God's merciful guidance in the life of himself and his people, that means in history" (Birkeland, 5). Later in the work Birkeland adds: "It might be objected that the divine guidance was only one of the many aspects of Muhammed's original experience of god. That is true. But when this aspect is so strangely emphasized in Surahs of that incontestable old age, it must have been of a special and fundamental importance. Structurally it is prior to the belief in reward and punishment. For the god must be a reality before he can appear as a judge" (Birkeland, 133).

13. On divine mercy in the Qur'ān see Johan Bouman, *Gott und Mensch im Koran: Eine Strukturform religiöser Anthropologie anhand des Beispiels Allah und Muhammad* (Darmstadt: Wissenschaftliche Buchgesellschaft, 1977), 151–53.

14. Interestingly, on each occasion it is a Biblical character who uses this turn of phrase to refer to God. Moses—asking forgiveness after the golden calf episode (Q 7:151; but notably only for Aaron and himself, not for the Israelites as a whole)—Jacob (12:64), Joseph (12:92), and Job (21:83). See Jacques Jomier, *Dieu et l'homme dans le Coran: L'aspect religieux de la nature humaine joint à l'obéissance au prophète de l'islam* (Paris: Cerf, 1996), 49.

15. A position commonly articulated in Islamic tradition is that *raḥmān* refers to a dimension of God's mercy that is universal (notably the blessings of nature), whereas *raḥīm* refers to a dimension of mercy (for

example, the forgiveness of sins) that is reserved for believers. On this
see, for example, Ibn Kathīr (d. 1373), who reports the following opinion in his Qur'ān commentary: "[*Al-Raḥmān*] carries a broader scope
of meanings pertaining to the mercy of Allāh with His creation in
both lives. Meanwhile, [*al-raḥīm*] is exclusively for the believers." See
Ibn Kathīr, *Tafsīr*, trans. S. al-Mubarakpuri (Riyadh: Dar-us-Salam,
2003), 1:67. There is no clear basis for this distinction in the Qur'ān.

16. A. Ambros, with S. Procházka, *A Concise Dictionary of Koranic Arabic* (Wiesbaden: Reichert, 2004), 205.

17. See C. Robin, "Le judaïsme de Himyar," *Arabia* 1 (2003): 71–172, 114.
As Robin explains, *raḥmānān* is used by both South Arabian Jews for
God and by South Arabian Christians for God the Father. In North
Arabia as well, we find that in pre-Islamic times people would call on
God, or a god, as "the merciful." A North Arabian inscription (in a
variety of "Ancient North Arabian" known as Safaitic) has an appeal
to a god who is referred to with a term related to Arabic *al-raḥīm* and
al-raḥmān: "O Merciful One (*ḥ rḥm*) and O One who causes death
(*ḥ ymyt*), and O *Rḍw* may the people be established [in this place]."
See Ahmad al-Jallad, *An Outline of the Grammar of the Safaitic Inscriptions* (Leiden: Brill, 2015), 241. Tellingly, the Qur'ān regularly
speaks of Allah as one who causes death (*yumīt*; see Q 2:258; 3:156;
7:158; 9:116, etc.).

18. Theodor Nöldeke argues that Muḥammad (whom he saw as the author of the Qur'ān) began to use *al-raḥmān* at a specific moment,
what he calls the "2nd Meccan" period. Nöldeke argues further that
this name is particularly associated with this period: it appears only
once in (what Nöldeke sees as) earlier Suras (Q 55:1), and only a few
times in Suras from the "3rd Meccan" period (Q 13:29; 41:1). Nöldeke
accordingly wonders why Muḥammad ceased using this name. He
speculates: "It could possibly have been his intention to avoid being
suspected of worshipping two deities." See Nöldeke et al., *History*, 99.

19. Of the 20 occasions in the Qur'ān that speak of God's wrath, 14
seem to involve the Israelites. Many Muslim exegetes, both traditional and modern, identify those who have "incurred God's wrath"
in Q 1:6 as the Jews. See, for example, the classical exegesis known
as *Tafsīr al-Jalālayn*. See Jalāl al-Dīn al-Maḥallī (d. 1459) and Jalāl al-
Dīn al-Suyūṭī (d. 1505), *Tafsīr al-Jalālayn*, ed. Marwān Siwār (Beirut:

Dār al-Jīl, 1410/1995); and Q 1:7; English trans. F. Hamza (Louisville, KY: Fons Vitae, 2008). For a modern example see the Qur'ān translation of Taqi al-Din Hilali and Muhsin Khan, which adds "such as the Jews" in parentheses after the reference to divine anger in Q 1:7. See *Interpretation of the Meanings of the Noble Qur'ān in the English Language* (Riyadh: Maktaba Dar-us-Salam, 1993).

20. Qara'i renders *maqt* as "outrage," perhaps concerned by the notion of divine loathing or hate. Ambros (p. 257) defines *maqt* as "a loathing, hatred."

21. Fazlur Rahman, *Major Themes of the Qur'ān*, 2nd ed. (Chicago: University of Chicago Press, 2009), 6. In his (over)emphasis on divine mercy, Rahman was evidently responding to what he felt was an antagonistic portrayal of the God of the Qur'ān in earlier Western scholarship. He writes: "Many a Western scholar (through a combination of ignorance and prejudice) has depicted the Qur'anic God as a concentrate of pure power, even as brute power—indeed, as a capricious tyrant" (Rahman, 1).

22. See David Marshall, *God, Muhammad and the Unbelievers: A Qur'anic Study* (Richmond, Surrey: Curzon Press, 1999), 79.

23. On the first page of *Major Themes of the Qur'ān*, Fazlur Rahman declares: "Mercy is as ultimate an attribute of God as power, and is in a definite sense synonymous with creation." We have already seen that it is not exactly accurate to think of mercy as an "ultimate" attribute of God (if by "ultimate" Rahman means "unconditional"). He is right, however, to emphasize the connection between creation and mercy and the Qur'ān.

24. The two dimensions of creation are joined in Qur'ān 10:31: "Say, 'Who provides for you out of the sky and the earth? Who controls [your] hearing and sight, and who brings forth the living from the dead and brings forth the dead from the living, and who directs the command?' They will say, 'Allah.' Say, 'Will you not then be wary [of Him]?'"

25. See, for example, Q 2:164; 6:99; 7:57; 20:53; 35:27; 79:33.

26. Rahman, 1. Elsewhere Rahman writes to this effect: "The problem is not how to make man come to belief by giving lengthy and intricate 'theological' proofs of God's existence, but how to shake him into belief by drawing his attention to certain obvious facts and turning these facts into 'reminders' of God." Rahman, 2.

27. To Marshall, the concentration of punishment stories in the Meccan period reflects a phase of Muḥammad's developing convictions. In Mecca, Muḥammad was convinced that his job was only to communicate the message (*balāgh*) given to him, since God would eventually punish those who refused to listen to that message. In Medina, Muḥammad came to see himself as the agent of divine punishment through his wars against the unbelievers, a conviction (for Marshall) epitomized by the "Medinan" verse 9:14: "Make war on them so that Allah may punish them by your hands and humiliate them and help you against them, and heal the hearts of a faithful folk." See Marshall, 156. Marshall holds, however, that while Muḥammad's attitude toward the unbelievers changes over time in the Qur'ān, that of God does not: "I have come to the conclusion that the main thrust of God's attitude to unbelievers remains constant" (Marshall, 88).

28. C. Gilliot, "Réflexions sur les raisons qui peuvent conduire à se convertir à l'Islam," *Lumière et Vie* 276 (octobre–décembre 2007): 105.

29. The notion that divine revelation is fundamentally a sort of warning is found in Q 28:43, where the divine voice of the Qur'ān declares: "Certainly We gave Moses the Book, after We had destroyed the former generations, as [a set of] eye-openers, guidance and mercy for mankind, so that they may take admonition." My attention to this verse was drawn by Bouman, 168.

30. By contrast, the Baghdādī Muʿtazilī school held that God chooses to help humans—that is, provide them with *lutf*—out of His generosity.

31. M. McDermott, *The Theology of al-Shaikh al-Mufīd* (Beirut: Dār al-Mashriq, 1978), 76.

32. O. Leaman, "Luṭf," *EI2*, 5:833b. Referring to Shahrastānī, *Nihāyat al-iqdām fī 'ilm al-kalām* (Baghdad: Maktabat al-Muthannā, 1964), 411. The Muʿtazilī perspective is generally followed also by Shiʿites such as al-Ḥillī (d. 1325).

33. ʿAbd al-Jabbār, *Mutashābih al-Qur'ān*, ed. ʿAdnān Zarzūr (Cairo: Dār al-Turāth, 1969), 2:734.

34. Nadwī, *Guidance from the Holy Qur'an*, 13.

35. Ibid., 14.

36. Ibid.

37. On this see Marshall, 79.

38. This perspective leads to certain theological problems, namely why God did not send more prophets to more peoples, and why God did not send any prophets after Muḥammad. The Qur'ān insists that God sent a prophet to each nation ("There is an apostle for every nation," Q 10:47), but of course one searches in vain for Muslim prophets sent to most nations on earth. Moreover, if only one prophet is sent to one generation of a certain nation, one wonders why other generations (earlier or later) did not receive a prophet. It seems that in the Qur'ān only the Israelites received more than one prophet.

39. The importance of asking God for forgiveness is also found in Q 4:64. Here, however, we find that not only is it important to ask for forgiveness from God; it is important to ask the Prophet to ask for forgiveness on one's behalf. "We did not send any apostle but to be obeyed by Allah's leave. Had they, when they wronged themselves, come to you and pleaded to Allah for forgiveness, and the Apostle had pleaded forgiveness for them, they would have surely found Allah clement and merciful."

40. One might compare Q 4:105–7, a passage in which the Qur'ān warns its audience against praying for "traitors" (*khā'inīn*).

41. The number 70 appears in two other places in the Qur'ān: Q 69:32 and Q 7:155. The former speaks of a chain in hell that is "seventy cubits" long; the latter is a reference to the 70 elders whom Moses selects in Numbers 11:25. It is thus possible that the Qur'ān's author simply liked the number 70, and the connection of Q 9:80 with Matthew 18 is coincidental. However, inasmuch as both Q 9:80 and Matthew 18:21–22 are concerned with forgiveness, I find it more likely that the two are connected.

42. Marshall, 82. Bouman agrees (p. 173) that mercy is ultimately subordinate to justice.

43. "Therefore I tell you, every sin and blasphemy will be forgiven men, but the blasphemy against the Spirit will not be forgiven" (Mat 12:31; cf. Mar 3:28–30 and Luk 12:10).

44. On this see Bouman, 178.

45. On the other hand, the example of Noah in the Qur'ān suggests that it is permissible to pray for the *destruction* of the unbelievers: "And Noah said, 'My Lord! Do not leave on the earth any inhabitant from

among the faithless. If You leave them, they will lead astray Your servants, and will beget none except vicious ingrates. My Lord! Forgive me and my parents, and whoever enters my house in faith, and the faithful men and women, and do not increase the wrongdoers in anything but ruin'" (Q 71:26–28).

According to later Islamic teaching, one may also pray for the *guidance* (not the forgiveness) of unbelievers in the hope that they will convert to Islam. This idea is sometimes based on a hadith, found in the collection of Muslim, according to which certain companions of the Prophet report to him that a tribe (named Daws) rejected him. The companions wish for the tribe to be destroyed, but the Prophet invokes God for their conversion: "[Ṭufayl and his companions said] 'Allah's Messenger, the tribe of Daws has disbelieved and has belied you, so invoke curse upon them.' It was said: 'Let Daws be destroyed,' whereupon he (Allah's Messenger) said: 'Allah guide aright the tribe of Daws and direct them to me.'" Muslim, *Ṣaḥīḥ*, 44, "K. Faḍā'il al-Ṣ aḥāba." For the English translation and Arabic text, see *Sahih Muslim*, trans. N. al-Khattab (Riyadh: Dar-us-Salam, 2007), 6:388.

46. In Sura 26 the Qur'ān quotes Abraham's prayer: "Forgive my father, for he is one of those who are astray" (Q 26:86).

47. Abū l-Ḥasan al-Wāḥidī, *Asbāb nuzūl al-Qur'ān*, ed. Kamāl Zaghlūl (Beirut: Dār al-Kutub al-ʿIlmiyya, 1411/1991), 268; English trans. M. Guezzou, *Al-Wāḥidī's Asbāb al-Nuzūl* (Louisville, KY: Fons Vitae, 2008), 95.

48. Qara'i renders the Arabic expression *lā yuḥibbu* in both verses as "does not like." I have modified this to "does not love."

49. Q 6:54 seems to make the point even more clearly that God's mercy is only for penitent sinners: "When those who have faith in Our signs come to you, say, 'Peace to you! Your Lord has made mercy incumbent upon Himself: whoever of you commits an evil [deed] out of ignorance and then repents after that and reforms, then He is indeed all-forgiving, all-merciful'" (Q 6:54). On the link between divine forgiveness and human repentance see Bouman, 166.

50. This poignant scene shows Muḥammad's affection for his uncle, who had protected him at a time when the nascent Islamic community was threatened. See Muslim *Ṣaḥīḥ*, 1, "K. al-Imān"; English trans: 1:119–22.

51. "Gabriel thrust mud from the sea into his mouth, lest [God's] mercy embrace him." *Tafsīr al-Jalālayn*, ad Q 10:90 (p. 224 of the English trans.).

52. *Tafsīr al-Jalālayn* (ad Q 15:56; English trans.: 274) identifies the astray as the "disbelievers."

53. See al-Dhahabī, *K. al-Kabā'ir*, ed. Abī 'Abd al-Raḥmān b. Sa'd (Beirut: Dār al-Kutub al-'Ilmiyya, 2006).

54. See W. Montgomery Watt, *Islamic Creeds* (Edinburgh: Edinburgh University Press, 1994), 43.

55. Watt, 44.

56. Watt, 52. In al-Ṭaḥāwī's creed we have a hint that the mechanism by which sinful believers are saved is through the intercession of the believers ("We seek forgiveness for their evil deeds"). The question of the role of the intercession of the faithful, and the special intercession of the Prophet Muḥammad, is the subject of different hadith and the object of a distinct debate among Muslim theologians (which I will not enter into here). See A. J. Wensinck and D. Gimaret, "Shafā'a," *EI2*, 9:177b–179a.

57. Watt, 45.

58. In recent years many Muslims have labelled Salafi-Jihadis as Khārijites because of their attacks on fellow Muslims. When the Saudi regime made this charge against Bin Laden, he responded by noting that his movement, unlike Khārijites, does not consider sinful Muslims to fall into the category of unbelief: "We should respond to some of the regime's [Saudi's] allegations, whose repetition has upset people both day and night throughout the past two years. It has accused the *mujahidin* of following the path of the Kharijites, but they know that we have nothing to do with such a school of thought. Our messages and conduct attest to this.... We believe that no sin besides that of unbelief makes a believer step outside his faith, even if it is a serious sin, like murder or drinking alcohol. Even if the culprit died without repenting of his sins, his fate is with God, whether He wishes to forgive him or to punish him." *Messages to the World: The Statements of Osama bin Laden*, ed. B. Lawrence; trans. J. Howarth (London: Verso 2005), 262.

59. "They think it proper to pray for the welfare of the imams of the Muslims, not to rebel against them with the sword, and not to fight in civil strife" (Watt, 45).

60. The notion that all souls will come to the brink of the fires of hell is in part a response to Q 19:71–72, a passage that could actually be read as implying that all souls will enter *into* the fire before some are saved: "There is none of you but will come to [or 'into' *wārid*] [hell]: a [matter that is a] decided certainty with *your* Lord. Then We will deliver those who are Godwary and leave the wrongdoers in it, fallen on their knees." The meaning of this passage turns on the interpretation of the active participle *wārid*.

61. Bukhārī, *Ṣaḥīḥ*, 81, *K. al-Riqāq*, "Bāb al-ṣirāṭ jisr Jahannam." English trans.: 8:305–8. See also the version in Bukhārī, *Ṣaḥīḥ*, 10, *K. al-Adhān*, "Bāb faḍl al-sujūd."

62. Watt, 78, from al-Ghazālī's work *The Revival of Religious Sciences*. "Monotheist" here is a euphemism for "Muslims." However, elsewhere (in his *Fayṣal al-tafriqa bayna al-Islām wa-l-zandaqa*) al-Ghazālī entertained the possibility that non-Muslim monotheists could be saved, but only those who had not heard the call of Islam. On this see Mohammad Hassan Khalil, *Islam and the Fate of Others: The Salvation Question* (Oxford: Oxford University Press, 2012), 30–39.

63. The Mu'tazilī exegete al-Zamakhsharī finds the apparent sense of this tradition impossible to reconcile with his strict idea of divine justice. He accordingly concludes that the unbelievers will not be relieved of punishment; they will simply have a new sort of punishment. He writes: "If the Tradition according to Ibn al-ʿĀṣ is sound, then its meaning can only be that the unbelievers will come out of the heat of the fire (and) into the cold of severe frost." This translation from Zamakhsharī's *tafsīr* is taken from H. Gätje, *The Qur'ān and Its Exegesis: Selected Texts with Classical and Modern Muslim Interpretations*, trans. A. Welch (London: Routledge, 1976), 183. For the Arabic see al-Zamakhsharī, *Al-Kashshāf ʿan ḥaqāʾiq ghawāmiḍ al-tanzīl* (Beirut: Dār al-Kitāb al-ʿArabī, 1947), 2:432.

64. On this see J. Hoover, "Islamic Universalism: Ibn Qayyim al-Jawziyya's Salafi Deliberations on the Duration of Hell-Fire," *Muslim World* 99 (2009): 181–201.

65. Notably the following report of Ibn ʿAbbās: "It is not necessary for anyone to judge God with respect to His creatures or to assign them to a garden or a fire." See Hoover, 186.

66. Ibn Taymiyya also notes Q 78:23, which reports that the damned will be in hell not "eternally" but rather "for ages" (*aḥqāb*). On Ibn Taymiyya's use of both passages, see Hoover, 186.

67. He argues creatively that the phrase "except what your Lord may wish" redounds not to the end of punishment, but to the end of punishment with fire: "The inhabitants of the hell-fire will not always remain only in the punishment of the fire; rather, they will also be punished through severe frost and in other ways." Gätje, 182. See al-Zamakhsharī, 2:430.

68. "God in the Koranic Weltanschauung does not subsist in His glorious self-sufficing solitude and stand aloof from mankind as does the God of Greek philosophy, but deeply involves Himself in human affairs." Toshihiko Izutsu, *God and Man in the Koran* (Tokyo: Keio Institute of Cultural and Linguistic Studies, 1964), 95.

69. On the "sealing" of hearts see also: 2:7; 6:46; 7:101; 9:87; 10:74; 16:108; 30:59; 40:35; 45:23; 47:16; 63:3. As one might surmise, al-Zamakhsharī offered alternative views of God's "sealing" of hearts—views that preserved an element of human freedom. See al-Zamakhsharī, 1:49–52.

70. Other passages that join together divine mercy and judgment/vengeance include: 6:133, 147, 156; 7:156; 13:6; 40:3; 41:43; 67:2; 76:31.

71. David Marshall argues that the mention of mercy in Q 6:12 is best understood in the light of the preceding verse, Q 6:11, where the Qur'ān alludes to the punishment that God has unleashed on the unbelievers: "Say, 'Travel over the land, and then observe how was the fate of the deniers.'" It is meaningful, Marshall concludes, that the declaration of God's mercy in Q 6:12 is "surrounded by menacing references to God's judgment." See Marshall, 81.

72. "When those who have faith in Our signs come to you, say, 'Peace to you! Your Lord has made mercy incumbent upon Himself: whoever of you commits an evil [deed] out of ignorance and then repents after that and reforms, then He is indeed all-forgiving, all-merciful'" (Q 6:54). One might compare the conclusion of Sura 20 where God (speaking to the Israelites) declares: "I indeed forgive those who repent, become faithful, act righteously, and thereafter follow guidance'" (Q 20:82).

73. Bouman, 174.

74. Marshall, 83.

75. Izutsu, 120.

76. Thus, Q 2:164: "Indeed, in the creation of the heavens and the earth, and the alternation of night and day, and the ships that sail at sea with profit to men, and the water that Allah sends down from the sky—with which He revives the earth after its death, and scatters therein every kind of animal—and the changing of the winds, and the clouds disposed between the sky and the earth, *there are signs for a people who exercise their reason.*" On this verse the medieval exegete al-Bayḍāwī (d. 1286) reports the following, attributed to the Prophet: "Woe to him who recites this verse but pays no attention to it." See Gätje, 152.

77. On this see Izutsu, 134.

78. Q 10:57 and 16:64 are similar. Q 31:3 (cf. 7:55) makes revelation "a guidance and mercy for the virtuous."

79. *Tafsīr al-Jalālayn,* ad Q 1:3 (trans. p. 1).

80. Izutsu proposes that we might see nature and revelation as two sorts of *āyāt.* The first is non-verbal, and the second is verbal. Comparing the two he writes: "The non-verbal *āyāt* have one conspicuous advantage: they can be and *are* actually addressed to mankind at large without any discrimination; moreover they can be given directly without any intermediary, while the verbal type can be given directly only to one particular person, the Prophet, and only indirectly and mediately to mankind" (p. 136). See his full discussion, pp. 135–39.

Works Cited

'Abd Al-Jabbār. *Mutashābih al-Qur'ān,* edited by 'Adnān Zarzūr. Cairo: Dār al-Turāth, 1969.

Al-Dhahabī. *K. al-Kabā'ir,* edited by Abī 'Abd al-Raḥmān Ibn Sa'd. Beirut: Dār al-Kutub al-'Ilmiyya, 2006.

Al-Jallad, Ahmad. *An Outline of the Grammar of the Safaitic Inscriptions.* Leiden: Brill, 2015.

Al-Maḥallī, Jalāl al-Dīn, and Jalāl al-Dīn Al-Suyūṭī. *Tafsīr Al-Jalālayn,* edited by Marwān Siwār. Beirut: Dār al-Jīl, 1995.

Al-Maḥallī, Jalāl al-Dīn, and Jalāl al-Dīn Al-Suyūṭī. *Tafsīr Al-Jalālayn,* edited by Ghazi bin Muhammad Ibn Talal; translated by Feras

Hamza. Amman, Jordan: Royal Aal al-Bayt Institute for Islamic Thought, 2007.

Al-Wāḥidī, 'Alī ibn Aḥmad. *Asbāb Nuzūl Al-Qur'an*, edited by Kamāl Zaghlūl. Beirut: Dār al-Kutub al-'Ilmiyya, 1991.

———. *Asbāb Al-Nuzūl*, edited by Mokraine Guezzou and Yousef Meri. Amman: Royal Aal al-Bayt Institute for Islamic Thought, 2008.

Al-Zamakhsharī. *Al-Kashshāf 'an ḥaqā'iq ghawāmiḍ al-tanzīl*. Beirut: Dār al-Kitāb al-'Arabī, 1947.

Ambros, Arne A., and Stephan Procházka. *A Concise Dictionary of Koranic Arabic*. Wiesbaden: Reichert, 2004.

Baljon, J. M. S. *Modern Muslim Koran Interpretation (1880–1960)*. Leiden: Brill, 1961.

Birkeland, H. *The Lord Guideth: Studies in Primitive Islam*. Oslo: Aschehoug, 1956.

Blachère, Régis. *Le Coran*. Paris: Maisonneuve, 1957.

Bouman, Johan. *Gott und Mensch im Koran: Eine Strukturform religiöser Anthropologie anhand des Beispiels Allah und Muhammad*. Darmstadt: Wissenschaftliche Buchgesellschaft, 1977.

Gätje, H. *The Qur'ān and Its Exegesis: Selected Texts with Classical and Modern Muslim Interpretations*, translated by A. Welch. London: Routledge, 1976.

Gilliot, Claude. "Réflexions sur les raisons qui peuvent conduire à se convertir à l'Islam." *Lumière et Vie* 276 (2007): 99–106.

Gimaret, D. *Les noms divins en Islam*. Paris: Cerf, 1988.

Hilali, Taqi al-Din, and Muhsin Khan. *Interpretation of the Meanings of the Noble Qur'ān in the English Language*. Riyadh: Maktaba Dar-us-Salam, 1993.

Hoover, J. "Islamic Universalism: Ibn Qayyim Al-Jawziyya's Salafi Deliberations on the Duration of Hell-Fire." *Muslim World* 99 (2009): 181–201.

Izutsu, Toshihiko. *God and Man in the Koran*. Tokyo: Keio Institute of Cultural and Linguistic Studies, 1964.

Jomier, Jacques. *Dieu et l'homme dans le Coran: L'aspect religieux de la nature humaine joint à l'obéissance au prophète de l'Islam*. Paris: Cerf, 1996.

Khalil, Mohammad Hassan. *Islam and the Fate of Others: The Salvation Question*. Oxford: Oxford University Press, 2012.

Marshall, David. *God, Muhammad, and the Unbelievers: A Qur'anic Study*. Richmond, Surrey: Curzon Press, 1999.

McDermott, M. *The Theology of Al-Shaikh Al-Mufīd*. Beirut: Dār al-Mashriq, 1978.

Messages to the World: The Statements of Osama bin Laden, edited by B. Lawrence; translated by J. Howarth. London: Verso, 2005.

Nadwī, Abū l-ḥasan ʿAlī. *Guidance from the Holy Koran*, translated by Abdur Raheem Kidwai. Markfield: The Islamic Foundation, 2005.

Nöldeke, Theodor, Friedrich Schwally, Gotthelf Bergsträßer, and Otto Pretzl. *The History of the Qurʾān*, edited and translated by Wolfgang H. Behn. Leiden and Boston: Brill, 2013.

Qaraʾi, Ali Quli. *The Qurʾan with Phrase-by-Phrase English Translation*. New York: Tahrike Taarsile Qurʾān, 2007.

Rahbar, D. *God of Justice: A Study in the Ethical Doctrine of the Qurʾān*. Leiden: Brill, 1960.

Rahman, Fazlur. *Major Themes of the Qurʾān*. 2nd edition. Chicago: University of Chicago Press, 2009.

Robin, C. "Le judaïsme de ḥimyar." *Arabia* 1 (2003).

Watt, W. Montgomery. *Islamic Creeds*. Edinburgh: Edinburgh University Press, 1994.

Chapter Six

RECOGNIZING THE DIVINE IN THE OTHER'S RELIGION: AN ISLAMIC PERSPECTIVE

Nayla Tabbara, Adyan Foundation, Lebanon

It is not difficult for a believer, especially a Christian or a Muslim believer, to recognize the divine at work in the lives of people from other religions. When we see a person filled with grace, we cannot but recognize it. Yet we usually associate this grace with our own religion instead of asking ourselves if it might be carried within the other's religion. Thus, we say they are anonymous Christians or anonymous Muslims, depending on the religion to which we belong. The question that is begged, though, is this: Can we find beauty in the other religion per se, not in the person from another religion? Can we recognize the divine in other religions, not only in the believers of other religions?

In the following pages I will try to articulate a reply to this question from an Islamic theological perspective while referring to Christian theology, as I believe that the dialogue of theologies is a beneficial methodology that enriches theologians when dealing with common issues that we grapple with in our different religions.[1]

The Truth Is Not a Ball

I believe that the text of "The Declaration on the Relation of the Catholic Church to Non-Christian Religions," proclaimed in 1965

at the end of Vatican II and entitled *Nostra Aetate*, represented
a major breakthrough in regard to the question of valuing other
religions in themselves. Besides its title, which recognized other
religions as a fact, the text stated: "The Catholic Church rejects
nothing that is *true and holy* in these religions. She regards with
sincere reverence those ways of conduct and of life, those precepts
and teachings which, though differing in many aspects from the
ones she holds and sets forth, nonetheless often reflect *a ray of that
Truth* which enlightens all men."[2]

In recognizing what is "true and holy"—that is, coming from
God—in other religions, and in advancing the idea that those
other religions, although different from Christianity, reflect a *ray
of that Truth*, or a ray of the divine, the text of *Nostra Aetate* and
the position of the Catholic Church created a shift in the way
religions usually perceive each other and the way in which they
perceive truth. To put it as simply as possible, we usually tend to
perceive truth as a ball that is either with me or with the other. On
that basis, either my revelation is true and yours is false, or yours is
true and mine is false. In this case, all goodness, beauty, or grace
that I find in the spiritual experience of another cannot be from
his religion, but from mine, hidden in a way in him and in his/
her experience.

Nostra Aetate's declaration portrayed the diversity of religions
and the relation to truth in a different manner. It put Truth—
that is, God—above us all, sending us rays through revelations.
Although the Catholic Church holds that the plenitude of revelation is in Christianity, it nonetheless viewed, in *Nostra Aetate*,
other religions as containing rays of revelation from the Truth.
The church was thus able to recognize the truth in other religions
while upholding its own religion as the best path to the Truth. It
opens thus the way for Christian believers for a new perception
and a new position: seeing grace in others, they can now ascribe
it not only to the personal spiritual path of others but also to the
religion of those others that was the vehicle allowing them to
receive this grace.

From Nostra Aetate *to the Qur'ān*

Transposing this to Islam and placing seemingly contradictory Qur'ānic verses about the other and about diversity of religions against this backdrop was a second breakthrough for me.

I had been working for some time on an Islamic theology of other religions. In doing so, I had gathered all Qur'ānic verses that refer to other religions and tried to make sense of them in a holistic, chronological, and contextual way. Two frames of reference appeared in my research. The first is theological verses—verses about diversity, about revelation, about the dogma of other religions, and about salvation with regard to other religions. The second frame of reference is verses about behavior toward the Other and the relation to diversity. The first type of verse presents the Qur'ānic position toward other religions and is less contextual than the second.

The second category of verses relates more to the change in context during the 23 years of revelation of the Qur'ān and echoes the growing mistrust and tension between Muslims and others, including the polytheists of Mecca and the Jewish tribes of Medina, leading to bloody wars. Yet it ends up on a more positive note of openness: a call to reconciliation, to opening up to difference, and a call to go out and meet those different, to vie with one another in the performance of good deeds, and to have more convivial relations with each other, including eating together and intermarrying.[3] What I will present here are the theological verses about diversity, about the dogma of other religions, and about ways of salvation. I will explicate the apparent contradiction between them and the three possible ways of bridging this contradiction, one of them being the method set by *Nostra Aetate*.

Does the Qur'ān Call for Acceptance of Diversity or for Exclusivism?

Some verses in the Qur'ān make life very easy for the theologians of other religions. These are verses that clearly portray religious diversity as willed by God. They can be seen in the framework of other verses that describe the beauty of creation in its diversity and the diversity of tongues and colors of humans as willed by God. These are verses such as Q 2:148: *"Every person has his direction to which he turns, so vie with one another in good works. Wherever you may be, God will bring you all together; surely God has power over all things."*[4] The word *direction* here is to be understood as direction of prayer, and thus the verse is referring to diversity in rituals and religions. Another verse upholding diversity is Q 5:48, which is even more explicit: *"To every one of you, We have appointed a divine law and a way. If God had willed, He would have made you one community, but that He may try you in what He has given to you. So vie with one another in good works; to God you shall all return, and He will then inform you of that in which you differed."*

Adding to these verses, others clearly indicate that salvation is not only for Muslims but for people of other religions and for all people who uphold the three Qur'ānic principles: belief in God, belief in the Last Day, and doing good. Such are the verses Q 2:62, *"Surely those who believe, and those of who follow Judaism, and the Christians, and the Sabaeans, whoever believes in God and the Last Day, and performs righteous deeds—their wage is with their Lord, and no fear shall befall them, neither shall they grieve,"* and Q 4:123–24: *"Not your desires, nor those of the People of the Book (can prevail): whoever works evil, will be requited accordingly. Nor will he find, besides God, any protector or helper. If any do deeds of righteousness—be they male or female—and have faith, they will enter Heaven, and not the least injustice will be done to them."* I must confess that these last two verses from An-Nisa' are among my favorites in the Qur'ān, as they clearly show that salvation is not a matter of identity for Muslims or for others, but a matter of abiding by faith through good deeds.

Yet these two sets of verses are easily contradicted by another set of verses: Q 3:19, *"Religion for God is Islam,"* and Q 3:85, *"Whoever desires a religion other than Islam, it shall not be accepted from him, and in the Hereafter he shall be among the losers."* There are three possibilities for dealing with this contradiction. The first and the easiest one is the exclusivist stance, considering solely the last-mentioned two verses, and that Islam is the only religion accepted by God. This is taught today in the Islamic education books used by ISIS in schools under their control, but has also been taught in many traditional Islamic circles since the earliest times.

Those who hold this position specify that the other verses that portray diversity as willed by God and that promise salvation for believers and good-doers from other religions—namely, Judaism, Christianity, and Sabianism—are invalid after the Islamic revelation. By this is meant that other religions were paths of salvation before the coming of Islam, but now that Islam has been revealed, it has become the only path of salvation. Yet this position has been opposed from the beginning by the fathers of Qur'ānic interpretation, among them the first commentator, al-Ṭabarī, who says that God does not revoke His promises.[5]

The second position defines Islam as meaning Islam in the broad sense. The Qur'ān, in fact, uses the term Islam as synonymous with Hanifiyya, or the path of Abraham. It even provides a definition of it in verse Q 4:125: *"And who is fairer in religion than he who submits his purpose to God and is beneficent, and who follows the creed of Abraham as a hanīf? And God took Abraham for a close friend."* The Qur'ān also refers to Jesus' Apostles, Moses, Aaron, Joseph, Jacob, Solomon, and the Queen of Sheba, and even Noah, as Muslims.[6] In this sense, the verse Q 3:85, *"Whoever desires a religion other than Islam, it shall not be accepted from him and in the Hereafter he shall be among the losers,"* can be understood as referring to Islam in the wide sense, the submission—or, rather, the abandoning of oneself—to God in confidence, and the expression of this confidence though beneficent action. This is in line with the verse *"Religion which is pure is that which is devoted to God"* (Q 39:3). In this sense, many other religions of the world, besides the most well-known monotheistic religions and the ones mentioned in the Qur'ān itself (Judaism, Christianity, Sabianism, and the religion of the Magians), can also be considered paths of devotion to God or of confidence in God and ways to benevolence. This is corroborated by two verses in the Qur'ān, the first of which is Q 4:163–65:

> We have revealed to you as We revealed to Noah, and the prophets after him, and We revealed to Abraham and Ishmael and Isaac, and Jacob, and the Tribes, and Jesus and Job and Jonah and Aaron, and Solomon, and We gave to David the Inscribed Book, and messengers We have told you of before, and messengers We have not told you of—and God spoke directly to Moses—messengers bearing good tidings and warning so that people might have no argument against God after the messengers. God is ever Mighty, Wise.

A second is Q 35:24: *"Truly We have sent you with the truth, as a bearer of good tidings, and a warner. And there is not a community which did not receive a warner (from God)."* From these verses it can be inferred that God's revelation is beyond the religions mentioned in the Qur'ān and that each people have had their prophet. This opens the way for interpreters and theologians of religions to consider a large number of religions in the world as being aligned with Islam in the broad sense.

Yet this second position alone can lead to a certain relativism. For if all these religions are paths to God and can be considered as Islam in the wide sense, they could all be considered as equal paths to God and to salvation, or to success (*falāḥ*), which is the Islamic counterpart of the more Christian concept of salvation.

This is why I argue for, in order to avert relativism, an articulation between this second position and a third position. The third position is inspired by *Nostra Aetate*, and thus by the possibility of considering one's religion as the one with the plenitude of meaning, the one with the most complete revelation, and at the same time considering that other religions are paths to God and to salvation, although not as completely as our own. I thus call for reading the verse Q 3:19, *"Religion before God is Islam,"* in this sense—that is, as meaning that the best religion for God is Islam, here Islam in the strict sense, without denying that other religions are paths to salvation, yet less complete and containing more man-made interferences. This is especially so given that the verse continues: *"Those who were given the Scripture differed only after the knowledge came to them through transgression among themselves."*

This understanding is corroborated by the beginning of the verse in Al Ma'ida that I cited previously:

> And We have revealed to you the Book with the truth confirming the Book that was before it and superseding it. So judge between them, according to what God has revealed, and do not follow their whims away from the truth that has come to you. To every one of you, We have appointed a divine law and a way. If God had willed, He would have made you one community, but that He may try you in what He has given to you. So vie with one another in good works; to God you shall all return, and He will then inform you of that in which you differed. (Q 5:48)

This verse comes, in fact, after a series of verses recognizing the Torah and the Gospels as revealed by God and as containing light and guidance. It thus confirms them yet says that the Qur'ān supersedes or overrides the Bible and the Torah in the points of divergence. Then the verse goes on to insist that diversity of religious paths is willed by God, and that He will explain to us our differences once we go back to Him. This verse thus presents at once diversity, acceptance and recognition of other religions, and precedence of Islam over them in the strict sense.

With this articulation, we can have an Islamic theology of other religions that advances three ideas:

1. Religious diversity is willed by God.
2. The best religion is Islam, yet other religions are also paths to salvation and are also sent by God.

3. A large number of religions in the world fall under the ap-
    pellation of Islam in the wide sense and have in common
    with Islam in the strict sense three pillars of faith and ac-
    tion: belief in God, belief in the Last Day, and beneficence.

What about Infidelity?

Yet if Christianity and Judaism and Sabianism are considered as Islam in the wide sense and are perceived as religions coming from
God and paths of salvation, what do we do with the verses that
clearly talk of disbelief or infidelity (*kufr*) in the dogma of these religions? My claim is that *kufr*, or disbelief, in those verses indicates the
points of divergence in the dogma, and not the whole belief system.

The main points of divergence are, in fact, disbelief in Muhammad and the Qur'ān, disbelief in Jesus as Messiah by the Jews, and
dogmas of divine filiation and the Trinity, although as one studies
the verses, it becomes clear that the Qur'ān is not talking about the
Trinity but about a triad. The clearest verse in this sense is Q 5:73:
*"They are indeed disbelievers, those who say, 'God is the third of three,'
when there is no god but the One God. If they do not desist from what
they say, those of them who disbelieve shall suffer a painful chastise-
ment."* The verse condemns the belief in three gods, and not in the
Trinity, with the expression "third of three." Another verse explains
what is meant by "third of three": *"And when God says, 'O Jesus, son
of Mary, did you say to mankind, "Take me and my mother as gods,
besides God?" He says, 'Glory be to You! It is not mine to say what I
have no right to. If I indeed had said it, You would have known it.
You know what is in myself, but I do not know what is within Your
Self: You are the Knower of things unseen"* (Q 5:116). From these
verses it is therefore apparent that the dogma that is refuted by the
Qur'ān is not the Trinity but a call for the worship of God, Mary,
and Jesus as a Triad, just as polytheists had pantheons with three
major divinities, a father god, a mother goddess, and a son or a
daughter god/dess.

The second divergence in dogma involves the question of divine sonship. The motif of divine filiation is also very much related to the polytheists of Mecca, who worshipped three daughters of Allah in their pantheon. Thus a large number of verses refuting divine filiation are addressed to the polytheists. Yet some are addressed to Christians and, strangely enough, to Jews: *"The Jews have said: 'Uzayr is a son of God!' The Christians have said: 'The Messiah is the son of God!' Such is the word that comes forth from their mouths; they copy that which the unbelievers said before them"* (Q 9:30). What is interesting to note here is the appellations. Although the Qur'ān refutes the sonship dogma and considers it to be disbelief, the text is very clear in its appellation, for it uses disbelievers (*kuffār*) for the polytheists and calls Christians and Jews by their names (Naṣārā for Christians, Yahūd for Jews).

The third divergence in dogma is the divinization of Jesus—or, more precisely, considering that God is the Messiah, which is not the belief of Christians per se, as what is portrayed in the verses is an equating of God with Jesus without the backdrop of the Trinity:

> They show disbelief those who say, "God is the Messiah, son of Mary." Say: "Who then can do anything against God if He desires to destroy the Messiah, son of Mary, and his mother, and all those who are on earth?" And to God belongs the kingdom of the heavens and the earth, and all that is between them. He creates what He will. God has power over everything. (Al Ma'ida 5:17)

And:

> They demonstrate disbelief those who say, "Indeed God is the Messiah, son of Mary." For the Messiah said, "O Children of Israel, worship God, my Lord and your Lord. Verily he who associates anything with God for him God has made Paradise forbidden, and his abode shall be the Fire; and for wrongdoers there shall be no helpers." (Q 5:72)

And the verse Q 4:171 summarizes both points:

> O People of the Scripture, do not go to extremes in your
> religion and do not say about God except the truth: the
> Messiah, Jesus the son of Mary, was only the Messenger
> of God, and His Word which He cast to Mary, and a
> spirit from Him. So believe in God and His messen-
> gers, and do not say, "Three." Refrain, it is better for
> you. Verily, God is but One God. Glory be to Him, that
> He should have a son! To Him belongs all that is in the
> heavens and in the earth. God suffices as a Guardian.

This verse is addressed to the People of the Book—that is, both
Christians and Jews—because the Qur'ān also admonishes Jews
and considers disbelief the fact that they did not believe in Jesus as
Messiah and Prophet from God:

> God then said: "O Jesus! I am going in truth to call you
> again to Myself, to raise you up to Me, to purify you
> from those who disbelieve [in you], and to place those
> who have followed you above those who have disbe-
> lieved [in you] until the Day of Resurrection. Soon you
> will return to Me; I will judge then between you and I
> will pronounce on your differences." (Q 3:55)

This last verse is among the very rare instances in the Qur'ān where
the expression "those who disbelieve" (*alladhīna kafarū*) is used for
the People of the Book, for the Qur'ān usually refers to Christians
and Jews either by calling them People of the Book or Christians and
Jews. Although it mentions diverging points in dogma as disbelief, it
does not call them "unbelievers" (*kuffār*). The Qur'ān in fact uses the
terms "unbelievers" (*kuffār*) and "associators" (*mushrikūn*) for Meccan polytheists only. Many Muslim preachers and jurists, though,
ignore this and apply these two terms to the People of the Book, thus
altering the meaning of the Qur'ānic message.

In fact, even if the Qur'ān points out divergences in dogma with the People of the Book, it emphasizes the commonalities in the most important tenets of faith—namely, that the God in whom all these religions believe is the same God, and that this God sends us revelations, and that we as believers ought to have confident trust in God:

> And do not dispute with the People of the Scripture unless it be with that, bettering the most virtuous way, except [in the case of] those of them who have done wrong, and say: "We believe in that which has been revealed to us and revealed to you our God and your God is one [and the same], and to Him we submit." (Q 29:46)

And, to make sure that the Islamic message stresses the salvation of the People of the Book and the recognition of their religions, despite the differences in dogma, the Qur'ān reiterates at the end of its revelation a verse that was revealed at the beginning of the Medinan period, that is, at the moment in which a real encounter between Muslims and the People of the Book began taking place in Arabia. Thus the verse appears first in Q 2:62, at the beginning of the Medinan period: *"Those who believe, and those who follow Judaism, and the Christians and the Sabians—any who believe in God and the Last Day, and work righteousness, shall have their reward with their Lord; on them shall be no fear, nor shall they grieve."* A slightly different version of it reappears toward the end of the Qur'ānic revelation in Q 5:69: *"Those who believe, those who follow Judaism, the Sabians and the Christians—any who believe in God and the Last Day, and work righteousness—on them shall be no fear, nor shall they grieve."*

I call this the bracket example, as if the Qur'ān were indicating that all divergences in dogma, and in actual life, are "contained" within this "doubled" verse, that these religions remain divine paths of salvation despite the problematic points of dogma. The Lebanese scholar Mahmoud Ayoub also considers this double verse as an emphasis of what is most important in the Qur'ānic message with regard to other religions.[7]

It can thus be summarized that the Qur'ān recognizes other religions, asserts the divine aspect of these other religions and the fact that these religions lead to salvation, and at the same time condemns some dogmas and other aspects of those religions as man-made additions to these religions.

Recognition beyond Respect

With this recognition of other religions, it is not enough to stop at mere passive and distant "respect" of other religions, without any effort to know more about them. I claim that we are called to get to know these religions and to value them. The verse Q 49:13 is an invitation to this: "*O you, human beings! We have created you of a male and of a female, and We have formed you into peoples and tribes so that you might have knowledge one of another. In truth, the most noble among you before God is the one who behaves with piety. God is all-knowing, he is aware of everything.*" The verse seems to be advancing the notion that the reason for God's creation of diversity among people, nations, and communities or religions is so that people get out of their comfort zones and make an effort to meet and know each other, as well as each other's cultures and religions. They gain from that a form of humility and personal responsibility, for the best humans are the most faithful and the most beneficent, across creeds and nationalities.

We are thus called not only to respect these other religions but to learn about them and value them. Although this position is quite removed from reality—where, besides exclusivism, we find much disdain of, if not fear of, the symbols, practices, and even texts of other religions—the Qur'ān itself upholds these symbols, practices, and texts.

The Qur'ān in fact praises the Torah and the Gospel as carriers of light and guidance, as mentioned earlier: "*Surely We revealed the Torah, wherein is guidance, and light"* (Q 5:44) and *"And We caused Jesus son of Mary to follow in their footsteps, confirming the Torah before him; and We gave to him the Gospel, wherein is guidance and light, confirming the Torah before it, and as a guidance and an admonition to the God-fearing"* (Q 5:46). Although the Qur'ān has precedence over the Torah and the Gospel as per verse Q 5:48, and although some verses in both books are considered altered textually or in their interpretation, the Qur'ān nonetheless considers both books as divine sources of light and guidance. A Muslim believer is thus called to discover this guidance and light in those books revealed by God, and, when there are points of divergence between these books and the Qur'ān, the Muslim then gives precedence to the Qur'ān. It is regrettable that the popular rigorist view of alteration, coupled with the exclusivist stance, has resulted in very few Muslims knowing the Torah and the Gospel. Indeed, many of them even dread reading them for fear of contamination by erroneous beliefs. This position not only shows a lack of respect for other books and for other faiths but is also an indicator of a lack of faith in oneself and of one's own commitment to one's faith, as if this faith were weak and needed to be protected from anything slightly dissimilar.

The Qur'ān also mentions the houses of worship of other religions: *"Say [O Muhammad]: 'My Lord has ordained equity. Lift up your faces towards Him in every place of prayer. Call upon Him, offering Him sincere worship'"* (Q 7:29) and *"O children of Adam, clothe yourselves beautifully for each place of worship"* (Q 7:31). Here the recognition goes beyond Judaism and Christianity and involves all houses where God is worshipped. What it also entails is the respect of the rituals of other religions, as houses of worship are the houses of communal rituals. Yet in reality much is done to dissuade Muslims from going to other places of worship and to dissuade others from entering Muslim houses of worship, except if they are interested in converting. Likewise, many believers tend to disdain the practices of other religions instead of seeing in them both a holy aspect and a beautiful human aspect of collective elevation and communion. The Qur'ān nonetheless stresses that this diversity of practice and ritual across religions is willed by God: *"And for every community, We have appointed a [holy] rite that they might mention God's Name over the livestock that He has provided them. For your God is One God, so submit to Him. And give good tidings to the humbly obedient"* (Q 22:34) and *"For every community We have appointed a [holy] rite which they are to observe. So do not let them dispute with you about the matter, but summon [people] to your Lord. Indeed you follow a straight guidance"* (Q 22:67). These verses, in addition to verse Q 2:148, which highlights the diversity of directions of prayer, demonstrates the Qur'ānic appreciation of rituals of other religions and the esteem given to them as coming from God.

Recognizing the divine in other religions therefore entails encountering these religions, their books, their places of worship, their practices, and their believers and their spiritual experiences. Although the Qur'ān sometimes admonishes believers from other religions for their deviations, it also lauds the believers of other religions who are true to their faith:

> ...some of the People of the Scripture are a community upright, who recite God's verses in the watches of the night, prostrating themselves. They believe in God and in the Last Day, enjoining decency and forbidding indecency, vying with one another in good works; those are of the righteous. And whatever good they do, they shall not be denied it, and God knows the God-fearing. (Q 3:113–15)

In fact, faith in the Qur'ān is not a communal quality but a personal path and commitment. This is why the Qur'ān lauds "some of the People of the Scripture" as it admonishes a group of Muslims from the Arab Bedouins: *"The Bedouins say: 'We believe!' Say to them: 'You do not believe, but say rather: 'we have embraced Islam' for the faith has not yet entered your hearts"* (Q 49:14).

It can thus be inferred that the motivation behind the call to go and meet people from different religions is not only to learn about their religions and practices but also to learn about how they live their faith and their own individual spiritual experience, rooted in their religion. We thus return to valuing personal experiences and relation to God and reception of grace, yet this time while recognizing the religious framework that allowed this personal relation to God to flourish.

All this goes against what is usually the norm between religions, for, in general, people do not dare to value anything in other religions for fear that such an act would be a betrayal of their own religion. Yet if they accept other religions as coming from God, they would be open to seeing God's signs in those religions, without it meaning a relativization of their own faith. One can without any guilt value spiritual and wisdom texts from other religions, forms of worship in other religions, and cultural aspects in other religions without diminishing an iota of their own faith in their religion.

Valuing God's Beauty in Valuing Other Religions

In verse Q 5:83, the Qur'ān advances the idea of speaking to some Christians in the context of the relation between Muslims and the People of the Book in Medina: *"And when they hear what has been revealed to the Messenger, you see their eyes overflow with tears because of what they recognize of the truth. They say, 'Our Lord, we believe, so inscribe us among the witnesses.'"* Although for some this is to be interpreted as Christians who ended up believing in Islam and becoming Muslims, the fact that they are described in the preceding verse as saying, *"Verily, we are Christians,"* is to me a clear indication that the verse is meant to praise people who do not leave their faith but stay firmly rooted in it while recognizing what is from God in other faiths. I also maintain that the Qur'ān asks the same of Muslims, for whatever the Qur'ān asks of the People of the Book, it also asks of Muslims.

Another verse, Q 32:15, describes the sensibility of those who believe in signs from God wherever they find them: *"Only those believe in Our signs, who, when they are reminded of them, fall down in prostration and make glorifications in praise of their Lord, and they do not disdain."* Finally, the verse Q 8:2 is the most explicit in describing real believers of any faith as those who recognize God's signs anywhere, and who love the mention of God wherever it is found: *"Real believers are those whose hearts are moved when God is mentioned. And when His signs are enumerated, this adds to their faith. They put their trust in God."* According to the Qur'ān, Divine Beauty infuses creation; it is the signs of God that are in the horizons and in us: *"We shall show them Our signs in the horizons and in their own souls until it becomes clear to them that it is the truth. Is it not sufficient that your Lord is witness to all things?"* (Q 41:53).

If we look more closely, we realize that these signs, this Divine Beauty, lie in diversity within Creation: *"And whatever He has created for you in the earth, diverse in hue. Surely in that there is a sign for people who remember"* (Q 16:13), and:

> Have you not seen that God sends down water from the heaven, wherewith We bring forth fruits of diverse hues? And in the mountains are streaks white and red, of diverse hues, and [others] pitch-black? And of humans and beasts and cattle, there are diverse hues likewise. Indeed, only those of God's servants who have knowledge fear Him. Truly God is Mighty, Forgiving. (Q 35:27–28)

Besides the beauty in the diversity of plants, animals, and humans, the beauty of God's creation lies in the diversity of tongues and colors: *"And of His signs is the creation of the heavens and the earth and the differences of your tongues and your colors. Surely in that there are signs for all peoples"* (Q 30:22).

Could it not be argued, then, that the beauty of God's creation lies also within the diversity of religions according to God's will? That we can laud the beauty of God and the beauty of creation by finding beauty in the Other and in the religion of the Other? However, this demands that we get rid of the mutual fear and competition for truth that have characterized the relations among religions throughout the ages.

Furthermore, the following verses note a clear correlation between diversity and a reviving of life after death: Q 45:4–5 states: *"And in your creation, and what He has scattered of animals, there are signs for a people who are certain; and the alternation of night and day, and what God sends down from the heaven [in the way] of provision with which He revives the earth after it is dead, and the circulation of the winds, there are signs for a people who understand."* And Q 2:164 says:

> Surely in the creation of the heavens and the earth, and the alternation of the night and day, and the ships that run in the sea with what profits men, and the water, God sends down from the heaven with which He revives the earth after it is dead, and He scatters abroad in it all manner of crawling thing; and the disposition of the winds, and the clouds compelled between heaven and the earth—surely there are signs for a people who comprehend.

Both verses end with a call to read the signs and try to comprehend what is behind them. Thus, could the metaphor also mean that valuing diversity in all its forms, including religious diversity, and engaging with it, vivifies the human heart and the spiritual path of each believer as the diversity of creation vivifies the earth?

Notes

1. Theological research undertaken at the Institute of Citizenship and Diversity Management at the Adyan Foundation is done, in most cases according to the methodology of "theologies in dialogue."
2. "*Nostra Aetate*: Declaration on the Relation of the Church to Non-Christian Religions," 1965. The Holy See, Vatican, website <http://www .vatican.va/archive/hist_councils/ii_vatican_council/documents/ vat-ii_decl_19651028_nostra-aetate_en.html>.

3. For the full study of the verses, see Fadi Daou and Nayla Tabbara, *Divine Hospitality: A Christian-Muslim Conversation* (Geneva: World Council of Churches Publications, 2017).

4. I use the translation of the Royal Aal al Bayt Institute: <http://www.altafsir.com/ViewTranslations.asp?Display=yes&SoraNo=1&Ayah=0&Language=2&LanguageID=2&TranslationBook=3)> and add my own changes to this translation where necessary.

5. Ṭabarī, *Tafsīr al-Ṭabarī* (*Jāmi' al-bayān fī ta'wīl āy al-Qur'ān*) (Beirut: Dār al-kutub al-'ilmiyya, 1999), I:361–65.

6. See Q 10:72 regarding Noah: *"My reward is from God alone, and I have received the order to be of those who submit themselves (to Him: muslimīn),"* and Q 12:101, about Joseph: *"O my Lord! You have invested me with sovereignty and you have taught me the interpretation of events. Creator of the heavens and the earth, you are my Protector in this world and in the other. Grant that I may die as one who submits to You (muslim) and place me among the righteous!"* Further, see Q 3:52, regarding the apostles: *"When he has noticed their disbelief, Jesus said: 'Who are my helpers in the way of God?' The apostles said: 'We are the helpers of God; we believe in God; witness that we are those who submit themselves (muslimūn)!'"*; Q 10:84, about Moses and his people: *"Moses said: 'O my people! If you believe in God, return to Him if you are submitted to Him (muslimīn)'"*; and Q 7:126, about Moses and Aaron: *"Moses and Aaron spoke to Pharaoh: 'You wish to take revenge on us simply because we have believed the signs of our Lord when they came to us.' Lord! Grant us patience and let us die in a state of submission!"* Also, Q 2:133, about Jacob and his sons: *"Were you witnesses, when death came to Jacob and he said to his sons: 'Who are you going to worship after me?' They said: 'We will worship your God and the God of your fathers: Abraham, Ishmael and Isaac, a unique God! And to him we will be submissive (muslimīn)!'"* And about Solomon and the Queen of Sheba: *"She said: 'My Lord! I have wronged myself, and I submit with Solomon to God, Lord of the worlds!'"* (Q 27:44).

7. Mahmoud Ayoub, "Religious Pluralism in the Qur'an," in *Mutual Perceptions Between Christians and Muslims in the Past and Present* (Arabic: *Al-Naẓarāt al-Mutabādala bayna al-Masīḥiyyīn wa'l-Muslimīn fī'l-Māḍī wa'l-ḥāḍir*) (Lebanon: University of Balamand, 1997), 24.

Works Cited

Ayoub, Mahmoud. "Religious Pluralism in the Qur'an." In *Mutual Perceptions Between Christians and Muslims in the Past and Present* [Arabic: *Al-Naẓarāt al-Mutabādala bayna al-Masīḥīyyīn wa'l-Muslimīn fī'l-Māḍī wa'l-ḥāḍir*]. Lebanon: University of Balamond, 1997.

Daou, Fadi, and Nayla Tabbara. *Divine Hospitality: A Christian-Muslim Conversation*. World Council of Churches Publications, 2017.

Ṭabarī. *Tafsīr al-Ṭabarī* [*Jāmi' al-bayān fī ta'wīl āy al-Qur'ān*]. Beirut: Dār al-kutub al-'ilmiyya, 1999.

Chapter Seven

THE QUR'ĀN, SALVATION, AND THE BEAUTY OF THE OTHER

Mun'im Sirry, University of Notre Dame

The Qur'ān's attitude toward other religions has been the subject of much discussion, yet it would be a mistake to assume that the Qur'ān has a coherent ethical position about how Muslims should treat the other. There are many passages in the Qur'ān that seem to allow for religious diversity and promote a peaceful coexistence among different religious communities. However, other passages can be understood as polemical in the sense that they not only negatively describe other religious communities—notably Jews and Christians—but also criticize them both in terms of doctrines and social interactions.[1] As is known, several passages in the Qur'ān criticize Jews and Christians for their erroneous beliefs. This Qur'ānic criticism of other religions has often been used by some Muslims to promote hatred and violence against the other. Even seemingly ecumenical passages have been interpreted to mean the opposite.

In this paper I focus on identical passages in the Qur'ān in 2:62 and 5:69 (with a slightly different wording), which have often been understood as scriptural proof-texts for interreligious harmony. At the least, these parallel passages appear to be positive and unequivocal allusions to other religious communities, such as the Jews and Christians. Muslims and non-Muslims alike have used these two identical passages as proof-texts for the Islamic tradition of tolerance and regard for the People of the Book (*ahl al-kitāb*). As such, these verses form an important locus for the continuing discourse between Muslims and other religions. The main argument put forth in this paper is that the lack of seeing the beauty in the other has led some Muslim scholars to obscure the peaceful message of the Qur'ān to such an extent that they strive to find ways to understand the inclusivist passages differently.

Theological Differences and Inclusive Attitudes

There is no question that the Qur'ān offers a distinctive theology that became the foundation of Islamic teaching, which is different from that of Christianity. While vigorously repudiating the Christian conception of God, the Qur'ān criticizes Christians for their belief in the divinity of Jesus or the doctrine of the Trinity (e.g., Q 5:17, 73, 154). However, despite these serious theological differences, the monotheistic nature of Christianity is not denied. The Qur'ān seems to reflect this position when it unequivocally confirms that Christians worship the God of the Qur'ān, while at the same it strongly criticizes them for their belief in trinitarian monotheism. When asking Muslims to debate the People of the Book in the best way possible, the Qur'ān also instructs them to say, "Our God and your God is one" (Q 29:46). This is the one and same God whose name is invoked in monasteries, churches, synagogues, and mosques (Q 22:48).

At least in three verses, different religious groups—including, among others, the believers, Jews and Christians—are mentioned together in a positive tone. Q 2:62, which is repeated in Q 5:69, is a good example of the believers being mentioned along with Jews, Christians, and Sabians. The verse reads as follows: "Truly those who believed (*al-ladhīna āmanū*) and those who became Jews (*al-ladhīna hādū*) and Christians (*naṣārā*) and the Sabians (*Ṣābi'īn*), whoever believes (*man āmana*) in God and the Last Day and does right, to them is their reward near their Lord; there is no fear for them, nor shall they grieve."

This is perhaps one of the most oft-quoted verses of the Qur'ān as a proof-text to support the idea of religious inclusivism in Islam.

It is hardly surprising that scholars have paid much attention to this passage to argue that Islam extends salvific promise to other religious communities. In the above passage, the condition for salvation is only twofold: true faith in God and the Last Day and righteous deeds. The passage can be understood to say that, as long as they believe in God and the Day of Judgment and do good deeds, the Muslims, Jews, Christians, and Sabians will be saved. Even the belief in the prophethood of Muhammad is not a condition for salvation.

Since this verse is included in chapters 2 and 5, it is unlikely that it has been abrogated by the later, more exclusive passages. Based on the traditional chronology of the Qur'ān, while chapter 2 (*al-Baqara*) was revealed to Muhammad soon after he arrived in Medina, chapter 5 (*al-Mā'ida*) is among the last chapters that Muhammad claimed to receive. Therefore, the theory of abrogation cannot be applied in this regard. This theory of abrogation, or *naskh wa mansūkh* (abrogating and abrogated verses), was developed by Muslim scholars to deal with seemingly conflicting passages of the Qur'ān. It is generally defined as the supersession of a certain verse by a later revelation, thereby rendering it inactive. The fact that this verse occurs at the beginning and end of Muhammad's prophetic career at Medina means that "neither the words nor the purport of these two identical verses were abrogated."[2]

In chapter 22 (*al-ḥajj*), verse 17, the Qur'ān again (though less explicitly) offers a positive assessment by confirming the obvious fact of religious difference. It is stated, "Surely those who believe, those who are Jews, the Sabians, the Christians, Magians and those who associated other gods with God, God will judge among them on the day of Resurrection. God is Witness over all things." Here, the fact of religious difference is recognized, and the Qur'ān leaves the ultimate judgment as to the validity of faith to God alone. Six different religious communities are mentioned together in the passage. Interestingly, the label of polytheism or idolatry (*shirk*) is not imputed to any of the recognized religious traditions. Rather, the passage places those who associate other gods with God in a separate category. The

Qur'ān condemns *shirk* as an unforgivable sin (Q 4:48), but it nevertheless does not associate this greatest sin with Jews or Christians.

Returning to the parallel passages of Q 2:62 and 5:69, there are many issues that have posed exegetical difficulties for Qur'ān commentators from quite early on. Who are these groups? When referring to Jews, why does the Qur'ān use the phrase *"al-ladhīna hādū"* (those who became Jews) rather than *"yahūd"* (Jews)? Why does the Qur'ān use the term *"naṣārā"* when referring to Christians, a term that is not used by Christians themselves? What is the etymology of the term *"naṣārā"*? Who were the Sabians? Grammatically, one may notice the inconsistency in the Qur'ānic usage of the term *"Ṣābi'īn"* (genitive) in Q 2:62 and *"Ṣābi'ūn"* (nominative) in Q 5:69. I will not address these questions. My primary concern is this: How has this passage been understood by Muslims throughout history? From a cursory reading it seems that the Qur'ān extends salvific promise to others in the sense that the condition for salvation is true belief in monotheism (belief in God and the Last Day) and doing righteous deeds. Is this the way the verses ought to be understood?

Indeed, many modern scholars answer positively. In his recent work titled *Islam and the Fate of Others*, Mohammad Hassan Khalil makes several references to Q 2:62 and 5:69, saying that these passages "portend the salvation of righteous, faithful Jews and Christians and a mysterious group called the Sabians."[3] Mahmoud Ayoub contends that the Qur'ān's main theme is faith, not religion. He criticizes the exclusionary orientation of Muslims who downplay or ignore the Qur'ānic texts like these that claim that salvation is open to anyone who believes in God and the Last Day and does good deeds.[4] In his widely read study *The Call of the Minaret*, Kenneth Cragg notes that this verse is conciliatory toward Christians.[5] It should also be noted that the positive tone of the verse is not only applicable to Christianity, but also other religious traditions. In the words of Geoffrey Parrinder, this verse and others "recognize the worth of other religions, if they had scriptures and believed in one God."[6]

It is the beauty of recognizing the salvation of others that is lacking in some Muslim commentaries on the above passage. As will be discussed in the following pages, Muslim commentators of the Qur'ān find various ways to interpret it differently. In fact, this verse is more ambiguous than it seems to be at first glance. As I will demonstrate later, most Qur'an commentators (*mufassirūn*) develop hermeneutical strategies to understand the relation between "those who have faith" (*al-ladhīna āmanū*) and "whoever believes" (*man āmana*), because for them it is redundant to say "whoever believes among those who have faith." The following is a general survey of what the *mufassirūn* have said about the identical verses mentioned above. Several Qur'ān commentaries examined in this paper reflect different views across the theological divide throughout the centuries.

Restricting the Others' Salvation

Let's begin with *Tafsīr Muqātil.* Muqātil b. Sulaymān (d. 150/767) is the earliest *mufassir* whose work is extant, known as *al-Tafsīr al-kabīr*, or simply *Tafsīr Muqātil.* Muqātil begins his explication by alluding to the occasion of revelation (*asbāb al-nuzūl*) of Q 2:62. He mentions a short version of the narrative of *asbāb al-nuzūl*, which is expanded by later *mufassirūn*, saying that this verse was revealed to Salmān al-Fārisī, who came to the Prophet and embraced Islam. He mentioned to the Prophet the situation of a Christian monk and his companions who were sincere in their religion, praying and fasting. The Prophet responded by saying that they are among the people of Hell; then this verse was revealed "on anyone among them who believes in the prophethood of Muhammad and what he brings forth (*fī-man ṣadaqa minhum bi-muḥammad wa-bimā jā'a bihī*)."[7] So, for Muqātil, the Qur'ānic phrase *man āmana bi-l-lahi wa l-yawm al-ākhir* (whoever believes in God and the last day) must be restricted to those who hold the faith of Islam among the four groupings. In his exegesis of Q 5:69, he emphasizes the point that the divine reward is only for "those who did good deeds (*'adda al-farā'iḍ*) before the prophethood of Muhammad and whoever remains alive to the time of the Prophet, no faith for him except to believe in Muhammad."[8]

Abū Jaʿfar ibn Jarīr al-Ṭabarī (d. 310/923), who wrote an encyclopedic *Tafsīr* titled *Jāmiʿ al-bayān ʿan taʾwīl āy al-Qurʾān*, addresses the difficulty of the relation of *man āmana* with the preceding *al-ladhīna āmanū*. He distinguishes the "believing" of a believer (*muʾmin*) from that of a Jew, a Christian, or a *Ṣābiʾ*. For the latter, "believing" means "coming to believe"—turning from a previous belief in the Torah (in the case of Jews) or in Jesus (in the case of Christians) to an acceptance of Muhammad. The "believing" of *muʾmin* does not mean his shifting from one religion to another, that is, his "coming to believe." Rather, it means his "standing firm in belief and not changing."[9] Had conversion from one belief system to another been intended, the statement would have been: "they believed (*āmanū*) in Muhammad and what he brought." With this understanding, Ṭabarī does not feel that the verse contradicts the overtly exclusivist passage of the Qurʾān (e.g., Q 3:85: "If anyone seeks a religion other than *al-islām*, it should not be accepted and in the Hereafter he will be among the lost"). Therefore, he rejects the idea of abrogation (*naskh*) attributed to the Companion Ibn ʿAbbās.[10] Interestingly, many modern scholars, including Mahmoud Ayoub, applaud Ṭabarī for rejecting the idea that Q 2:62 has been abrogated by the more exclusivist verse.[11] What they ignore is that Ṭabarī himself offers an exclusivist understanding of 2:62 in such a way that it means the opposite of what Ayoub has proposed.

Another tenth-century *mufassir*, al-Samarqandī (d. 375/985), in his *Baḥr al-ʾulūm*, proposes two possible interpretations of the relation of *man āmana* with *al-ladhīna āmanū*. First, *man āmana* refers to the last three groups (Jews, Christians, and Sabians), which means that whoever among Jews, Christians, and Sabians believes in the oneness of God, they shall have their rewards from their Lord. He is quick to add that the belief in the One God also includes the belief in Muhammad for the simple reason that one is not a believer in God unless he also believes in what is sent down to Muhammad as well as to other prophets. Second, *al-ladhīna āmanū* (those who have faith) refers to hypocrites, those who believe with their mouths but not with their heart.[12] According to this understanding, *man āmana* refers to all the four groupings who sincerely believe in God and follow what is brought by Muhammad.

The Shī'ī exegete of the tenth century, al-Ṭūsī (d. 385/995), follows the pattern set by earlier *mufassirūn* such as Ṭabarī. He, too, is preoccupied with the relation of *man āmana* to the preceding four categories (*al-ladhīna āmanū, al-ladhīna hādū, al-naṣārā,* and *al-Ṣābi'īn*). He solves the problem as Ṭabarī did by positing an implied "among them" (*min-hum*) so that the entire first part of the verse functions as a nominal absolute followed by quasi-conditional: "Truly those who have faith and those Jews, Christians and Sabians, whoever among them believes in God and the Last Day, will have their reward near his Lord."[13] He rejects the idea that *al-ladhīna āmanū* (those who have faith) refers to the hypocrites, as proposed by earlier scholars. Al-Ṭūsī also feels obliged to counter the interpretation of another group, the Murji'ites, who claim that *īmān* (belief) does not involve *'amal Ṣāliḥ* (action/good conduct).[14] The fact that God placed *man āmana* before *'amila Ṣāliḥan* is proof for him of its primacy.

An important *mufassir* of the eleventh century, al-Tha'labī (d. 427/1035), focuses on the identity of "believers or those who have faith" (*al-ladhīna āmanū*) instead of "whoever believes" (*man āmana*). He offers several possibilities: the believers are "those who believe in Jesus but never become Jews nor Christians nor Sabians" (*hum al-ladhīna āmanū bi 'īsā thumma lam yatahawwadū wa-lam yatanaṣṣarū wa-lam yuṣabbi'ū*), and they wait for the coming of Muhammad; the believers are "seekers of the true religion" (*ṭullāb al-dīn*) such as ḥabīb al-Najjār, Qais b. Sa'āda, Zayd b 'Amru, Waraqa b. Nawfal, and so forth, who believed in the Prophet before the time of Muhammad; or they are the "believers of previous communities" (*mu'minū al-umam al-māḍiya*).[15] As such, it's no longer redundant to say that "whoever among the believers, Jews, Christians and Sabians believes in God and the Last Day" because the believers are understood to refer to a specific group of people before the advent of Muhammad.

Another eleventh-century Muslim scholar, al-Māwardī (d. 450/1058), in his *al-Nukat wa al-'uyūn*, spends a great deal of time discussing the etymological problem of the terms "*hādū*" and "*naṣārā*." However, at the end of his exegesis of Q 2:62, he argues that either this verse refers to the people before the messengership of Muhammad who already acknowledged his prophecy or that it is abrogated by Q 3:85: "If anyone seeks a religion other than *al-islām*, it should not be accepted and in the Hereafter he will be among the lost."[16] Al-Māwardī is one of the earliest Muslim scholars to argue for the abrogation of the seemingly ecumenical passages with the more overtly exclusive ones.

Unlike the above exegetes, who restrict salvific promise to those who accept the prophethood of Muhammad, the Sufi exegete al-Qushayrī (d. 465/1072) contends that salvation transcends the groupings. "The difference of way (*ṭarīq*) with the unity of principle (*aṣl*) does not prevent the beauty of acceptance," he argues; "therefore, whoever trusts God in his signs and believes in what is told about his right and attributes, the divergence of laws and the difference of labels are not obstacles in attaining the divine pleasure."[17] He makes it explicit that "those believers, Jews, Christians and Sabians who agree on the divine knowledge (*ma'ārif*), for all of them is the beautiful place of return."[18] With regard to Q 5:69, Qushayrī offers the following exegesis: "God explains that—even though their situations differ into different groups—once the principles of tawhid unite them they (all the four groups) will attain safety from a threat and victory with abundance."[19]

Al-Zamakhsharī (d. 538/1144), a mu'tazilite Qur'ān commentator, is very much preoccupied with grammatical issues. In his exegesis of Q 5:69, for instance, he spends most of his time discussing how to understand the nominative case of *Ṣābi'ūn*, instead of *Ṣābi'īn* (genitive), as in Q 2:62. He briefly offers an interpretation

of *al-ladhīna āmanū* as "those who pay reluctant lip-service to belief" (*āmanū bi-alsinatihim min ghayr muwāṭa'a al-qulūb*) and *man
āmana* as "whoever among the unbelievers (*al-kafara*) believes sincerely and enters the religion of Islam completely."[20] A grammatical
discussion of the syntax of *man āmana* closes Zamakhsharī's remarks. He acknowledges two syntactical possibilities: (1) *man
āmana* can be read as the subject of a nominal sentence in which
fa-la-hum ajruhum is the predicate; or (2) *man āmana* can be read
as one of the accusatives following *inna*, so *fa-la-hum ajruhum*
functions as a predicate for all that comes after *inna*.[21]

By the time of Ibn al-Jawzī (d. 597/1201), there must have been
several theories developed by the *mufassirūn* in dealing with the
ambiguity of this verse. He identifies five possible referents for
al-ladhīna āmanū and seven explanations about who the Sabians
are. He provides a neat summary of the views expressed by previous commentators on the identity of believers (*al-ladhīna āmanū*)
as follows: (1) according to Ibn 'Abbas, that was a group who believed in Jesus before Muhammad was sent; (2) in the opinion of
al-Suddī, they are those who believed in Moses and lived in accord
with the Mosaic law until the coming of Jesus. After Jesus came,
they believed in him and followed his law until the time of Muhammad; (3) Sufyān al-Thawrī said that *al-ladhīna āmanū* were
the hypocrites; (4) they are the ones who were searching for Islam,
such as Qass b. Sā'ida, Baḥira, Waraqa b. Nawfal, and others; and
(5) they are the believers from among this *umma*.[22] As for the relation of *man āmana* to *al-ladhīna āmanū*, he summarizes three
explanations: (1) since groups of unbelievers (*kuffār*) are mentioned
together with the *mu'minūn*, the phrase *man āmana* refers to the
former; (2) the phrase *man āmana* means one who persists in his
belief; and (3) *al-ladhīna āmanū* refers to the hypocrites confessing
islām, while *man āmana* connotes true, heartfelt belief. He also alludes to the problem of abrogation, but he does not reveal his own
position on this and on other issues mentioned earlier.[23]

A similar approach is adopted by both Sunni and Shī'ī exegetes
of the late eleventh century onward. The Sunni exegete Fakhr al-

Dīn al-Rāzī (d. 606/1209) begins his exegesis by saying "*ikhtalaf al-mufassirūn fī al-murad min-hu* (the *mufassirūn* differ on the meaning of it)," and then enumerates their views oftentimes without revealing his own position.[24] The problem, as he understands it, lies in the ambiguity of the relationship between *al-ladhīna āmanū* and *man āmana*, as has been discussed above. Similarly, the Shi'i exegete al-Ṭabarsī (d.548/1153) begins his explication of *al-ladhīna āmanū* by saying, "*ikhtalafa fī hā'ula' al-mu'minīn man-hum* (they disagree on those believers: who are they)."[25] A complete departure from this approach is the Sufi *Tafsīr* by the famed Ibn 'Arabī (d.638/1240). As we know, Ibn 'Arabī has not formally written a complete *Tafsīr*, and his exegesis of Q 2:62 is very brief. The lexical, grammatical, and historical concerns that have preoccupied other exegetes are almost entirely absent. No reference at all is made to narratives of *asbāb al-nuzūl*, nor is any attempt made to refer to Prophetic hadiths. Ibn 'Arabī begins his exegesis by delving into a deeper meaning of the four groupings, equating *al-ladhīna āmanū* with "those who believe with uncritically accepted beliefs (*īmān taqlīdī*)," Jews with "those who take things literally (*ẓāhiriyyūn*)," Christians with "those who find hidden meanings (*bātiniyyūn*)," and Sabians with "those who worship the angle of reasons for their argumentation with rationalities and the stars of power for their argumentation with hallucinations."[26] In order to enjoy an enduring spiritual reward (*al-thawāb al-bāqī al-rūḥānī*), Ibn 'Arabī contends, "ones must believe sincerely in God, and they ascertain the knowledge of *tawhid* (one-ness of God) and resurrection and do what fits them for meeting God and attaining happiness in the Hereafter." At the very end of his exegesis, he remarks that "the whole is an interjection (*i'tirād*) in the midst of the (divine) address to the *Banū isrā'īl*."[27]

While the diversity of views continues to be preserved by the later *mufassirūn*, including al-Qurṭubī (d. 671/1272), al-Bayḍāwī (d.685/1286), Abū ḥayyān (d. 745/1344), Ibn Kathīr (d. 774/1373), and al-Suyūṭī (d. 911/1505), the discussion on the question of abrogation becomes more widespread. Qurṭubī closes his exegesis on Q 2:62 by presenting the opinion of Ibn 'Abbas, who argues that this verse has been abrogated by Q 3:85. Even if it is not abrogated, he contends, the verse is concerned only with those who hold a firm belief among the believers in the Prophet Muhammad.[28] Ibn Kathīr extends the theory of abrogation to the idea of supersessionism of pre-Islamic religions with the advent of Islam. "The implication of Ibn 'Abbas' view," Ibn Kathīr argues, "is that no one's belief and action will be accepted unless it's conforming with the shari'a of Muhammad after his prophethood."[29] Suyūṭī refers to the work of Abū Dāwūd al-Sijistānī titled *al-Nāsikh wa al-mansūkh*, in which the latter includes this verse as having been abrogated.[30]

The concern with the relation of *man āmana* with *al-ladhīna āmanū* is also evident in the Zaydi exegete al-Shawkānī (d. 1250/1834), of the late eighteenth century. He rejects the idea that *al-ladhīna āmanū* means the hypocrites. For Shawkānī, since the term is mentioned in reference to other religious groups, such as Jews, Christians, and Sabians, it is intended to explain that the condition of the Islamic religion (*milla islāmiyya*) and the rest of religions, in fact, returns to a single issue—namely, anyone among them who believes in God and the Last Day and does right is entitled to attain the divine reward. However, he is quick to add that what is meant by "belief" is that which the Prophet explained when he was asked by the angel Gabriel concerning it. Thus, Shawkānī argues, "no one can claim to have faith unless he accepted the Islamic religion. Whoever does not believe in Muhammad nor the Qur'ān, he is not a believer. Whoever believes he becomes a believing Muslim and will not remain a Jew nor Christian and Magian."[31] Shihāb al-Dīn Maḥmūd al-Alūsī (d. 1854) relates the verse to God's threatening statement about Jews in the previous passage, and the function of their being mentioned here along with the believers is to show "that the condition of each religion before abrogation necessitates reward and after abrogation prohibition."[32]

Among twentieth-century *tafsīr*s, we notice some sort of departure from pre-modern Qur'ān commentaries. It is worth noting that no reference at all is made in the modern *Tafsīr*s to the divergence of opinions that early exegetes entertained in their exegetical works. The discussion on the ambiguity of the relationship between *al-ladhīna āmanū* and *man āmana* is also entirely absent. Sayyid Qutb (d. 1966), for instance, understands *al-ladhīna āmanū* as simply the Muslims (*wa l-ladhina āmanū ya'nī bihim al-muslimūn*).[33] Likewise, Abū Bakr al-Jazā'irī (d. 1921), Ibn 'Ashur (d. 1973), and Tantawi (d. 2010) gloss the term to mean "the Muslims who believe in the Prophet Muhammad."[34] The Egyptian Muhammad al-Sha'rawi (d. 1998) offers an interesting interpretation of *al-ladhīna āmanū* as referring to a natural faith (*īmān al-fitra*) that came with Adam on earth until the time of Muhammad. He then says, "Those who believe previously with Adam or other prophets, those who came afterward to diagnose the errors that took place, some of whom call themselves Jews and others Christians and Sabians, that God wants to tell them that it's now over. Whoever believe in Muhammad there is no fear for them nor shall they grieve. It is as if Muhammad's message came to purify all the previous religions."[35] Most modern exegetes examined in my study are explicitly in favor of the idea of supersessionism that with the advent of Islam all other religions have become invalid.

Two modern Qur'ān commentators (Muhammad husayn Tabat abā'ī [d. 1981] from Iran and Rashīd Ridā [d. 1935] from Egypt) seem to offer a somehow different take from the supersessionist approach. The only criterion for salvation, according to Tabatabā'ī, is the real belief in God and the Last Day, accompanied by good deeds. One cannot be saved from punishment merely by claiming to be a believer or a Jew or a Christian. Tabatabā'ī especially rejects the insertion of implied *min-hum* (among them) that earlier *mufassirūn* have suggested, for such an understanding denotes some recognition to those labels/names.[36] Rashīd Ridā goes even further, claiming that "there is no problem without stipulating belief in the Prophet Muhammad because the discourse here is about God's treatment of all groups and communities that believe in a prophet and a revelation particular to them."[37] No one can claim salvation, Ridā argues, simply by claiming to be a Muslim, Jew, Christian, or Sabian, because its attainment lies not in religious sectarian allegiances. He cites Q 2:111–12: "And they say: 'Only Jews and Christians will enter the Garden.' Such are their fancies! Say to them: 'Show me your proof if you speak the truth.' Yes, indeed. He who surrenders his face to God in all piety shall receive his reward from his Lord. No fear shall fall upon them, nor shall they grieve" as God's response to the wrangling of Jews, Christians, and Muslims, each asserting claims to ultimate superiority. He closes his exegesis of Q 2:62 with the following statement: "Indeed, if the people of divine religions (*ahl al-adyān al-ilāhiyya*) believe in God and the Last Day in the right manner as explained by their prophet and do righteous deeds they will be saved and rewarded in God's eyes."[38]

However, Riḍā's take on Q 5:69 is more polemical in tone. For him, the context of this verse in the Qur'ān is to show that:

> the People of the Book have not upheld God's religion and what God enjoins them to do, including religious duties and its intents. Neither have they preserved the text of scriptures entirely nor have they avoided the literal meanings nor have they believed in God and the Last Day in the right manner as exemplified by their pious forefathers nor have they done good deeds, except a few among them hidden in different times or various mountains and corners of nations. They were punished for (their belief in) the oneness of God and accused of being heretics because of rejection of the Church's traditions.[39]

Encountering the Conservative Legacy of the Past

Up to this point, it seems clear that Q 2:62/5:69, which seems to extend God's salvation to all humans who possess faith and do good deeds, has been understood differently by Muslim commentators. They develop various strategies to circumscribe the ecumenical nature of the verse, for instance, by claiming that it refers only to Jews or Christians or Sabians who had adhered to the pristine faith before the advent of Islam. Some argue that the verse has been abrogated by subsequent revelation. It is true that the Qur'ān contains plentiful calls for religious tolerance, pluralism, and respect for diversity. However, even the oft-quoted verse exemplifying the Qur'ānic manifesto of pluralism has been understood to mean the opposite. What is interesting to note is that this intolerant reading of the Qur'ān is more prevalent than is generally assumed. It is often argued that the Qur'ānic vision of tolerance has been misappropriated by radical or fundamentalist Muslims—whatever that term means. The fact of the matter is that the narrow and conservative reading of the Qur'ān is so widespread that it makes the task of constructing tolerant societies among Muslim populations immeasurably difficult.

As discussed earlier, Q 2:62/5:69 is so arresting in its breadth and clarity that it would seem to leave little room for controversy. To repeat, however, mainstream Qur'ānic interpreters have found ways to problematize it by suggesting that, with the advent of the Muslim community, all other pre-Islamic religions are no longer valid as they have been annulled by Islam. Contrary to the pluralistic spirit of the Qur'ān, most Qur'ān commentators restrict the salvation of the other in such a way that non-Muslims today cannot claim to be among those who will attain salvation. Thus, the fate of non-believers has become one of the most contentious issues. One should not fail to note that these Qur'ān commentaries were written during the time when Muslims enjoyed extensive political power. And this imperialistic moment has had a profound impact on the way Muslim *mufassirūn* interpret the Qur'ān relating to the fate of others. Although we find plentiful resources for religious pluralism in the Qur'ān, the tradition of Qur'ānic exegesis exerts itself to prove the opposite.

This failure to see the beauty of peaceful coexistence among different religious communities is also evident in post-Qur'ānic discriminatory regulations. One example of these discriminatory regulations practiced in early Islam is what is known as the *Shurūṭ 'Umariyya* (Ordinances of Umar). Although the historicity of their attribution to 'Umar is questionable, at least in the eyes of Western scholars, the *Shurūṭ* are well-documented in the Muslim sources. Amād ibn al-ḥusayn al-Bayhaqī (d. 1066) cites the *Shurūṭ* in his *Al-sunan al-kubrā*. In *Tārīkh madīnat Dimashq*, Ibn 'Asākir (d. 571/1176) adduces five different versions of the document that have minor variations among them. In his *Aḥkām ahl al-dhimma*, Ibn Qayyim al-Jawziyya (d. 751/1350) cites two versions almost identical to some of the above.[40] The *Shurūṭ* contain, among other things, clauses stipulating that non-Muslims are not to build new churches within a city, are not to restore destroyed churches within Muslim quarters, are not to mount crosses on the outsides of churches, are not to display crosses or (holy) scriptures publicly in the market quarter of the Muslims, are to refrain from processions and other religious celebrations in public, are not to own slaves jointly with Muslims, are to wear particular accessories—a belt, head covers, shoes—and so forth.[41]

Ibn Qayyim devotes a long chapter to the interpretation of this document, saying that it is so famous that he could dispense with its *isnād*, as it was accepted by the imams, inscribed in their books, and referred to by them; the text of the *Shurūṭ* was continuously on their tongues and in their books; the Caliphs implemented it and acted in accordance with it.[42] I have discussed elsewhere that when the 'Abbasid Caliph al-Mutawakkil (d. 247/861) endeavored to stop the inter-religious dialogues and scholarly disputations that his predecessors had notably encouraged, he based his order on these very *Shurūṭ* of 'Umar.[43] It is worthwhile to quote the laws passed by the Caliph al-Mutawakkil, as recorded by the historian Ṭabarī:

> In the year (235/850), al-Mutawakkil gave orders that the Christians and the dhimmis (protected non-Muslims) in general be required to wear honey-colored hoods (*taylasān*) and girdles (*zunnār*); to ride on saddles with wooden stirrups and with two balls attached to the rear.... He gave orders to destroy their churches which were newly built and to take the tenth part of their houses. If the place was large enough, it was to be made into a mosque; if it was not suitable for a mosque, it was

to be made an open space. He forbade their employment in government offices and any official business where they would have authority over the Muslims. He forbade their children to attend Muslim schools or that any Muslim should teach them.[44]

Professor Abdulaziz Sachedina is correct in saying that, contrary to the spirit of tolerance in the Qur'ān, Muslim jurists encouraged a state-sponsored institutionalization of the inferiority of non-Muslims as necessary to the well-being of the Muslim public order, which eventually led to the adoption of a contemptuous attitude toward non-Muslim minorities. Sachedina is critical of the post-Qur'ānic discriminatory regulations, arguing that "most of the past juridical decisions treating non-Muslim minorities have become irrelevant in the context of contemporary religious pluralism."[45] His endeavor to confront the conservative legacy is to be applauded, for the Qur'ān still speaks to millions of the faithful through the voices of its classical commentators.

This negative attitude, arising from the spirit of enforced uniformity and stability in the community, also extended to fellow believers who failed to meet the criteria of pure faith, which puts the cornerstone of Qur'ānic pluralism at stake. While the Qur'ān seems to favor an overall tolerance of religious pluralism and allow for religious freedom, the social ethics delineated by the Muslim commentators and jurists regarded pluralism as a source of instability and social unrest in the Muslim public order.[46] I would argue that this conservative legacy of the past must first be admitted in order for us to be able to exert a new exegetical course. The exegesis is the product of its own time and place. Even some Qur'ānic verses reflect the circumstances of the time and place in which they were revealed. I agree with Khaled Abou El Fadl that the relation of the text to the reader plays a critical role in determining its meaning. For Abou El Fadl, "the meaning of the text is often only as moral as its reader. If the reader is intolerant, hateful, or oppressive, so will be the interpretation of the text."[47]

I also agree with Wilfred Cantwell-Smith that there is no fixed meaning of the Qur'ān. Cantwell-Smith says: "The real meaning of the Qur'ān is not any one meaning but is a dynamic process of meanings, in variegated and unending flow."[48] Certainly, the Qur'ān is polemical toward Christianity and Judaism, but it was further interpreted by the classical commentators who lived in what John Wansbrough calls a "sectarian milieu."[49] The result, as expected, is a bunch of Qur'ānic exegeses that advocate a supremacist view of Islam over other religions. Even the most powerful commandment of religious pluralism and tolerance in Q 2:62/5:69 has been interpreted to mean the opposite. However, as Cantwell-Smith argues, this is not the single, final meaning of the Qur'ān. The interpretation of modern Muslim scholars examined in this study shows a significant departure from the classical exegeses. In order to chart a new exegetical course in the light of religious diversity in the modern context, we need to emphasize the beauty of living together side by side in harmony.

Notes

1. For a detailed discussion of polemical passages in the Qur'ān, see Mun'im Sirry, *Scriptural Polemics: The Qur'ān and Other Religions* (Oxford: Oxford University Press, 2014).

2. Maḥmoud Ayoub, "The Qur'ān and Religious Pluralism," in Roger Boase (ed.), *Islam and Global Dialogue: Religious Pluralism and the Pursuit of Peace* (Burlington, VT: Ashgate, 2005), 277.

3. Mohammad Hassan Khalil, *Islam and the Fate of Others* (Oxford: Oxford University Press, 2012), 8.

4. See Maḥmoud Ayoub, "Nearest in Amity: Christians in the Qur'ān and Contemporary Exegetical Tradition," *Islam and Christian–Muslim Relations* 8.2 (1997): 145–64; see also Ayoub, "The Qur'ān and Religious Pluralism," 273–81.

5. Kenneth Cragg, *The Call of the Minaret* (Oxford: Oxford University Press, 2000), 260.

6. Geoffrey Parrinder, *Jesus in the Qur'ān* (London: Faber and Faber, 1965), 154.

7. Muqātil ibn Sulaymān, *Tafsīr Muqātil bin Sulaymān* (Beirut: Dār al-kutub al-'ilmiyya, 2003), I:35.

8. Ibid., 313.

9. Ibn Jarīr al-Ṭabarī, *Jāmi' al-bayān fī ta'wīl āy al-Qur'ān* (Beirut: Dār al-kutub al-'ilmiyya, 1992), I:379.

10. Ibid., 372–73.

11. Mahmoud Ayoub, *The Qur'an and Its Interpreters* (Albany: State University of New York Press, 1984), I:110.

12. Al-Samarqandī, *Baḥr al-'ulūm* (Beirut: Dār al-kutub al-'ilmiyya, 2006), I:120.

13. Muhammad ibn al-Hasan al-Ṭūsī, *al-Tibyān fī tafsīr al-Qur'ān* (Beirut: Dār al-alamira, 2010), II:345.

14. Ibid., 347.

15. 'Abd al-Rahmān ibn Makhlūf al-Tha'labī, *al-Jawāhir al-ḥisān fī tafsīr al-Qur'ān* (Beirut: Maktabah 'asriyya, 1997), I:76–77.

16. Al-Māwardī, *al-Nukat wa al-'uyūn* (Beirut: Dār al-kutub al-'ilmiyya, 2007), I:133.

17. Al-Qushayrī, *Laṭā'if al-ishārāt* (Beirut: Dār al-kutub al-'ilmiyya, 2000), I:50.

18. Ibid.

19. Ibid.

20. Zamakhsharī, *al-Kashshāf* (Beirut: Dār al-kutub al-'ilmiyya, 1995), I:139.

21. Ibid.

22. Ibn al-Jawzi, *Zād al-masīr fī 'ilm al-tafsīr* (Beirut: Dār al-kutub al-'ilmiyya, 1994), I:79–80.

23. Ibid., 80.

24. Fakhr al-dīn al-Rāzī, *Mafātīḥ al-ghayb* (Beirut: Dār al-fikr, 1981), III:111.

25. Al-Ṭabarsī, *Majma' al-bayān fī tafsīr al-Qur'ān* (Beirut: Dār al-kutub al-'ilmiyya, 1997), I:187.

26. Ibn 'Arabī, *Tafsīr ibn 'arabī* (n.p.; n.d), I:39.

27. Ibid.

28. Al-Qurṭubī, *al-Jāmi' li-aḥkām al-Qur'ān* (Beirut: Dār al-kitāb al-'arabī, 2012), I:474.

29. Ibn Kathīr, *Tafsīr al-Qur'ān al-'azim* (Beirut: Maktaba al-hilāl, 1986), I:152.

30. Al-Suyūṭī, *al-Durr al-manthūr fī al-tafsīr al-ma'thūr* (Beirut: Dār al-kutub al-'ilmiyya, 1990), I:145.

31. Muhammad ibn 'Ali ibn Muhammad al-Shawkānī, *Fatḥ al-qadīr* (Beirut: Dār al-kutub al-'ilmiyya, 1994), I:62.

32. Shihāb al-dīn Mahmūd al-Alūsī, *Rūḥ al-ma'ānī* (Beirut: Dār al-kutub al-'ilmiyya, 2001), I:280.

33. Sayyid Qutb, *Fi Zilāl al-Qur'ān*, trans. Adil Salahi and Ashur Shamis as *In the Shade of the Qur'ān* (Leicester, UK: The Islamic Foundation, 2001), I:92.

34. Abu Bakr al-Jazā'irī, *Aysar al-tafāsīr* (Beirut: Maktaba al-'ulum, 1997), I:65; Ibn Ashūr, *al-Taḥrīr wa al-tanwīr* (Beirut: Muassassa al-tārīkh, 2000), I:521; Muhammad Sayyid Ṭanṭāwī, *al-Wasīṭ fi tafsīr al-Qur'ān al-karīm* (Cairo: Matba'a al-sa'āda, 1985), I:198.

35. Muhammad Mutawallī al-Sha'rāwī, *Khawāṭir*, known also as *Tafsīr al-Sha'rāwī* (Cairo: Dār akhbār al-yawm, 1991), I:370.

36. Muhammad Husayn Ṭabatabā'ī, *al-Mīzān fi tafsīr al-Qur'ān* (Beirut: Muassasah al-a'lami, 1997), I:192.

37. Muhammad Rashīd Riḍā, *Tafsīr al-manār* (Beirut: Dār al-fikr, 2007), I:244.

38. Ibid., 246.

39. Ibid.

40. See R. Levy-Rubin, "*Shurūṭ* 'Umar and Its Alternatives: The Legal Debate on the Status of Dhimmis," *Jerusalem Studies in Arabic and Islam* 30 (2005): 171–206.

41. See Albert Noth, "Problems of Differentiation Between Muslims and Non-Muslims: Re-reading the 'Ordinances of 'Umar (*al-Shurūṭ al 'Umariyya*),'" in L. I. Conrad and R. Hoyland (eds.), *Muslims and Others in Early Islamic Society* (Burlington, VT: Ashgate Variorum, 2004), 103–24.

42. Ibn Qayyim al-Jawziyya, *Aḥkām ahl al-dhimma* (Damascus: Maktabat Jami'a Dimasq, 1963).

43. Mun'im Sirry, "Early Muslim–Christian Dialogue: A Closer Look at Major Themes of the Theological Encounter," *Islam and Christian–Muslim Relations* 16/4 (2005): 361–76.

44. See Bernard Lewis, *Islam, from the Prophet Muhammad to the Capture of Constantinople* (New York: Harper & Row, 1974), II:224–25.
45. Abdulaziz Sachedina, *The Islamic Roots of Democratic Pluralism* (London: Oxford University Press, 2001), 68.
46. Ibid., 100; see also Sachedina, "Freedom of Conscience and Religion in the Qur'ān," in D. Little, J. Kelsay, and A.A. Sachedina (eds.), *Human Rights and the Conflict of Cultures: Western and Islamic Perspectives on Religious Liberty* (Columbia: University of South Carolina Press, 1988), 53–90.
47. Khaled Abou El Fadl, *The Place of Tolerance in Islam* (Boston, MA: Beacon Press, 2002), 23.
48. W. Cantwell-Smith, "The True Meaning of Scripture: An Empirical Historian's Nonreductionist Interpretation of the Qur'ān," *International Journal of Middle East Studies* 11/4 (1980): 504.
49. See John Wansbrough, *Sectarian Milieu: Content and Composition of Islamic Salvation History* (Oxford: Oxford University Press, 1978).

Works Cited

Abou El Fadl, Khaled. *The Place of Tolerance in Islam.* Boston, MA: Beacon Press, 2002.

Alūsī, Shihāb al-Dīn Mahmūd. *Rūḥ al-maʿānī.* Beirut: Dār al-kutub al-'ilmiyya, 2001.

Ayoub, Mahmoud. "Nearest in Amity: Christians in the Qur'ān and Contemporary Exegetical Tradition." *Islam and Christian–Muslim Relations* 8.2 (1997): 145–64.

———. *The Qur'ān and Its Interpreters.* Albany: State University of New York Press, 1984.

———. "The Qur'ān and Religious Pluralism." In *Islam and Global Dialogue: Religious Pluralism and the Pursuit of Peace*, edited by Roger Boase. Burlington, VT: Ashgate, 2005, 273–81.

Cantwell-Smith, W. "The True Meaning of Scripture: An Empirical Historian's Nonreductionist Interpretation of the Qur'ān." *International Journal of Middle East Studies* 11/4 (1980): 487–505.

Cragg, Kenneth. *The Call of the Minaret.* Oxford: Oxford University Press, 2000.

Ibn 'Arabī, *Tafsīr ibn 'arabī* (n.p.; n.d).

Ibn Ashūr. *al-Taḥrīr wa al-tanwīr.* Beirut: Muassassa al-tārīkh, 2000.

Ibn al-Jawzī. *Zād al-masīr fī 'ilm al-tafsīr.* Beirut: Dār al-kutub al-'ilmiyya, 1994.

Ibn Kathīr. *Tafsīr al-Qur'ān al-'aẓīm.* Beirut: Maktaba al-hilāl, 1986.

Ibn Qayyim al-Jawziyya. *Aḥkām ahl al-dhimma.* Damascus: Maktabat Jāmi'a Dimasq, 1963.

Ibn Sulaymān, Muqātil. *Tafsīr Muqātil bin Sulaymān.* Beirut: Dār al-kutub al-'ilmiyya, 2003.

Jazā'irī, Abū Bakr. *Aysar al-tafāsīr.* Beirut: Maktaba al-'ulūm, 1997.

Khalil, Mohammad Hassan. *Islam and the Fate of Others.* Oxford: Oxford University Press, 2012.

Levy-Rubin, R. "*Shurūṭ* 'Umar and Its Alternatives: The Legal Debate on the Status of Dhimmis." *Jerusalem Studies in Arabic and Islam* 30 (2005): 171–206.

Lewis, Bernard. *Islam, from the Prophet Muhammad to the Capture of Constantinople.* New York: Harper & Row, 1974.

Māwardī. *al-Nukat wa al-'uyūn.* Beirut: Dār al-kutub al-'ilmiyya, 2007.

Noth, Albert. "Problems of Differentiation Between Muslims and Non-Muslims: Re-reading the 'Ordinances of 'Umar (*al-Shurūṭ al 'Umariyya*).'" In L. I. Conrad and R. Hoyland (eds.), *Muslims and Others in Early Islamic Society.* Burlington, VT: Ashgate Variorum, 2004, 103–24.

Parrinder, Geoffrey. *Jesus in the Qur'ān.* London: Faber and Faber, 1965.

Qurṭubī. *al-Jāmi' li-aḥkām al-Qur'ān.* Beirut: Dār al-kitāb al-'arabī, 2012.

Qushayrī. *Laṭā'if al-ishārāt.* Beirut: Dār al-kutub al-'ilmiyya, 2000.

Qutb, Sayyid. *Fi Zilāl al-Qur'ān.* Translated by Adil Salahi and Ashur Shamis as *In the Shade of the Qur'ān.* Leicester, UK: The Islamic Foundation, 2001.

Rāzī, Fakhr al-Dīn. *Mafātīḥ al-ghayb,* also known as *al-Tafsīr al-kabīr.* Beirut: Dār al-fikr, 1981.

Riḍā, Muhammad Rashīd. *Tafsīr al-manār.* Beirut: Dār al-fikr, 2007.

Sachedina, Abdulaziz A. "Freedom of Conscience and Religion in the Qur'ān." In D. Little, J. Kelsay, and A. A. Sachedina (eds.), *Human Rights and the Conflict of Cultures: Western and Islamic Perspectives on Religious Liberty.* Columbia: University of South Carolina Press, 1988: 53–90.

————. *The Islamic Roots of Democratic Pluralism*. London: Oxford University Press, 2001.

Samarqandī. *Baḥr al-'ulūm*. Beirut: Dār al-kutub al-'ilmiyya, 2006.

Sha'rāwī, Muhammad Mutawallī. *Khawāṭir,* known also as *Tafsīr al-Sha'rāwī*. Cairo: Dār akhbār al-yawm, 1991.

Shawkānī, Muhammad ibn 'Ali ibn Muhammad. *Fatḥ al-qadīr*. Beirut: Dār al-kutub al-'ilmiyya, 1994.

Sirry, Mun'im. "Early Muslim–Christian Dialogue: A Closer Look at Major Themes of the Theological Encounter." *Islam and Christian–Muslim Relations* 16/4 (2005): 361–76.

————. *Scriptural Polemics: The Qur'ān and Other Religions*. Oxford: Oxford University Press, 2014.

Suyūṭī. *al-Durr al-manthūr fi al-tafsīr al-ma'thūr*. Beirut: Dār al-kutub al-'ilmiyya, 1990.

Ṭabarī, Ibn Jarīr. *Jāmi' al-bayān fi ta'wīl āy al-Qur'ān*. Beirut: Dār al-kutub al-'ilmiyya, 1992.

Ṭabarsī. *Majma' al-bayān fi tafsīr al-Qur'ān*. Beirut: Dār al-kutub al-'ilmiyya, 1997.

Ṭabatabā'ī, Muhammad Husayn. *al-Mīzān fi tafsīr al-Qur'ān*. Beirut: Muassasah al-a'lam, 1997.

Ṭanṭāwī, Muhammad Sayyid. *al-Wasīṭ fi tafsīr al-Qur'ān al-karīm*. Cairo: Matba'a al-sa'āda, 1985.

Tha'labī, 'Abd al-Rahman ibn Makhlūf. *al-Jawahir al-hisan fi tafsir al-Qur'ān*. Beirut: Maktabah 'asriyya, 1997.

Ṭūsī, Muhammad ibn al-Hasan. *al-Tibyān fi tafsīr al-Qur'ān*. Beirut: Dār al-alamira, 2010.

Wansbrough, John. *Sectarian Milieu: Content and Composition of Islamic Salvation History*. Oxford: Oxford University Press, 1978.

Zamakhsharī. *al-Kashshāf*. Beirut: Dār al-kutub al-'ilmiyya, 1995.

Part III

BEAUTY AND HINDUISM

Chapter Eight

TRAVELING THE *VIA PULCHRITUDINIS*—BOTH WAYS

Francis X. Clooney, S.J., Harvard University

Introduction

The welcome announcement of the 2015 conference that led to this volume invited us to travel the way of beauty: "Convinced that beauty is indeed a means for touching the human heart, and recognizing the rich role of beauty in the history of Christian theological thought, we plan to explore how beauty can be found in religions and cultures, and how the beauty of the Christian gospel should be communicated in different religious and cultural settings." Thus offered to us are fresh possibilities holding rich promise within the Catholic community itself in the renewal of our presentation of the faith. In encountering the beautiful, we go deeper into ourselves, and yet also step beyond ourselves, by a desire that recognizes the face of the immanent-transcendent. That we should recognize and not take for granted the beauty of the Gospel is an important insight, lest we reduce the Good News to its truth or moral goodness. The project has also invited us to think of "how beauty can be found in religions and cultures." Here I would add a further possibility, not only that this discovery shows us how the beauty of the Gospel can be communicated in those religions and cultures, but also how we might encounter God in that beauty, beyond possibilities accounted for by truth and goodness.

How to think and say more about this way of beauty? I suppose that the way to proceed here would most sensibly be by way of aesthetic exploration, experiencing instances of beauty in the visual and aural and tactile arts: meditations on the beautiful that are not merely apprehensions of its truth and goodness. But I will for the moment forgo that possibly more satisfying route and instead travel a path of words, considering what has been said about the way of beauty and then reflecting on some verbal representations of the beautiful, words that evoke the beautiful in the mind's eye. For the sake of clarity in what follows, in Part I, I put in place some documentation on the use of *via pulchritudinis* ("way of beauty") in the contemporary Roman Catholic Church, and then draw on the work of Hans Urs von Balthasar to play out more amply the dynamics of the beautiful in relation to the human and divine. This background is necessary, lest we speculate very broadly about beauty and the beautiful, without the discipline of attention to the meaning of *via pulchritudinis* in modern Catholic teaching.

In Part II, my primary contribution to our conversation, I take the words of the invitation in a new direction, exploring "how beauty can be found in religions and cultures, and how the beauty of the Christian gospel should be communicated in different religious and cultural settings" by considering whether this path allows for two-way traffic, as the beauty of other religions finds its way also into the experience of the Christian. For that purpose, I give one extended example, an instance of the beautiful divine in a Hindu tradition. If eyes are opened to the beauty of the Gospel and the beautiful in non-Christian cultures, can we not also view the divine in traditions such as the Hindu? In search of an answer, I will be reflecting on the *Saundarya Lahari* (*Flood of Beauty*), a Hindu text considered at length in my 2005 book *Divine Mother, Blessed Mother: Hindu Goddesses and the Virgin Mary*.[1] I conclude this second, constructive part of the paper by assessing honestly the difficulties arising when we open the way of beauty to two-way travel.

Part I:
The Via Pulchritudinis *and a Catholic Theology of Beauty*

Documentation of the Term *"Via Pulchritudinis"*

First, to be clear on the contours of this project as a comparative venture, it is worthwhile to understand the lineage of the very idea of the *via pulchritudinis* in modern Catholic theology, particularly since this usage seems not to have been thoroughly documented by historians. I therefore lay out here, in a straightforward manner, some relevant texts, supplementing each by a brief comment.

1. AN EARLY—THE EARLIEST?[2]—use of the term *via pulchritudinis*: An intriguing place to start is with an essay by the art historian and theorist Étienne Souriau. In his "Via Pulchritudinis" (1959),[3] he speaks of spontaneous apprehensions of beauty, the spontaneous and ecstatic momentary recognition of beauty in certain experiences, often in nature. But he then turns to the second possibility, a *way* of beauty, a pathway and ascent to the divine by the third of the three transcendentals:

> The second (approach) takes up the ontological legitimacy of the *via pulchritudinis* in order to reach God by one of his three transcendental attributes. As for the austere admonitions against rationalism or the criticism to which any of them is susceptible, we can ignore those here, since they do not matter in this context. What is positive, in each case, is the direction of the soul. Thanks to an aesthetic sign of the divine, real or supposed, this direction traces the course of a drive that traverses nature in order to try to go beyond it.[4]

Souriau offers us an interesting contrast between a sudden apprehension of the beautiful and a gradual apprehension of beauty. This *via pulchritudinis* can be learned and practiced and does not eschew intellectual inquiry or close attention to the natural. In keeping with the great tradition of the Church, the direction of this path is upward, to ascend through the natural to a realm beyond it. Souriau is relying on the notion of the three transcendentals—truth, goodness, and beauty—and bringing needed attention to the third.

2. PAUL VI, DISCORSO, CONGRESSI MARIOLOGICO E MARIANO, MAY 16, 1975

By contrast, it is interesting to note that Paul VI does not appeal to those three transcendentals, but simply compares the way of truth and the way of beauty. The latter is attractive because it is easier and accessible to all, yet energized by the mysteries of the Virgin Mary and the Holy Spirit.

> In this matter a double path is opened for us, and the first is the way of truth. This is clearly the way of study that is Biblical, historical, and theological. It looks to the proper place of Mary established in the mystery of Christ and the Church. You follow this way of learned men, and it is very useful to the studies to be undertaken in Mariology.
>
> But there is another way, a way accessible to all, even to people of humble condition, which we call the way of beauty: to this path leads that precious, marvelous and most beautiful doctrine of Mary and the Holy Spirit, into which the investigations of this Marian Congress ought to delve. Surely Mary is "entirely beautiful," and likewise "the mirror without blemish.... Surely the work for us is to look to Mary and turn our eyes to her uncontaminated beauty, especially since often the false images of beauty in this world offend our eyes and as it were blind them. The contemplation of Mary's exalted beauty, on the contrary, is able to generate the finest senses of the soul...."[5]

This teaching of Paul VI, brief as it is, seems to be at the origin of modern Catholic reflection on the *via pulchritudinis*.

3. HOMILY OF BENEDICT XVI, APRIL 24, 2005

> There is nothing more beautiful than to be surprised by the Gospel, by the encounter with Christ. There is nothing more beautiful than to know Him and to speak to others of our friendship with Him. The task of the shepherd, the task of the fisher of men, can often seem wearisome. But it is beautiful and wonderful, because it is truly a service to joy, to God's joy which longs to break into the world.

This passage often figures in the modern teaching on the *via pulchritudinis*, even if Benedict does not use here the term "way of beauty." Key is that he grounds the preaching of the Gospel in its beauty, its capacity to open the way to Christ. By extension, it also instigates the Christian desire to share that beauty with others, in a joyful manner that avoids the dichotomies of true and false, good and evil.[6]

4. CONCLUDING DOCUMENT OF THE PLENARY ASSEMBLY (2006) convened by the Pontifical Council for Culture, on "The *Via Pulchritudinis*, Privileged Pathway for Evangelisation and Dialogue."

> In this perspective, the *Way of Beauty* seems to be a privileged itinerary to get in touch with many of those who face great difficulties in receiving the Church's teachings, particularly regarding morals. Too often in recent years, the *truth* has been instrumentalised by ideologies, and the *good* horizontalised into a merely social act as though charity towards neighbour alone sufficed without being rooted in love of God. Relativism, which finds one of its clearest expressions in the *pensiero debole*,[7] continues to spread, encouraging a climate of miscomprehension, and making real, serious and reasoned encounters rare.[8]

Note that this document, too, refers to truth, goodness, and beauty, but concedes the limitations of the former two, while the third has a hitherto not fully explored capacity to manifest God to seekers:

> Beginning with the simple experience of the marvel-arousing meeting with beauty, the *via pulchritudinis* can open the pathway for the search for God, and disposes the heart and spirit to meet Christ, who is the Beauty of Holiness Incarnate, offered by God to men for their salvation. It invites contemporary Augustines, unquenchable seekers of love, truth and beauty, to see through perceptible beauty to eternal Beauty, and with fervour discover Holy God, the author of all beauty.[9]

It is notable that this passage from the same document combines in a single flow what Souriau had wisely distinguished: sudden apparitions of the beautiful, and traveling a measured path to the apprehension of beauty. While the sudden experience of the first may prompt one to embark on the latter, this should not be taken for granted.

Yet the document continues with hesitations, too, about the adequacy of the beautiful in today's cultures:

> All cultures are not equally open to the transcendent and welcoming of Christian Revelation. Not all expressions of beauty—or moments which pretend to be so—favour an acceptance of the message of Christ and the intuition of His divine beauty. As their artistic expressions and aesthetic manifestations are marked by sin, cultures can attract and imprison one's attention until it folds in on itself creating new forms of idolatry.[10]

It is interesting that the terminology is vague enough that even cultures with long Christian histories can be indicted, though one might expect that in this document non-Christian cultures would be particularly judged to be suspect.[11] The remedy is to make sure beauty is firmly bonded to the true and the good:

> Perception requires an education, for beauty is only authentic in its link to the truth—of what would brilliance be, if not truth?—and it is at the same time "the visible expression of the good, just as the good is the metaphysical expression of beauty." And again, "Is not beauty the surest route to attain the good?" asked Max Jacob.[12]

The beautiful, like the true and the good, requires interrelation with the others in this triad. The danger at this point is the foreclosure of any real freedom for beauty, and the document does not further clarify how that eventuality is to be avoided.[13]

5. POPE FRANCIS, EVANGELII GAUDIUM (2013)

Finally, we can note Pope Francis's well-known and well-received encyclical letter, *Evangelii Gaudium.*

> Every form of catechesis would do well to attend to the "way of beauty" (*via pulchritudinis*).[14] Proclaiming Christ means showing that to believe in and to follow him is not only something right and true, but also something beautiful, capable of filling life with new splendour and profound joy, even in the midst of difficulties. Every expression of true beauty can thus be acknowledged as a path leading to an encounter with the Lord Jesus.[15]

Francis thus hearkens to "true beauty" and places emphasis on a way to Christ through the beauty of the Good News.

> This has nothing to do with fostering an aesthetic relativism which would downplay the inseparable bond between truth, goodness and beauty, but rather a renewed esteem for beauty as a means of touching the human heart and

enabling the truth and goodness of the Risen Christ to radiate within it. If, as Saint Augustine says, we love only that which is beautiful, the incarnate Son, as the revelation of infinite beauty, is supremely lovable and draws us to himself with bonds of love. So a formation in the *via pulchritudinis* ought to be part of our effort to pass on the faith....

Francis goes on to exhort his listeners to allow freedom to the beautiful, that it might flourish, unconstrained by overly familiar forms:

We must be bold enough to discover new signs and new symbols, new flesh to embody and communicate the word, and different forms of beauty which are valued in different cultural settings, including those unconventional modes of beauty which may mean little to the evangelizers, yet prove particularly attractive for others.[16]

The way of beauty is a way of preaching the Gospel. He also points us, however vaguely, to the beauty in various cultural settings and to "unconventional modes of beauty," but gives no explicit indication that he is thinking of the religions of the world.

To conclude this section: In the preceding pages I have cited key essays and documents attesting to the importance of the *via pulchritudinis*. Beauty is therefore to be honored as an attractive, more intimate, and perhaps, in our era, more efficacious way of access to the mysteries and realities of Christ and of the Christian faith. The emerging and consistent teaching of the Catholic tradition since Paul VI's 1975 teaching is the hope that the *via pulchritudinis* can speak freshly to people in today's world, stepping beyond (even if not contradicting) the rational dynamics of the truth and moral dynamics of the good. Attention to beauty, of course, opens into the realm of the aesthetic, and this indicates an approach that has its own requirements and sensitivities and thus its own potential. The teaching is forward-looking and generates hope with respect to reaching new audiences. Implicit, too, is the hope that it can also open new ways of reaching non-Christians, who are put off by the appearances of Christian rationalism and moralism.[17]

Giving Form to the Beautiful: Some Insights from Hans Urs von Balthasar

But for our fuller understanding of the *via pulchritudinis*, we also need a more comprehensive theology of beauty. Here I can only indicate the contours of that theology by noting the aesthetic theology of Hans Urs von Balthasar. Given his emphasis on the centrality of the beautiful to theological discourse, it is no surprise that I should point here to his views, and not be the first to do so even with respect to the *via pulchritudinis*.[18]

In Section II.3 of the 2006 synodal "Concluding Document" of the Council for Culture, cited above, attention has already been drawn to his writing:

> In proposing a theological aesthetic, von Balthasar sought to open the horizons of thought to the meditation and contemplation of the beauty of God, of the mystery of Christ in whom he reveals Himself. In the introduction to the first volume of his major work, *The Glory of the Lord*, the theologian speaks of "what for us will be the first," beauty, and explains its value compared with the good which "has lost its power of attraction," and where "the proofs of truth have lost their conclusive character."

A note in the same document fills out this observation through an extended quote from Balthasar's *The Glory of the Lord* (Volume One), which I reproduce here:

> Beauty is the word that shall be our first. Beauty is the last thing which the thinking intellect dares to approach, since only it dances as an uncontained splendour around

the double constellation of the true and the good and their inseparable relation to one another. Beauty is the disinterested one, without which the ancient world refused to understand itself, a word which both imperceptibly and yet unmistakably has bid farewell to our new world, a world of interests, leaving it to its own avarice and sadness. No longer loved or fostered by religion, beauty is lifted from its face as a mask, and its absence exposes features on that face which threaten to become incomprehensible to man. . . .

He goes on to lament a world that either debases beauty in a cheap fashion, or finds it embarrassing and best passed over in silence.[19]

In a later section of the same volume, "The Task and the Structure of a Theological Aesthetics," Balthasar spells out the dynamics of the beautiful, noting that there are two elements to it, as indicated in my summary of his words. First, there is *forma*—the beautiful is materially grasped, even subjected to numerical calculation, and yet at the same time, reaching into the deep, arousing delight; this is the sacrament of depth, and of the self-revealing Being, self-representation.[20] Second, there is *lumen*, the radiance turning us to the visual as it reaches the eyes of our minds and leads us to a mediating second vision, rapture, transport. This is a seeing, beholding, perception of the invisible now made visible,[21] an apprehension of the splendor of the mystery that evokes an enrapturing *amor* (*eros*).[22] The *forma* draws us to itself; the *lumen* shines toward us, onto us, as if from outside us, yet drawing us outside ourselves. These are the objective (*forma*) and subjective (*lumen*) sides of the phenomenon of beauty. Balthasar emphasizes that the resultant engagement with the desired and beautiful lord is not a yearning for the unreachable. Rather, by faith—*eros* and ecstasy occur always in the context of salvation history[23]—we know that the ultimate reality is at the same time reaching out to us.[24]

Balthasar then distinguishes two theoretical lenses through which to view the dynamics of the beautiful, respectively related to the *forma* and the *lumen*. First, there is *a theory of vision*, such as regards the perception of the form of God's self-revelation; second, there is *a theory of rapture*, such as regards the incarnation of God's glory and the consequent elevation of the human to participate in that glory.[25] He further explains this pairing of *vision and rapture* as a path, a road:

> To be sure, there is a road which the human spirit takes as it seeks for the Christian truth (*intellectus quaerens fidem*), and this search may be fostered by variously showing and making visible in an appropriate way the form of God's revelation, which conceals itself from the eyes of the world and of salvation history *sub contrario*, as Luther has it. As we have said, however, this road itself already stands in the rays of the divine light, a light which, in an objective sense, makes the form visible and which, in a subjective sense, clarifies and illumines the searching spirit, thus training it in an act and a *habitus* which will become perfect faith once the vision has itself been perfected.[26]

To travel this road is to approach *forma*, drawn from the start by the grace of *lumen* shining in that *forma*. All of this then suggests a theology of the *via pulchritudinis*, though Balthasar seems not to have used the term.

Indeed, it is no surprise that Balthasar too, would be thinking of the path of beauty—the "road." He does us the service of grounding the conversation about beauty by still deeper insights into the divine-human relationship as a matter of light and form, apprehension, desire, and the ecstatic, as the beholder reaches out beyond her own capacity into the mystery of God. Beauty is no additional and attractive bonus that merely enhances good feeling; it is solidly at the core of the Christian faith as holistically and dramatically understood. The beautiful is there for us to behold, and we seek it out, the object of our deep desire; yet it, too, steps beyond itself and draws us beyond ourselves to it. In the beautiful, we yearn for God, and God keeps surprising us by reaching us first. But can God do this outside the Christian context, accessible through other forms and illumining us by light already shining there?

Part II:
The Via Pulchritudinis
Mapped across Other Religions

With the documentary and theological starting points of Part I in place, we can now turn to the key further question about this way of beauty: how do we travel this path in practice, specifically in relation to our encounter with other traditions? The documents catalogued at the start of this essay highlight the beauty of Christ and beauty of the Gospel, and intimate the role beauty might play in non-Christian cultures in disposing people to receive the message of Jesus.

But what about other apprehensions of beauty? Does the *via pulchritudinis* cross that terrain, too? Recall this paragraph from the 2006 statement, which expresses seemingly a priori doubts likely to preempt two-way travel on the *via pulchritudinis*:

> All cultures are not equally open to the transcendent and welcoming of Christian Revelation. Not all expressions of beauty—or moments which pretend to be so—favour an acceptance of the message of Christ and the intuition of His divine beauty. As their artistic expressions and aesthetic manifestations are marked by sin, cultures can attract and imprison one's attention until it folds in on itself creating new forms of idolatry.

Above I noted that this statement is vague enough that any culture could be the subject of assessment here, not just cultures without long Christian heritages. In every culture, the beautiful must be assessed in accord with norms regarding true and integral beauty. Yes, but here I add that the authors are clearly thinking of a reception by the non-Christian of the Christian mystery in terms of the beauty of Christ, which in turn will redeem what may in some imperfect way be beautiful in those non-Christian traditions. Some cultures are not ready to receive this beauty; perhaps their own aesthetic standards are an obstacle to the reception of the beauty.

In "The Task and the Structure of a Theological Aesthetics," cited earlier, Balthasar moves quickly to abrupt judgment on other traditions, and his enumeration of what are to him their very apparent flaws: "the religious and aesthetic enthusiasms of extra-Biblical religions with all their empty systems of divine epiphanies and avatars," their "distortions and confusions," and the "ineffective rhetoric" of an *eros* that remains incomplete because "it excludes God's redemptive grace"[27] (123). Though the beautiful subsists in the particular, Balthasar speaks abstractly and without any examples whatsoever of what he indicts here. Rather, his judgment is a priori: the distorted and ineffective "is the most man's religious eros can attain to once one excludes redemptive grace."[28] He thus adheres closely to a divine and Christian beauty, available to others, but not reflecting on what we might see, receive, as beauty approaches us from other sources. The beautiful in other religions can never be truly beautiful.

But surely we can do better than this. The *via pulchritudinis* is hardly a fresh or promising way forward, if the presence of the beautiful in other faiths—by paths that cross into territories not our own—is ruled out in advance. Pope Francis encourages us to think more productively. As we have seen, in *Evangelii Gaudium*, he invites us to think more expansively and generously of a variety of cultures: "We must be bold enough to discover new signs and new symbols, new flesh to embody and communicate the word, and different forms of beauty which are valued in different cultural settings, including those unconventional modes of beauty which may mean little to the evangelizers, yet prove particularly attractive for others."[29] If there is to be this aesthetic exchange and communication, we need to be able to apprehend and honor the beautiful in the other *religious* tradition as we encounter it, learning to apprehend there what is to us "unconventional" and perhaps inaccessible by the paths of the true and the good. And this is a mandate to learn of beauty by traveling the *via pulchritudinis* in another religious tradition.

An Encounter with the Beautiful in the Hindu Tradition

While I cannot spell out here a theology of beauty according to Hinduism, much less world religions more broadly, we can explore in some detail traces of a way or ways of beauty in Hinduism, the topic of this panel. Since beauty exists not in theory, but in the particular, it is advisable here to forgo tracing the concept of beauty in the Hindu and Sanskrit contexts, and instead offer just a single pellucid instance of the *via pulchritudinis* in Hinduism.[30] Turning to a text of meditative practice, focused entirely on divine beauty, is the most efficacious way to proceed here: the appropriately entitled *Saundarya Lahari* (*Flood of Beauty*). The *Saundarya Lahari* is a Hindu poetic text of 100 verses, often attributed to the great Vedanta theologian Sankara. By its name—*saundarya-lahari*, flood of beauty—we know that the 100 verses are signally about beauty. The hymn puts a beautiful goddess before us, for contemplation, and charts a path through bliss, to beauty, to Devi. By tradition, the *Saundarya Lahari* contains two floods, an interior—the divine within us—flood of bliss (*ananda-lahari*), and then an exterior—the divine beyond us—flood of beauty (*saundarya-lahari*):[31]

1–7	Opening meditation
8–41	*Flood of bliss*: Devi in relation to the tantric tradition ("The Flood of Bliss")
42–91	*Flood of beauty*: Meditation on her, head to toe ("The Flood of Beauty")
92–95	Climax, attainment
96–100	Concluding meditation and prayer

Let us consider each flood in turn, with an eye toward how the one leads us to the other.

On the Flood of Bliss

The Flood of Bliss reconfigures the tantric world to ensure that no truths or goods block the way to focusing on her, the beautiful one. It is a preparation, defending a tantric bhakti, in which, then, it makes sense to say that contemplating her can become the primary thing. Verses 8–41 include a complex yet discernible progression:

1. Meditating on her tantric identity, in the chakras and the yantra of triangles that is the Sri Chakra (8–14)
2. The power of meditating on her (15–22)
3. Devi, the gods, and Siva (23–31)
4. Setting up the contemplation (32–34)
5. The contemplation of Devi, in the chakras (34–41)

The point of this first Flood is to make the case for her supremacy, with respect to ordinary deities, of course, but also in relation to the entire apparatus of esoteric meditation, including the chakras, the secret syllables of her name, the Sri Chakra (a geometric configuration of her person and face). Even her consort Siva is likewise put in his place in relation to her greater reality. Devi, this beautiful goddess, is supreme. In the Flood of Bliss, we can detect three transformations: the spiritual-material (from the ordinary body to the charged power points that are the chakras), the auditory (from ordinary names to her holy mantra name), and the visual (from her visible appearance to the Sri Chakra). These transformations elaborate the initial insight of verse 1, that Devi is not primarily a mythically imagined expender of power as is her spouse but, instead, Power itself.

Let us take just the first transformation as our example. In the Flood of Bliss, Devi is situated with respect to the chakras, material/spiritual centers of power usually located within the (human) body at specific locations: anus (*muladhara*), genitals (*svadhisthana*),

navel (*manipura*), heart (*anahata*), throat (*visuddhi*), and brow (*ajña*).
Above them, and as the point toward which the goddess energy rises
(as the *kundalini* serpent), is an opening at the top of the head, the
thousand-petaled lotus (*sahasrara*) and the ultimate point of transcendent power. It is not clear whether these chakras are established
as points in Devi's own body or simply as centers of energy within
her wider domain; perhaps both. But this traditional knowledge is
evoked not for its own sake or merely to warn us about the com-
plexity of *tantra* and its accessibility to the few, but to assert Devi's
superiority over *tantra* and its universe. *Tantra* is powerful and complex; Devi is still greater, and it all comes to completion in her:[32]

> *You pierce earth in the muladhara chakra, water in the*
>   *manipura chakra,*
> *Fire in the svadhisthana chakra, wind in the anahata*
>   *chakra and the ether above that, and*
> *Mind in the chakra between the brows.*
> *Thus you pierce the entire kula path and then take plea-*
>   *sure with your Lord*
> *In the secrecy of the thousand-petaled lotus. (9)*
> *You sprinkle the evolved world with a stream of nectar*
>   *flowing from beneath your feet, and*
> *From the resplendent abundance of the nectar moon*
> *You descend to your own place, making yourself a serpent*
>   *of three and a half coils, and*
> *There you sleep again in the cave deep within the founda-*
>   *tion. (10)*

Verse 14 indicates her superiority to the elements and presumably
to the chakras. Passing them by, one seeks her feet:

> *Fifty-six rays in earth, fifty-two in water, sixty-two in fire,*
> *Fifty-four in air, seventy-two in the heavens, sixty-four in*
>   *the mind:*
> *But far above them all are your lotus feet. (14)*

She is beyond the lotuses taken to symbolize the chakras, and in the end salvation depends simply on viewing her:

> *Slender as a streak of lightning, the essence of sun, moon,*
>   *and fire;*
> *Though seated in the great forest of lotuses, you stand high*
>   *above even the six lotuses;*
> *If great souls in whose minds impurity and illusion are*
>   *obliterated look upon you,*
> *They gain a flood of highest delight.* (21)

In verses 36–41, the chakras are described as belonging to her. In them, Siva and the lesser consort reside. The chakra physiology, a physical-psychological-spiritual symbiosis, is accepted as subsumed within her larger and personal reality.

In a Christian theological way of speaking, we might say that the Flood of Bliss is not only asserting that she is the source and site of bliss, but also that she is transcendent over, and free with respect to, even the concepts, images, and practices of *tantra*. However powerful *tantra*'s conceptions of the divine within the body may be, she is also beyond those constrictions. More simply: she is a Person who, with her consort Siva, is accessible to whoever will come to her and take refuge at her feet.

On the Flood of Beauty

The challenge, then, is how one is to reach her: what is the *via*? It is a way of beauty, and this is the program of the second major part of the text, the Flood of Beauty (42–91), an extended meditation on her beauty, her *forma*. For it is all about her, the beautiful one, and so one contemplates Devi in an extraordinarily detailed manner that takes up fifty verses, beginning with the crown on her head, and ending at her feet.[33] Elements of this contemplation include:

1. The long contemplation of her, from head to toe;

2. Emphasis on the concrete, particular;
3. Full, spiritual bodiliness, gendered, but also physical, bodily sites contextualized by myth, filled with deities and dramatizations;
4. Culturally determined beauty;
5. Beautiful in a stylized way, with poetic tropes, deliberately remaining on the surface.

The entire Flood Beauty is an extended contemplation of Devi's form, but the viewer is not in charge, and Devi is not merely an object of vision. To view her is not merely to gaze at an available object of scrutiny, but to encounter her, to be drawn into her world.

Here, by way of example, is the opening section of the Flood of Beauty, verses 42–46:

> *If someone praises your golden crown inlaid with every*
> *jeweled celestial gem—*
> *O daughter of the snow-capped mountain—*
> *Won't he imagine it as the crescent moon spread manifold*
> *By the luster radiating from the varied gems set there—*
> *or as Sunasira's bow? (42)*
> *Blessed one, your locks of hair, thick, shining and soft, are*
> *a field of blue lilies in bloom:*
> *May they scatter the dark enveloping us.*
> *Even the sumanas flowers from trees in the garden of*
> *Vala's slayer dwell here*
> *In order to realize their own fragrance—or so I imagine.*
> *(43)*
> *Wearing red as intense as a ray of the newly rising sun*
> *Held hostage by enemy hordes of the dark's most powerful*
> *elements:*
> *Such is the flow of the line parting your hair;*
> *Like a surging torrent is the flood of beauty from your face:*
> *May it set forth our welfare. (44)*
> *Surrounded by curls resembling young bees,*

> *Your face mocks the luster of the lotus, while*
> *Your smile—attractive, delicate, fragrant—and*
> *The sparkle of your teeth intoxicate those honey bees,*
> *The eyes of Memory's destroyer. (45)*
> *I think of your forehead, flawless in its loveliness and*
> 　　*radiance,*
> *As a second crescent adorning your brow;*
> *Placed there out of order but then becoming one,*
> *Together these crescents, seamed with a smear of nectar,*
> 　　*turn into the full moon goddess. (46)*

These verses—and all that follow—are both meditations on details of her physical form and richly contextualized cultural and religious readings of that form. One might say that at issue is intelligent beauty, a beauty that is informed by the true and even the good.

Where Contemplation Leads

But the process is not the goal; there is a culmination that alone can satisfy the practitioner who desires most deeply the beauty of Devi. The progression of the Flood of Beauty maps a descent toward the final goal. The climax is in self-surrender at her feet, indeed, under them, even in them:

> *Ever giving wealth to the helpless according to their desire,*
> *Quickly scattering honey, a mass of beauty,*
> *As blessed as a bouquet of mandara flowers, such are your*
> 　　*feet:*
> *May I plunge my life into them like the six-footed bee, my*
> 　　*senses my feet. (90)*

Devi's feet like flowers, since both are fragrant and auspicious: in a poetic manner, they *are* flowers. In turn, the poet's six senses, which enjoy her feet, are portrayed as the six feet of the bee delving into the flower as the object of its delight. We see a graded comparison here, from flower to the enjoyment of the flower, the poet's six senses as bees, the bees as indulging their pleasure. By the mention of his own self and his senses, the poet implicitly invites the listener, after the entire Ocean of Beauty, to enter deeply and with pleasure into the experience of Devi.

The final verses of the *Saundarya Lahari*, 98–100, are best taken as words of praise in her presence, there at her feet. These last verses catch the spirit of the encounter:

> *I desire wisdom, Mother, so tell me,*
> *When I shall drink that essence of chewed betel juice red-*
> *   dened with lac dye,*
> *The water that washed your feet,*
> *The essence of betel from Vani's lotus mouth*
> *That makes poets even of those mute by birth? (98)*
> *Whoever is devoted to you will play with Sarasvati and*
> *   Laksmi, rival Vidhi and Hari,*
> *Have a beautiful form that melts even Pleasure's chastity,*
> *Live a long life free from the bonds that bind beasts, and*
> *Enjoy the taste known as "highest bliss." (99)*
> *Illumining the sun with small flames,*
> *Bathing the moon whence nectar flows with drops from*
> *   moonstones,*
> *Satisfying the ocean with its own drops of water—*
> *And me too, praising you with your own words,*
> *O Mother of all words. (100)*

By these words the destination is both reached and longed for. And so, the *Saundarya Lahari*, long before the modern popularization of the way of beauty in the Catholic community, had mapped and popularized a very similar route indeed.

If we take seriously that the *Saundarya Lahari* is a text of theological and spiritual practice, 8–41 can be said to prepare for 42–91, by showing her supremacy, and emphasizing that attention must be paid to her, exclusively. This ordering—bliss, then beauty—is counter-intuitive in a way, since it means that the complexities of tantric practice, the complex geometrical design of the Sri Chakra, and the situated power centers that are the chakras are all beneath her feet, which are reached most easily by contemplating her beauty. And if so, they are to be superseded by the loving and long contemplation of her beauty, a contemplation that reaches from her head down to her feet. This is surely a way of beauty, is it not? While traveling such a path would not therefore be necessarily simple, access to it seems simpler than by way of *veritas* and *bonum*.

A Comparative Aesthetics of the Beautiful

My hope is that this brief excursion into a Hindu example of the beautiful, and indeed a truly Hindu *via pulchritudinis*, plausibly indicates that the experience, practice, and theology of the beautiful is not a Christian preserve. Enlivening our sense of the *via pulchritudinis* in Christian tradition should prompt us to welcome examples from other traditions that, similarly pedagogical in form, invite us to step beyond the truth and the good as interreligious categories and learn from the beautiful across religious boundaries. By the logic of the beautiful, which is not merely subordinate to the true or the good, we can and should explore learning the *via pulchritudinis* in accord with the *Saundarya Lahari*, too.

Here, too, we must proceed slowly, since hasty generalizations, even benevolent ones, do not aid our overall project, and I close by proposing two strategies. First, let us now return to Balthasar, to map the achievement of the *Saundarya Lahari* in accord with his categories. As we saw earlier, he makes a series of distinctions that categorize component dynamics of beauty. These can, for the sake of our explorations, be applied to Devi as presented in the *Saundarya Lahari*, in a chiastic ordering, a–b and then b–a, that draws in both the Flood of Bliss and Flood of Beauty sections of the hymn:

a. Balthasar: *forma*, in which the beautiful is materially grasped, even subjected to numerical calculation, and yet at the same time, reaching into the deep, arousing delight; this is the sacrament of depth, and of the self-revealing Being, self-representation:

Application: *in the Flood of Bliss*, even mathematical calculations are used to locate Devi with respect to tantric tradition yet beyond it too; these practices present to us Devi's formal reality, the fact of her beauty.

b. Balthasar: *lumen*, which turns us to the visual, as this radiance reaches the eyes of our minds, and leads us to a mediating second vision, rapture, transport. This is a seeing, beholding, perception of the invisible now made visible, an apprehension of the splendor of the mystery that evokes an enrapturing *eros*:

Application: *in the Flood of Beauty*, the mysteries previously presented with a certain abstract precision related to forms are now presented in vivid visibility, in the details of her gracious presence, as she looks to those who love her. This is why it is important to note that in each verse in the "Flood of Beauty," she is active, drawing the devotee into her bountiful and beautiful world.

b. Balthasar: *a theory of vision*, such as regards the perception of the form of God's self-revelation:

Application: *in the Flood of Beauty*, we find a seeing that is nuanced and refined with respect to her self-presentation in her material reality. Yet this, too, is further signified in terms of natural and mythic connections, which serve to intensify her self-revelation to those contemplating her.

a. Balthasar: *a theory of rapture*, such as regards the incarnation of God's glory and the consequent elevation of the human to participate in that glory:

Application: *in the Flood of Bliss*, we can make sense of the precisely detailed location of her with respect to the angles of the Sri Chakra and in the chakras within the body. This is nothing but a practice by which to see how the human, by insight and self-knowledge, is drawn into her larger reality even as she inhabits human reality as well.[34]

While this correlation is provisional and to some extent artificial, it helps us to open up the complex and dense dynamics of the *Saundarya Lahari* according to Balthasar's aesthetics, so apt to appreciation of the way of beauty promoted in the documents cited at the start of this essay. Not only are there gestures toward the beautiful in the Hindu tradition—beautiful nature, beautiful images, beautiful myths—such as a Christian visitor might appreciate at first glance, but there are also intentionally designed and intensified mappings of beauty—and the concomitant desire, rapture, encounter—as a theologically useful frame in which to speak effectively of Devi.

Receiving This Great Beauty: Seeing Her with the Virgin Mary

Second, by this excursion into the world of the *Saundarya Lahari*, I have taken rather literally the challenge to travel the *via pulchritudinis*, recognizing beauty as a bridge between religions that might facilitate encounters and engagements that might not be possible by calculations of truth or the good. Given the strong sense in ecclesial and theological documents that beauty is a powerful manner of access to the Christian revelation, my contribution has been to ask whether the beautiful in the Hindu tradition can be an entrée, for us who are Christian, to better receive the Hindu. So let us conclude by assessing the prospects for the reception of the *Saundarya Lahari* into the Catholic context.

Because she is supreme, Devi is neither a product of *tantra* nor entirely ruled by its strictures. She can show herself to whoever wishes to see her. Similarly, here, one might draw on Balthasar and others to insist that truth, configured and constrained by one or another series of conceptualizations, not be allowed to predetermine what is possible for and by the intuitive, dramatic, and graced apprehension of the beautiful: the *forma* and the *lumen*, the vision and the rapture, have an aesthetic logic to them that is not merely a side road into the *via veritatis*. However, we grasp the truth and the good in Christian tradition, and expect them to extend interreligiously, the reality of the divine, luminous and beautiful, is always greater still.

This way forward allows beauty to encounter beauty by taking seriously both the goddess text and Marian parallels accessible not first by theology but by a recognition of the beautiful. In my 2005 book, I recognized that by a way of truth there would be no chance of an easy path from a Christian theology, even a feminist theology, to Devi, and from there back to Christian theology. I chose instead to stay on the way of beauty, juxtaposing the *Saundarya Lahari* with the Marian hymn *Stabat Mater*,[35] the bliss of the beautiful encountering the tragedy of that same beautiful.

The *Stabat Mater* offers a loving contemplation of Jesus the Crucified in its first verses, but gradually and more intensely contemplates and encounters Mary, who stands and grieves at the cross, in a vision accessible only to those willing to look and to see in a steady fashion:

> *The sorrowful mother was standing in tears*
> *Near the cross as her son was hanging there, and*
> *Through her sighing soul that shared his sadness and was*
> *   sorrowing,*
> *Pierced a sword.* (1)
> *O how sad and afflicted*
> *Was that blessed mother of the only-begotten,*
> *As she was bewailing and sorrowing and trembling,*
> *As she stood looking upon the punishments of her re-*
> *   nowned son.* (2)
> *Who are those who would not weep*
> *Should they look upon the mother of Christ in such*
> *   torment?*

> *Who would be unable to share the sadness of the holy*
> *mother,*
> *Should they contemplate her sorrowing with her son?* (3)
> *She looked upon Jesus suffering torments,*
> *Beaten down with whips for the sins of his own people,*
> *She looked upon her own sweet child, dying, abandoned,*
> *Until he sent forth His spirit.* (4)

While Mary's *beauty* is not on our minds in that terrible scene, there is no doubt about the compelling nature and efficacy of a long, loving, and chastened contemplation of her standing there. We cannot look away.

Verses 5–10 of the hymn are addressed directly to Mary, for in contemplation lies the way to the salvation now opened in her son, who has died:

> *O Mother, font of love,*
> *Make me feel the force of sorrow, that I might lament*
> *with you,*
> *Make my heart burn in loving Christ, God,*
> *That I might be pleasing to Him.* (5)
> *Holy Mother, do this—*
> *In my heart firmly fix the wounds of the crucified,*
> *Share with me the punishments*
> *Your so worthy, so wounded Son suffered for me.* (6)

The *via pulchritudinis* is a way of learning, and by word, contemplation, and vision, we need to take the time to travel through examples like this, between Mary and Devi. Seeing Mary, seeing Devi.

Beauty is not jealous, but rejoices in the beautiful. The beauty of Christ is light, but it ought not blind us to the beauty of the Other. It illumines rather than overshadows, and does not obscure that beautiful Other. The awakening of desire for the beautiful has an objectivity that is neither slight nor entirely in our control, and perhaps at first neither to our liking.[36]

If we place this contemplation within the purview of efficacious seeing, and allow for a diverse palette of what we see, including the beautiful and the sorrowful, then from Devi, contemplated in the *Saundarya Lahari*, back to Mary in the *Stabat Mater* is indeed a way of beauty, riveting in its own way and not to be blocked by doctrinal concerns familiar on the *via veritatis*. Traveling this other, less traveled path is neither easy nor predictable, but it seems a necessary and truly new complement to ways that suit our minds and morals. Is this not the call of Pope Francis, and the hope underlying this volume and the conference that preceded it?

Notes

1.   New York: Oxford University Press, 2005.
2.   I say "modern" theology, since, despite the use of Latin, the *via pulchritudinis* seems not to have a premodern lineage. I have not (yet) found any earlier use of the term *"via pulchritudinis"* than Souriau's essay, and he gives no sources; none of the later documents below refers to Souriau's work. I welcome instances of the term *via pulchritudinis* from before 1959.
3.   *Dieu*, n.s. 3 (juillet/septembre 1959): 333–40.
4.   Souriau, 33; my translation from the French.
5.   From Section III of the Latin, in my own translation.
6.   Worthy of note, too, is a section of Pope Benedict's brief remarks on the documentary film *Art And Faith*—Via Pulchritudinis: "One could say that the artistic patrimony of Vatican City constitutes a kind of great 'parable' through which the Pope speaks to men and women of every part of the world, and so from many cultures and religions, people who might never read one of his Discourses or Homilies. This brings to mind what Jesus said to his disciples: to you the secret of the Kingdom of God has been given, but to those on the 'outside' everything is said 'in parables' (Mk 4:10–12). The language of art is a language of parables, endowed with a special universal openness: the *'via Pulchritudinis'* is a path to guide the mind and the heart to the Eternal, to elevate them to the heights of God." (Address given at the Vatican, October 25, 2012).

7. The notion of "weak thought" can be traced most obviously to the writings of Gianni Vattimo. See, for instance, Gianni Vattimo and Santiago Zabala, "'Weak Thought' and the Reduction of Violence: A Dialogue with Gianni Vattimo" (Yaakov Mascetti, trans.), *Common Knowledge* 8.3 (2002): 452–63. There, Vattimo says that "thinking is no longer demonstrative but rather edifying, it has become in that restricted sense weaker" (452).

8. II.1.

9. Ibid.

10. Ibid.

11. See also *Doctrinal Note on Some Aspects of Evangelization* (2007): "Although non-Christians can be saved through the grace which God bestows in 'ways known to him,' the Church cannot fail to recognize that such persons are lacking a tremendous benefit in this world: to know the true face of God and the friendship of Jesus Christ, God-with-us. Indeed 'there is nothing more *beautiful* than to be surprised by the Gospel, by the encounter with Christ. There is nothing more beautiful than to know him and to speak to others of our friendship with him.' The revelation of the fundamental truths about God, about the human person and the world, is a great good for every human person, while living in darkness without the truths about ultimate questions is an evil and is often at the root of suffering and slavery which can at times be grievous" (n. 7).

12. Ibid.

13. We can note here also "The New Evangelization for the Transmission of the Christian Faith" (2012). This document notes the growing interest in the Church in the way of beauty as deeply akin to faith. "The knowledge coming from beauty, as in the liturgy, is able to take on a visible reality in its originally-intended role as a manifestation of the universal communion to which humanity and every person is called by God.... This fundamental role of beauty urgently needs to be restored in Christianity. In this regard, the new evangelization has an important role to play. The Church recognizes that human beings cannot exist without beauty. For Christians, beauty is found within the Paschal Mystery, in the transparency of the reality of Christ" (n. 157). If "for Christians" the universally appealing beauty is discovered in the Paschal Mystery, the implication is or should be

that "for non-Christians" beauty might be discovered in other places, including the liturgies of those traditions.

14. A note here points to Proposition 20 of the 13th Ordinary General Assembly of the Synod of Bishops, 2012: "In the New Evangelization, there should be a particular attention paid to the way of beauty: Christ, the 'Good Shepherd' (cf. *Jn* 10:11) is the Truth in person, the beautiful revelation in sign, pouring himself out without measure. It is important to give testimony to the young who follow Jesus, not only of his goodness and truth, but also of the fullness of his beauty. As Augustine affirmed, 'it is not possible to love what is not beautiful' (*Confessions*, Bk IV, 13.20). Beauty attracts us to love, through which God reveals to us his face in which we believe." The document goes on to emphasize that beauty and the sacred arts are essential to priestly formation, catechesis, and the liturgy.

15. n. 167.

16. n. 167.

17. For a salutary critique of the *via pulchritudinis* with respect to Marian theology, see Johann G. Roten, S.M., "Mary and the Way of Beauty," *Marian Studies* (Annual Publication of the Mariological Society of America, Marian Library, Dayton University) 49 (1998): 109–27. See also Sr. Thomas Mary McBride, O.P., "Beauty, Contemplation, and the Virgin Mary," <http://www.christendom-awake. org/pages/mcbride/beauty.htm>, and Carolyn Pirtle, "The Via Pulchritudinis, Fauré's Requiem, and the Eucharist," *Logos* 19, no. 2 (2016): 127–49.

18. Certainly, other theologians can offer bases for a consideration of the way of beauty. Even among the documents I cited earlier, the essays by Souriau (1959) and Roten (1998) give us starting points for grounding the ecclesial statements, and if we do not become distracted from the practical purpose of this *via pulchritudinis* by theorizing beauty, a still wider set of studies would be appropriate.

19. Note 12 in Hans Urs von Balthasar, *Herrlichkeit: Eine theologishe Ästhetik, I: Schau der Gestalt*, 1961. English translation taken from *The Glory of the Lord, A Theological Aesthetics, I. Seeing the Form* (Edinburgh: T. & T. Clark, 1982), 18–19.

20. *The Glory of the Lord*, 18–19.

21. Ibid., 120.

22. Ibid., 121.

23. Ibid., 124.

24. Ibid., 122. In elaborating these points, and to highlight how "man's transport to God" grounds the Aristotelian and Neo-Platonic notion of that which is loved "in an antecedent and condescending divine *ekstasis* in which God is drawn out of himself by *eros* into creation, revelation, and Incarnation," Balthasar offers an exegesis of a passage from the *Divine Names* of Dionysius (122–24). For Dionysius, God is active and dynamic, stepping outside himself, leaving his "transcendent throne" "to dwell within the heart of all things in accordance with his super-essential and ecstatic power whereby he nonetheless does not leave himself behind." God is, according to Dionysius, zealous in his *eros* toward all beings, even spurring "them on to search for him zealously with a yearning *eros.*" According to Dionysius, "both to possess *eros* and to love erotically belong to everything Good and Beautiful, and *eros* has its primal roots in the Beautiful and the Good: *eros* exists and comes into being only through the Beautiful and the Good." But Balthasar feels obliged to assert that Dionysius too must be purified: "Delete from this text, if you will, everything which appears too Neo-Platonic" (ibid., 123). Is this a deletion of what is not true, thus bringing Truth, the third transcendental into play?

25. Ibid., 125.

26. Ibid., 126.

27. *Glory of the Lord*, 123.

28. Ibid.

29. *Evangelii Gaudium*, n. 167.

30. I should first of all admit that it would be a very interesting and long detour to think more specifically about beauty in the Hindu context, or about the meanings of beauty (*saundarya*) in Hindu tradition in general. A good introductory volume on the topic is Venkatarama Raghavan's *The Concept of the Beautiful in Sanskrit Literature* (Madras: Kuppuswami Shastri Research Institute, 1988).

31. In the following pages, I use *Saundarya Lahari* as the title of the entire work, and "Flood of Beauty" (*saundarya lahari*) to indicate its section of visualization, 42–91.

32. The translations of verses from the *Saundarya Lahari* given here and below are my own, but (as indicated in *Divine Mother, Blessed*

Mother), they are indebted to previous translations noted in the bibliography of that volume. See also that book for further explanation of words in the verses, etc.

33. On this manner of head-to-toe, or toe-to-head meditation, see also Steven P. Hopkins, *Singing the Body of God: The Hymns of Vedantadesika in Their South Indian Tradition* (New York: Oxford University Press, 2002), chapter 5, "A God from Toe to Crown."

34. The "theory of rapture" might also be applied to the Flood of Beauty section of the text.

35. Here, too, I use my own translation which, as noted in *Divine Mother, Blessed Mother*, is indebted to older translations of the hymn.

36. We can hardly avoid a certain subjectivity here, even if we do not reduce beauty to merely individual tastes. It is fair to notice and ponder the cultural rootedness of beauty: with all her ornaments, her vividly exaggerated features highlight the challenge of the extravagant poetry of the text, and a culturally specific language of beauty, even aside from theological problems that might arise. Perhaps, to put it too simply, she is not beautiful enough for us, or she is not beautiful enough in a Western manner. Perhaps the *Saundarya Lahari* is not to our taste; perhaps we find the Virgin Mary beautiful, a spiritual beauty radiating through the material form, but not Devi. Mary is familiar to us, after all. But even so, it may also be because we are not sufficiently educated so as to be able to appreciate the subtlety of the verses, and the elegant practices by which the author brings out the multi-dimensional nature of her every feature. We may not appreciate the allusions we see in the texts, and the tropes of the Sanskrit tradition may remain stubbornly foreign to us. The images of Devi in the *Saundarya Lahari* may seem odd or exaggerated to us at first, if we are not part of its aesthetic culture. If so, they will never do justice to her dramatic, participatory beauty until we enter upon that culture. Patience is required, and the work of appropriating the text. The larger problem, of course, may be one of truth. It is almost always thought that there is no room in the Catholic mind or heart for actual Goddesses. Whatever the beauty of this or that image of Devi, it cannot be or become—the skeptical theologian will insist—that beauty, in its full, personal, and interpersonal form, may not become a *via pulchritudinis* that the Christian can travel. Truth

may again stand as a roadblock, barring what the eye sees and the heart moves toward impulsively, ecstatically. Perhaps one cannot, as a Catholic, travel the way of beauty without first and last traveling the way of truth.

Works Cited

Balthasar, Hans Urs von. *The Glory of the Lord: A Theological Aesthetics, I. Seeing the Form.* Edinburgh: T. & T. Clark, 1982. (German edition: Herrlichkeit: Eine theologishe Ästhetik, I: Schau der Gestalt, 1961.)

Clooney, Francis X., S.J. *Divine Mother, Blessed Mother: Hindu Goddesses and the Virgin Mary.* New York: Oxford University Press, 2005.

Hopkins, Steven P. *Singing the Body of God: The Hymns of Vedantadesika in Their South Indian Tradition.* New York: Oxford University Press, 2002.

McBride, Sr. Thomas Mary, O.P. "Beauty, Contemplation, and the Virgin Mary," 2002 <http://www.christendom-awake.org/pages/mcbride/beauty.htm>, accessed September 16, 2017.

Pirtle, Carolyn. "The Via Pulchritudinis, Fauré's Requiem, and the Eucharist." *Logos* 19, no. 2 (2016): 127–49.

Raghavan, Venkatarama. *The Concept of the Beautiful in Sanskrit Literature.* Madras: Kuppuswami Shastri Research Institute, 1988.

Roten, Johann G., S.M. "Mary and the Way of Beauty." Marian Studies (*Annual Publication of the Mariological Society of America,* Marian Library, Dayton University) 49 (1998): 109–27.

Souriau, Étienne. "Via Pulchritudinis" *Dieu* n.s. 3 (juillet/septembre 1959): 333–40.

Vattimo, Gianni, and Santiago Zabala. "'Weak Thought' and the Reduction of Violence: A Dialogue with Gianni Vattimo." Translated by Yaakov Mascetti. *Common Knowledge* 8, no. 3 (2002): 452–63.

Chapter Nine

THE MYSTERY OF THE INFINITE IN THE HINDU SPIRITUALITY AND THEOLOGY OF NON-DUALITY

Bradley Malkovsky, University of Notre Dame

Preliminary Remarks

Hinduism, which is really a cluster of religions rather than a single unified entity with one creed for all, is notoriously difficult to summarize. This is especially true with regard to Hindu views of the divine. Though the overwhelming majority of Hindus orient their lives to the ultimate mystery, the particular way they understand this reality, its presence to the world, and its various activities differs enormously from one group to another. One finds in Hindu thought not only strict monotheisms, but also various brands of polytheism, and very often one discovers the belief in a supreme reality co-existing with lesser gods. As to the nature of this ultimate reality, one finds belief in divine personhood, mercy, and love, but also teachings advocating a non-relational impersonal Absolute. This fluid acceptance of deity is one of the most noticeable features of Hindu faith and, for outsiders, one of the most confusing. But one might also regard the idea that there are many legitimate and complementary ways of thinking about the divine as one of Hinduism's greatest strengths and attractions.

Responding to the Christian
Charge of Idolatry and Polytheism

The Christian outsider, often enough ignorant of Hindu faith, is sometimes quick to brand Hinduism as essentially idolatrous, superstitious, and polytheistic. A closer look, however, reveals a quite different picture. The long-standing Christian accusation of Hindu idol worship, for example, turns out in many—perhaps most—cases not to be a worship of the finite as such, but rather the worship of the transcendent divine as freely dwelling *within* the material of the finite. Here Hindu worship before physical objects should be seen as the proper human response to the free and deliberate "descent" of the merciful and all-powerful Lord into the physical realm (*arcavatara*), whereby God graciously draws near to the devotee, much like the event of the Incarnation in Christian belief. God, who is already present to the world as its hidden ground, now becomes present to the devotee in a more visible, tangible, and interpersonal way. This new interpersonal presence of the divine through the medium of finite physical objects enables a deeper spiritual communion between God and devotee to take place. Thus, what had appeared to be idolatry, from the initial Christian point of view, turns out rather to be a particular Hindu version of sacramental presence.

As to an alleged Hindu polytheism that would eclipse or obscure monotheism, though I believe it does exist to some extent among Hindus, especially at the popular level, it is not clear just how widespread this belief is.[1] Further, we might ask why exactly Christians have so readily regarded Hinduism as essentially polytheistic. There are three reasons, I think, for this widespread assessment. The first is that many Christians are unfamiliar with the notion that in Hinduism there are many legitimate names given to the one creator God, even within a single Hindu theological tradition.[2] These names do not refer to many gods, but are rather many names for the one God. Second, a person only superficially acquainted with Hinduism may be unable to distinguish these names for the one creator God from the many names and images for the multitude of minor deities or gods that also exist, many of whom are represented in very different ways in stone and wood. The third reason why Christians are often quick to judge Hinduism as being polytheistic is that they are often preconditioned by their reading of the Bible to expect to find the idolatrous worship of "false gods" in other religions. Biblical warnings against polytheism and worship of "other gods" are frequently laden with severe threats of divine punishment. It is all too easy, then, to misread the many Hindu representations of the divine as a result of this Biblical preconditioning. The situation is not helped by the fact that Hindus themselves often refer to their material depictions of the Absolute as "idols," though in the Hindu context the term does not have the negative connotations normally associated with Biblical religion.

Certainly, in the many *formal theologies and philosophies* of various Hindu schools over the centuries, in contrast to popular Hinduism, a polytheism that would simply obscure awareness of the supreme reality is largely absent.[3] One finds instead an *enormous variety of monotheisms*, that is, complementary and at times competing theologies extolling Vishnu, Shiva, or the Goddess (Shakti, Kali, Durga, et al.) as a grace-giving and merciful creator, each theology and divine name expressing in its own unique way a particular understanding of how the one God relates to the world both ontologically and soteriologically. Here I am not talking about various names for God from within a single theological tradition, but rather understandings and names for God across many Hindu traditions (*sampradayas*). These traditions share much conceptually, despite their marked differences. Though the theologies and names for the Lord may be different, many of the same attributes for the one personal God are found across a broad spectrum of Hindu theologies. Hence, the supreme Lord, regardless of sectarian profession, is consistently understood to be infinite, eternal, all-powerful, omniscient, all-pervasive, and interactive, responding mercifully to the entreaties of the yearning devotee.

The great majority of Hindus, then, like Christians, believe in a merciful and loving creator. They also recognize the value of compassion as essential to authentic spirituality, they believe that God has appeared in creaturely form for the benefit of all humanity, and they see liberating union or communion with the divine as the final goal of all existence. From my Christian perspective I find all this to be commendable, even admirable. There are nevertheless significant differences, to be sure, between Hindu and Christian teaching on the final goal and purpose of divine activity, as well as what means God uses to achieve this end. But that is not the focus of this paper.[4]

A Different Understanding of Reality

In addition to these many Hindu theologies and spiritualities that are oriented to the divine as Person and to which the great majority of Hindus subscribe, there is another Hindu approach that is quite different, one that contrasts markedly with both Christian and Hindu devotionalism and which is the main topic of this essay. Here the goal of the spiritual life is not love but enlightenment, the blissful awakening to the natural presence of the divine as one's very Self. This is a different experience of oneness than the oneness of love. The Sanskrit term for this oneness is *"advaita,"* literally "non-duality." The teaching of non-duality is embodied especially in a scripture-based theological and spiritual tradition called Advaita Vedanta. This tradition of wisdom and experience stretches back to ancient India and exists today both in India and in the Hindu diaspora. In what follows I will briefly summarize some basic features of this theological tradition. I hope to show how, despite a widely perceived belief that Hindu non-dualistic teaching is incompatible with Christian teaching and spirituality, it has been regarded by a number of Christians in recent times, especially by those living in India, as being not only compatible with Christian faith, but also as presenting a potentially valuable enrichment to Christian theology and spirituality. But, as we shall see, the compatibility of non-dualistic thought with Christian

theology will ultimately depend on the particular way one understands non-dualistic or advaitic ontology.

Upanishads and Advaita Vedanta

All Vedanta schools, of which there are many, attempt to articulate,
each in its own way, the true meaning of the Upanishads.[5] The
ontologies represented by these schools differ widely, so much so
that the name taken by each school identifies its particular way of
understanding the relation of the world to its transcendent source.[6]

The Upanishads themselves are a collection of ancient revealed
writings dated roughly 700–200 B.C.E. and which are based on oral
traditions that stretch back possibly several centuries earlier. Their
common spiritual teaching is that liberation from suffering comes
with right insight into the true nature of reality and self, in a shift
away from awareness filtered by ego, desire, fear, and delusion to an
awareness that is pure consciousness.

The Upanishads as a whole mark an important milestone in
Hindu spirituality in that they indicate a transition from a widely
practiced sacrificial ritualism to something more interior and
potentially more valuable: the cultivation of an awareness of a supreme, all-pervading reality that is the source and ultimately the
true goal of all human life. The name for this ultimate reality is
brahman. Brahman is infinite eternal being and pure consciousness. The awakening to *brahman* as one's true center or Self (*atman*)
brings perfect peace and bliss. The goal of Advaita practice is to
awaken to this deep serene awareness, which is untouched by life's
constant changes, its transient pleasures and fears, and thereby to
find true freedom. No longer identifying with body and mind, one
awakens to what one already is.

The reason why the many Vedantic schools, with their broad
spectrum of ontological positions about the relation of *brahman* to the world, can all base themselves on the Upanishads[7] is
because the Upanishads themselves do not present a unified or

monolithic ontology, despite their common focus on *brahman* as being the supreme and innermost reality of all things. The famous Indian historian of religion S. N. Dasgupta believed there to be no fewer than three main currents of ontology displayed in these texts.[8] The three ontologies appear to be contradictory when read without the help of a higher synthesis. When taken in isolation, however, the individual Upanishadic texts may appear to propound very different teachings about the relation of the world to its source. In some scriptural passages *brahman*, the ultimate ground of existence, is presented as the sole reality; the world is but a mere appearance or illusion. This will eventually become the position of mainstream Advaita Vedanta. One may also read verses in the Upanishads that seem to represent a pantheistic view of the universe. Finally, some Upanishadic verses appear to teach a sort of transcendental theism, in which *brahman* is regarded as a distinct world-governing creator and Lord. Many other interpretations of the Upanishads have been added over the centuries, as evidenced by the emergence of a great variety of competing Vedantic schools. This variety of philosophical and theological interpretations is an indication that the mysterious divine presence is not easy to grasp and conceptualize. Even when experienced in a mystical insight, it eludes all attempts at precise human articulation and does not easily translate into a single system of human thought. That is why, according to the Upanishads, it is more correct to say what the supreme reality is not (*neti neti*) than to say what it is. This approach, of course, is reminiscent of the *via negativa* of Christian theology.

Advaita Vedanta, then, means the "non-dualistic interpretation of the Upanishads." Among all Vedanta schools it is the one that has perhaps exercised the greatest influence on Hindu intellectual history. This is in large part due to Shankara (ca. 700 B.C.E.), who is Advaita Vedanta's most illustrious, but also its most controversial, theologian and defender. I shall return to Shankara in a bit for the purpose of using him as a springboard to reflect on two competing understandings of non-duality. But first I would like to examine one particular Upanishadic text, in order to show the richness and beauty but also the ambiguity of foundation texts that would bear witness to the mystery of the divine presence.

The Non-Duality of the World and Its Source

The notion of divine immanence is one of the hallmarks of Vedanta teaching. Its chronological starting point is the Upanishads. Among the Upanishads there are some passages that are especially well known for their praise of the Absolute that is manifested in and present to all things. One example is Shvetashvatara Upanishad 4.3–4. This Upanishad is fairly late, as far as the Upanishads go, probably appearing around 200 B.C.E. or perhaps a few centuries later. The fact that the supreme reality is addressed here as a "You" is striking, since the earliest Upanishads, appearing half a millennium or more before this particular Upanishad, did not tend to express the reality of *brahman* in such personalistic language.

This passage, like so many others in the Upanishads, uses ecstatic language to proclaim the wondrous presence of the divine to the world. This is not an exercise in systematic theology or philosophical thought or an apologetics intended to win a debate about the proper way to articulate the relation of the many to the One. It is rather an expression of amazement and wonder at the divine presence. The proclamation is intended to open the eyes of those individuals whose minds are already somewhat disposed to experience for themselves the oneness that is announced. The creator who is praised here is not a God who is removed or distant from the world. This is a transcendent source that is manifested in everything that is, yet always eludes our conceptual grasp. Nor is this creator one who is actively engaged with the world, calling people into a personal relationship or commanding them to do good and avoid evil. Though there are similarities between this Upanishad and the Psalms with regard to their teaching that all creation gives glory to God, there is a greater emphasis in this Upanishadic passage on the mystery of presence. The Psalms teach that the majesty and goodness of the creator are reflected in the gratuitous created nature of all things, such that all creation worships and praises the creator.[9] The Psalms, moreover, also maintain a very clear emphasis on the distinction between creator and creature. The creatorship and lordship of God is always the point of such Psalms. The teaching of Shvetashvatara Upanishad, by contrast, if it can be called a teaching at all, is more about the mysterious oneness or perhaps "not-two"-ness[10] of the creator and creation. Notice here the many assertions about the creator being closely linked to the created world:

> 3. You are the woman. You are the man. You are the youth and the maiden, too. You, as an old man, totter along with a staff. Taking birth, you have your faces everywhere.

> 4. You are the dark-blue moth, you are the green (parrot) with red eyes. You are (the cloud) with the lightning in its womb. You are the seasons and the seas. You, indeed, are without beginning. You exist as the Omnipresent, from whom have sprung all the worlds.

In this passage a hidden reality manifests itself, shining through the manifold forms of beauty, goodness, and power found in nature. This is not merely praise of nature's loveliness; it is at the same time and perhaps even more an expression of praise of the creator's miraculous presence in creation. The passage *announces* to the listener God's presence to the world without *explaining* it. God is at the same time both manifest and hidden in all earthly realities: in the faces and forms of human beings, in young and old, male and female, but also in the insect and bird, all the way up to the flash of lightning in a thunder cloud and in the vastness of the ocean. All things, great and small, not only express the invisible creator— as, for example, a work of art expresses something of the artist's mind and intention—but, even more, they reveal its living *presence*.

Brahman is identified with everything that exists, even with the passing of the seasons, and yet *brahman* is revealed to transcend everything in its own perfect mystery and being.

There is a sense of inexplicability in these verses that speak of the not-two-ness of creation and creator. There is wonder at existence itself, but also wonder at the disclosure of the supreme reality. Nevertheless, a doubt remains. Might such passages from the Shvetashvatara Upanishad be finally regarded as pantheism? Are God (*brahman*) and the world perhaps the very same reality? The language of these verses might suggest this. After all, the passage says that the creator *is* the world. "You are" all these things, "you are" all people, "you are" all of nature, "you are" all that exists. It is passages like these, as well as other famous passages such as "All this is *brahman*" (Chandogya Upanishad 3.14.1) that have led many non-Hindu readers to conclude that the Upanishads teach pantheism, that everything is purely and simply God, and that there is finally no real distinction between God and the world, after all. It has often been said by Christians, when first exposed to passages like Shvetashvatara Upanishad 4.3–4, that the Upanishads—and Hinduism in general—do not have a clear enough understanding of divine transcendence, since they take the world to be God.

Advaita Vedanta teaching, however, which is rooted in the Upanishads, is very clear that the Upanishads do not teach pantheism. The world is not simply God. *Brahman* is in many ways different from the world as well as transcendent to it. *Brahman* is the original and eternal reality, the transcendent ground of the visible changing world, changeless and limitless, utterly simple and undivided, nameless and ineffable, beyond all name and form, beyond all the beings of the world, completely transcending human thought and speech. It is the all-pervasive reality, not only the ground of being but also the ground of all consciousness. In many ways, then, *brahman* is very unlike the world. But if pantheism is ruled out, what does advaita or non-duality mean? What kind of oneness is this?

Mainstream Advaita Vedanta, while rejecting pantheism, has, for the most part, interpreted non-duality as illusionistic monism, which is a different teaching of oneness than pantheism. Here the world is a mere appearance, and only *brahman* truly exists. But if such a monism teaches that only *brahman* exists, the world that is perceived to be real and full of the presence of the divine cannot really exist at all. It is but a passing appearance that vanishes with right awareness in the experience of enlightenment. Only *brahman* exists. This would appear to be a logical and obvious conclusion. If *brahman* is limitless, the world cannot exist alongside it. Nothing can be added to infinity, and if creation were indeed real, it could only exist by subtracting something from the being of *brahman*. But then *brahman* would no longer be the infinite and changeless reality. One reaches this conclusion through reliance on thinking and reason. This, then, is the standard understanding of non-duality in the tradition of Advaita Vedanta: the world is an illusion; only *brahman* exists. There is only an apparent creation. The standard Advaitic formulation is summarized as: "*Brahman* is real, the world is an illusory appearance; the individual soul is *Brahman* alone, not other." Such a doctrine attempts to safeguard the transcendence and plenitude of the absolute reality, but it does so at the cost of the world's reality.

Advaita Vedanta's Critique of Christian Teaching

Moreover, Advaita teaching, which might be summarized as acosmic monism, has often critiqued Christian teaching on God's relation to the world as lacking insight and depth. Hindu Advaitins often regard the Christian doctrine of creation as a form of cosmological dualism, because the world's reality seems to them to be apart from or "outside" God, and therefore to set limitations on the infinity and absoluteness of the divine. Here the God of Christians and the world are two realities that would add up to a larger reality than either of them. Also, from the perspective of Advaita Vedanta, the Christian view of the world, basing itself on the Bible, is a place where, prior to revelation, God would seem to be absent. Though the world is created by God, and though God's glory is reflected in all that exists, it is only after some time that the divine word truly enters the world (at first through the many prophets and finally through the incarnation) from outside it. It is difficult to avoid spatial metaphors here; from the Advaitic perspective, God and the world in the Christian sense appear in relation to each other as limited parts of a larger whole. God is outside the world, and the world is outside God. The two exist alongside each other in their separate realms. And only in the course of time does God freely choose to become truly present to the world. Therefore, from the perspective of Advaita, the God of Christians cannot be regarded as a true Absolute, since God is merely a ruler "over" the world, one who enters history from the "outside," as it were, from the sphere "above," a God who is not, therefore, the infinite and total reality. Advaita challenges what it sees to be the logic of this Christian ontology: how, finally, could anything or anyone co-exist alongside that One (*tad ekam*) who is by nature the plenitude of being? Does not Hindu scripture (Taittiriya Upanishad 2.1) teach that *brahman* is "Reality, Knowledge, Infinite"? It is axiomatic for Advaitins generally that the affirmation of a being's relationality amounts to a denial of its independence, transcendence, and infinity. So the Christian God, who is conceived in relational terms as creator and redeemer of the world, does not appear to enjoy the absoluteness and transcendence of the Advaitic *brahman*, beside which nothing could exist to take away from the plenitude of its being.

Further, it is not uncommon for Advaitins to regard Christian talk of a personal God as an anthropomorphic projection.[11] In the Biblical account, God has all-too-humanlike qualities: Yahweh makes decisions, stretches out a hand, speaks a word to be obeyed, favors one people over another, becomes angry, destroys nations, repents of anger, rejoices, and even sings. God is a father, a mother, a judge, a teacher, a friend, and a king, but he is not the changeless ground of all being (*sat*), pure consciousness (*cit*), and serene beatitude (*ananda*). What has the God of the Bible to do with the *brahman* of the Upanishads? There seems to be little agreement

and few if any points of contact between Christianity and Advaita
Vedanta about either the nature of the supreme reality or the relation of the Absolute to the phenomenal world.

Thus, from the perspective of mainstream Advaita, when Christians speak of the centrality of the incarnation and resurrection
of Christ for human salvation, when hope is placed in the eschatological consummation of the world brought about in accord
with a divine plan, they reveal that they are trapped on a lower
level of awareness (*vyavahara-avastha*) in which distinctions and
separation are perceived and trusted to be real. Christians need to
transcend the distinction of creator and creature, God and world,
self and other, and realize the infinite impersonal *brahman*, which
is without distinction and relation.

Christian Rejection of Advaita

What of Christian attitudes to Advaita? The broadest Christian
approach to non-dualistic Vedanta, whether Catholic or Protes-
tant, with but few exceptions, takes the strict illusionistic tradition
of Advaita Vedanta at its word. Because Advaita Vedanta denies
the reality of the created world and history and, therefore, of the
incarnation; because it teaches that the Absolute is impersonal
rather than personal; and because its spirituality is oriented to
knowledge and identity rather than to love and to a communion
of persons, it is not surprising that many Christians have written off Advaita teaching, believing they have nothing to learn
from Advaita, because Advaita is basically false teaching. In this
view there is a complete incompatibility between Christian and
Advaitic teaching. This is the stance taken especially by many
Evangelical Christians in India and abroad, for Advaita confirms
their conviction that non-Christian religions and philosophies are
nothing more than futile strivings of sinful and misguided humans, deprived of grace, to attain salvation through their own
efforts. In addition, a high percentage of Christians in India called

Dalits (formerly known as Untouchables) react especially strongly against Advaita teaching, since, in their view, this doctrine that espouses the unreality of the world has done nothing to improve the lot of the poor and downtrodden.

Yet despite legitimate Christian grievances about the traditional lack of engagement of Advaitins with social issues, the Christian critique, for the most part, has not recognized the possibility of a truly liberating experience or awareness lying at the root of Advaitic teaching, nor do they recognize that such an interior liberation might even have implications for engagement to overcome social ills and prejudices.[12] Conversely, there also seems to be little recognition on the part of Advaitins that Christian doctrine, too, is ultimately grounded in the liberating experience of God actively engaged in human history.

Non-Duality as a Refined Teaching about the Mystery of Creation

There is another way of understanding Advaita or non-duality, one that is not illusionistic, an interpretation that is accepted by a minority of Hindu Advaitins, but which has also found support among some leading Christian theologians and contemplatives living in India during the past half-century. According to this interpretation, a proper understanding of non-duality and the world is able to avoid the extreme view of illusionistic or acosmic monism that would deny the reality of the world. In this view non-duality is a subtle Hindu teaching about a real creation. In this understanding the mysterious emergence of creation through the absolute power of the divine results in no change whatsoever in the creator. A passage from the Brhadaranyaka Upanishad (5.1.1) supports this:

> *That is fullness. This is fullness.*
> *From fullness comes fullness.*

When fullness is taken from fullness,
Fullness remains.

What this means is that with the creation of the world nothing is added to or taken away from the infinite reality of God. The world is a totally contingent reality that expresses in a limited way the infinite reality of God or *brahman*. Support for this alternative understanding of advaita, that is, a realist non-duality, is sometimes based on a re-evaluation of Shankara's writings, a scholarly development that began in the 1950s. We recall that Shankara is the great theologian of Advaita Vedanta. He has tremendous authority as an interpreter of the Upanishads. All contemporary Advaitins cite him in their works. The modern scholarly rereading of Shankara, one that does not interpret him only through the lens of illusionistic-minded Advaitins who came after him, but rather examines Shankara's writings on their own terms, concludes that Shankara, in fact, sees the world as being very real.[13] This reevaluation of Shankara, as might be expected, is controversial, and is rejected by the majority of Advaitins.

According to this realist understanding of advaita or non-duality, the created world and the uncreated *brahman* cannot be added up as two realities, simply because they do not exist on the same level of being. The teaching that God and the world are "not-two" is intended to preserve the reality of the world while also safeguarding the transcendence and fullness of the creator. *Brahman* is the infinite reality, and the world is very real, but it does not exist with the same degree of being as its source. It is being-by-participation in the Being of the eternal divine.

This realist interpretation of non-duality has been welcomed by a number of Christian thinkers for a variety of reasons. It coheres well with Christian teaching. It teaches a real creation. And, more important, it also broadens and deepens Christian thinking about the miraculous nature of creation.

This realist teaching of non-duality might thus serve to correct widespread popular Christian misconceptions about creation and

God's relation to the world. Often enough God's transcendence is mistakenly understood by Christians—not necessarily Christian *theologians*—to mean that God is a distant reality separate from creation. That is one way of thinking of God's transcendence—using spatial terms—but it is problematic. Advaitins have pointed this out, as I indicated earlier in this essay. To set God apart from the world is to set spatial limits on God. But God is the infinite reality, "whose center is everywhere and whose circumference is nowhere."[14] But the attempt by monistic Advaita to safeguard God's infinite reality does not allow for the existence of a real world and is thus unacceptable to Christians and to most Hindus.

It is remarkable that two leading twentieth-century Catholic systematic theologians, both Jesuits—the German Karl Rahner (1904–1984) and the Dutch Piet Schoonenberg (1911–1999)—discovered the value of Hindu teaching on non-duality very late in life and recognized its potential importance as an aid in thinking more correctly about the mystery of God's relation to the world. In a talk presented at a dialogue conference of Hindus and Christians in 1983,[15] Rahner noted the widespread tendency in popular Western thought of imagining God's transcendence to the world in spatial categories: as two realities existing side by side ("die Anschauung eines räumlichen Nebeneinander von Gott und Welt"[16]) or as God existing outside the world. Hindu non-dualistic teaching would be a viable way of correcting this widespread misconception.[17] Here the world and God are seen to be, using Advaita language, "not-two"; there is distinction here but no separation. God, of course, as the self-existent reality, can exist independently of the world, while the reverse is not possible. This understanding of creation ontology is what the late Sara Grant, RSCJ (1922–2002), trained in both Thomism and in Shankara's Advaita teaching, and who referred to herself as a "non-dualist Christian," called a "non-reciprocal dependence relation."[18]

Schoonenberg, like Rahner, believed in the conceptual compatibility of Hindu non-dualism with the Christian doctrine of creation. After discovering the Hindu teaching of advaita, he was reminded of a medieval Christian theological teaching that expressed essentially the same truth of non-duality, namely that with the act of creation the result was "plura entia sed non plus esse" ("more beings but not more Being").[19] Similarly, St. Bernard of Clairvaux spoke of God as (Deus est) "qui suum ipsius est, et omnium esse," or "God is He who is His own being and the being of all."[20] These are examples of non-dualist ontology coming from some of the greatest representatives of the Christian theological and spiritual tradition.

For Richard De Smet, Shankara's non-duality finally amounted to a particular understanding of creation, one that guaranteed both the absolute reality of the creator and the relative reality of the world. Shankara's teaching was thus in harmony with Christian teaching. De Smet went so far as to assert that non-duality, properly understood, was the ontological presupposition of all Christian doctrine. "Mainstream Christianity implies a refined sort of non-dualism," he wrote.[21] His understanding of non-duality, moreover, unlike illusionistic Advaita, presupposed and guaranteed a place for personalism, relation, and love, the kind of things typically missing from mainstream Advaitic thought. This is what made it distinctively Christian.

From Concept to Presence: Non-Dual Experience as a Challenge to Hindu and Christian Theology

Not all Christians involved in the encounter with Hindu Advaita give primary concern to the theoretical or conceptual reconciliation of non-duality and Christian doctrine, as did Rahner and Schoonenberg. For some, it is not enough to draw conceptual parallels between the ontology of Aquinas and Shankara or to find echoes of Advaita in the non-dualistic-sounding articulations of the Christian past or to attempt to articulate a more refined theological understanding of creation for our time. For some Christians, one does not truly understand or grasp the significance of non-duality prior to the actual experience of it. Once one is engulfed by the awareness of advaita, any theology that would pretend to explain it, even with a logically acceptable doctrine of creation, should be regarded as suspect.

It was the Catholic monk Swami Abhishiktananda[22] (originally Henri Le Saux, 1910–1973) who most forcefully warned against the dangers of conceptual reductionism in speaking of advaita or non-duality. His writings are a reminder that behind all the Upanishadic articulations and the scholastic teachings of Vedanta is the mystical experience of non-duality, which escapes all attempts at articulation and objectification. He did not, however, deny the presence of advaita in the Christian tradition. He affirmed that advaita "is already present at the root of the Christian experience. It is simply the mystery that God and the world are *not two*."[23] Like De Smet, he spoke of "the advaitic dimension of revelation and of Christianity."[24] Yet, as he immersed himself more and more in non-dualistic spirituality, through his meditation on the Upanishads and with the help of Hindu Advaitins, Abhishiktananda grew increasingly impatient with theologians who, he felt, merely wrote and thought about non-duality rather than lived non-duality as an awakening to true selfhood after the death of the ego. The Christian, he declared, ran the risk of "constructing for his own use a Christian version of Advaita which excludes on principle anything that does not fit into a previously determined framework—and this, even before he has made any attempt to enter into the advaitic experience from within."[25] For Abhishiktananda, the challenge to Christian theology and Christian faith derived from the experience of non-duality, not merely from the way it might be conceptualized to fit Christian faith.

Abhishiktananda also felt that the same challenge existed for some Hindu academics and philosophers of non-duality. Advaita was too often regarded, even for them, as a "magnificent idea" for the mind to reflect on rather than an overwhelming and transforming experience in the depths of one's being. The intense non-dual experience of pure consciousness, devoid of relation, devoid of the old "I," shatters all previous notional understandings of self and God. We see here that the Catholic monk living in India was struggling to maintain the value of his previous experience of a personal God in the face of an entirely new experience of the Absolute. Both experiences revealed themselves as true and liberating, yet it was difficult to see how two very different kinds of awareness could be conceptually reconciled. One experience affirmed the reality and value of the creature and of relation; the other seemed to obliterate it.

In speaking of Abhishiktananda's radical openness to all experience, the late Jacques Dupuis, who knew Abhishiktananda personally, remarked that "one must have an interior experience of the encounter of the religious experience of both traditions and allow them to react upon each other in one's own person, while remaining completely open to what might be produced by the shock of the encounter which surely had never before taken place at the necessary and intended depth."[26] Dupuis goes on to summarize Abhishiktananda's experience of non-duality in the following words:

> At the awakening of the experience of advaita, the onto-logical density of the finite seer vanishes. The awakening to absolute awareness leaves no room for a subjective awareness of self as finite subject of cognition; there remains only the *aham-* ("I") awareness of the Absolute.... What abides is the awakening of the one who knows to the subjective consciousness of the Absolute itself. And it is not an objective knowledge of the Absolute by a finite me. In the process of illumination, the human "me" gives way to the divine *Aham.* Such is the radical demand of *advaita.*[27]

What is noteworthy about Abhishiktananda's own writings on advaita was his success—despite certain acosmic tendencies—in steering away from controversies as to whether or not non-duality ultimately meant acosmic illusionism, that is, whether or not the world really existed. His focus was more on interiority and inner awakening and less on speaking about the ontological status of the world. His language was seldom argumentative or polemical; his primary goal was not so much directed toward convincing Hindus of a world-affirming interpretation of non-duality, as De Smet had done, as it was directed "to sensitize Christian thought to the treasures that await it"[28] in the deep silence of non-dual experience. He saw himself as a witness to an experience of interior freedom that is seldom understood or appreciated by Christians.

Shankara himself taught that to really know the supreme reality, and not just to have correct thoughts about it, what is required of the one seeking to know is a complete inner purification and preparation. As valuable as thinking is, it is not enough. Reason left to itself with regard to ultimate matters is inconclusive, he taught. There is no end to the clash of reasoned opinion. The seeker must therefore be guided by revealed scripture. But what is often overlooked is that Shankara taught something else, too. He taught that a highly intelligent and learned mind is, of itself, incapable of grasping the truth proclaimed by the Upanishads. What is required is a "childlike" (Sanskrit: "*balya*") mind, one that is pure and guileless.

Ramana Maharshi: Modern Sage of Non-Duality

Non-dualistic teaching and self-realization have been propagated in India for more than 2,500 years. Over the centuries, Advaita Vedanta, the most influential of all the Vedantic schools, has systematically cultivated and nurtured attitudes, practices, and teachings intended to foster a non-dualistic vision of life leading eventually to spiritual awakening and inner liberation. It is a tradition rich in commentaries and sub-commentaries on authoritative texts. Advaita Vedanta's most famous exponent, as we have seen, was Shankara, who was, before anything else, a commentator on sacred writings. He is the author of only one independent treatise, the *Upadeshasahasri*.[29] Shankara himself wrote nothing autobiographical, and we have no statement from him anywhere in his writings about any personal experiences he might have had as a follower and propagator of non-dual teaching.

Arguably the most influential Hindu representative of non-dual teaching in modern times, and a person who advocated a quite different path to enlightenment than that offered by Shankara and Advaita Vedanta, was Ramana Maharshi (1879–1950),[30] a man who had an enormous impact on the spiritual quest of Swami Abhishiktananda and who has had a lasting impact on other well-known Christian contemplatives in the twentieth and twenty-first centuries. In fact, Maharshi is one of the most famous modern sages to emerge from any religion. Nearly seventy years after his death, he continues to have a worldwide following.

The account Maharshi gave of his sudden and unexpected awakening to non-dual awareness around the age of sixteen in July 1896 is one of the most famous spiritual narratives in modern Hindu literature.[31] In it he describes his breakthrough into a higher unitive awareness of selfhood. From that time onward his focus was continually on the Self, the true Self that we are, as opposed to the everyday understanding of self that we normally think we are. This was not an abstract theory. His awakening changed him and liberated him forever, centering his attention on an inner spiritual reality that was more him than his own body and mind. The sage spoke with a quiet unshakeable authority, rooted in a profound inner experience. Though he preferred to teach through silence, he allowed himself to enter into spiritual dialogue with others. In these dialogues he never said, "I think that…" or "This is my opinion." He was also, unlike Shankara, completely uninterested in theological debate. He simply asked his conversation partners to investigate for themselves what their real nature was. They should do this by following the first pronoun singular, "I," to its source. If they did not turn back in fear in their interior search, they would uncover their true identity as pure consciousness, at the same moment that their old identity dissolved into nothingness.

Maharshi's emphasis on the availability of non-dual awareness for all people and without the condition of any prior training in the proper reading of the Upanishads or in metaphysical argumentation has made him more accessible and attractive to the modern searcher of truth than Shankara.

Ramana Maharshi may be seen as a modern embodiment of the Upanishads, both because of the continual focus of the Upanishads on Self-realization and because of their fluid and indeterminate teachings on ontology. Like the Upanishads, Maharshi is unconcerned with a systematic formulation of ontology. Sometimes his thinking sounds more realist, at other times more illusionist. But always at the center of his teaching is the reminder that we are in essence the self-shining eternal light of consciousness.

I include below a link to the most famous photo of Ramana Maharshi ever taken, as he nears the end of his life.[32] Notice the beauty, serenity, kindness, even holiness of his face. His face shows us that non-duality is more than a mere idea or theological notion. It is because of that face that the words of Maharshi are so credible to so many people of so many religions or of no religion at all. Though his teachings are so challenging to our everyday ideas about ourselves and God, his face continues to invite us to probe deeper into our self-awareness and discover what is truly lasting and real about ourselves.

I must confess that I am very attracted to this teaching, even though I'm not sure how well it can be harmonized with my own Christian faith and experience. But perhaps we don't have to understand everything of another religion to appreciate its beauty or be able to frame it in theological language that would integrate it into our own view of life. The exact significance of non-dual experience, especially that of Ramana Maharshi, for Christian faith must remain unanswered for now. But perhaps, in the words of the late Murray Rogers, an Anglican contemplative and a friend of Abhishiktananda, we might learn to be as thankful for what we do not yet fully understand as for that which we do understand.[33]

Notes

1. I recall a public disagreement between two famous Hindu scholars some years ago at the annual convention of the American Academy of Religion. One of the two remarked that many Hindus are, in fact, polytheists, whereas the other asserted that polytheistic faith does not exist at all among Hindus.

2. Lord Vishnu, for example, is addressed by more than a thousand names by Vaishnavites, i.e., worshippers of Vishnu.

3. But some Hindu systems are non-theistic—for example, Mimamsa and most of Samkhya.

4. From the Christian point of view the purpose of God's activity is basically twofold: to bring justice, peace, and harmony to the human race as well as to integrate all of creation into the divine life. This integration and transformation includes all worldly matter and all dimensions of the human person, both physical and spiritual, in what is called the resurrection.

5. The etymology of the word "Upanishad" is not clear, though some scholars take it to mean something like "sitting down near." The understanding here is that for more than two millennia the teachings of the Upanishads have been handed down from teacher to student, the latter being understood as sitting in close proximity to the master.

6. Thus Dvaita Vedanta (dualism), Vishishtadvaita Vedanta (the non-duality of the qualified Brahman), etc.

7. Along with the Upanishads, two other texts constitute the "triple canon" or "triple foundation" (*prasthana-traya*) of Vedantic schools. They are the Bhagavad-Gita (ca. 200 B.C.E.) and the Brahma-Sutra (estimates of its final form vary widely, situating it as late as 400 C.E.). But the Upanishads are the texts with the greatest authority in this canon.

8. See S. N. Dasgupta, *A History of Indian Philosophy*, Vol. 1 (Delhi: Motilal Banarsidass, 1988), 50.

9. See Psalms 66:4, 19:1, 96:13, 97:6; 98:4–9, etc.

10. See Anantanand Rambachan, *A Hindu Theology of Liberation: Not-Two Is Not One* (Albany: State University of New York Press, 2015).

11. This Advaita critique applies to all other anthropomorphically expressed theisms as well: Hindu, Muslim, etc.

12. For a new interpretation of non-duality that gives meaning and value to the world, one that would inspire a greater engagement with human rights issues see Rambachan, *A Hindu Theology of Liberation*.

13. This sifting of the real teaching of Shankara from later misinterpretations is similar to the way in which twentieth-century Christian theologians learned to distinguish the real teaching of Thomas Aquinas from later Neo-Thomist doctrine.

14. A number of possible sources of this sentence have been offered by scholars.

15. The conference took place outside Vienna, in Mödling. Illness prevented Rahner from attending, so his paper was read aloud by another scholar.

16. Karl Rahner, "Welt in Gott: Zum christlichen Schöpfungsbegriff," in Andreas Bsteh, ed., *Sein als Offenbarung in Christentum und Hinduismus* (Mödling: Verlag St. Gabriel, 1984), 74–75. My translation. This essay has never been translated into English, according to email correspondence I received from the Karl Rahner Archive in Munich in October 2015.

17. Note the title of Rahner's talk: "World in God."

18. See her *Toward an Alternative Theology: Confessions of a Non-Dualist Christian* (Notre Dame: University of Notre Dame Press, 2002).

19. Piet Schoonenberg, "Gott als Person und Gott als das unpersönlich Göttliche: Bhakti und Jnana," in Gerhard Oberhammer, ed., *Transzendenzerfahrung, Vollzugshorizont des Heils* (Vienna: Indological Institute of the University of Vienna, 1978), 229.

20. *De Consideratione*, 5.6.13. This quote is given in *Doctrine de la non-dualité* (Paris: Dervy-Livres, 1982). The book was written by an anonymous Christian monk familiar with Hindu Advaita teaching.

21. See De Smet, "Interphilosophical and Religious Dialogue in My Life," in A. Pushparajan, ed., *Pilgrims of Dialogue: A Collection of Essays Presented to Fr. Albert Nambiaparambil in Honour of His 60th Birthday* (Munnar: Sangam Dialogue Centre, 1991), 5.

22. "Abhishiktananda" is a Sanskrit word coined by Le Saux meaning "the bliss of Christ."

23. *Hindu-Christian Meeting Point: Within the Cave of the Heart* (Delhi: ISPCK, 1976), 100: his emphasis.

24. Ibid., 101.

25. Ibid., 95.
26. See Jacques Dupuis, *Jesus Christ at the Encounter of World Religions* (Maryknoll, NY: Orbis Books, 1991), 67.
27. Ibid., 61.
28. Letter to R. Panikkar, dated May 18, 1966, in *Swami Abhishik-tananda: His Life Told through His Letters*, ed. James Stuart (rev. ed.; Delhi: ISPCK, 1984), 180.
29. The text has been translated as the "Thousand Teachings."
30. His original name was Venkataraman Iyer.
31. The traditional account of Mahashi's enlightenment experience is related by Arthur Osborne, *Ramana Maharshi and the Path of Self-Knowledge* (Tiruvannamalai: Sriramanasramam, 2002), 7–9. This account has been challenged in its details by David Godman, perhaps the foremost living authority on Ramana Maharshi. Godman draws on two 1930 conversations between Maharshi and B. V. Narasimha Swami. See Godman, "Bhagavan's Death Experience," *The Mountain Path* (1981): 67–69. More recently, J. Glenn Friesen has argued that Maharshi's narrative of his enlightenment experience was influenced by exposure to modern religious ideas centered on the value of personal experience. See *Ramana Maharshi: Interpretations of His Enlightenment* (Calgary: Aevum Books, 2015).
32. G. G. Welling, *Sri Ramana Maharshi. 1948.* <http://www.luminous-lint.com/app/image/382537481911238063240/>, accessed July 1, 2017).
33. See Murray Rogers, "Grounds for Mutual Growth," *Hindu-Christian Studies Bulletin* 14 (2001): 3.

Works Cited

Abhishiktananda, Swami. *Hindu-Christian Meeting Point: Within the Cave of the Heart.* Delhi: ISPCK, 1976.

Dasgupta, N. *A History of Indian Philosophy*, Vol. 1. Delhi: Motilal Banarsidass Publishers, 1988.

De Smet, Richard. "Interphilosophical and Religious Dialogue in My Life." In *Pilgrims of Dialogue: A Collection of Essays Presented to Fr. Albert Nambiaparambil in Honour of His 60th Birthday*, edited by A. Pushparajan. Munnar: Sangam Dialogue Centre, 1991.

Dupuis, Jacques. *Jesus Christ at the Encounter of World Religions.* Mary-knoll, NY: Orbis Books, 1991.

Friesen, Glenn J. *Ramana Maharshi: Interpretations of His Enlightenment.* Calgary: Aevum Books, 2015.

Godman, David. "Bhagavan's Death Experience." *The Mountain Path* (1981).

Grant, Sara, RSCJ. *Toward an Alternative Theology: Confessions of a Non-Dualist Christian.* Notre Dame, IN: University of Notre Dame Press, 2002.

Osborne, Arthur. *Ramana Maharshi and the Path of Self-Knowledge.* Tiru-vannamalai: Sriramanasramam, 2002.

Rahner, Karl. "Welt in Gott: Zum christlichen Schöpfungsbegriff." In *Sein als Offenbarung in Christentum und Hinduismus*, edited by Andreas Bsteh. Mödling: Verlag St. Gabriel, 1984.

Rambachan, Anantanand. *A Hindu Theology of Liberation: Not-Two Is Not One.* Albany: State University of New York Press, 2015.

Rogers, Murray. "Grounds for Mutual Growth." *Hindu-Christian Studies Bulletin* 14 (2001).

Schoonenberg, Piet. "Gott als Person und Gott als das unpersönlich Göttliche: Bhakti und Jnana." In *Transzendenzerfahrung, Vollzugshorizont des Heils*, edited by Gerhard Oberhammer. Vienna: Indological Institute of the University of Vienna, 1978.

Stuart, James, ed. *Swami Abhishiktananda: His Life Told through His Letters* (rev. ed.). Delhi: ISPCK, 1984.

Chapter Ten

CONTEMPLATING THE DIVINE WITH A SENSE OF WONDER

Anantanand Rambachan, St. Olaf College

In the previous essay in this collection, "The Mystery of the Infinite in the Hindu Spirituality and Theology of Non-Duality," Professor Bradley Malkovsky offered rich suggestions for deepening the dialogue between the Hindu and Christian traditions. In this brief response, I build upon and amplify some of these directions.

Bhagavadgītā 2:29 speaks of the infinite *brahman* and repeats, three times, the Sanskrit word "*āścaryavat.*"[1] *Āścaryavat* conveys the sense of wonder, marvel, and awe. *Brahman,* according to this Bhagavadgītā text, can be contemplated only with a sense of wonder (*āścaryavat paśyati kaścidenam*). One can speak of it only with wonder (*āścaryavadvadati tathaiva cānyaḥ*), and the one who hears does so with wonder (*āścaryavaccainam anyaḥ śṛṇoti*). This verse concludes with the observation that, even after hearing (*śrutvā api*), one never fully understands (*enam veda na caiva kaścit*). *Brahman* is unlike the objects of our world that are objectified and may be described with the features of sense objects. Bhagavadgītā 2:29 seems to echo Kaṭha Upaniṣad 2:7, which describes the speaker and the knower as wonderful (*āścaryaḥ*):

> *Wonderful is the speaker of it, skilled the winner of it,*
> *Wonderful the knower of it, taught by a skilled one.*[2]

I cite these texts from the Bhagavadgītā and the Upaniṣad that connect *brahman* with the sense of wonder, since I think that the experience of beauty includes wonder. Wonder or marvel (*adbhuta*) is one of the eight sentiments listed by Bharata in his *Nāṭya Śāstra*.[3] There is a dimension of the inexplicable in that which evokes wonder and which is experienced as beautiful. *Brahman* evokes wonder also for the fact that it eludes all conventional words and symbols and can never be known as an object of the mind or senses.

The experience of beauty and wonder in relation to *brahman* is not possible in the absence of the manyness of the universe. A non-dual *brahman*, without the self-multiplying process of creation described in the Upaniṣads, is not describable as wonderful or beautiful.[4] In the absence of manyness, there is only being and silence. There is no knower, object of knowledge, and process of knowing. To speak of *brahman* with words like "beauty" or "wonder" is to do so from a context and place of diversity and speak relationally.

It is also true, however, that the experience of beauty and wonder is made possible through a particular characterization of the relationship between *brahman* and the world of manyness. It is very appropriate, therefore, to focus—as Malkovsky does—on some of the historical ways in which this relationship is articulated.

In spite of persistent mischaracterizations, the Advaita tradition does not understand the *brahman*-world relationship as pantheistic. Pantheistic interpretations of Advaita ignore the many Upaniṣadic texts that emphasize *brahman*'s transcendence. The Advaita understanding of *brahman* emphasizes *brahman*'s immanence as well as transcendence. Although emphasizing that *brahman* exists in everything and everything exists in *brahman*, Advaita does not equate *brahman* simplistically with the world, or limit *brahman* to the world. As the Īśā Upaniṣad (5) puts it, "That (*brahman*) moves. That does not move; That is far off, That is near; That is inside all this, and That is also outside all this." The famous *Puruṣa Sūkta* hymn of the Ṛg Veda underlines the transcendence of *brahman* by stating that *brahman* pervades the world by one-fourth of *brahman*'s being, while three-fourths remain beyond it.

In addition, pantheism does not allow for liberation (*mokṣa*), predicated on the availability of *brahman*, free from the limits of time and space. The knowledge of a *brahman* that has become or is simply transformed into the world is not liberating. I contend also that a *brahman* (or cause *kāraṇa*) that transforms itself into the universe (or effect *kārya*) does not evoke the sense of wondrous beauty spoken of in the Bhagavadgītā. There is no *āścaryavat* in speaking about such a *brahman*.

The second interpretation of the *brahman*-world relationship is monism. Here, unlike in pantheism, the transcendent non-duality of *brahman* is emphasized. This, however, is done at the cost of the world. The world is likened to an illusion that we project because of our ignorance of *brahman*, the true reality. When *brahman* is known, the world recedes in significance and meaning, and even disappears. This is similar to the error of taking a rope to be a snake. When the perceiver realizes his error, the snake disappears and the rope alone exists. This is a pervasive understanding of the Advaita tradition and one that is more challenging to refute than pantheism. More difficult, for me, is that this interpretation of *brahman*-world relationship is associated with a negativization of the world. The world is equated with ignorance (*avidyā*) and suffering, and liberation (*mokṣa*) is construed as freedom from the world. When the reality of the world is questioned in this manner, it is not consistent for one to be troubled by events within it. Interpretations like these often provide justification for world-negation and renunciation. Taken to their extremes, these interpretations make it difficult to take the issues of the world, such as poverty and injustice, seriously. The world and its problems are regarded as illusory.

Like pantheism, monism does not invite the experiences of wonder, marvel, or beauty. Such a response may be construed as conferring a false value upon the world. Monism invites indifference and detachment to the world. There is a third possibility, one acknowledged by Malkovsky, that avoids both pantheism and monism. It avoids also a radical *brahman*-world dualism. This is the interpretation that I seek to develop in my own writings.[5] It is grounded in those Upaniṣad passages, such as Taittirīya Upaniṣad 3.1.1, that speak of *brahman* as "That from which all beings

originate, by which they are sustained and to which they return."
Other Upaniṣads (e.g., Chāndogya Upaniṣad 6.2.1–2), speak of
brahman as the indivisible and uncreated One from which the
many emerge. The Upaniṣads contest the existence of anything but
the One *brahman* before creation, and the emergence of the world
from anything other than *brahman*. The universe does not spon-
taneously appear from non-existence but is willed into being by
an intentional creative act of *brahman*. *Brahman* brings forth the
world from itself, without any depletion of *brahman*'s plenitude
(*pūrṇatva*). The many is an expression of *brahman*'s fullness or being (*ānanda*). Taittirīya Upanisad (III.6) describes this fullness as
the source of everything in the following words:

> From joy beings are born; by joy, being born, they live;
> into joy they enter when they pass on.[6]

What I read in these Upaniṣad passages is a somewhat describable but inexplicable and asymmetrical relationship between
brahman and the world in which *brahman* is not lost or depleted
in the act of self-multiplication but remains single and non-dual
(*ekamevādvitiyam*). Its relationship with the world may be described as not-two (*advaita*), since the existence of the world cannot
be denied, even though *brahman* is the being (*sat*) of all that exists.

This invites wonder and astonishment. It is the marvel that Ar-
juna is asked to ponder (*paśya me yogamaiśvaram*) by Krishna in
the Bhagavadgītā (9:5). It is the marvel that is described in the
beautiful poetic paradoxes of the thirteenth chapter (14–16):

> Having hands and feet everywhere, eyes, heads and
> faces everywhere, having ears everywhere, That stands,
> enveloping everything in the world.
>
> Shining by the function of the senses, yet freed from
> all the senses, unattached yet maintaining all, free from
> qualities yet experiencing the qualities.

> Outside and inside beings, those that are moving and
> not moving, because of its subtlety. This is not compre-
> hended. This is far away and also near.

There is beauty in seeing our world as *brahman*'s marvelous
outpouring and as a celebratory expression of *brahman*'s fullness.
Its value is derived from the fact that it originates from, exists in,
and shares the nature of *brahman*, even though, as a finite process,
it can never fully express *brahman*. *Avidyā* (ignorance) is not the
world itself but a particular way of seeing it. It is to see the many
and to be unaware of the One. *Avidyā* also is to think that seeing
the One requires the negativization or even the mental negation
of the many. What the Advaita tradition offers is a special way
of seeing the One and the many; seeing the many as unique expressions of the one. This is a seeing that is imbued with awe and
wonder. We are certainly invited into this mode of seeing when the
Bhagavadgītā (15:12) asks us to see the radiance (*tejaḥ*) of God in
the light of the sun, moon, and fire, and to experience the divine
in the taste of water (7:8), in the fragrance of the earth (7:9), and
in the gift of reason (7:10), and when the Īśā Upaniṣad (1) implores
us to wrap all things in God (*īśā vāsyam idam sarvam yat kiñca
jagatyām jagat*). To see the creation wrapped in the One who is its
source, support, and end is to see with beauty and reverence. This
is sacred seeing (*darśana*).

This vision of beauty embraces in a special way the *jīvan mukta*
(the living liberated), who is not blind to the world but who sees
the world with new and radiant eyes. Living liberation reminds
us that *mokṣa* is not freedom from the world or its negation. It is
fully consistent with life in the world. In his commentary on the
Bhagavadgītā 2:29, with which I began this short essay, Śankara
gives an alternative interpretation in which he speaks of the living
liberated as a rare being of wonder. This opens up for us the possibility of speaking of beauty in relation to the life of the human
being who embodies the vision of Advaita and who exemplifies
compassion. The *jīvan mukta* who sees creations with eyes of

wonder is herself a being of wonder. Wonder is experienced by one who herself embodies wonder.

Notes

1. See *The Bhagavadgītā*, trans. Winthrop Sargeant (Albany: State University of New York Press, 1984). Translation modified.
2. Valerie J. Roebuck, trans. and ed., *The Upaniṣads* (London: Penguin, 2003).
3. See Michelle Voss Roberts, *Tastes of the Divine* (New York: Fordham University Press, 2014).
4. "He desired: 'Let me become many! Let me be born,'" Taittirīya Upaniṣad 2.6.
5. In several of my publications I have attempted to refute a monistic interpretation of Advaita and to advance this alternative one. See especially *The Advaita Worldview* (Albany: State University of New York Press, 2006) and, more recently, *A Hindu Theology of Liberation* (Albany: State University of New York Press, 2015).
6. *Anandadhyeva khalvimani bhutani jayante, anandena jatani jivanti, Anandam prayanty-abhisam-viçanti.*

Works Cited

Rambachan, Anantanand. *The Advaita Worldview*. Albany: State University of New York Press, 2006.

———. *A Hindu Theology of Liberation*. Albany: State University of New York Press, 2015.

Roberts, Michelle Voss. *Tastes of the Divine*. New York: Fordham University Press, 2014.

Roebuck, Valerie J., editor & translator. *The Upaniṣhads*. London: Penguin, 2003.

Sargeant, Winthrop, translator. *The Bhagavadgītā*. Albany: State University of New York Press, 1984.

Part IV

BEAUTY AND BUDDHISM

Chapter Eleven

FINDING BEAUTY IN THE OTHER: BUDDHIST PERSPECTIVES

Donald W. Mitchell, Purdue University

The Buddha

At first reading, "Finding Beauty in the Other" would seem to be problematic for early Buddhism in India. Let me explain with a summary of the Buddha's analysis of the experience of beauty and ugliness, and a present-day example. In doing so, I will present his teaching about "dependent arising" (*paṭicca-samuppāda*).

In the twelve-link chain of dependent arising of sensory, mental, and life experience, one comes to the point where the senses give rise to contact with an object of sense. There arises from this contact certain sensations and feelings. Some of these feelings can give rise to desire or "craving," which can then generate attachments that produce an unwholesome process of life, or what the Buddha calls "becoming." To better understand this process of dependent arising, let us take as an example the experience that a Thai novice monk shared with me. He was standing in line with his fellow monks, begging for food in the early morning. He kept his head down so as not to see the persons who were putting food in his begging bowl. But in front of one woman, he saw that her toenails were painted bright red. This perception gave rise to feelings that produced sexual desire. He said that he then had to deal with the sense perception and emotional sensation in order to decide if he would be able to become a member of the Buddhist order of monks.

Turning back to the process of dependent arising taught by the Buddha, my friend's sense of sight contacted an object that gave rise to certain feelings that in turn gave rise to sensual desire. Now at that point, the Buddha teaches, one has the freedom to reflect on this process and not allow the desire to become an attachment that negatively affects one's life process. My friend had the freedom not to allow the desire he experienced to lead to an attachment that would result in his leaving the Buddhist order—his present form of becoming.

When the Buddha discussed this linkage of dependent arising, he often spoke of the perceptions of "beauty" and "ugliness." To see beauty can lead to sensations or feelings that result in "craving" (*taṇ hā*—"thirst"). One can begin to crave or thirst to possess what one sees. This state of mind can generate "greed," which is one of the three "root causes" of evil. On the other hand, seeing ugliness in someone or something can lead to a second kind of craving—the desire to be rid of what one sees. This "aversion" can generate "hatred," which is the second of the three root causes of evil. I would add that the third root cause of evil is "delusion." This refers to being deluded in thinking that by possessing what one craves and by being rid of that to which one has an aversion, one will find happiness. Instead, "pulling" to oneself persons, objects, or situations one craves, and "pushing" away persons, objects, or situations to which one has an aversion in order to find happiness lead to negative states of mind and evil actions. These actions are not ones that are motivated by the four relational virtues of loving-kindness, compassion, sympathetic joy, and equanimity. These are the four "divine abodes" taught by the Buddha that characterize true relational happiness and define relationships in Nirvana.

For the Buddha, it is necessary to be "unmoved" by perceptions and sensations in negative ways. For example, an early text speaks of a monk who had an advanced skin disease and whose fellow monks kept him separate from them because of their being "moved" by aversion to his condition and "fear" of being infected by it. The Buddha, when he visited that community of monks, instead took a basin of water and a towel and washed the monk himself. He admonished the monks, saying, "Monks, you do not have a mother or a father here who can tend to you. If you, monks, do not tend to one another, who is there to take care of you? Remember that whoever tends a sick person, as it were, tends to me."[1]

So what about beauty? Is there a positive experience of beauty according to the Buddha and early Buddhism? In fact there is. The Buddha taught over and over that the dress and the demeanor of the monks should be "pleasant" or "pleasing" (*pāsādika*) to the sight. Note here that the Buddha connects the beauty of dress to the beauty of demeanor. Also, the monastery should be built and kept up so that it is pleasing to the sight and provides the peace needed for meditation. Again, note that the beauty of place is connected to the beauty of spiritual growth. For example, the Venerable Sappaka speaks of finding beauty and being delighted by it on the banks of the Ajakaraṇī River, near which he practices meditation in his cave:

> *When the crane with its beautiful white wings,*
> *Startled by fear of the dark thundercloud,*
> *Flees, seeking shelter—*
> *Then the River Ajakaraṇī delights me....*
> *Who wouldn't be delighted*
> *By the rose-apple trees*
> *That adorn both banks of the river there,*
> *Behind the cave of my hermitage?*
>
> *... The lazy frogs croak:*
> *"Today isn't the time to stray from mountain streams;*
> *Ajakaraṇī is safe, pleasant, and delightful."*[2]

The Buddha also taught what are called the Eight Liberations. The third is when one is "intent only on the beautiful (*sobhana*)."[3] This liberation comes about when the forms of our perceptual experience cease and meditation is focused on a beautiful mental image. Here beauty is used to lift and purify one's mind. The Buddha takes this view of beauty a step further. He states: "Not by eloquence or by lovely features is a person beautiful if he or she is jealous, self-ish, or mean. But the person who has completely uprooted these vices and is free from hatred, that person is really beautiful."[4] Here we see that the beautiful is not just an object of meditation to purify the mind. But when one is pure in mind, speech, and action, he or she is "beautiful." Complete purity and beauty are found in Nirvana. In early Buddhism, this is represented by the lotus that grows in the murky water and breaks the surface, blossoming with a beautiful flower and a delightful fragrance.

Theravāda Buddhism

The great systematizer in the Theravāda tradition was Buddha-ghosa, the fifth-century C.E. composer of the classic entitled *The Path of Purification* (*Visuddhimagga*). In this text, he speaks of how loving-kindness meditation can purify the mind and heart in a way that frees one from attachment to visual beauty and enables one to find universal beauty. He says about loving-kindness meditation that it can "pervade one's heart" so that "Everywhere and equally, one dwells pervading the entire world with loving kindness from the heart, abundant, exalted, measureless, free from enmity, and free from all afflictions."[5]

With this loving kindness pervading one's heart and seeing the world through it, one is said to realize that others are "unrepulsive," and "ugliness disappears."[6] Then one can see the truly "beautiful" in all beings: "For all beings are unrepulsive to one who abides in loving kindness. Being familiar with the unrepulsive aspect... loving kindness is the basic support for the liberation by the beautiful."[7] With this heart-love experience of the beautiful beyond the visual beauty tied to perception, one is able to practice love of others based on this deeper awareness of the true beauty of all beings.

Here it is important to note that for the Buddha as for Buddhagosa, what is discovered through this wisdom insight into the beautiful is a step toward finding Nirvana. Experiencing the beautiful in others is connected with the purity of mind and the loving kindness of the heart that sees past perceptions of ugliness and beauty. This degree of liberation is a basis for the final liberation of Nirvana. In this regard, it is important to note that the attainment of Nirvana, according to the Buddha and Theravāda, is not "produced" by morality, meditation, or wisdom. Rather, it is described as "unborn," or "unproduced." It is like metal that is covered with rust. Once the rust is removed, the underlying metal is discovered. It was there all the time. This is the highest inner beauty that one glimpses in the beautiful found in wisdom of mind and loving kindness of heart.

So, turning to "Finding Beauty in the Other," one could say that if Nirvana is unproduced, it must already exist. It is a matter of realizing it, awakening to it, becoming enlightened to its highest beauty. For Theravāda, this means we must follow a Path of Purification until we "blow out" the conditions of our ordinary life and realize our full potential—the attainment of Nirvana. One then finds Nirvana hidden in the other, the highest beauty. To see this in others, as something that is already but not yet as we Christians might say, is to find real beauty in the other. Here are some passages from a guided meditation by Ven. Ayya Khema of the Theravāda tradition that speaks of discovering this beauty in oneself and in the other:

> Look into your heart and see that there is a shining jewel in there, *beautiful*, translucent, giving off many colors, the most valuable thing that one can find in the universe, the seed of enlightenment.... And now look at people everywhere... there isn't one that doesn't have that same jewel in their heart. And it's easy to love these people, to feel connected... and to know that's the only way they can live together in peace.... Wherever we look, each heart has it, it's of the greatest *beauty* and magnificent value. And so our love can flow easily everywhere unimpeded.[8]

Mahāyāna Buddhism

A new literature was written in India during the third and fourth
centuries C.E. (two or three centuries before Buddhaghosa). These
new Mahāyāna *sūtras* introduced the notion of *Tathāgata-garbha,* or
"womb/embryo of the Buddha." *Tathāgata* is a title for the Buddha,
and *garbha* means both "womb" and "embryo." The texts state that
all living beings are like wombs that contain within the embryo of
Buddhahood. It is important to note that in Mahāyāna Buddhism,
the goal in life is not simply to attain Nirvana, but to attain Buddhahood: to become a Buddha. The Bodhisattva Path of Mahāyāna that
leads to Buddhahood entails a number of stages that enable one to
create a celestial Buddha realm and reside there for eons as a celestial Buddha in touch with all living beings helping them to achieve
Awakening and Buddhahood. In Theravāda Buddhism, each person
who gains Nirvana in this life goes to final Nirvana after death.

So, as the Buddha taught that Nirvana is unborn, unproduced, and
therefore something potentially realizable by all living beings, in these
new *sūtras* it is said that we contain within us the unborn "embryo"
of Buddhahood. The goal of Mahāyāna Buddhism is the Awakening
of this *Tathāgata-garbha.* The reality that is being referred to here is
the pure, luminous, and nirvanic essence of the Dharma-body (or
Truth Body) of the Buddha. It is hidden within like an embryo in a
womb, or in the language of the *sūtras,* like a "resplendent" Buddha
statue covered with a rag. According to one such *sūtra,* it is "Like a
Buddha in a faded lotus flower, like honey covered by bees, like a fruit
in a husk, like gold within its impurities, like a treasure hidden in the
dirt...like a valuable statue covered with dust, so is this [*Tathāgata-
garbha*] within all beings."[9] It is the true beauty of self and other.

It is clear that Buddha-nature in all beings is a "pure" reality
hidden by "impurities," somewhat like Nirvana is described in
Theravāda. What is explicit in both cases is that our Buddha-nature
or Nirvana is concealed by the defilements of ignorance, hatred,
greed, and delusion. What is implied is that in our ordinary defiled
condition, we cannot produce Buddhahood or Nirvana—just as

a rag cannot produce the Buddha statue within it. And it is also implied that this reality is found in all others "like a treasure hidden in the dirt." In Mahāyāna, the stories of the bodhisattvas who choose the path to full Buddhahood often describe their loving and compassionate gaze at living beings, seeing the hidden beauty of their true nature and at the same time their suffering condition due to their ignorance and other defilements.

The bodhisattvas's experience of the other became the model for how Buddhists are to see beauty in the other, the gold Buddha in the rags of the human condition. For example, in the *Lotus Sūtra*, Never Despise Bodhisattva would speak the same words of praise to everyone he met from the lowly in society to those of high rank: "I would never despise you or treat you with arrogance... you will surely attain Buddhahood someday."[10] Through the eyes of this bodhisattva, all others are beautiful. All Buddhists of this tradition seek to follow the Bodhisattva Path to gain these eyes of Enlightenment to see beauty in self and other.

Buddhism in East Asia

In the south of China during the fourth century C.E., translations of Buddhist texts from India were being made using Daoist and Neo-Daoist terms and concepts. For example, in some Neo-Daoist texts, the world of phenomena is the functioning of the Dao such that the essence of each being in the world is the Dao itself. The Mahāyāna Buddhist translators conveyed this idea through the *Tathāgata-garbha* texts, which state that all beings have the same essential nature. The translators rendered *Tathāgata-garbha* as "Buddha-nature" and affirmed that one can realize this original nature through Enlightenment. By Awakening in the Mahāyāna tradition, one can discover Buddha-nature in oneself and in others. This line of thought became very influential in all of East Asia.

Another concept that is linked to Buddha-nature is "suchness" (*tathatā*). The suchness of all beings is their emptiness of the independence that the discriminating mind attributes to them. In the suchness of existence, all beings have Buddha-nature. Existence in its suchness manifests luminous Buddha-nature in all phenomena. This means that in Awakening to our Buddha-nature, we discover Nirvana in *saṃsāra*. The inner "unborn nature," the Buddha-nature of all beings, shines in the interdependent suchness of all beings. These ideas influenced the evolution of East Asian Buddhism. In relation to our topic, one finds true beauty in oneself and the other within the interrelated suchness of all beings. In East Asia, this opened the door to seeing the functioning of the natural world as an interrelated whole made up of beings that are innately pure and beautiful. In this viewpoint we can also see the influence of Daoism.

From the writings of Huisi, the Second Patriarch of the Tiantai Buddhist tradition in China, we read a passage that puts all these elements together:

> The mind is the same as the Pure Mind, True Suchness, Buddha-nature, and the Dharma-body.... Although the mind has always been obscured by mental states based on ignorance, its true nature has always been pure; thus it is called Pure Mind.... The Buddhas past, present and future as well as all living beings have this Pure Mind as their essence.... It is therefore called the True Suchness of all beings.... This Pure Mind is called Buddha-nature because "Buddha" means Awakening, and "nature" means mind. The mind is called the Dharma-body because the meaning of "Dharma" consists in functioning, and the meaning of body consists of establishing.... The functioning of the Dharma establishes the basis of this one mind in all beings.... Therefore, the mind is called the Dharma-body.[11]

In short, the essence of the mind is the one Pure Mind that is in all beings as their Buddha-nature. In the Tiantai School of Chinese

Buddhism, we find the metaphor of water and waves. The waves on the surface are in motion, but the water below is still. The movement of the waves does not affect the still nature of the water below. So, too, the mind experiences motion due to the perceptions that move it. But the deeper Pure Mind is always still and unmoved by the surface movement. It is this inner purity that gives real beauty to all beings to be discovered in oneself and others.

A second Buddhist tradition in China is Huayan. It adds another dimension to the notion of beauty presented by Tiantai. While it confirms the inherent purity and beauty of Buddha-nature in all beings, it expands the understanding of that nature and also stresses the relational element. In the text *Treatise on the Golden Lion*, the author, the famous Fazang, writes: "When we see a lion [made out of gold] coming into existence as a form...there is nothing apart from the gold."[12] In other words, Buddha nature is not something inside beings like a golden statue in a cloth, but all beings *are* Buddha-nature. When we realize Buddha-nature, we see that all beings "shine." In addition, the text goes on to say, "[A]nd the jointly arisen beings mutually shine."[13] Because all beings arise together and are Buddha-nature in all their aspects, there is a relational mutuality that also shines with purity and beauty. All things are interwoven in the beauty of perfect balance and harmony.

To make his point, Fazang is said to have built a tower of mirrors for Empress Wu. The tower was round with mirrors on the walls, and in the center was a Buddha statue with a light beside it. When Empress Wu looked down into the tower, she saw that the Buddha statue was shining in each of the mirrors. And the mirrors were placed so that each of them reflected its image of the Buddha statue to the others. Therefore, each contained all the images from the other mirrors. Huayan speaks of this as "mutual penetration" and "mutual containment." In short, we are each Buddha-nature and we are present in each being in the universe, and the universe of beings is present within us. The purity of Buddha-nature *is* us, and we contain, due to the mutual arising of all beings, the purity of Buddha nature that *is* all other beings. To be Awakened is to realize this relational beauty as who we are and to see it shining as all other beings. Fazang concludes his treatise by noting that, through this wisdom, one enters "the sea of perfect knowledge... Whether one sees beauty or ugliness, the mind is calm like the sea.... [T] here are no negative mental formations.... This is called the entry into Nirvana."[14] This Nirvana *is* the beautiful. It shines in all beings from their Buddha-nature, and we contain all beings within ourselves as all beings contain us.

Something of this view is expanded on by the great Buddhist Son (Zen) scholar in Korea, Chinul. He said:

> If in one thought moment a person can trace back the luminosity of his or her mind and his or her original nature, that person will discover that the ground of this nature is innately free of any defilements.... Therefore, one eliminates what is unwholesome without eliminating anything; and one cultivates what is wholesome without cultivating anything either. This is true cultivation and true elimination.[15]

The point here is that in tracing back the luminosity of our mind, we discover that the luminosity is radiating from our Buddha-nature. When we discover this we also discover that in truth there is nothing to eliminate and nothing to cultivate. At root, all is in perfect balance/harmony from beginningless beginning to endless end, as the Zen saying goes. *Saṃsāra is* Nirvana, and we *are* Buddha-nature. In this we discover the universal beauty of existence, of self and other. This is our "original nature," like the still water below the "ordinary" waves of good and evil on the surface. As Chinul says: "The original wisdom of universal brightness is the very essence of all living beings and Buddhas.... [W]e understand from Awakening that all living beings and Buddhas perfectly interpenetrate in the wisdom of universal brightness."[16] This mutual interpenetration echoes the Huayan teaching of the luminous beauty of the relationality of interpenetration and the mutuality of containment of all beings.

Finally, Buddhism in East Asia affirms that all beings, not just human beings, have Buddha-nature. Therefore, there is an emphasis on nature. To take Japan as an example, the temple gardens originally inspired by Chinese and Korean Buddhist temples became models for Japanese landscape architecture where naturalism is primary. The stone gardens of the late Muramachi period created a new style across Japan. The larger boulders represent mountains or islands, while the planes of moss or sand symbolize the boundless sea of life. On another level, the boulders represent beings that are constituted by the sand that surrounds them. The sand is raked to represent a dynamic process that produces beings. Also the arts of calligraphy, stone lanterns or water basins, water flowing from a bamboo pipe, tea houses, flower arranging, and ink paintings portray the beauty of the natural world.

Finding Beauty between Self and Other

In conclusion, I would propose the following comparative question about beauty *between* self and other. If two persons find this kind of beauty in self and other, what is the mutuality of the relation like? I asked the following question decades ago to Keiji Nishitani, the famous Buddhist philosopher and leader of the Kyoto School at his home in Kyoto: "You speak of the movement from 'self-centeredness' to 'other-centeredness' that reflects the unity and compassion of ultimate reality.... If we do this together with others, are we creating what you call 'a field of force' that gathers all beings in their 'Home Ground'?"[17] Nishitani answered:

> Yes, and when we attain deeper realization of unity, we find the fundamental truth of community...or what has been called *circuminsessional* interpenetration. This is to be aware of the fundamental way of being, unity.

> Here in unity, each person can realize his or her true self.
> But the true self is always other-centered so it also means
> to become aware of... the true freedom of our being. To
> discover our True Self, or what we call Buddha-nature,
> is at the same time the realization of true unity. It is, in
> fact, the self-realization of the unity itself.[18]

For Nishitani, "unity" is the interrelated dynamic of Buddha-nature that is what he calls the "Home Ground" of all beings. All beings are fundamentally united in this Home Ground. It is the Ground of all beings and the true Home that they seek. When they do, they are at home in this ground of unity. The Home Ground of Unity is a collective reality in that it is not only Buddha-nature within, but a reality in which all beings share as their true Home.

Nishitani's point is that Awakening is not just the realization of the potential of Nirvana or Buddhahood *in* oneself. It is the self-realization of Nirvana or Buddhahood *between* oneself and all beings. It is their collective Home Ground. What is of comparative interest is Nishitani's use of the word "*circuminsessional.*" This term is used to describe the dynamic of unity within the Trinity. It is obvious that Nishitani understood something about the mutual indwelling of the Persons of the Trinity that reminded him of the total self-giving dynamic of beings united in their Home Ground on the basis of Buddha-nature.

Here, Nishitani was echoing the teachings of Shin'ichi Hisamatsu, the great Zen Master of the early Kyoto School. At Kyoto University in 1942–43, students went to Hisamatsu in crisis over the war. "The students and the teacher became one," according to Masao Abe, one of the students, who went on to become a major figure in the Kyoto School.[19] Hisamatsu called this communal oneness "the ideal of a post-modern age." He sought to build a community overcoming the individualism of modernity. His communal spirituality called for what he termed an "active love" in which people give themselves as gifts to each other in a relational interpenetration that is an image of the interpenetration of the Dharma-body (*Dharmakāya*)—the True Body of the Buddha that includes all existence and is our Buddha-nature.

Hisamatsu says that this active mutual love is like a fire:

> It will be warm and congenial. If we spread this warmth externally, in the same way as a charcoal fire lights in one spot and spreads, everyone in this room will become warm. When each of us becomes a charcoal fire, this warmth can extend to those around us, the places we find ourselves, and the places to which we go.[20]

For Hisamatsu, this mutuality of love as a dynamic unity is beauty of a specific kind. He names it *"yūgen"* (profound).[21] The depth of this profound beauty is glimpsed in the profound, beautiful "locus" of tranquility and harmony of the tea ceremony, where there is a "collapse of the distance" between self and other.[22] Here the two become one with totality.

In the Catholic tradition, Piero Coda, Tom Norris, and other members of the Abba School in Rome are developing a Trinitarian theology based on a communal spirituality similar to Hisamatsu's.[23] One of their points is that in the past, being created in the image of God has been interpreted on an individual and internal basis. But from a Trinitarian point of view, the image of God can be seen as a collective and lived "imaging" of the Trinity. It is a *"circuminsessional* interpenetration,"* to quote Nishitani, that defines the mutuality of the total kenotic love of the Trinity. Herein lies the beauty *between* self and other that is the Home Ground that embraces both in mutual love.

Notes

1. Mahāvagga, 8:26.
2. Theragāthā, 4.11.

3. Digha Nikāya, 15.
4. Dhammapada, 262–63.
5. Visuddhimagga, IX:44.
6. Ibid., IX:120.
7. Ibid.
8. See <www.leighb.com/seedofel.htm> (April 10, 2006): 1.2; italics mine.
9. Ratnagotra-vibhāga Sūtra, 96, 97.
10. Chapter 20.
11. Dacheng zhiguan famen, I-II.
12. Jin shizi zhang, 5.
13. Ibid., 7.
14. Ibid., 9, 10.
15. Susim kyōl, Q/A 3, 7.
16. Wondon sōngbullon, Q/A 3–4.
17. Donald W. Mitchell, "Compassionate Endurance: Mary and the Buddha: A Dialogue with Keiji Nishitani," *Bulletin of the Vatican Secretariat for Non-Christians* 21 (1986): 287.
18. Ibid.
19. Abe Masao, "A History of the F.A.S. Zen Society," *The Eastern Buddhist* (1984): 5.
20. Donald W. Mitchell, *Spirituality and Emptiness: The Dynamics of Spiritual Life in Buddhism and Christianity* (New York: Paulist Press, 1991), 157.
21. For more on this topic, see William R. LaFleur, *The Karma of Words: Buddhism and the Literary Arts in Medieval Japan* (Berkeley: University of California Press, 1986), 102.
22. LaFleur, 103.
23. See Piero Coda, *Dalla Trinità: L'avvento di Dio tra storia e profezia* (Rome: Città Nuova Editrice, 2011); and Thomas J. Norris, *The Trinity: Life of God, Hope of Humanity: Towards a Theology of Communion* (New York: New City Press, 2009). For my comparison between the work of the Abba School and Hisamatsu, see: Donald W. Mitchell, "Unity and Dialogue: A Christian Response to Shin'ichi Hisamatsu's Notion of FAS," *FAS Society Journal* 1 (Spring 1986): 6–9.

Works Cited

Coda, Piero. *Dalla Trinità: L'avvento di Dio tra storia e profezia.* Rome: Città Nuova Editrice, 2011.

LaFleur, William R. *The Karma of Words: Buddhism and the Literary Arts in Medieval Japan.* Berkeley: University of California Press, 1986.

Masao, Abe. "A History of the F.A.S. Zen Society." *FAS Society Journal* (Autumn 1984): 1–12.

Mitchell, Donald W. "Compassionate Endurance: Mary and the Buddha: A Dialogue with Keiji Nishitani." *Bulletin of the Vatican Secretariat for Non-Christians* 21 (1986).

———. *Spirituality and Emptiness: The Dynamics of Spiritual Life in Buddhism and Christianity.* New York: Paulist Press, 1991.

———. "Unity and Dialogue: A Christian Response to Shin'ichi Hisamatsu's Notion of FAS." *FAS Society Journal* 1 (1986).

Norris, Thomas J. *The Trinity: Life of God, Hope of Humanity: Towards a Theology of Communion.* New York: New City Press, 2009.

Chapter Twelve

SEEING BEAUTY IN EVERYDAY LIFE ACCORDING TO THE *LOTUS SUTRA*

Gene Reeves, Rissho Kosei-kai

I'm tempted to launch into a talk about this thing called "Buddhism."[1] Buddhism is, as you know, a very, very rich tradition involving several different cultures, and for me at least it's very difficult to talk about Buddhism in general. There are some things one can say, but very few with accuracy. So I'm here representing, in a way, one particular, really quite small Buddhist tradition.

As you heard in the introduction, I'm from Rissho Kosei-kai, a Buddhist institution that was founded in 1938. It is not very old and not very big; we probably have six to seven million people. But it is a tradition that goes back through other Buddhist traditions in Japan and China, particularly the Nichiren tradition, which is quite large, especially in its influence. With only one exception, all of the modern Buddhist movements in Japan are rooted in Nichiren Buddhism.

Nichiren Buddhism is rooted in Chinese Tiantai Buddhism (Tendai in Japanese), which takes us back to the seventh century. So there is a long history of connections here, but there are a lot of Buddhisms in this world. From other papers we've heard from South Asian and Southeast Asian Buddhism (Theravada), we've heard from Tibet, and we've heard from China. There is a sense in which my wife and I represent Japan here this morning. One thing about Japanese Buddhism is that it is more recent in its inception than Chinese Buddhism or Southeast Asian Buddhism (although it is not more recent than Tibetan Buddhism). One important thing about Japanese Buddhism in general, especially contemporary Japanese Buddhism, is its generosity of spirit—as I like to say, a kind of openness to others and to other Buddhist traditions.

Well, I was invited to this conference originally to comment on Robert Gimello's paper, which I did not get to see until just before the conference. So I've not had much time to think about it. There is, however, one thing I'd like to say about that paper—I liked that paper, I learned a lot from it, and I think all of us can learn from it. But I wondered whether it isn't after all, in the end, very Christian, rather than Buddhist. Very Christian in the sense, well, almost in the Barthian sense, that it takes these two kinds of aesthetics, these two kinds of beauty—which are there, there's no denying that they're there—and kind of pushes them apart more than needs to be. He makes them totally different from one another in a way that they really are not in Buddhist art.

There are lots of little things we could talk about in this paper, but to take one example: for Prof. Gimello, otherworldly Buddhist images are perfectly symmetrical. Yet in my experience I do not think I have ever—and I need to do some research to see if this is true—seen a Buddhist image that is perfectly symmetrical. They all have elements of difference between the left and the right, between the upper and the lower. There is no perfect symmetry. They are more symmetrical than some other images, that's for sure. But it's a matter of degree, not a matter of complete symmetry. So I would take this as just one little symptom of something one might think about: whether Prof. Gimello is pushing the difference between worldly and otherworldly to a kind of extreme that is classically found, typically, in Christianity, but not so much in Buddhism.

I would also like to make one quick comment about Donald Mitchell's paper, though not really so much about the paper itself. The title of Don's paper (as presented at the conference) has to do with Theravada Buddhism, Southeast Asian Buddhism, but he winds up in the last third of the paper or so talking about East Asian Buddhism, which is fine. Now this may be just a prejudice or bias on my part, but it's true that you can find in a text that the robe should be worn in a certain way that is pleasing, and that the temple should be pleasing and so forth—but it has always seemed to me that in Theravada Buddhism (today at least), beauty is something to be shunned. Beauty is not to be found in the other, beauty is not to be found anywhere, if we're to follow the monastic rules. And this seems to go beyond monastic life. It seems to me that in Theravada Buddhism there is very, very little appreciation for beauty anywhere. Even the temples are really not beautiful compared with East Asian temples, or compared with Western churches.

So those are the two things I would like to say off the top of my head about the two papers.

As I was thinking about speaking at this conference, I thought about the title of this conference: "Finding Beauty in the Other." I'd like to tie my remarks to the three key terms in that title: "finding," "beauty," and "other." I think that my Buddhist perspective on those three terms is a little different from the perspective of some others.

First, "finding." It is a word we do not use very much in Buddhism; it can be used, of course, but it's not used very much. When I first started thinking about this title, I thought that "beauty" and "other" would be very simple and not be problematic, but that "finding" might be problematic because in English "finding" means different things. Finding can be the result of a search: "I found my wallet in the bedroom." Or finding can be the result of an accident: "I found a dollar in the street." Or it can be to recognize the presence of something: "Sugar is found in soft drinks." Or it can be a matter of becoming aware of something: "The detective found the girl's killer." Or finding can be a matter of declaring something to be the case: "The killer was found guilty." So we have many different uses of "find" or "finding," and there are also other obscure uses of "find": "to find oneself," "to find God." What do these "finds" mean?

What does it mean, then, to find beauty in the other, or in a religious tradition other than one's own? Well, for those of us who are devoted in some way to the *Lotus Sutra*, as Don Mitchell suggests, beauty can be found everywhere. Don would say "hidden beauty," but I'm not sure that for us beauty is always, or even usually, hidden, as it's always there, not to be found, but to be seen. Well, maybe seeing is a kind of finding, I'm not sure.

Prof. Mitchell mentions the bodhisattva named Never Disrespectful, who appears in Chapter 20 of the *Lotus Sutra*. I think it's a very important story illustrating what we need to talk about. In this story Never Disrespectful Bodhisattva, we're told, did not study or recite *sutras* so never learned anything from them, and this bodhisattva becomes, toward the end of the story, an earlier embodiment of Shakyamuni Buddha. So this is not a story about any old bodhisattva; this is a story about the future Buddha. His practice is not sitting in meditation, not reciting *sutras*, nor doing any of a lot of other practices that Buddhists follow.

His practice is the very simple one of going to everyone he meets and telling them, "I would never disrespect you because you too can become a buddha." This is the central teaching of the *Lotus Sutra*: not that everyone can become a buddha—that would be impossible—but that *anyone* can become a Buddha. Any one of us in this room can become a buddha today by helping some other person. You or I can be a Buddha for someone else.

So this Never Disrespectful Bodhisattva is a kind of model of what we can be for each other. It also has the opposite meaning: it means not only that each and every one of us can become a buddha for someone else, it means that anyone else can become a buddha for us. The person you meet in a subway car, the spouse you greet at home, the teenage kid you don't get along with very well—any person you meet, any person you encounter, can become the Buddha for you.

Beauty. What is found or seen, at least in the Buddhist context, may not fit very well with Western understandings or definitions of beauty. Nowhere in the *Lotus Sutra*—and here I suppose I am quarrelling a little bit with Don Mitchell—nor really explicitly in any Buddhist text I can think of, is it suggested that what is seen or found in the Other is "Truth" (with a capital "T"), Goodness, and Beauty, the three transcendentals of Western philosophy and theology. Of course, one can find them if you want to look hard for them. You can find suggestions of such things, but actually this is really Christianizing or at least Westernizing Buddhism.

Similarly—despite Nishida, who is very influenced by nine-teenth-century German philosophy—I do not think you can find much of a "true self" in Buddhism. Occasionally you do find it, perhaps especially in today's American Buddhism, but not in the *Lotus Sutra* do you find anything equivalent to a "true self." There is no true or ideal self. There is only the self which actually is.

Still, there is beauty in the Lotus. I'm speaking from the *Lotus Sutra* tradition, where the flowering of the lotus is a powerful image. There is something beautiful about the lotus, with its roots in the mud and its flower facing the heavens. But sometimes—especially in Western interpretations of that imagery—we are told that the flower is what is beautiful and the roots in the mud are ugly. Yet for *Lotus Sutra* Buddhists, that is never the case. What is the case is that the whole process of a beautiful flower emerging from the muddy water, or from the mud in which its roots are located, that very process is what is beautiful. It is the whole lotus that is beautiful, not just its flower. It is the flowering of the whole plant, including its muddy roots.

Part of this idea (and this I think is related to Prof. Gimello's paper) is that beauty emerges from the ordinary. Beauty emerges from the ordinary, but that does not mean that it leaves the ordinary behind. Without the ordinary, there is no beauty.

In Chapter 15 of the *Lotus Sutra* there is an interesting story about bodhisattvas. It is a long story and I don't have time to tell all of it here. In an earlier chapter, Chapter 11, a lot of buddhas and bodhisattvas have come from other worlds to this world in order to visit Shakyamuni Buddha and another buddha, Abundant Treasures Buddha, who is from the past and is now extinct. And when it is time for these buddhas and bodhisattvas to go home, some of the bodhisattvas go up to Shakyamuni Buddha and they ask him if they could stay behind to help him out in this world. They realize that he's living in this world where people are difficult to deal with, and they think maybe they can help out. In response, Shakyamuni Buddha basically says, "Well, thank you very much, but no thanks; we've got plenty of bodhisattvas of our own." As he says that, an uncountable number of bodhisattvas emerge from the Earth. The tradition has understood that those bodhisattvas emerging from the earth are a symbol of bodhisattvas emerging from everyday life.

This suggests that *you* can be a bodhisattva, today, because of your rootedness—we could say rootednesss in mud but that is probably making it too ugly—your rootedness in everyday life. For the *Lotus Sutra*, and for much of Buddhism, beauty always is connected to the ordinary. It's not as two different things but one thing, which is a process, a process of the beautiful emerging from the ordinary, or the other-worldly emerging from the this-worldly.

Finally, a word about the "Other." I am probably the only Buddhist in this conference. So I should be in a good position to speak about otherness. Here I'm the Other. Yet many of you or at least several of you in this conference are old friends of mine. We have known each other for years. You have eaten in my home. You know my wife. So it's awfully hard for me to believe that because I'm Buddhist, I'm simply "Other."

It does not work that way, it seems to me, in our lives and in reality. Similarly, the *Lotus Sutra* proclaims that no one is merely "Other"; that there is no really, finally, or no totally "Other." We find Buddha-nature in others because it arises in ourselves, and it only arises in ourselves if we see it in others.

Otherness, of course, emphasizes diversity, the reality of which cannot be denied. But the *Lotus Sutra* and many forms of Buddhism tend to emphasize the opposite, to emphasize unity, togetherness, commonality. Anyone, according to the *Lotus Sutra*, anyone without exception, has the potential to be a buddha. Whether rich or poor, female or male, young or old, healthy or sick, beautiful or ugly, moral or immoral—and we have stories to sort of account for each of these. Anyone, absolutely anyone, has an ability to embody the Buddha in his or her life and thereby find or see the Buddha in others. So maybe for *Lotus Sutra* Buddhists, it's not enough to find beauty in some "Other." At our best, we find common ground in others, and the fantastic power to make a difference in this world. And we can do this, at least in part, because others are not simply or merely other. They are like ourselves.

For Rissho Kosei-kai, that is what makes interfaith relations, interfaith cooperation, interfaith understanding, interfaith dialogue—what makes interfaith relationships terribly important. We live in a troubled world, a very troubled world, a world which badly needs peace. The founder of Rissho Kosei-kai, Nikkyo Niwano, has said: "It's ridiculous to believe that any one religious sect, or any one religion, can solve the problems of this world." Interfaith cooperation, seeing beauty in others, is absolutely essential for the future of the world, in order for there to be movement toward world peace.

Notes

1. This contribution was originally delivered as a response to a paper by Donald Mitchell, which was revised for publication in this volume, and one by Robert Gimello, which, sadly, could not be included in the publication because of the many images without copyrights in it. Little attempt was made to alter the informal mode of delivery or the dialogical nature of this paper. In spite of the references to a work that is not available here, the reflections by Reeves still offer a new take on how Japanese Buddhism and the *Lotus Sutra* find beauty in the other. —*The Editors*

Part V

BEAUTY AND AFRICA

Chapter Thirteen

OF RAINBOW NATIONS, KENTE CLOTH, AND THE VIRTUE OF PLURALISM: NAVIGATING THE BEAUTY AND DIGNITY OF DIFFERENCE IN SEARCH OF A LIVABLE FUTURE IN AFRICA

Teresia Hinga, Santa Clara University

This paper begins with the observation that Africa is character-ized by diversity in multiple, intersecting ways. Culturally, Africa is home to at least 3,000 different ethnic groups, each of which boasts a distinct and customized expression or embodiment of what is generically called "African culture." Kenya, for example, has 40 different ethnic groups, each of which speaks a great diversity of languages. In terms of religion, Africa is heir to what has been dubbed a "triple heritage"—namely, Indigenous Religions, Chris-tianity, and Islam. These three are also internally diverse, there being several forms of Islam (e.g., Ismaili, Sunni), Christianity (e.g., Catholic, Methodist, Pentecostal), and indigenous religions (e.g., Zulu, Igbo, Kikuyu, Masai).

The paper examines how Africa has dealt with this reality of pal-pable difference(s) and the consequences that follow for a continent seeking a livable future. With suitable examples, it proposes that failure to adequately see, engage, and even embrace the "beauty and

Dignity" of the (racially, ethnically, and religiously) "Other" has too often led to violent conflicts that have radically compromised human and other forms of flourishing on the continent. Conversely, it proposes that embracing the beauty and dignity of the Other is a moral imperative for a continent seeking a livable future.

Contextualizing the Title

The title evokes the language and metaphors used by several key persons who have taken the time to reflect deeply on the reality of difference in Africa (and, indeed, the world today) and who have contemplated the deadly consequences of a failure to adequately embrace and viably navigate this difference. These persons include Desmond Tutu, who used the metaphor of the rainbow to describe his vision for a society that embraces difference, specifically racial difference as it embraces a beautiful rainbow. It also includes Mercy Amba Oduyoye, who, reflecting on the tensions and conflicts and even violence perpetrated because of a failure to see beauty in gender difference, introduces the metaphors of beads of many colors and Kente cloth to describe her vision of a society that values all persons, regardless of gender.

The title also invokes Rabbi Jonathan Sacks, who, in his book *The Dignity of Difference: How to Avoid the Clash of Civilizations*, calls upon us not only to celebrate the beauty of difference but also to honor the dignity of the different other. He wrote his book to counteract the view that when different nations, people, and communities meet, there is inevitably going to be a clash of civilizations. In his words:

> The *Dignity of Difference* is a plea—the most forceful I could make—for tolerance in an age of extremism. I see in the rising crescendo of ethnic tensions, civilization clashes and the use of religious justification for acts of terror, a clear and present danger to humanity.[1]

Meanwhile, in her rather autobiographical book *Encountering God: A Spiritual Journey from Bosman to Banaras,* Diana Eck introduces the notion of "pluralism" as virtue and proposes that pluralism ought to be the moral response to the fact of diversity or plurality in the world. For her, pluralism is a virtue that needs to be embraced and nurtured as an antidote to the vices flowing from failure to honor the dignity and beauty of difference. She argues that pluralism calls for a recognition of spiritual and other forms of interdependence and a larger sense of *we,* and she provides examples of people in history who have been propelled by this virtue and who have called for a larger sense of we.[2] Motivated by this virtue, people such as Gandhi (whose case she cites) have tried to re-create an imagined community marked not just by mere tolerance of each other, but by mutual respect and engagement.

In this paper, I focus specifically on two such exemplars from Africa whose lives are, at least in my view, propelled by the virtue of pluralism. I explore their experiment with the virtue of pluralism and unpack the metaphors they use to describe their vision of society and the larger sense of we. I refer to Desmond Tutu and his re-imagination of South Africa as a Rainbow Nation and as an antidote to apartheid and racism, and to Oduyoye's notion of threading beads of many colors and weaving a new Kente cloth of humanity out of different strands. Oduyoye's dream of a larger sense of we is concretized and, to an extent, exemplified in the Circle of Concerned African Women Theologians, a group she founded. This is an actual community of women who, though marked by difference,[3] are determined nonetheless to weave a new and beautiful tapestry out of their differences.

Understanding the Diverse African Landscape

Desmond Tutu and Mercy Oduyoye offer strategies for more viably navigating the diverse African context. What is the nature of this diversity, and what forms does it take? Below is a preliminary—

even tentative—mapping of the several ways in which diversity and difference are made manifest in the African landscape. These include religio-cultural diversity, diversity of identities (racial, ethnic, and gender), and instances of multiple belonging, hybridity, overlapping, and hyphenated identities.[4]

Religio-Cultural Diversity

In discussing diversity in the African context, a key feature that one must reckon with is Africa's tremendously diverse heritage of religions and cultures. As stated above, Africa is heir to what has been described as the triple heritage of AIRs (African Indigenous Religions), Christianity, and Islam. These three heritages are also internally quite diverse, with each tradition having multiple versions based on the interpretation of key ideas within that tradition. For example, the vexing issue of polygamy in Africa is evaluated differently in the three traditions. In Islam, as well as in African indigenous religions, polygamy—though not morally obligatory—falls within the realm of the morally permissible. In Christianity, however, monogamy is the ideal, and divorce and remarriage are frowned upon. Underlying these differences in the ethical evaluation of polygamy is a diversity of interpretations regarding the meaning and goals of marriage, as well as the nature of family and obligations therein.[5] The implications of this religio-cultural diversity for a determination of the role and value of religion in helping human forms of flourishing should be considered. At the very least, religio-cultural diversity demands that we abstain from generalized, essentializing, and generic responses to such questions as those concerning marriage. Any dialogue regarding the fact of plurality of religion in Africa would have to name and shame the ways in which religious chauvinism and exclusivism have been a source of pain for many. In fact, the continent as a whole has been on the receiving end of extreme racial chauvinism and exclusivist approaches to diversity, as a result of which Africa has been defined as "the Dark Continent" on ethnocentric grounds.[6] This "invention" of Africa as a Dark Continent has had tragic and far-reaching consequences and has generated substantial amounts of Afrophobia and Afro-Pessimism.

Diversity of Identities

The African context is characterized by the presence of *Diversity of Identities*. Not only is there diversity in ethnic,[7] racial, and religious identity; there is also diversity in gender identity. The latter form of identity tends to be ignored, resulting in questions such as the one about marriage being treated generically or, even worse, andro-centrically. As we press for viable ways in which to deal with difference, there is a need to integrate gender into the analysis and to recognize women not just as victims of chauvinism and exclusivism, but as human beings with moral agency and therefore with much to contribute in the search for social transformation. Attention and concern must also be given to the fact that many are transgendered or "differently gendered" and have been subjected to persecution and harassment because they are outsiders in a heteronormative society.[8]

Hybridity, Intersecting Multilayered, Overlapping, and Hyphenated Identities

Moreover, much of the contestation and even conflict arises out of the failure to handle appropriately the reality of multiple, sometimes competing, intersecting, overlapping, hyphenated, and multilayered identities.[9] Thus, for example, in recent times in Kenya, ethnic identity and legitimate pride degenerated into ethnic chauvinism or negative ethnicity, which conflicted sharply with national identity and pride. This conflict resulted in deadly clashes after the 2007 elections seemed to favor one or the other side in the ethnic divide. In the bloody and violent clashes that ensued, those who had married across ethnic lines were particularly vulnerable. The children in such families became the targets of both sides of the warring groups. While in Kenya the failure to recognize and honor ethnic diversity caused much pain and loss of life, in Rwanda, this failure led to outright genocide. In 1994, almost a million people were killed in Rwanda because they were "different."

The plight of children caught in this catastrophic ethnic violence is well captured by Uwem Akpam in his book *Say You Are One of Them*. In one of the several stories that the book comprises, Akpam invites us to listen to Monique, a half-Tutsi, half-Hutu child, as she acknowledges her vulnerability. Under pressure from his fellow Hutu, her father has just killed her Tutsi mother. Monique is running away from her house, in which some Tutsi are hiding. She meets a Tutsi mob en route to her house to avenge her mother's death. She describes the scene in sordid and heartbreaking detail:

> ... we limp on into the chilly night ... the blood has dried into our clothes like starch ... there is a smaller mob coming towards us. Monsieur Henri is among them ... these are our people on Maman's side ... they are shouting how they are going to kill Papa's people ... some of them have guns. If Papa could not spare Maman's life, would my mother's relatives spare mine? Or my brother's? ... I slip into the bush, with Jean on my back.[10]

Elsewhere, national identity is compromised by ethnic identity expressed in a chauvinist manner. This is often further compounded by diversity of religious identity, also expressed in a chauvinistic manner. In Nigeria, for example, the question of diverse ethnic identity is compounded by diverse religious identity. It is a context in which religious identity and ethnic identity at times overlap, but also a context in which religious identity does not quite follow the national boundaries. Often, the Muslim identity and Christian identities are part of a global dynamic that transcends national and ethnic boundaries and which leads to overlapping and competing identities, a situation that is volatile and often explodes in violence.

It is this explosive context and its outcome that Akpam describes in another story in the above collection. In "Luxurious Hearses," Akpam describes through the voice of Jibril the hostilities between northern Nigeria, largely Islamic, and the south, largely Christian. Jibril, the son of a Christian mother (a southerner who has migrated north), converts to Islam. When trouble breaks out between Muslims and Christians, Jibril's mother recommends that he flee back to the south to take refuge with his father. He must ride in a bus full of southerners, running away from persecution in the north. Unfortunately, he cannot camouflage his Islamic identity, since one of his arms has been amputated to punish him for some wrongdoing under Islamic laws.

Pressured to fully identify himself and facing violence from the fellow fugitives, Jibril's mind is full of questions:

> ...the events of the previous two days had knifed through his Muslim identity, running in the bush from Khamfi, Jibril's mind has become a whirlwind of questions: Allah, is it true that once a person is baptized as my mother said I was at birth he remains a Christian forever...never to remove the mark from his soul? Are you punishing me for this infant baptism? You know that as far as I can remember I have always felt every inch a Muslim.... If the world will not accept me as a Southerner–Northerner, will you also condemn me as a Christian–Muslim? Though I attacked Musa and Lukeman for being fake Muslims, Please Allah, give me the wisdom to convince the Christians in this bus that I am truly one of them...lead me home Allah, lead me to Peace. Allah, your religion is a religion of Peace....[11]

I submit that factoring in the phenomenon of hybridity, multiple-belonging, and overlapping or hyphenated identity to our analysis and response to the challenge of difference in Africa will help us to understand the plight of many (that is, probably all of us) who, like Jibril, inhabit multiple sites of identity simultaneously. In so doing, we might discover, as Jibril does rather belatedly, that religious and other forms of identity (gender, ethnic, or racial) have been manipulated particularly by those in power to enhance their own "blessings," often in ways that are a bane to those without power.[12] More positively, we might also discover the best practices with respect to how to celebrate and navigate this diversity of identities, or even how to mobilize it as a resource in Africans' quest for a place to feel at home in the world.[13] In the above story, Jibril gains much-needed insight when, in his bid to escape persecution, he receives help from both Christians and Muslims. It is to these kinds of Muslims and Christians that he dedicates his final moments before he is to be lynched by Christians who, in their fanaticism and fear, expect him to identify either as Muslim or Christian and not *both* Muslim and Christian:

> Jibril attempted to convey the mangled story of his religious identity... but their murderous looks told him it was useless.... [T]hese were not the stares of Catholics, or born again Christians or ancestral worshippers.... His conversion meant nothing to them. Their stares reminded him of his fundamentalist Muslim friends Musa and Lukman. When they started jeering at him again, it was not so much at his Northerner–Southerner claims but at his supposed Christo–Muslim identity... they (sarcastically) told him to lift his cut wrist so that Mohammed would come to his rescue. He did not argue. He obliged them... raising the stump as high as he could.[14]

Jibril recognizes the sheer absurdity of fundamentalism masquerading as religion, yet he does not condemn religion qua religion.

> Knowing very well that these people were not going to spare him, he returned to his God of Islam, the one he truly knew, although this journey had altered his fanatic worldview. He flushed the desire to be a Christian from his soul. With all he had seen and experienced, he could not forget the sources of Allah's help during his flight. He raised his stump for Mallam Abdullahi and his fam-

ily, for showing him another way [to escape]. He raised it to celebrate the Christians who had held a Muslim prayer-mat for him.[15] He raised it for Yusuf,[16] who refused, when the crucial moment came, to abandon his faith; he [Jibril] felt one with him, though they belonged to different faiths and worlds now....[17]

Through this story, Akpam laments the folly and tragedy of Africa's failure to honor the reality of multiple intersecting and overlapping identities such as the ones that shaped Jibril's life. Many have lost their lives to the failure of Africa to acknowledge and embrace that reality. Failure to see beauty and dignity of the other coupled with religious chauvinism has fueled many tragedies and massive loss of life. Considering specifically the question of how best to navigate the challenges of diverse religions, the enduring ethical question can be phrased thusly: to what extent are the woes haunting Africa related to a failure to discern adequately and evaluate the multiple religions and spiritualities that prevail in Africa? How are the tragic consequences such as the ones Jibril faced related to Africa's failure to distinguish true, life-giving spirituality from its deadly counterfeits[18] or, in theological parlance, heresies? How might a better recognition and application of the virtue of pluralism become a prophylactic to such tragedies, which are seemingly ubiquitous? This is the ethical question to which Tutu and Oduyoye have responded with bold proposals regarding the imperative to embrace pluralism.

Defining the Virtue of Pluralism: Mapping the Opportunities and Challenges in Africa

Considering the challenges posed by the fact of multiple religious traditions in the world, Diana Eck observes that

> the greatest source of tensions is not the divide between western and non-western traditions or between mystical

and prophetic traditions: rather, the tensions arise because of the way people respond to diversity both *within
and across religions.*

Eck identifies a spectrum of responses that are to be found in
all religious traditions: exclusivism, inclusivism, and pluralism.[19]
She explains that the "tension is between exclusivists and plu-
ralists, fundamentalists and liberals, wall builders and bridge
builders."[20]

Of the three responses, she proposes that pluralism is the most
morally viable response to the fact of diversity. She proceeds to
define pluralism mainly by distinguishing it from what it is not. As
she explains, pluralism[21]

1. is not the sheer *fact of plurality* but active engagement
   with this *plurality.*
2. is not mere *tolerance*, for tolerance is a deceptive virtue
   since it assumes a hierarchy, with the tolerator being on
   top. Tolerating does not necessitate the "tolerator" understanding the "tolerated."
3. is not *syncretism* (i.e., lumping all differences into one
   or cherry picking among differences and homogenizing
   them). Rather it assumes a genuine respect of difference
   and commitment to engage with it.
4. is not *relativism* (i.e., a view that any and all perspectives
   are valid). Pluralism assumes commitment, even religious commitment. One does not check one's religious
   (or other) commitment at the door en route to the table
   of dialogue. Rather, one brings it along and engages the
   other from the vantage point of one's committed-ness.
   One is open to the fact that what is true is always true for
   someone and that there is always a point of view!

Eck concludes that, while matters of truth and value are relative
to our conceptual framework and worldview, nihilistic relativism

is problematic: if everything is more or less true, I do not give myself to anything in particular. Such relativism too often becomes a dangerous excuse for inaction against injustice.

It is in the context of tension and conflict that the idea of "interfaith dialogue" has been proposed as a part of the solution. Reflecting on the role of interfaith dialogue in diffusing the tensions around difference, including religious difference, Eck considers pluralism both as a means and a goal of interfaith dialogue. She prefers pluralism since, as she points out, "the isolationism of the exclusivist is not open to dialogue, while the inclusivist is open to dialogue but does not quite *hear* or even accept the self-understanding of the other."[22] The inclusivist accepts or tolerates the Other often by redefining the Other in his or her own terms as a precondition for acceptance. In her words:

> The biggest difference between the inclusivist and the pluralist is the self-consciousness of one's understanding of the world and God.... [However,] if we are inclusivists we include others into a worldview that we already know and on the terms we have already set. If we are pluralists we recognize the limits of the world we already know and seek to understand others in their own terms, not just ours....[23]

She considers dialogue as a way to the goal of social transformation but clarifies that dialogue is *not debate about two competing positions*, wherein the goal is to "win" the other to one's side of the contest; rather, dialogue is "a seeking of relationship through encounter and engagement for *mutual transformation*."[24]

Propelled by the virtue of pluralism, the goals of dialogue are a genuine quest for mutual understanding and mutual transformation. Such dialogue, Eck opines, would also pave the way for much needed interfaith cooperation toward the transformation of our global and local cultures so that they are more conducive to the flourishing of all.

Dialogue across (Religious) Differences and the Virtue of Pluralism in the African Context: Opportunities and Challenges

Africa is a religious continent—palpably so. We are heir to what the late Ali Mazrui dubbed a triple religio-cultural heritage of AIRs, Christianity, and Islam (in chronological order). How we have responded or are responding, or will respond, to this diversity is not an academic matter. It is often a matter of life and death.[25] At the same time, however, one recognizes the many blessings and positive outcomes that have been occasioned by interpretations and practices and application of religion that stay close to the ethical core of the triple heritage of the religio-cultural traditions that Africa has inherited, as I will demonstrate below. Propelled by the core values of their respective faith traditions, many Christians, Muslims, and even practitioners of AIRs have interpreted and practiced their faith in ways that have well served human and other forms of flourishing on the continent.[26]

In recognition of this potential for religion to be a blessing, I present here two exemplars and socially engaged scholars (Tutu and Oduyoye) who have examined the question of religious, racial, and gender diversity and made, in my view, valid proposals as to what is wrong and how to remedy it. At the same time, as indicated above, religion has been manipulated or expressed in aggressive competitive and chauvinistic ways that make many consider religion a bane to the well-being of Africa and its peoples.[27] In agreeing with Tutu and Oduyoye, I argue that Africa's plurality of religion and cultures need not be the "curse" that it is threatening to become. It has been and can continue to be a blessing and a resource. These exemplars argue that the solutions coming from cultivating and nurturing pluralism and acceptance of the beauty of difference will help us to gain better traction and hence enable us to make greater strides on the path to enhanced human and other forms of flourishing. This, however, entails owning up to and acknowledging the ambiguous ways in which we have interpreted religion in the past, and a renewed commitment to overcoming such ambiguity henceforth. Such acknowledgment of past errors and ongoing ones will help not only to pre-empt future woes and injustices arising out of such ambiguity, but also facilitate the much-needed healing of trauma from past injustices, particularly where such injustices are rooted in distorted and unethical interpretations and practices of religion in Africa.

Two Road Maps to Pluralism: Tutu's Call for Rainbow Nations and Oduyoye's Proposal for Weaving a New Kente Cloth from the Different Strands in Africa

Regarding the issue of diversity, there seems to be an emerging consensus among significant persons and organizations that there can be no future without embracing pluralism.[28] This is the attitude that sees diversity not as a problem to be overcome, eliminated, or wished away, but a welcome reality that is here to stay and that can be an asset. In this context, Desmond Tutu encourages Africans to celebrate the beauty of diversity, a beauty reminiscent of the "rainbow," while Mercy Oduyoye invites us to think of the beauty and unity in diversity in Africa, which reminds her of beads of many sizes and colors, threaded together to create beautiful jewelry, or different-colored strands of fabric that can be woven into beautiful Kente cloth. For both of these writers, our diversity is a resource and an occasion to celebrate—as long as we approach it with a sense of pluralism.[29]

The Rainbow People of God: Desmond Tutu's Vision of Inclusive Community Rooted in Both Christianity and African Religions

Desmond Tutu, an Anglican bishop from South Africa, is well known for his role in the Truth, Justice and Reconciliation Commission in South Africa.[30] In his writings and sermons, Tutu envisions a new South Africa characterized by mutual respect and acceptance on the part of the people of that country. This vision is articulated in several places but most clearly in the title of one of his books, *The Rainbow People of God*, which is a collection of sermons, speeches, and letters addressing what he refers to as "the making of a peaceful revolution."[31] He speaks primarily from the context of apartheid in South Africa and unequivocally defends the moral imperative of embracing the beauty, honor, and dignity of the (racial) other, since this imperative is key to the flourishing and well-being of all. He thus encourages, as a matter of ethical duty, seeing the "different others" as "a rainbow people of God." In calling for us to embrace difference among people in the same way that we embrace the beauty of the different colors of the rainbow, Tutu is inspired by ethical sensibilities and imperatives to be found both in Christianity and in indigenous African religions, two of the several "different" religions that Africa has inherited from the past.[32]

One theo-ethical sensibility is the idea rooted in the Bible to the effect that human beings are made "in the image of God." This means that each person is of intrinsic value and dignity and that all human beings share a common identity and common destiny. They therefore have in common a responsibility to take care of each other and the earth, their home. It is on the basis that all are made in God's image and therefore have intrinsic worth, dignity, beauty, and moral agency that Tutu appealed in 1976 to B. J. Vorster, then prime minister of South Africa. He urged him to take action in light of the escalating desecration of people of color that had culminated in the Soweto uprisings of 1976.

> I am writing to you as one who has experienced the joys and anguish of family life, its laughter and its gaiety, its sorrows and pangs. I am writing to you sir as one passionately devoted to a happy and stable family life as an indispensable foundation of a sound society. I am writing to you as a human person to another person gloriously created in the image of the selfsame God and redeemed

by the very same Son of God and sanctified by the very same Holy spirit God who works inwardly in all of us to change our hearts of stone into hearts of flesh....[33]

He reminds Vorster,

> This Jesus Christ, whatever we may have done, has broken down all that separates us irrelevantly—such as race, sex, culture, status etc. In this Jesus Christ we are forever bound together as one redeemed humanity, black and white together.[34]

The notion that all are made in the image of God makes it imperative that all persons work to dismantle apartheid as a matter of theological and ethical duty. For, as Tutu argued,

> ...we are each a God Carrier, a tabernacle of the Holy spirit.... To treat one such as less than this is not just wrong.... It is to spit in the face of God. Consequently injustice, racism, exploitation, oppression are to be opposed not as a political task but as a response to a religious, a spiritual imperative.[35]

Desmond Tutu's vision of an inclusive community marked by pluralism, respect, and honor for the "different other" is also inspired by ethical sensibilities that flow from the African worldview, a worldview R. Sambuli Mosha discusses in his book *The Heartbeat of Indigenous Africa*.[36] Dr. Mosha identifies four aspects of this worldview and continues to analyze the ethics and virtues that flow from it. The four aspects of the African worldview are:

1. Belief in God (a belief shared by Christianity)
2. Belief in the intrinsic link between individual and society
3. Belief that all is in constant process of formation and transformation

4. Belief that the world is a living, interconnected, and interdependent whole[37]

In making the ethical case for pluralism, Tutu frequently appeals to aspects of this worldview and applies the ethics that flow from it. In particular, Tutu leverages the African notion of the person, perhaps best captured by the multilayered notion of *Ubuntu*.

According to African understanding, the person "is a person through others" (Ubuntu Ngubuntu Ngabantu). One with Ubuntu recognizes and lives up to the insight of the second aspect of the African worldview to the effect that "the individual's humanity is bound up with that of others" and that there is an intrinsic unity between the individual and the community. As John Mbiti, a Kenyan theologian, aptly puts it, while in the Western notion of the person the motto is "I think therefore I am," in the African understanding the motto is "we are therefore I am." Tutu captures this thought even more concisely when he affirms that a person with authentic Ubuntu recognizes and lives up to the insight that "we belong to the bundle of life."[38] He explains:

> A person with ubuntu is open and available to others, affirming of others, does not feel threatened that others are able and good, for he or she has a proper self-assurance that comes from knowing that he or she belongs in a greater whole and is diminished when others are humiliated ... or treated as if they were less than who they are.[39]

Ubuntu also refers to the quality of the person, the quality of being authentically human. To describe someone as having Ubuntu is a celebration of such a person's virtue-driven life and the "ethical qualities" that define the authentic person. Such persons, according to Tutu, are "generous, hospitable, friendly, caring and compassionate [and] they share what they have."[40]

In Tutu's vision of a mutually caring, inclusive community, the idea of Ubuntu becomes crucial for his argument against apartheid.

In his words, "Racial hatred diminishes me, in fact it diminishes all when one is diminished. We all belong to the bundle of life regardless of who we are and of what color."[41]

Another dimension of the African worldview that boosts the quest for pluralism and an inclusive, mutually respectful community is the notion of interdependence and interconnectedness of everything. Recognizing the validity and implications of this aspect of the African worldview for a people divided on racial grounds, Tutu constantly reminded his audience of the folly of thinking that racism affects only the victims. He reminds his audience that it affects all of us, not only because we belong to the bundle of life, but also because we are interdependent. He appeals to all to consider that becoming a rainbow nation is a collective communal project, and that we must become a rainbow nation together. For Tutu, there is not an us or them, just a we—a larger sense of we. As he explains:

> We are all fellow South Africans. We are compatriots. People shared newspapers, picnic lunches, stories—and they discovered (what a profound discovery!) that they were human together and that they actually seemed to want much the same things—a nice house in a secure and safe neighborhood, a steady job, good schools for the children, and, yes, skin color and race were indeed thoroughly irrelevant.[42]

Tutu concludes:

> God does not make us self-sufficient. We have our own gifts and that makes us unique, but I have gifts that you do not have and you have gifts that I do not have. The totally self-sufficient person, if ever there could be one, is subhuman. The first law of our being is that we are set in a delicate network of interdependence with our fellow human beings and with the rest of God's creation.[43]

A third pertinent aspect of the African worldview is the thought that in African understanding all is in process of transformation, all is in process of *becoming*. It is in recognition of the validity of this thought that Tutu was convinced that South African society held the possibility of transformation from a nation marked by racism and bigotry to a rainbow nation. In traditional society, rituals to recognize, celebrate, and signify individual and community transformations were created and practiced.[44] It is in this context that we can understand Tutu's role as overseer of the Truth, Justice and Reconciliation Commission, a national ritual of transformation, reconciliation, and healing for a South Africa en route to becoming a rainbow nation.

Regarding the traumas of the legacy of ambiguity and conflicts that have haunted the continent, especially South Africa, Desmond Tutu proposes that there cannot be a future without forgiveness. Reconciliation and restorative justice will only be achieved if we avoid the extremes of "historical amnesia" and "Nuremberg" approaches to (retributive) justice. He proposes "the third way" of "truth, justice and reconciliation" for a church of the "third day," marked by resilient hope.[45] The humanity of both victims and perpetrators (that is, all of us, according to Tutu) needed to be recognized. A third way of truth and reconciliation would honor the intrinsic worth of even the perpetrator (who is also made in God's image and whose Ubuntu is radically diminished, but not extinguished).[46]

Understood in this way, Ubuntu is an antidote to the wounds arising from a divided community. As Battle concludes: "We will grow in the knowledge that they (white people) too are God's children, even though they are our oppressors, though they may be our enemies... paradoxically, and more truly, they are truly our sisters and our brothers because we have dared and have had the privilege to call God, Abba, our father. Therefore, they belong together with us in the family of God, and their humanity is caught up with our humanity as ours is caught up with theirs."[47]

Given the reality that we are all interconnected and interdependent, chauvinism (of any kind) is, at best, folly and often morally reprehensible. Tutu reinforces the thought with the parable of a light bulb who thought he/she was a "light" all unto himself. Tutu tells the story:

> There was once a light bulb which shone and shone like no other light bulb had shone before. It captured all the *limelight* and began to strut about arrogantly, quite unmindful of how it was that it could shine so brilliantly, thinking that it was all due to its own merit and skill. Then one day somebody disconnected the famous light bulb from the light socket and placed it on the table, and try as hard as it could, the light bulb could bring forth no light and brilliance. It lay there looking so disconsolate and dark and cold—and useless. Yes, it had never known that its light came from the power station and that it had been connected to the dynamo by little wires and flexes that lay hidden and unseen and totally unsung. . . .[48]

Walking the Talk of Pluralism, Threading Beads of Many Colors, and Weaving a New Kente Cloth: Oduyoye and the Circle of Concerned African Women Theologians

While Desmond Tutu evokes the image of a rainbow to demand respect and reverence to the beauty of racial difference, Mercy Oduyoye uses the image of beads of many colors, as well as Kente cloth made of different strands, to describe her imagined inclusive community marked by mutual respect, reverence, and fairness. Her vision was concretized in her deliberate founding of an international community of diverse women, determined to nurture and grow pluralism among themselves for their own sake and for the benefit of society at large. Under her mentorship, the women committed themselves to working systemically across differences and in solidarity with each other to unmask various injustices, but also to make proposals regarding the way forward toward a sustainable and just peace.

I refer specifically to the Circle of Concerned African Women Theologians (hereafter the Circle). This organization was founded in 1989 by Mercy Oduyoye, an Akan woman from Ghana who was then one of the deputy directors of the World Council of Churches. The primary goal of the circle was/is to systematically examine the role of religion and culture in Africa in facilitating injustice—particularly that of sexism. The goal was/is also to examine ways in which religious beliefs and practices could facilitate peace, justice, and other freedoms that define and enhance *Ubuntu, true humanity.*

Recognizing that religion and culture are pivotal in shaping women's lives for good or ill, and proceeding on what feminists elsewhere have dubbed "the hermeneutics of suspicion," the women embarked on a seven-year (later reduced to five-year) cycle of sustained analysis of religion and culture, with several specific objectives in mind:

1. To encourage and empower the critical study of the practice of religion in Africa.
2. To publish theological literature written by African women with a special focus on religion and culture.
3. To undertake research that unveils (and names) both positive and negative religio-cultural factors, beliefs, and myths that affect, influence, or hamper women's development.
4. To promote a dialogical approach to religious and cultural tensions in Africa and beyond.
5. To strive toward the inclusion of women's studies in religion and cultures and in academic research institutions in Africa.
6. To empower African women to contribute to the cross-cultural discourse on women's issues through engagement in critical cultural hermeneutics.
7. To promote ecumenism and cultural pluralism.[49]

Living the Dialogue by Embracing Pluralism: The Circle's Response to the Challenge of Difference

Over the last thirty years or so, the Circle has sought to fulfill its goals by publishing a number of monographs from its five-year Pan-African conferences. While neither time nor space allows me to explain here what the women have said in each of the many volumes that they have published individually or collectively to date, I have in other essays cited representative samples of the writing and explained in some detail and in a synthesized manner how, through this particular community of dialogue and solidarity, concerned African women are responding to and engaging issues of injustice and lack of peace on the continent.[50]

More pertinently for the purposes of this essay and its theme, the women have identified the mishandling of the fact of diversity, which characterizes humanity today, as a key obstacle to peace in Africa and beyond. In their analysis, the women have also noted that in Africa, as elsewhere, much of the violence and pain is occasioned by a failure to adequately come to terms with and appropriately respond to the reality of religio-cultural, ethnic, gender, and other forms of difference. They have also noted that much of the violence is feminized, leading to the emergence of a category of violence known in the discourse as "gender-based violence." Sexism, a major manifestation of the failure to navigate gender difference in morally viable ways, has led to much pain, particularly for women caught up in sexist structures and social arrangements.[51]

Moreover, women are often caught at the intersection of multiple systems of chauvinism and domination rooted in the failure to see beauty and dignity in the different Other. Racism, colonialism, and classism weave a deadly web for many. Such chauvinism manifests directly in the exclusion, rejection, and often violence against those who are seen as "different." As we have seen above, ethnic chauvinism in its extreme manifestation leads to frequent violent ethnic clashes and even, in the case of Rwanda, genocide. Racial chauvinism has informed the exploitation of black people and their resources for centuries under colonialism, with apartheid in South Africa being an example of racism gone wild. Sexism—gender-based chauvinism—has also led to violence against women and loss of life for thousands of them.[52] As Charlotte Bunch, a leading scholar and advocate of women's rights as well as human rights, has put it: Sexism kills![53]

Chauvinism also manifests more subtly in the conditional tolerance and inclusion of the *different others*, provided they change in the direction dictated by those in power. This kind of chauvinism is perhaps best exemplified in Africa in the often coercive proselytization projects by dominant religions, sometimes using "charity" and other alleged benefits for affiliating with the dominant traditions as "bait" for such conversion. At other times, chauvinism has been nurtured among indigenous peoples by those who insist that their religion or denomination is superior. Consequently, conflicts among Christians and Muslims in Africa have been fanned by outsiders fighting for a greater share of Africa as a "spiritual territory." In the case of transgendered identities, the stigma against such persons has often escalated into deadly violence—exemplified, for example, by so-called correctional rape, ostensibly designed to "convert" gay people to heteronormativity.[54]

Against this background, and with the realization that religiocultural and other forms of diversity are a major given in Africa and elsewhere in the world, and that many tensions and conflicts in Africa are attributable to chauvinism and a gross mishandling of difference, Circle women have entered into a covenant "to promote a dialogical approach to religious–cultural and other tensions in Africa."[55]

Further, instead of just promoting the idea of dialogue as a means to pluralism, they have in practice adopted pluralism and a radical inclusivism, thus living the dialogue rather than simply speaking about it. For example, recognizing that the religio-cultural diversity is a given, and in their efforts to implement their covenant to embrace pluralism and dialogue, the Circle opened its membership to all women, regardless of their faith tradition—be it Islam, Christianity, Hinduism, or Judaism. Most important, despite the

Christianized background of most of the founding members, the Circle includes women who continue undeterred to practice the indigenous African religions, despite the many years of propaganda against them. While such openness to all faith traditions operating in Africa does not necessarily mean that the Circle members are themselves beyond chauvinism, it does signify their commitment to practicing rather than just speaking about dialogue and pluralism. Though not an easy course to follow—indeed, some of the Christianized women of the Circle have rather uncritically accepted the alleged superiority of imported Euro-Christianity—the commitment to embrace women from all faiths in the Circle has not only been a challenge but also an opportunity for them to understand each other and the various faiths with which they affiliate. Having members from the various faith traditions allows for a collective, insiders' critique of sexism and other forms of injustice as they become manifest in and through the faith traditions. It also allows women to detect and reject misrepresentations and caricatures of their faith as they explain to each other the beliefs and practices of those faiths in an atmosphere of mutual respect. Armed with a better understanding of each other and how the respective faith traditions shape their experiences as women, they are better positioned to launch a more credible religio-cultural critique and thus pave the way for social transformation.

Women in the Circle also commendably manifest a pluralist mindset as they recognize that there are even differences among them, and that there is no such a thing as a generic African woman. They recognize the problematic that could arise out of elitist and chauvinistic attitudes among women themselves. For this reason, and in order to respond adequately to diversity among women themselves, the Circle deliberately names and rejects classism and elitism. In their efforts to transcend classism and elitism within the circle, for example, membership to the Circle is not (at least so far) contingent on the payment of dues. Neither is a university degree a requirement for membership. The necessary and sufficient conditions are one's willingness and commitment to work in dialogue and sisterly solidarity with other women across Africa's many borders, both physical and metaphorical. Membership also calls for a commitment to a radical inclusivism that the Circle women not only recommend but also embody in practice.[56] In thus practicing pluralism and inclusivism, the Circle does not just talk about dialogue but strives to "walk the talk." It is an example of living the dialogue in a community where women from diverse backgrounds feel affirmed and in communication with each other for mutual enrichment and empowerment.

Circle Praxis and the Promise of Transformative Dialogue

While at face value the above list of goals and objectives seems to suggest that the Circle pursues a variety of different, unrelated tasks, a closer look reveals that in reality the goals are but various facets, aspects, or dimensions of a two-pronged Circle project: the eradication of injustices, particularly those based on sexism, among other systems of domination, as well as the quest for a radical pluralism without which peace and justice are unattainable. Thus, in the members' writings, they demand and engage in transformative dialogue with church and society on crucial issues of concern to women, including issues of violence that are often rooted in a failure to embrace and navigate difference more viably. Such dialogue with church and society also becomes a major ingredient in the overall quest for justice and peace on the continent.[57] Participating in and even calling for such dialogue is an imperative—or even a duty—that they have embraced. As Oduyoye writes in her articulation of this imperative:

> Any strategy to achieve greater power for women must be accompanied by voicing... for if we do not deliberately attempt to break the silence about our situations as African women, others will continue to maintain it....

> We must not let our voices grow quiet, for simultaneously with our cries for change a vigorous campaign is being waged by *both men and women*....[58]

Oduyoye speaks also for the Circle women when she reminds us that such naming and voicing become socially transformative only if the women are listened to and their naming is taken seriously. Failure to listen to women—or worse, silencing them as they attempt to name and address the deadly structural violence that targets them—is simply not acceptable. Through their work, they address church and society, demanding that on matters of justice, society listen and respond to women by acknowledging and engaging them and their agency in the project of a humanizing society in Africa and beyond.

In Oduyoye's words,

> Dealing justly with African women must begin by taking seriously women's questions and concerns about their status. Trivializing women's concerns does more harm than good...[instead] women's voices should be listened to when they speak about the God-given dignity of every person and the consequent need for each person for respect. To expect women to uphold all that which is humanizing in African culture and yet deny them participation in the politics of the family and the nation is a like asking them to make bricks without straw.... [W]e must acknowledge that women are not merely symbols of morality but are also human. Perhaps then we can remove the obstacles in women's paths to self-actualization...and continue our path to democratization based on the full participation of all women and men.[59]

Demanding transformative dialogue as a prelude to transformative action in church and society is therefore a legitimate strategy for African women, as exemplified in the work of the Circle in the last three decades. The hope is that the world is listening to them as they assert their agency and work toward a lifetime in service of social change.

Circle women have also recognized the fact that, quite often in history, oppressed people have fought back against their oppressors and reversed the situation. Many of the coups in Africa are based on this principle, wherein the liberators of today become the dictators of tomorrow, since, in fact, all that has been accomplished in a coup is a reversal of the status quo. The idea of *transforming* the systems of domination is hardly ever given any thought, and the notion of power as dominion or as power over others remains unchallenged. In a critical response to this situation, women in Africa—like many of their sisters across the world—are beginning to re-think the question of power and have taken significant baby-steps toward practicing alternative ways of wielding power and authority. The emphasis (at least *de jure*, if not entirely in practice) is to nurture the idea of "power for" and "power with" other women.[60]

It is in this context that we begin to understand the symbolic significance of the fact that these African women theologians deliberately chose to call themselves the "Circle" of Concerned Women. This term signifies the women's intentions to overcome the kind of hierarchical thinking that supports and facilitates the use of power as domination and also fuels exclusivism and deadly chauvinism. To actualize their goal of overcoming hierarchical thought and practices that engender Kyriarchies, it was determined quite early that leadership of the Circle would be exercised by a steering committee. It was also decided not to use terms such as *president* and *chairman*, which suggest hierarchy. The leaders serve on a voluntary basis and for limited terms. The overall coordinator of Circle activities is simply designated "Circle Coordinator." By deliberately replacing hierarchical thinking with "Circle thinking" dialogue and practice, the women have taken a step in the direction of pluralism that thrives on and simultaneously inspires inclusive communities marked by justice, solidarity, and mutual respect. Circle thinking and practice, in lieu of hierarchical and pyramidal thinking, is recommended and modeled by the women as a significant ingredient in the quest for peace and justice.[61] In embracing Circle thinking and practice, then, African women embody and model what they long for: transforming power so that it is in the service of Ubuntu, human dignity, rather than in the service of exploitation and vandalization of humanity.

Dialogue, Conscientization, and the Transformation of Consciousness

One of the greatest insights on the part of feminist analysts of culture and society in the face of sexism and its basis in essentializing and "demonizing"[62] the Other is that one is not born a woman or a man but rather becomes a man or woman. In other words, notions of manhood and womanhood are learned rather than innate.[63] The insight that gender is socially constructed implies that there is no such thing as a generic woman or a generic man, and gender essentialism is therefore a fallacy. This also implies that much of the behavior that manifests as sexism and gender violence is learned behavior, acquired through the various strategies by which society transmits its notions of manhood and womanhood. It follows that if sexism is not innate but learned, it can be unlearned. Concerned women argue that the same process of socialization that is used to ingrain sexist views of men and women in society can be re-claimed and re-channeled to help people unlearn those negative and destructive ideas—for example, the view that aggressiveness is essential to manhood, while passivity is essential to womanhood, or the equally destructive view that "men don't cry" but "women are hysterical" and therefore weak and unreliable.

Against this background, women in Africa, as elsewhere, have realized that dealing effectively with social injustices demands conscientization, the awakening of awareness of such problematic mindsets in society, as well as the awakening of a desire to do something about them. Such awakening and transformation of consciousness is necessary, since no amount of calling for justice, preaching peace, or sending troops to keep peace will work on its own until we begin to learn the practice of peace. In fact, women themselves have had to unlearn internalized sexism (along with other *-isms* such as racism and tribalism) and acquired self-deprecation. Only then can they make an effort to transform their own consciousness in order to deal with the enemy within that is an obstacle in their path to freedom and justice. They are also legitimately calling for a similar unlearning of hateful and violent behavior in others, both in church and society. Moreover, they are reclaiming their roles as formatters and nurturers of consciousness through their role as educators of their children. For them, rethinking socialization and its potential for transforming society toward justice and peace is a key piece to the puzzle. Like Tutu, their belief is that change is possible.

Oduyoye's Vision and Roadmap to a Livable Future: Threading Beads of Many Colors and Weaving a New Kente Cloth

It is the recognition of the viability and imperative of seeing difference as an asset rather than a problem that inspired Oduyoye to pursue the formation of the Circle and to mentor the women in their not-so-easy journey toward becoming a community marked by mutuality and solidarity across differences, a community determined to embody what they hope for: a society marked by justice, mutuality, respect, and reverence for all.

Oduyoye describes and makes the case for her vision of this ideal community in her book *Daughters of Anowa*. Specifically, in the last chapter of the book, titled "Conclusion: Beads and Strands," she describes her vision and her assessment of women's role in creating the imagined society more "poetically" and vividly by invoking several metaphors drawn from the world of women and their traditional roles in society—that is, bead-making and weaving.

To begin with, she describes her vision for an inclusive society and the creative work and moral imagination that goes into the work of becoming a society in ways that remind her of women and bead-making. In her words:

> ...as I look at the world of African women today, I think of beadwork. When I look at the variety of beads, I think of the changing being of the African woman: my grandmother, my mother, myself, my nieces, and my grandnieces: different beads from the same pot, different shapes, sizes, colors, uses, ever changing patterns strung on new strings.
>
> I hear the deliberate, gentle, instructing voices of the older women evoke the rhythm of *sam-sina*, the action of drawing a bead off the thread or pulling the thread through a bead. Women threading beads. I watch the different colors and I see a pattern emerge as they reject some beads and pick up others. Deliberate choices and delicate handling.... We appear only in beads of our choice, strung on strong strings in patterns of our creation.[64]

Similarly, she is reminded of women as weavers and imagines their role in the weaving of a new society, bridging the gap across differences. She continues:

> I also think of weaving, of the multi-colored, ever new patterns of *Kente* and *Aso Oke* cloth. In my reflections I hear the rhythm of weaving. I see a Yoruba woman, sitting straight-backed on a stool facing the broad woman's loom. Weaving large and wide, she does not produce narrow strips to be sewn together, but a whole universe of cloth— several motifs and several colors, blending and clashing, but forming one piece. I think of wholeness, a whole being who mothers a whole universe and clothes it with love.[65]

Oduyoye infers that while the task of weaving a new tapestry of humanity is time consuming and challenging, it brings joy to the weaver. She concludes: "and I see [in the weaving woman] her transparent joy. I see shredded lives being bound together by intertwining them. I see her, with her back straight and her eyes straining to join two ends of a broken thread, creating a new pattern...."[66]

Oduyoye concludes her book and statement of her imagined society on a hopeful note—that is, that another world is possible since people can change. Like Tutu, she is hopeful that Africa can learn how to weave a beautiful tapestry of humanity from the different strands of human experiences, hopes, and dreams. She invites all, particularly women, to become active weavers of a new Kente cloth of humanity.

Notes

1. Jonathan Sacks, *The Dignity of Difference: How to Avoid the Clash of Civilizations* (London and New York: Continuum, 2002), vii.
2. For details, see Diana L. Eck, *Encountering God: A Spiritual Journey from Bozeman to Banaras* (Boston: Beacon Press, 1993), 204–10.
3. For example, members of the Circle of Concerned African Women Theologians are drawn from the spectrum of Africa's diverse religions, including Islam, Christianity, AIRs (African Indigenous Religions), and even Judaism. Being pan-African in geographical scope, its members are also drawn from among the thousands of different ethnic groups that inhabit the continent.
4. For commentary on what it means to live a hyphenated identity, see the documentary "Hyphen-Nation": <https://www.youtube.com/watch?v=3ZwRQBHoQwE>.
5. For example, the different evaluation of polygamy has caused tensions within African Christian families in which women in polygamous relationships and their children may be disinherited when the husband converts to Christianity and is expected to give up all but one wife at baptism. It is perhaps in recognition of the growing concern around the ethical complexities arising from diverse interpretations of marriage and family that Pope Francis recently called for a global study of the implications of the changing notions of family in the

modern pluralistic world. See the 2014–2015 Bishops Extraordinary Synod on the Family.

6. For a detailed analysis of the racist and ethnocentric roots of what he calls the Myth of the Dark Continent, see Patrick Brantlinger, "Victorians and Africans: The Genealogy of the Myth of the Dark Continent," *Critical Inquiry* 12.1 (1985): 166–203. For a rebuttal of this myth and what has been described as "a corrective to Africa's image as a dark hopeless place…a hopeful narrative about a continent on the rise," see Dayo Olopade, *The Bright Continent: Breaking Rules and Making Change in Africa* (Boston: Houghton Mifflin Harcourt, 2014).

7. There are at least 3,000 different ethnic groups on the continent. Though they share a common worldview with key defining features, these groups practice their religions in ways that are culturally customized. Thus, for example, while belief in God is common to all the groups, the way that God is conceptualized and named may differ from one ethnic group to another. Ethnic identity is also linked with the discrete ethnic group's history and ancestry. Ethnic diversity has been a major factor in shaping Africa's destiny and experience, with "negative ethnicity" and chauvinism giving rise to many conflicts and even genocide.

8. The failure to embrace the differently gendered has, for example, led to the horror of the so-called correctional rape. Such differently gendered people and their relationships have been threatened with the death penalty. For details, see the documentary *God Loves Uganda*, about the plight of the differently gendered in Uganda, where the death penalty has been proposed for them: *God Loves Uganda*, directed by Roger Ross Williams (Variance Films, 2013).

9. Consider the "hybrid," multilayered religious, cultural, and ethnic identities that have emerged, particularly in the African Diaspora, as depicted, for example, in a recent documentary, *The Neo-African-Americans*. The documentary analytically considers the people of African descent in America and distinguishes between those African Americans who are linked historically to the Transatlantic slave trade several hundred years ago and those people of African descent who came more recently to the US as asylum seekers, workers, or just immigrants, some from the continent and some from other parts

of the African Diaspora like Jamaica and Haiti. The documentary explores the ramifications of these diverse groups even among the New African Americans and the question this diversity raises for the politics of identity in America today. In short, these are "the Neo-African-Americans." For a link to the trailer, see: <https://www.youtube.com/watch?v=UJKV5roH244>.

10. Uwem Akpam, *Say You Are One of Them* (New York: Little Brown and Company, 2008), 353.

11. Ibid., 245.

12. Religion has been used to support the welfare of those in power. In apartheid South Africa, the Bible was read and cited to justify racism, while elsewhere, colonization and subjugation of peoples have been enacted in the name of religion.

13. Consider, for example, the role of "hybrid" or "Creole" religions, such as the Afro-American Black Church, *Santería*, and *Condomblé*, that have emerged in the diaspora and their role in helping Africans navigate the complexities of being "dispersed" and being "EDPs" (externally displaced peoples).

14. Akpam, 321.

15. During their flight, the fugitives had taken refuge with Mallim Abdullahi, a Muslim who had hidden them in his house under a pile of prayer mats. Jibril could not hold down his side of the mat because of his amputated wrist. A fellow fugitive hiding under the mat with him, a Christian, held it for him.

16. Yusuf was Jibril's brother who had been killed for refusing to give up his Christian faith.

17. Ibid.

18. Jibril distinguishes here between Mallim Abdullahi's more authentic form of Islam and Fanaticism, a counterfeit religion to which he himself had succumbed with dire consequences.

19. To illustrate the difference between these responses, she tells a story from which she gets the title of the chapter, "Is Our God Listening?" In the story, a Jew and a Christian are walking around in Japan when they stumble on a Japanese person deep in prayer. They wonder between themselves "Is our god listening? If he is not listening, why not? If he is, then what are we all about?" (i.e., why do we bother to be labeled "Jewish," "Christian," etc.?). She invokes this story to

demonstrate the distinction between exclusivism, inclusivism, and pluralism. The exclusivist would say our god is not listening to others, while inclusivists incorporate others into a world we already know, and in our own terms. For details see Eck, *Encountering God*, 166ff.

20. Ibid., 169.

21. For details see ibid., 191–99.

22. Ibid.

23. Ibid., 169.

24. Ibid., 197.

25. Even mass death, as in the case of Rwanda and South Africa during apartheid.

26. Consider, for example, the work of thousands of Christian missionaries who, over the years, have dedicated their lives to improving the quality of life of those on the continent. Many such missionaries are propelled by the core values of the gospel as they are summarized, for example, in the Sermon on the Mount. Or consider the work of exemplars like Wangari Maathai, who have tapped the ideals of indigenous Africa and Christianity and recommended the same in a bid to create a livable future for all on the continent.

27. Cf. Emmanuel Katongole, *The Sacrifice of Africa: A Political Theology for Africa* (Grand Rapids, MI: W. B. Eerdmans, 2011).

28. Consider, for example, the Parliament of the World's Religions and its Declaration Toward a Global Ethic, in which an unequivocal statement is made to the effect that "our different and cultural traditions must not prevent our common involvement in opposing all forms of inhumanity and working for greater humanness." For details, see <https://parliamentofreligions.org/pwr_resources/_includes/FCKcontent/File/TowardsAGlobalEthic.pdf>; and "Call to Our Guiding Institutions," <https://s3.amazonaws.com/berkley-center/991208CPWRCallOurGuidingInstitutions.pdf>.

29. This is a central thesis in Oduyoye's *Daughters of Anowa: African Women and Patriarchy* (Maryknoll, NY: Orbis Books, 1995), especially Chapter 10, "Beads and Strands."

30. Tutu himself is a good example of hyphenated identity: he is an African-Anglican bishop.

31. See Desmond Tutu, *The Rainbow People of God: The Making of a Peaceful Revolution* (New York: Doubleday, 1994).

32. The case against apartheid was also made on the basis of Islamic teachings and ethics. As Christians declared apartheid blasphemous and a heresy, Muslim activists propelled by Islamic teachings and theo-ethics also fought against apartheid. They were convinced that apartheid, a radical failure to see beauty in the racial other, is haram (i.e., sinful and forbidden by Islamic faith). For a detailed account of Muslim women's active participation in the struggle against apartheid and how they considered it unethical in light of Islamic teachings, see Georgina Jardim, "Muslim Women Against Apartheid: Muslim Women for Universal Values," *Journal of Scriptural Reasoning* 14:1 (June 2015).

33. Tutu, *Rainbow People of God*, 7.

34. Ibid.

35. Tutu, quoted in Michael Battle, *Reconciliation: The Ubuntu Theology of Desmond Tutu* (Cleveland, OH: Pilgrim Press, 1997), 48.

36. For details see R. Sambuli Mosha, *The Heartbeat of Indigenous Africa: A Study of the Chagga Educational System* (New York: Garland Publishing, 2000).

37. Paraphrased from Mosha, 7–15.

38. Desmond Tutu, *No Future without Forgiveness* (New York: Doubleday, 1999), 31.

39. Ibid.

40. Ibid.

41. Ibid.

42. Desmond Tutu, *God Has a Dream: A Vision of Hope for Our Time* (New York: Doubleday, 2004), 6.

43. Ibid., 25.

44. For a discussion of the transformative role of ritual in indigenous Africa, see Mosha, 68–78.

45. This is Desmond Tutu's thesis in *No Future without Forgiveness*, here at 30.

46. Ibid., 31.

47. Michael Battle, *Reconciliation*, 47

48. Desmond Tutu, "Response at Graduation of Columbia University's Honorary Doctorate," at University of Witwatersrand on August 2, 1982, as quoted in Battle, *Reconciliation*, 219.

49. Cited in Mercy Amba Oduyoye (ed.), *Transforming Power: Women in the Household of God* (Accra: Sam Woode Publishers, 1997), 5.

50. Teresia M. Hinga, "The Dialogical Imperative: Listening to Concerned and Engaged African Women," in Colleen M. Griffith (ed.), *Prophetic Witness: Catholic Women's Strategies for Reform* (New York: Crossroad, 2009), 83–96.

51. Gender-based violence is a key focus of the Circle research and advocacy. It was, for example, the theme for its 5th Pan African conference titled, *Transforming Faith Communities into Safe Space: Conversations on Gender, Health, Culture, and Empire* held at Kempton Park, Johannesburg, 7–11 August, 2013. For details, see the Circle website: <http://www.thecirclecawt.com/>.

52. For a harrowing and gendered account of violent conflict and its disproportionate and deadly impact on women, see *Documentary Lumo* from PBS, which features the excruciating plight of Lumo Sinai, one of the thousands of women in Goma, DRC, who were gang-raped and violated and left with painful and often irreparable fistulas. For an analytical account of the globally escalated gender-based "sexual violence in armed conflict" and its roots in what the author refers to as "(Globalized) Hegemonic masculinity," see Janie L. Leatherman, *Sexual Violence and Armed Conflict* (Cambridge, England: Polity Press, 2011), 150.

53. Charlotte Bunch, "Women's Rights as Human Rights: Toward a Re-Vision of Human Rights," *Human Rights Quarterly* 12:4 (1990): 486–98, here at 488.

54. Cf. Roger Ross Williams's documentary *God Loves Uganda*.

55. See Teresia Hinga, "The Dialogical Imperative," 86.

56. For example, with the inclusion of both men and non-African women in the dialogue.

57. Cf. Oduyoye, *Daughters of Anowa*.

58. Ibid., 170.

59. Ibid., 171.

60. Such a reconsideration and rethinking of the question of power within the church is urged, for example, by Letty Russell in her book aptly titled *Church in the Round: Feminist Interpretations of the Church* (Louisville, KY: Westminster/John Knox, 1993). In the book, she invokes the metaphor of a round kitchen table and the possibility of face-to-face conversations around such tables to signify the kind of ecclesiology that concerned women, even in Western feminist circles, long for. For details, see *Church in the Round*, 12.

61. Carrie Pemberton, *Circle Thinking: African Women Theologians in Dialogue with the West* (Leiden and Boston: Brill, 2003).

62. In the writings of the Church Fathers, women have been described as "the devil's gateway" for the role they allegedly played in the Fall of Man. See, for example, Tertullian, *On the Apparel of Women*, Book I, ch. 1 in: *From Ante-Nicene Fathers*, Vol. 4, ed. Alexander Roberts, James Donaldson, and A. Cleveland Coxe (Buffalo, NY: Christian Literature Publishing Co., 1885). Revised and edited for New Advent by Kevin Knight, available online at <http://www.newadvent.org/fathers/0402.htm>. See also Alvin J. Schmidt, *Veiled and Silenced: How Culture Shaped Sexist Theology* (Macon, GA: Mercer University Press, 1989), 43.

63. Simone de Beauvoir, *The Second Sex* (New York: Random House/Alfred A. Knopf, 2009).

64. Oduyoye, *Daughters of Anowa*, 209.

65. Ibid., 209–10.

66. Ibid.

Works Cited

Akpam, Uwem. *Say You Are One of Them*. New York: Little Brown and Company, 2008.

Battle, Michael. *Reconciliation: The Ubuntu Theology of Desmond Tutu*. Cleveland, OH: Pilgrim Press, 1997.

Brantlinger, Patrick. "Victorians and Africans: The Genealogy of the Myth of the Dark Continent." *Critical Inquiry* 12.1 (1985): 166–203.

Eck, Diana L. *Encountering God: A Spiritual Journey from Bozeman to Banaras*. Boston: Beacon Press, 1993.

Hinga, Teresia M. "The Dialogical Imperative: Listening to Concerned and Engaged African Women." In *Prophetic Witness: Catholic Women's Strategies for Reform*. Edited by Colleen M. Griffith. New York: Crossroad, 2009, 83–96.

Katongole, Emmanuel. *The Sacrifice of Africa: A Political Theology for Africa*. Grand Rapids, MI: W. B. Eerdmans, 2011.

Leatherman, Janie. *Sexual Violence in Situations of Armed Conflict*. Cambridge: Polity Press, 2011.

Mosha, R. Sambuli. *The Heartbeat of Indigenous Africa: A Study of the Chagga Educational System*. New York: Garland Publishing, 2000.

Oduyoye, Mercy Amba. *Beads and Strands: Reflections of an African Woman on Christianity in Africa*. Yaoundé, Cameroun: Editions Clé; Akropong-Akuapem, Ghana: Regnum Africa, 2002.

———. *Daughters of Anowa: African Women and Patriarchy*. Maryknoll, NY: Orbis Books, 1995.

——— (ed.). *Transforming Power: Women in the Household of God*. Accra: Sam Woode Publishers, 1997

Olopade, Dayo. *The Bright Continent: Breaking Rules and Making Change in Africa*. Boston: Houghton Mifflin Harcourt, 2014.

Pemberton, Carrie. *Circle Thinking: African Women Theologians in Dialogue with the West*. Leiden and Boston: Brill, 2003.

Russell, Letty M. *Church in the Round: Feminist Interpretation of the Church*. Louisville, KY: Westminster/John Knox, 1993.

Sacks, Jonathan. *The Dignity of Difference: How to Avoid the Clash of Civilizations*. London and New York: Continuum, 2002.

Tutu, Desmond. *God Has a Dream: A Vision of Hope for Our Time*. New York: Doubleday, 2004.

———. *No Future without Forgiveness*. New York: Doubleday, 1999.

———. *The Rainbow People of God: The Making of a Peaceful Revolution*. New York: Doubleday, 1994.

Williams, Roger Ross (director). *God Loves Uganda*. Variance Films, 2013.

Chapter Fourteen

AGWA BU MMA: VIRTUE AND BEAUTY IN AN AFRICAN COMMUNITY

Paulinus Ikechukwu Odozor, C.S.Sp.
University of Notre Dame

When the Igbo say *"Agwa bu mma,"* they mean, loosely trans-lated, that "character is beauty," or its corollary, that "beauty lies in character." It is a bold aphorism that asserts a relation-ship between physical beauty and moral goodness. Sometimes it also is not only a claim regarding the superiority of morality to aesthetics, but one that appears at first glance to collapse the cat-egories of aesthetics and morality into one, decidedly tilting the balance toward morality. Thus *agwa bu mma* contains some sig-nificant insights that are fraught with challenges. One of those challenges has to do with understanding the relationship of hu-man agency and divine enablement or capacitation among the Igbo. The other is the understanding of virtue among the Igbo and the relationship of virtue to beauty among human beings. This challenge leads to the discussion in this essay of the mean-ing of beauty among the Igbo and how it relates to the theory of virtue and of the approbation of human moral agency within this African community. To get as good a handle on our topic as possible, I will undertake an analysis of *The Concubine,* a novel by a Nigerian (Igbo) writer. But first I will provide a brief intro-duction to the Igbo.

The Igbo

The Igbo are an ethnic group in present-day Nigeria whose homeland lies between the Niger River and the Cross River. Most Igbo live in the area in the east, where the river makes its way down to the Niger Delta. However, a substantial minority of Igbo live to the west of the Niger River. Like other groups whose limits are not defined by obvious natural boundaries, the Igbo tend to merge into neighboring peoples.[1] The Igbo are bordered to the west, north, and southeast by neighbors whose histories are closely intertwined with theirs.

When we consider the Igbo or the Igbo-speaking peoples as a whole, in what sense are they to be regarded as a unit? First, they occupy a common territory. Second, they speak a common language, though with many slight variations. "With a few exceptions, these variations appear to be mutually intelligible, without undue difficulty, at least to those who are accustomed to traveling. The language is therefore...a unifying factor."[2] Third, the Igbo are also a culturally homogeneous group—with the same or identical kinship structures, religious practices and symbols, exogamic marriage patterns, and so forth. These make the Igbo a culturally distinct group and provide a unifying factor among them.

The Igbo are a very well-traveled people. Even though they occupy the Nigerian hinterland, which for many centuries was impenetrable to outsiders, especially those coming from the West, the Igbo nonetheless have, for a remarkably long period of time, maintained trade relations with neighbors to the north (the Igala), the west (the Edo and the Bini), and the south of Nigeria. Today the Igbo are found almost everywhere in the world, including here in the United States. As they migrate to different parts of the world, the Igbo carry with them their distinct patterns of kinship associations, language, preference for certain foods, and religious and metaphysical outlook. No one knows exactly how many Igbo there are in the world today. Some have put the number at about 18 percent of the population of Nigeria, which is itself unreliably estimated to be about 177 million. Other sources argue that the Igbo could number up to 71 million worldwide, if diasporic Igbo or descendants of the Igbo are counted. However we look at it, the Igbo constitute a very visible aspect of the life of the Nigerian nation.

The Igbo have also massively embraced Christianity. They are statistically among the most Christian groups in the world today. Over 90 percent of the Igbo consider themselves Christian in one form or another. Like other Africans, religion informs the life of the Igbo in its totality.[3] As in all other communities in Africa, Igbo Christians must contend with the reality of African Traditional Religion (ATR) as a backdrop to their faith. For the most part, ATR has become for most Africans an important preparation for the reception of Christianity, in that it supplies a wholesome religiosity and important theological insights into the encounter with the divine, which the African Christian carries over into the Christian faith. ATR also presents very crucial challenges to Christianity in various aspects. This is the basis for the ongoing dialogue between Christianity and ATR. At the center of this dialogue stands the African theologian. As Adrian Hastings once put it, "The chief non-Biblical reality with which the African theologian must struggle is the non-Christian religious traditions of his own people." In this way, African theology has become "something of a dialogue between the African scholar and the perennial religions and spiritualities of Africa."[4]

The dialogue between African primal religions and Christianity is often referred to as inculturation, a phenomenon that the Nigerian theologian Luke Mbefo has described as "a giant intellectual effort in faith to find a coherent and cogent interpretation of Christianity for any culture different from its Eurocentric matrix."[5] Conversely, inculturation as an intellectual undertaking in Africa can also imply an attempt to explain an African religious/philosophical phenomenon in categories that are familiar to or "brewed"[6] in Western philosophical or Christian categories. In any case, inculturation is always a two-way process involving some form of give-and-take among various cultures and traditions in search of greater clarity regarding certain human truths or values.[7]

The Concubine

The Concubine[8] is the first of three novels by Nigerian Igbo writer Elechi Amadi. Initially published in 1966 and set in a rural Igbo community in eastern Nigeria, the novel is about family, traditional values, rivalries, and love in an African community. It opens with the story of conflict between two young men, Madume and Emenike, over a disputed boundary line, a situation that leads to a physical altercation between the two neighbors. Although Emenike dies mysteriously sometime after this fight from what the traditional medicine man describes as "lock chest," many people in the community hold that his death is the result of the fight with Madume, whom they all consider greedy and unjust in his dealings with people. Sometime thereafter, when Madume—who always had a longing not only for Emenike's property but also for his beautiful wife, Ihuoma—tries to appropriate for himself a plantain tree that Ihuoma has on the same piece of property he (Madume) had wanted to wrest away from Emenike (Ihuoma's dead husband), he is struck blind by a cobra that appears suddenly from nowhere and spits in his eyes. Dejected, depressed, and abandoned by everyone, Madume later hangs himself.

The main theme of this book is love and desire, and at the center of it all is Ihuoma, a young woman of extreme beauty and mother of three children, who became a widow upon the death of Emenike only six years into their marriage. Ihuoma is described as the most desirable woman in her community. In Amadi's words, "Ihuoma's complexion was that of an ant-hill. Her features were smoothly rounded and looking at her no one could doubt that she was enjoying her husband's wealth."[9] Also, according to the author, Ihuoma's face had a youthful expression—alluring, deeply enchanting, and with a deeply bewitching subtlety that radiated an otherworldly beauty. However, what made Ihuoma stand out were not just her physical attributes.

> That she was beautiful she had no doubt, but that did not make her arrogant. It was her husband's boast that in their six years of marriage she had never had any serious

quarrels with another woman. She was not good at invec-
tives and other women talked much faster than she did.
The fact that she would be outdone in the verbal exchange
perhaps partly restrained her from coming into open verbal conflicts with her neighbors. Gradually she acquired
the capacity to bear a neighbor's stinging remarks without
repartee. In this way, her prestige among the womenfolk
grew until even the most garrulous among them was reluctant to be unpleasant to her. She found herself settling
quarrels and offering advice to older women.[10]

In various parts of the novel, Ihuoma is described as ready to forgive, industrious, caring, loving, peace-loving, and understanding.
In other words, her beauty is in her *agwa* (character). One of the
women echoes the general sentiment of everyone within the community when she says of Ihuoma that "she is easily the best woman
in the village. She can't do anything shameful."[11] Ihuoma is considered an *Ezigbo Mmadu* (a good person) by all within her community,
even those who are inclined to be envious of her beauty and near
perfection in terms of both character and aesthetics.

To be a virtuous person is to be an *Ezigbo Mmadu*. For the Igbo,
an *Ezigbo Mmadu* is seen to possess such moral virtues as truthful-
ness, reliability/dependability, justice, peacefulness, empathy, and
concern for others. Ihuoma is someone neighbors and acquain-
tances consider an *Ezigbo Mmadu*, a good person, because she is
known to be industrious, caring, peace-loving, understanding, and
ready to forgive. Two quick points to note are that although the
catalogue of the morally desirable virtues are the same for everyone,
some of the virtues are considered more sought-after than others.
Also, the ordering of the virtues can be gender-determined. Thus,
even though these virtues apply to both males and females, some
are considered more important in females than in males and vice
versa. Among the Igbo the virtue of peacefulness is highly prized
generally, but it is even more valued when a woman possesses it.
This is so because it is a valuable asset that she brings to her hus-

band's clan, among whom she will make her home as a married person. Also, the quality of industriousness is one that the Igbo culture expects of everyone, though it is more highly prized in a man, since he is expected in traditional Igbo society to be "man enough" to provide for his family's material needs. All this is to say that every culture, including the Igbo, has its concept of "the standards of good behavior, of what is to be admired, and what abhorred. Yet, by and large, within a single culture the fundamentals of what is decent and decorous possesses the elements of continuity."[12] As Thomas Aquinas puts it, "Virtue is a good quality (*habitus*) of the mind, by which we live righteously of which no one can make bad use; which God works in us, without us."[13] Aquinas states that the last clause in this definition applies to infused virtues—that is, those virtues that God bestows on us without action on our part. These include the so-called cardinal virtues of faith, hope, and charity. One of the questions that I will raise later in this chapter, in the context of the story of the various characters in Elechi Amadi's novel, is whether there is an understanding of the idea of virtues of the infused kind in African primal religions, and how this may compare with that same notion within Christianity.

A Contrasting Character

A second character of interest in the novel is Ahurole, a young woman from Omokachi village, the fiancée and later wife to Ekwueme. Ahurole is as beautiful as Ihuoma, but she is described as an immature character who cries over nothing. What irritates her husband most is "that any time she had this crying fit, she would sulk until he calmed her as he would a baby."[14] When she was not sulking, "Ahurole was vivacious and full of pranks. She would wrestle energetically with her husband amidst tumbling chairs, laughing happily." But when her tears set in, she presented an alarmingly contrasting picture. This picture was far from what Ekwueme had wanted in marriage. "He wanted a woman who would not only receive praise and encouragement but also give them in return; a mature woman, soothing and loving...." He wanted a self-motivated and contented person. On the contrary, "Ahurole is a unique type of woman altogether."[15] The difference lay in her *agwu*. It was her *agwu*'s fault that she was a bit neurotic. It was her *agwu* that led her to procure a love potion that drove her husband mad and nearly killed him. It was her *agwu* that made her eventually go away from her matrimonial home. It was her *agwu* that made Ahurole "a unique type of woman altogether." Her *agwu* needed to be tamed, for it was this same *agwu* that tainted her *agwa*.

Agwu is a widely employed term in Igbo cosmology:

> Agwu is of the category of spirits created by Chukwu-okike (the creator God) along with such deities as *Igwe*, *Anyanwu*, *Amadioha*, and *Ala*, whose respective natural symbols are the sky, the sun, the thunder and the earth. Unlike a mere spirit force, *agwu* exercises intellectual and volitive faculties and is believed to exercise immense influence in human affairs. He is the patron spirit of the *dibia* (diviner-cum-healer) and the inspirer of people of outstanding talent.[16]

Among the Igbo, *agwu* has also become a metaphor for "wickedness, madness, malice, perfidy, callousness, and everything that is evil."[17] In his book *Sacrifice in Ibo Religion*, Francis Arinze writes that *agwu* is regarded as "the spirit...who can be capricious to the extreme, but who also enriches his devotees."[18] Another Igbo scholar, Emefie Ikenga Metuh, speaks of *agwu* in these terms: "*Agwu* is the patron spirit of divination and diviners. It is called *mmuo nkpasa*, spirit of confusion.... *Agwu* afflicts its victims with psychological disturbance which sometimes takes the form of restlessness, wastefulness or even madness—*Ara Agwu*."[19] So, in this story, Ahurole is afflicted by an evil *agwu*, a situation that raises the question of moral culpability. For even though the community thinks of this woman as being under the influence of her *agwu*, they still expect her to be like Ihuoma and the other good women in the community.

While we grapple with the question of moral culpability in the case of Ahurole, the story of Ihuoma raises another issue—that of moral praise. In Amadi's book, Ihuoma is described almost in non-human terms. Her beauty and her character are almost otherworldly. We later discover that she is in fact (and unbeknownst to her) the human wife of the Sea-King, who has equipped her with all kinds of unimaginable qualities and who continues to guard and guide her in her earthly sojourn.

> Ihuoma belongs to the sea. When she was in the spirit world she was a wife of the Sea-King, the ruling spirit of the sea. Against the advice of her husband she sought the company of human beings and was incarnated. The Sea-King was very angry but because he loved her best of all his wives he did not destroy her immediately [after] she was born. He decided to humor her and let her live out her normal earthly span and come back to him. However because of his great love for her, he is terribly jealous and tries to destroy any man who makes love to her.[20]

Thus, Ihuoma's late husband, who was thought to have died of "lock-chest," was killed by the Sea-King; and Madume, the man who tried to dispossess her of her plantain trees and who himself secretly lusted after her, was actually killed by the Sea-King, who had assumed the form of a cobra.

Agwa *and* Agwu

The story of these two women, Ihuoma and Ahurole, raises many deeper ethical questions among the Igbo and in many other African societies. I will list a number of them here, especially as issues for further research and investigation. The first concerns the role of the divine in human affairs and, subsequently, the problem of human moral agency and freedom. The virtuous and beautiful Ihuoma is, in the end, discovered to be an incarnate divine person—the wife of the Sea-King. Was her character human or was she of good character because she was semi-divine? In a very telling passage in the book, the *dibia* Anyika, who was consulted by the would-be in-laws of Ihuoma, says to his clients, "Look at her [Ihuoma]....Have you seen anyone quite so right in everything, almost perfect? I tell you only a sea-goddess—for that is precisely what she is, can be all that."[21] This quotation points to something that anyone familiar with the Igbo religion would know—namely, the tendency sometimes to ascribe any perfection, moral or aesthetic—especially in a woman—to unseen powers from the dark world. This tendency can create two reactions: a devaluing of the moral or physical endowment in question or an exaggeration of its importance, whereby the person in question is elevated to near-mythical status. More important, this tendency contains a number of truths dear to the heart of the Igbo. The first is that (as I have already noted above) beauty is a divine endowment both in nature and in the human person. Second, "even the highest and brightest thing contains seeds of darkness. A beautiful girl can have a dark heart, just as a sweet-smelling soup can contain poison."[22] Among the Igbo, the eagle is a metaphor for beauty. Majestic in flight and able to soar, the eagle can be a thing of beauty. A beautiful girl is sometimes referred to as *Ugo*, an eagle. So is a handsome and well-built man. But despite being beautiful, the eagle is a fierce predator whose moral nature is not absolute. Therefore, "eagle metaphors are not as superficially simple as they may appear to be, and this is true of Igbo aesthetic/moral/philosophical thought as a whole."[23] Even the virtuous life is not considered to be absolutely so, since no one possesses virtue to the utmost degree or in all areas. As the Igbo would say, every human being goes to the toilet, and all lizards are capable of suffering a belly ache. On the other hand, it would seem to me that there is also an understanding in ATR—especially among the Igbo—of infused virtues; that is, of some virtues as good qualities "which God works in us, without us," as Aquinas puts it. As far as I know, there is no fully developed theory of virtue in the writings of African theologians today. But it would seem that there are grounds for a comprehensive comparative study of this notion in ATR and in moral theology.

In Amadi's novel, Ahurole's fortunes, like those of Ihuoma, are also affected by the spirits. In Ahurole's case it is her *agwu* that is controlling her *agwa*. Her *agwu* is a bad one, and it is this that makes her the kind of woman she is. Again, we see here the question of the value of human moral agency. Here we have what I believe to be a very big issue that must be addressed in any dialogue with African Traditional Religion, especially among the Igbo. ATR admits of many agents and intermediaries. Among the Igbo there are *chi* and *agwu*, among many others. The question is the extent to which human beings can be considered free agents if their *chi* or their *agwu* or any other divinities play such decisive roles in their lives. As Chinua Achebe points out:

> The Igbo believe that a man receives his gifts or talents, his character—indeed his portion in life in general—before he comes into the world. It seems there is an element of choice available to him at that point, and that his chi presides over the bargaining. Hence the saying *obu etu nya na chie si kwu*, which we often hear when a man's misfortune is somehow beyond comprehension and so can only be attributable to an agreement he himself entered into, at the beginning, alone with his chi; for there is a fundamental justice in the universe and nothing so terrible can happen to a person for which he is not somehow responsible.[24]

There is in this statement a bit of predestination and moral determinism rolled into one. For if someone has already received his or her talents in a metaphysical primordial past, and if someone's character is already set at that point, how can anyone blame this person for any wrongdoing committed in his real life? It is not sufficient to argue that the person has a say at the point of bargaining, for there certainly is no awareness of this fact by anyone I know. We are dealing here with the human agent's agency and freedom of action. Later in his essay, Achebe tries to wriggle out of this dilemma by asserting that *chi* is more concerned with success or failure than with righteousness and wickedness. But he quickly adds that "this is not to say that Chi is indifferent to morality."[25] The paradox here is that despite all the belief in the role of the divine in people's lives, the Igbo do, in fact, hold people accountable for their actions, both their failures and successes. But this accountability is mitigated by the metaphysical considerations that we have stated here. Where all of this leaves us is not always clear. What *is* clear, though, is that among the Igbo things are not always what they appear to be, even in morality. There is thus room for tentativeness and acceptance of ambiguity in human conduct and choices, for we do not always know. We can never totally determine what is motivating human action or driving human choices. It is also interesting that despite their belief in the human capacity for excellence due to hard work and industriousness, the Igbo always reserve room for divine enablement in human achievement, whether moral or otherwise.

Beauty: A Final View

Finally, what is beauty and what place does it have among the Igbo? Reading through Amadi's *The Concubine*, one is struck not only by the cultural aspects of the understanding of beauty but especially by the fact that there are common human aspects to this notion that are pertinent everywhere. An understanding of beauty that is suggested in one of the Socratic dialogues is that "the beautiful either is or depends upon what is beneficial or what pleases through the senses or what pleases through the senses of hearing and sight."[26] In the *Timmaeus*, Socrates states that beautiful things are so because they are made with care "in the due proportion of part to part by mathematical measurement." Important here are the qualities of measure and proportion. For St. Augustine, beauty involves a normative judgment. "We perceive the ordered object as being what it ought to be, the disordered object as falling short. The idea of beauty therefore connotes an ideal order divinely illuminated. This means that there can be no relativity in the understanding of beauty. There can be no relativity in it."[27] Ihuoma is beautiful because she is pleasing to the eye and possesses due proportion, both aesthetically and morally. Ahurole, on the other hand, even though she is pleasing to the eye, is not considered beautiful because she lacks moral proportion and measure.

In Thomas Aquinas's metaphysics, being is good, and to say that the thing is or exists is to say that it is good, in that everything that exists is in some way desirable. "The essence of goodness consists in this, that it is in some way desirable." And that thing is desirable insofar as it is perfect. Everything that exists is desirable in some way, but not absolutely, because although everything that exists is good, being is not ascribed to things univocally. Some things actually are, and other things have being in potentiality. By "its substantial being, everything is said to have being simply; but by any further actuality is said to have being relatively."[28] Beauty is "what pleases on being seen."[29] Here, seeing "extends to all cognitive grasp: the perception of beauty is a kind of knowing." And "beauty being part of goodness is an ontological term with different senses when applied to different things in different contexts. The concept signifies a whole family of qualities, for as Aquinas himself puts it, "each thing is beautiful in its own way."[30] Aquinas's most important remarks on beauty occur in the context of his discussion of St. Augustine's attempt to identify the persons of the Trinity with some of his key concepts—the Father with unity, the Son with truth, and the Spirit with concord. In this discourse, Aquinas says of the Son, "Species of beauty has a likeness to the property of the son." Beauty, he says, includes three conditions: "integrity" or "perfection," "proportion" or "harmony," and "brightness" or "clarity,"[31] which is that "splendor of form shining on the proportional parts."

There are a number of relevant insights to be gained from this brief presentation of the thought of Aquinas on beauty. The first is that, like Aquinas, the Igbo believe that there is a transcendental aspect to beauty. In fact, the Igbo believe that beauty is a divine endowment, whether in humans or in nature. But beauty, insofar as it is a human quality, is enhanced by virtue—hence, the saying *"agwa bu mma."* *Agwa* in Igbo can refer to action, to character, to someone's way of being and behaving. Here we are dealing with that stable aspect of one's personality that defines who one is and that makes the person recognizable as being such and such a person, as different from or opposed to being such and such a person who acts in this or that more or less stable manner. The *Oxford English Dictionary* defines character, inter alia, as "the sum of the moral and mental qualities which distinguish an individual or a people, viewed as a homogeneous whole; a person's or group's individuality deriving from environment, culture, experience, etc.; mental or moral constitution, personality." The dictionary also refers to character as "moral and mental qualities strongly developed or strikingly displayed; distinct or distinguished personality." There is an Igbo saying that states that you cannot eat beauty, desirable as it is. In other words, the truly beautiful and desirable individual is the truly morally upright person.

Finally, in a world where beauty and bodily endowments are being deified, traditional Igbo religion and Christianity share an important insight—namely, that it is all grace. Beauty in all or any of its forms, moral or physical, is grace. They are also limited goods and a partial reflection of God, the absolutely beautiful one.

Notes

1. Elizabeth Isichei, *The Igbo People and the Europeans: The Genesis of a Relationship—to 1906* (London: Faber and Faber, 1973), 17.
2. See Margaret M. Green, *Igbo Village Affairs: Chiefly with Reference to the Village of Umueke Agbaja* (London and Edinburgh: Frank Cass, 1947, 1964), 5.

3. Kwesi Dickson, *Theology in Africa* (London and New York: Darton, Longman & Todd/Orbis Books, 1984), 29.
4. Adrian Hastings, *African Christianity: An Essay in Interpretation* (London: Geoffrey Chapman, 1976), 50ff.
5. Luke Nnamdi Mbefo, C.S.Sp., *The True African: Impulses for Self-Affirmation* (Enugu, Nigeria: SNAAP Press, 2001), 45.
6. I am consciously borrowing the concept of inculturation as "a brew" from Agbonkhianmeghe E. Orobator's book, *Theology Brewed in an African Pot* (Maryknoll, NY: Orbis Books, 2008).
7. See Paulinus I. Odozor, *Morality, Truly Christian, Truly African: Foundational, Methodological, and Theological Considerations* (Notre Dame, IN: University of Notre Dame Press, 2014), 36.
8. Elechi Amadi, *The Concubine* (London, Ibadan, Nairobi: Heinemann, 1996).
9. Ibid., 14.
10. Ibid., 15–16.
11. Ibid., 119.
12. Anthony H.M. Kirk-Greene, "'Mutum Kirki': The Concept of the Good Man in Hausa," in *African Philosophy: An Anthology,* ed. Emmanuel Chukwudi Eze (Malden, MA/Oxford, UK: Blackwell Publishers, 1998), 121–29, quotation at 121.
13. Thomas Aquinas, *Summa Theologiae,* Vol. 1, translated by the Fathers of the English Dominican Province (New York: Benzinger Brothers, 1947), I–II, q.55, a.4; also, Sentences D 27, a.2.
14. Amadi, *The Concubine,* 176.
15. Ibid., 181.
16. Jude C.U. Aguwa, "Agwu Possession: Belief and Experience in Traditional Igbo Society," *Paideuma* 39 (1993): 279.
17. Ibid., 280.
18. Francis Arinze, *Sacrifice in Ibo Religion* (Ibadan: University of Ibadan Press, 1971), 23.
19. Emefie Ikenga Metuh, *God and Man in African Religion: A Case Study of the Igbo of Nigeria* (Enugu, Nigeria: SNAAP Press, 1999), 96.
20. Amadi, *The Concubine,* 254.
21. Ibid.
22. Herbert M. Cole and Chike Aniakor, *Igbo Arts: Community and Cosmos* (Los Angeles, CA: Museum of Cultural History, UCLA, 1984), 216.

23. Ibid., 219.
24. Chinua Achebe, "Chi in Igbo Cosmology," in *African Philosophy: An Anthology*, ed. Emmanuel Chukwudi Eze (Malden, MA/Oxford, UK: Blackwell Publishing, 1980), 69.
25. Ibid.
26. See Monroe C. Beardsley, "Aesthetics, Problems of," *The Encyclopedia of Philosophy*, Vol. 1 (New York: Macmillan Publishing Co. & the Free Press; London: Collier-Macmillan, 1967), 19.
27. Ibid., 23
28. Aquinas, ST, 1, q.5, art. 1.
29. Aquinas, ST, 1, q.5, art. 4
30. Beardsley, "Aesthetics, Problems of," 23.
31. Aquinas, ST, 1, q.39, art. 8.

Works Cited

Achebe, Chinua. "Chi in Igbo Cosmology." In *African Philosophy: An Anthology*. Edited by Emmanuel Chukwudi Eze. Malden, MA/Oxford, UK: Blackwell Publishing, 1980.

Aguwa, Jude C. U. "Agwu Possession: Belief and Experience in Traditional Igbo Society." *Paideuma* 39 (1993).

Amadi, Elechi. *The Concubine*. London, Ibadan, Nairobi: Heinemann, 1996.

Arinze, Francis. *Sacrifice in Igbo Religion*. Ibadan: University of Ibadan Press, 1971.

Beardsley, Monroe C. "Aesthetics, Problems of." In *The Encyclopedia of Philosophy*, Vol. 1. New York: Macmillan Publishing Co. & The Free Press; London: Collier-Macmillan, 1967.

Cole, Herbert M., and Chike Aniakor. *Igbo Arts: Community and Cosmos*. Los Angeles, CA: Museum of Cultural History, UCLA, 1984.

Dickson, Kwesi. *Theology in Africa*. London and New York: Darton, Longman, & Todd/Orbis Books, 1984.

Green, Margaret M. *Igbo Village Affairs: Chiefly with Reference to the Village of Umueke Agbaja*. London and Edinburgh: Frank Cass, 1947.

Hastings, Adrian. *African Christianity: An Essay in Interpretation*. London: Geoffrey Chapman, 1976.

Isichei, Elizabeth. *The Igbo People and the Europeans: The Genesis of a Relationship—to 1906.* London: Faber and Faber, 1973.

Kirk-Greene, Anthony H.M. "'Mutum Kirki': The Concept of the Good Man in Hausa." In *African Philosophy: An Anthology.* Edited by Emmanuel Chukwudi Eze. Malden, MA/ Oxford, UK: Blackwell Publishing, 1998.

Mbefo, Luke Nnamdi, C.S.Sp. *The True African: Impulses for Self-Affirmation.* Enugu, Nigeria: SNAAP Press, 2001.

Metuh, Emefie Ikenga. *God and Man in African Religion: A Case Study of the Igbo of Nigeria.* Enugu, Nigeria: SNAAP Press, 1999.

Odozer, Paulinus I. *Morality, Truly Christian, Truly African: Foundational, Methodological, and Theological Considerations.* Notre Dame, IN: University of Notre Dame Press, 2014.

Orobator, A. E. *Theology Brewed in an African Pot.* Maryknoll, NY: Orbis Books, 2008.

NOTES ON CONTRIBUTORS

MARIA CLARA LUCCHETTI BINGEMER is Professor of Theology at the Pontifical Catholic University, Rio de Janeiro, Brazil, and Dean of the Center for Theology and Human Sciences at the same university. In 2010 and 2012 she served as a senior fellow at DePaul University's Center for World Catholicism and Intercultural Theology. She is the author of *Jesus Cristo: Servo de Deus e messias glorioso* (2008) and *Simone Weil: Acción y contemplación* (2007).

PETER CASARELLA is Associate Professor of Theology in the Department of Theology, University of Notre Dame. Before coming to Notre Dame in 2013, he served as Professor of Catholic Studies at DePaul University, where he was also the director of the Center for World Catholicism and Intercultural Theology. His research and teaching interests include Latino/a theology, medieval Christian thought (especially Bonaventure and Nicholas of Cusa), and theological aesthetics. He is the author of *Word as Bread: Language and Theology in Nicholas of Cusa* (2017), *A World for All? Global Civil Society in Political Theory and Trinitarian Theology* (with William F. Storrar and Paul Louis Metzger; 2011), *Cusanus: The Legacy of Learned Ignorance* (2006), and *Christian Spirituality and the Culture of Modernity: The Thought of Louis Dupré* (with George P. Schner, S.J.) (1998).

FRANCIS X. CLOONEY, S.J., is Parkman Professor of Divinity and Professor of Comparative Theology and Director of the Center for the Study of World Religions, Harvard University. His primary areas of scholarship are theological commentarial writings in the Sanskrit and Tamil traditions of Hindu India, and the developing field of comparative theology. He is the author of numerous articles and books, including *The Truth, the Way, the Life: Christian Commentary*

on the Three Holy Mantras of the Srivaisnava Hindus (2008), and
Comparative Theology: Deep Learning across Religious Borders (2010).

CATHERINE CORNILLE is Professor of Theology and Chairperson
of the Department of Theology, Boston College. Her research
interests focus on the theology of religion, the theory of interreligious dialogue, concrete questions in the Hindu-Christian
and Buddhist-Christian dialogues, and the phenomenon of inculturation and intercultural theology. She is the author of *The
Im-Possibility of Interreligious Dialogue* (2008) and the editor of numerous multi-author collections.

TERESIA HINGA is Associate Professor of Religious Studies at Santa
Clara University. Her research focuses on religion and women's issues, particularly Africa, African religious history, and expression in
the global religious landscape, religion and public policy, and the
ethics of globalization. She is a founding member of the Circle of
Concerned African Women Theologians, a pan-African association
of women who study the role and impact of religion and culture on
African women's lives. She is author of *African, Christian, Feminist:
The Enduring Search for What Matters* (2014). She is also a member of
the Black Catholic Symposium, of the AAR and of the Association
for the Academic Study of Religion in Africa (AASR).

BRADLEY MALKOVSKY is Associate Professor of Theology, University
of Notre Dame. His area of specialization is the Hindu-Christian
encounter. He is the editor of *New Perspectives on Advaita Vedanta*
(2000) and the author of *The Role of Divine Grace in the Soteriology
of Samkaracarya* (2001). His book *God's Other Children: Personal
Encounters with Love, Holiness, and Faith in Sacred India* (2013),
which describes his interactions with Muslims, Hindus, and Buddhists, won the Huston Smith Prize.

DONALD W. MITCHELL is Professor Emeritus of Philosophy at Purdue University, and is now Permanent Visiting Professor at Sophia

University Institute (Italy). His publications include *Buddhism: Introducing the Buddhist Experience* (3rd ed., 2014), *The Gethsemani Encounter* (1997), and several other books, journal articles and book chapters. Mitchell has been an organizer and participant in all six of the Vatican's dialogues with Buddhism for the past 35 years, as well as co-founder of the Society of Buddhist-Christian Studies and co-editor of its journal. He is also founder and editor of *Claritas: Journal of Dialogue and Culture.*

PAULINUS IKECHUKWU ODOZOR, C.S.SP., is Associate Professor of Christian Ethics and the Theology of World Church, University of Notre Dame. His scholarly interests lie in foundational issues in moral theology/Christian ethics; the history of moral theology; contextual theological issues, including questions pertaining to inculturation; theology and society; African Christian theology; and the theology of marriage. His major publications include *Moral Theology in an Age of Renewal: A Study of the Catholic Tradition since Vatican II* (2003) and *Sexuality, Marriage and Family: Readings in the Catholic Tradition* (2001).

ANANTANAND RAMBACHAN is Professor of Religion, Philosophy, and Asian Studies at St. Olaf College in Northfield, Minnesota. He has been actively involved in the field of interreligious relations and dialogue, and as a Hindu participant and analyst. He is currently an advisor to the Pluralism Project at Harvard University. His many publications include *Accomplishing the Accomplished: Vedas as a Source of Valid Knowledge* (1991), *Gitamrtam: The Essential Teaching of the Bhagavadgita* (1993), *The Limits of Scripture* (1994), and *A Hindu Theology of Liberation* (SUNY, forthcoming).

GENE REEVES is an emeritus and retired from Meadville Lombard Theological School and the University of Chicago in the United States, from the University of Tsukuba in Japan, and from Renmin University of China. He is an International Advisor at Rissho Kosei-kai, a Japanese Buddhist organization in the Lotus

Sutra tradition that has been active in sponsoring scholarship on Buddhism and in fostering dialogue between Buddhism and non-Buddhist traditions.

GABRIEL SAID REYNOLDS is Professor of Islamic Studies and Theology, and Director of the Undergraduate Program at the Department of Theology, University of Notre Dame. In 2012–13, he directed The Qur'an Seminar, a year-long project with a team of 28 international scholars who are producing a collaborative scholarly commentary on the Qur'an (<quranseminar.nd.edu>). His research is focused above all on the Qur'an and Christian-Muslim relations. He is the author of several books, including *The Qur'an and Its Biblical Subtext* (2010) and *The Emergence of Islam* (2012).

MUN'IM SIRRY is Assistant Professor of Theology, with additional responsibilities for the Contending Modernities Initiative, University of Notre Dame. His primary research and teaching interests include modern Islamic thought, interreligious relations, Qur'anic studies, and political theology. He is the author of *Scriptural Polemics: The Qur'ān and Other Religions* (2014) and several journal articles and book chapters.

LAWRENCE E. SULLIVAN is Professor Emeritus of Theology and Anthropology, University of Notre Dame. He was Director of the Center for the Study of World Religions at Harvard University and Professor of World Religions at Harvard Divinity School. His research and teaching interests include native religions, ritual in postcolonial settings, religious beliefs and practices centered on health and healing, and arts and performances associated with ritual. He is the author of numerous books, including *Stewards of the Sacred* (2004), *Nature and Rite in Shinto* (2001), and *The Cosmos and Wisdom of Taoism* (2001).

NAYLA TABBARA is the Director of the Institute of Citizenship and Diversity Management at Adyan Foundation (a joint Muslim-

Christian association dedicated to advancing interreligious collaboration throughout the Middle East that she co-founded in 2006). She is also a faculty member at the Religious Studies Faculty of the Université de Saint Joseph in Beirut. She is the author (with Fadi Daou) of *Divine Hospitality: A Christian-Muslim Conversation* (2017), *Christianity and Islam in the Context of Contemporary Culture: Perspectives of Interfaith Dialogue from Russia and the Middle-East* (2009), and numerous journal articles.

INDEX